AF411984

R. Henry Migliore & Walter Thrun

PRODUCTION/ OPERATIONS

MANAGEMENT:

A

PRODUCTIVITY APPROACH

PRODUCTION/OPERATIONS MANAGEMENT

A Productivity Approach

by
R. Henry Migliore
Walter Thrun

ISBN 0-89397-403-X
Copyright © 1990 by
R. Henry Migliore & Walter Thrun
Managing for Success
P.O. Box 957
Jenks, Oklahoma 74037

Published by
Nichols/GP Publishing
11 Harts Lane
East Brunswick, NJ 08816

Contents

Foreword
by R. Henry Migliore

In my first planning responsibility as chief industrial engineer of a Continental Can Co., Inc. manufacturing plant in the mid-1960s, we went through the typical process. Everything starts with a marketing forecast and then all other parts of the organization adapt their planning process to the marketing plan. This is absolutely the wrong approach.

The marketing plan often can't see the financial implications, and most certainly has little insight into the production implications of some of its decisions. I learned that lesson as Manager of Press Manufacturing at another Continental plant two years later.

As I drove down the Dan Ryan Expressway one morning I heard an unusual "easy open" can being advertised for an automobile product. I remember thinking . . . "I'm glad I'm not in his production manager's shoes." Later that week my boss informed me that R&D was coming in to start adapting equipment and running experiments for developing the new easy open can for an automobile product. Clearly production and research were not involved in any of the planning. The product was advertised to be on the shelf in a big Memorial Day campaign. Independence Day found the top research and engineering people in the company assembled in Chicago trying to figure out why the manufacturing process wasn't working properly. Poor planning, marketing dominance and lack of input had created a monstrous situation.

Preface

During the initial preparation for this text, several educators expressed the feeling that such a text should be written by someone with actual experience in the production process. This same feeling was indicated on several of the questionnaires referred to in the introduction to this text. A typical "add on" comment was:

"Must include emphasis on practical, 'hands on' experience in addition to theoretical/academic learning."

The authors have extensive manufacturing and engineering experience. Both have been successful in developing model manufacturing organizations that show bottom-line results.

Dr. R. Henry Migliore is Professor of Strategic Planning and Management at Northeastern University/ University Center/ Tulsa, and was formerly dean of the School of Business at Oral Roberts University. Previous to this appointment, he served with Continental Can Co. in engineering and manufacturing positions.

In addition to his academic responsibilities, Migliore has served on the Board of Directors for T.D. Williamson Inc., a leading manufacturer and service company for pipelines. He is the author of books, articles and papers in the area of strategic planning, MBO and general management.

Migliore has the manufacturing experience of dramatically increasing productivity at Continental Can's St. Louis plant and directed the turnaround in Continental's Stockyards Plant press manufacturing operations. He directed the Industrial Engineering function at CCC's Elwood plant, with the notable accomplishment of setting up a cost-reduction program that was second in cost-reduction volume in the Central Division. Other manufacturing companies have used him to work on planning, production and related problems.

Walt Thrun recently retired as manager of manufacturing for a modern manufacturing facility owned by Tenneco Co. He previously served as controller, manager of industrial engineering and facilities manager for several other blue-chip firms, including Anaconda, AMAX, and Pepsico, Inc. He is presently a full-time instructor of management at Northeastern State University.

Thrun was a key player in bringing the break-even point for the Tenneco subsidiary from over 80% capacity to less than 45% capacity in a two-year time period.

He has been published in various periodicals ranging from engineering journals to *Management Accounting*. His most recent work was a five-part series on foundry productivity, which appeared in the industry's leading trade journal.

Introduction

This book, *Production/Operations Management: A Productivity Approach* addresses those production-related activities that are involved in implementing a firm's strategic plan — those activities that bring goods and services into being. A unique productivity approach is presented that emphasizes time as the universal benchmark with which to measure the productive opportunity of all production factors. Also emphasized is the importance of involving all functions in the strategic planning process. A concerted attempt is made to reflect the inherent integration of a firm's production system and its financial system.

The text is presented in five sections:

1. Strategic Planning and the Production Process

2. Productivity: Enhancing the Production Process

3. Productivity: Applicable to All Inputs of the Production Process

4. Planning, Tracking, and Controlling the Production Process

5. Bringing It All Together

Before explaining "why" the text is organized as it is, and before giving a brief synopsis of the contents of each section and chapter, it is appropriate to reveal the basic results of a questionnaire that was sent to 200 business schools during the initial stages of manuscript preparation. The purpose of the questionnaire was to determine which areas of production/ operations management present-day instructors feel are relevant and important.

Of the 42 questions on the questionnaire, the 10 that college/ university professors felt were most important are listed below in descending order:

1. Forecasting and inventories;
2. Production systems (design);
3. Quality control;
4. Analytical methods in production/operation management, i.e., cost analysis, linear programming and simulation models;
5. Project management, i.e, PERT and critical path applications;
6. Inventory control systems;
7. Production systems (management);
8. Material requirement planning (MRP);
9. Computers and Automation; and
10. Cost data for decision making (including break-even concepts).

Interesting results were also found in the business survey entitled "The 1983 Manufacturing Futures Project." The top five activities that industry planned to focus on in the mid-1980s were:

1. Developing new processes for new products;
2. Production/inventory control systems;
3. Defining a manufacturing strategy;
4. Integrating manufacturing information systems; and
5. Making existing systems work better.

Now, as we briefly explain the contents of each chapter of the text, the reader will note that leading-edge production/operation concepts are presented in such a manner as to address the needs of both academia and the business community.

Section 1, Strategic Planning and the Production Process, presents an overview of the text and its contents. Chapter 1, The

Production Process is the Implementation of the Firm's Strategy, introduces the reader to the role of production/operations management (POM) as it relates to the total firm. The futility of omitting production/operations managers from the strategic planning process is discussed. The production plan is expressed in terms of the implementation of the strategic plan. Chapter 1 also lists the rationale for the organization of the total text.

Section 2, Productivity: Enhancing the Production Process, outlines the methods used to accomplish the purpose of the text. Chapter 2, Productivity is the Key to Global Competition, provides a comprehensive argument justifying the productivity approach as the central theme for a POM text. The choice for this approach was made by the authors months before the AACSB revealed its thoughts on the subject: ". . . AACSB will urge business schools to tie course work in all disciplines, including finance, more closely to the issues of production and productivity."

The productivity approach was chosen by the authors because it was felt that productivity improvement is the key to maintaining/regaining world market share, especially in basic hard-goods industries. A close look at the steel and auto industries is presented to support this thinking.

Chapter 3, Productivity Measurement Is a Function of Time, examines the concept of time. Time is a point on the unending span and time is also the measure of the distance between any two points on this span. It is this latter aspect of time that qualifies it as a production input and is also the universal benchmark with which to gauge all productivity.

Section 3, Productivity: Applicable to All Inputs to the Production Process, introduces the various inputs to the production process. This section deals with the productivity of each of the several inputs from cash to energy. No input escapes the productivity opportunity.

Chapter 4, Productivity of Capital: The Initial Production Input, explains the key concepts of the text. The chapter is innovative as to content and unique in presentation. It explains the time value of money, but the major thrust of this chapter is to relate the productivity of all production factors to the benchmark of time.

Chapter 5, Working Capital: Cash to Cash, also containing subject matter that is unique to POM texts, is totally relevant to the POM field. The major concepts presented center on the idea that all factors of production begin with the exchange of cash. Productivity cannot be achieved until goods and services are once again in the form of cash from their sale. Simply stated, products remaining unsold in inventory, or services prepared but not rendered, do not generate financial outputs and, therefore, the productivity ratio cannot be established.

Chapter 6, Capital Planning for Production Facilities: Initial or Additions, presents the topic of capital budgeting. Varied ranking techniques are illustrated and the time value of money is stressed. The comprehensive examples presented are classic in nature. The productivity of capital is stressed. The capital: labor concept is explained along with several charts illustrating past United States capital: labor statistics.

Chapter 7, Measuring the Labor Input, concentrates on the quantitative aspect of the labor input. The chapter is basically one comprehensive example illustrating the measurement of labor effort. Also discussed are the varied uses of labor measurement data, i.e., bases for measuring employee performance, developing product cost, and capacity analysis.

Chapter 8, Motivation, Management, and Collective Bargaining, presents the argument that total factor productivity is a function of employee motivation. Also discussed is the inherent conflict between the goals and ideals of the firm. Current bargaining issues are described along with examples of negotiating strategies employed during times of recession. The Japanese management approach is discussed along with several other aspects of "participative management" concepts. This chapter contains numerous tables and graphs comparing United States productivity with the productivity of other nations.

Chapter 9, Materials: Composites, Substitutions, and Yield, also containing subject matter unique to POM texts, is devoted entirely to discussing materials as physical inputs. Dr. Merton Flemings, head of the Department of Materials Science Engineering at Massachusetts Institute of Technology (MIT), testified recently before the House Committee on Science and Technology that the United States needs a comprehensive materials research and development policy. Flemings stated that limitations of materials and materials processing represents today's engineering limitations for a wide variety of structures, devices, and machines. Both Japan and the United Kingdom are pursuing such programs already. The chapter presents the emerging concepts of "near net shape" as well as a comprehensive material substitution problem using linear programming.

Chapter 10, Facilities: Location and Installation/Project Management, defines "facility" as it relates to the production of goods and services. Also illustrated is the change in financial position for a firm when capital facilities are added. Facility additions are considered partial implementation of the firm's strategic plan. This chapter contains a comprehensive illustration of facility installations using PERT and critical path techniques.

Chapter 11, Energy as a Production Input, begins by defining energy, in universal terms as the most abundant resource or production factor. This chapter illustrates how to measure the energy input for a given firm as well as how to improve the productivity of energy. Illustrations show how to calculate the trade-off point between different available energy sources such as natural gas vs. electrical power. Extensive discussion is presented on the two major aspects of electric power, i.e., peak energy demand measured in kilowatts (kw) and energy demand per time period measured in kilowatt hours (kwh). Also presented is a discussion about electric rates relative to an electric power company's capacity utilization. A multiple regression model is used to illustrate how to estimate total energy consumption for a given time period. This chapter also includes a discussion of synthetic fuels.

Section 4, Planning, Tracking and Controlling the Production Process, deals with the management of the varied production inputs as they are associated with the production process, from their point of entry into the system until they exit the system to the appropriate distribution mechanisms.

Chapter 12, Selected Production/Inventory Topics, explains the front end of the production process, i.e., defining the demand for the goods and services of the firm. Classic quantitative tools are presented such as regression models and exponential smoothing techniques. Dependent versus independent demand is discussed. Not to be overlooked is the forecast of goods and services relative to the firm's strategic plan and general economic factors.

This chapter expands basic inventory concepts to include the "value added" concept as products progress through the production process. This chapter stresses the financial implications relative to inventory management. Also illustrated is the required integration of the data bases for both the operating system and financial system of the firm.

Chapter 13, Strategically Managing Quality, presents four different approaches to quality and how quality fits into the overall production plan. State-of-the-art measuring techniques are presented along with quality control relative to Dr. Ed Deming and the Japanese. The productivity of each production factor is discussed in light of effective quality control.

Section 5, Bringing It All Together, is designed to tie several key production and productivity concepts together with the financial status of the firm.

Chapter 14, Managing Constraints, consists of a comprehensive model of a firm that considers capital and strategic planning simultaneously. The model is unique not only to POM texts but to any current business text. It uses linear programming to define the firm's most desirable product mix in terms of contribution maximization. The model defines desirable and undesirable product lines. It also defines bottlenecks in the production process as well as quantifying the cash-flow advantage by the systematic removal of each bottleneck. The model points out that strategic plans, production plans, and capital plans need to be considered together.

The chapter points out that factor productivity begins with the proper product mix for any given production process. The concepts presented in this chapter are on the "leading edge" of today's business climate.

Chapter 15, Developing the Production Plan, presents the development of the production plan and shows how to put all the strategic items in motion.

Section 1

STRATEGIC PLANNING AND THE PRODUCTION PROCESS

Chapter 1
The Production Process
Is the Implementation of
A Firm's Strategy

Objectives

- *Understand the concept of strategic planning for the firm.*
- *See how the production manager fits into the planning process.*
- *Show how the production plan contributes to the overall strategic plan.*
- *Establish why the production plan is important and necessary.*
- *Introduce the systems approach to the production process.*
- *Set the stage for the book.*

Contents

It All Begins With the Firm's Purpose

The genesis of a business entity can be found in its mission statement. The mission statement summarizes the firm's very reason for being — the purpose for its existence. Most firms were conceived by a vision. Someone could see a need for a product or service that was heretofore not produced or provided, or perhaps there was a void in some market for an existing product or service. In any case the fulfillment of the envisoned need or void becomes a mission for an entrepreneur. The fulfillment of such a mission is expressed in terms of products (goods and/or services).

Now, once the vision is reduced to documentation, comes the task of bringing it to fruition. Between the mission and fulfillment, however, lies a wide gulf; the crossing of which has been the downfall of many throughout history.

Figure 1.1. The gulf between mission and fulfillment

What is required is the ability to look across the gulf and plot the most expedient path which begins with the mission and ends with its fulfillment.

A problem arises if we can't scan the gulf and clearly see the fulfillment. This condition prompts a journey that begins without direction. It brings to mind the words of Alice from the classic story of our favorite lost girl:

> Would you tell me please which way I ought to go from here? That depends a good deal on where you want go, said the cat. I don't much care where, said Alice. Then it doesn't matter which way you go, said the cat.

That outlook, though perhaps appropriate for Alice, is not adequate for a business entity. The voyage across the gulf must not begin without setting our compass; the heading of which is established only after we have determined the proper direction. As shown in Figure 1.2, the proper direction is established by way of the strategic planning process.

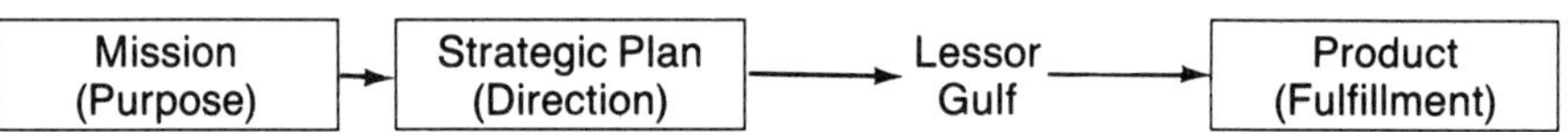

Figure 1.2. The gulf lessons with direction

The Eight Steps in Strategic Planning

Strategic planning is the philosophy of managing with a planning process. It is both a product and a process. The *product* is the plan itself. It is in writing and clearly defines where the organization intends to be in the long term, usually three to five years. The plan includes strategy and the short-term steps to ensure overall success. The *process* is the interaction that takes place in developing the plan. Everyone involved in executing the plan must be involved in its development.

The strategic planning process can be depicted in eight prescribed steps:

1. Defining an organization's or individual's purpose and reason for being;

2. Monitoring the environment in which one operates;

3. Realistically assessing strengths and weaknesses;

4. Making assumptions about unpredictable future events;

5. Prescribing written, specific and measurable objectives in principal result areas that contribute to the purpose;

6. Developing strategies on how to use available resources to meet objectives;

7. Making long- and short-range plans to meet objectives; and

8. Constantly monitoring performance to determine whether it is keeping pace with the attainment of objectives and is consistent with the defined purpose.

    a. There must be willingness to modify objectives, strategies and plans when conditions change.

    b. Purpose, environment, strengths, weaknesses, and assumptions must be reevaluated before objectives are set for the next time period.

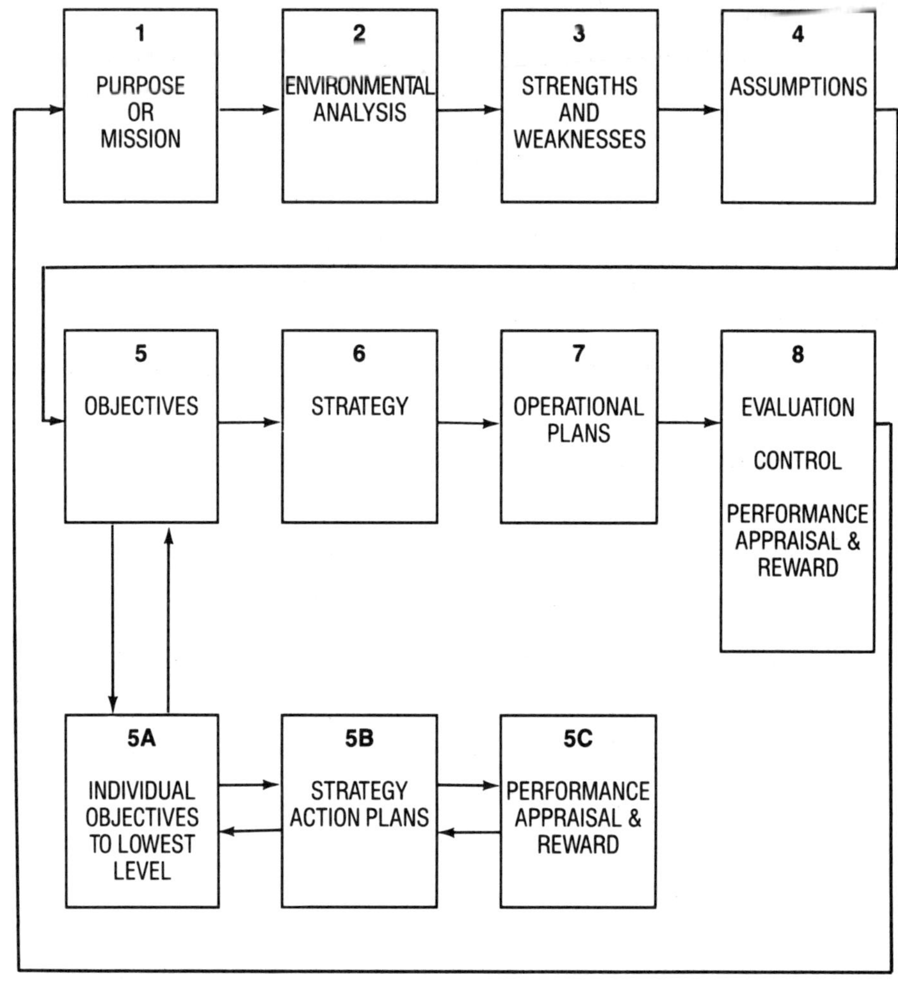

Figure 1.3. Strategic long-range planning process

Functional Plans Support Total Plan

Now that we've established an overall sense of direction, let's consider the following question: How many products are produced or services rendered in the board rooms of firms?

In other words, can and will the people at the top, who typically engage in the strategic planning process, bring the strategic plan to completion and fulfill their mission? Not hardly. While planning is typically done at the top, fulfillment depends on every layer in the organization right on down to the assembler on the shop floor or the food preparer in the kitchen. How futile it is to omit the "doers" from the strategic planning process.

The "doers" are represented by the different functional heads within the organization. Several of these functions include:

- marketing

- finance

- manufacturing (production)

- human resources

- engineering

Not only should functional heads participate in developing the firm's overall strategic plan, they should support the total plan with complementary functional strategic plans that support the organization's overall strategic plan. For example, a firm may decide to increase its global participation as a producer of video disc players. The overall plan may include such items as:

- Increase market share in several former Eastern Bloc countries.

- Introduce second-generation disc players before the competition does.

- Improve profitability by concentrating on selling higher-margin disc players.

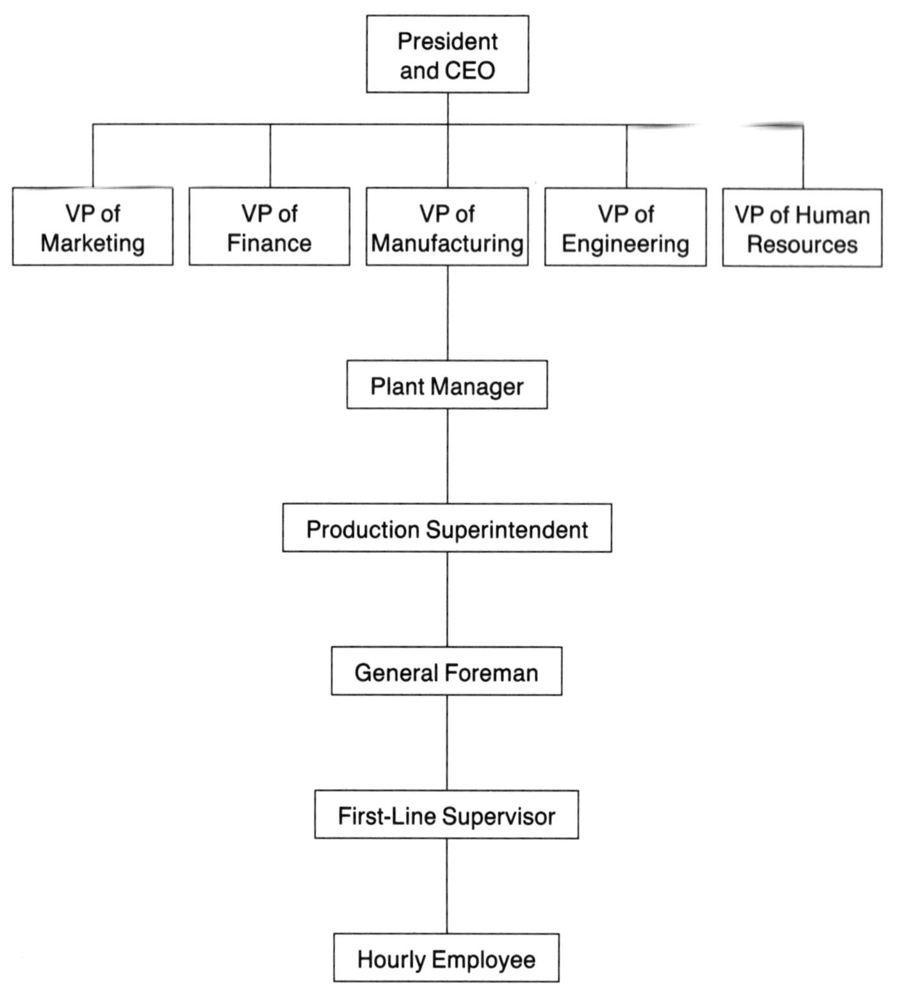

Figure 1.4. Organizational functions

Now then, even though the overall strategy of the company is to increase its global participation as a producer of video disc players, the above items are respectively:

- market driven

- engineering driven

- finance driven

If the firm's functional plans are prepared independently and without consideration of the overall strategic plan or other functional plans, several things might happen.

- The marketing plan may, for example, focus on East Germany. The marketing people may not be interested in introducing a new model disc player in view of the newly opened markets in the former Bloc countries. Furthermore, concentrating on higher-margin players may be contrary to improving market share in Eastern Europe.

- The engineering plan will focus on the product. The most functional new product may not appeal to Eastern European consumers. Additionally, the new model may produce a low margin on sales when it is introduced.

- The financial plan to improve profitability through selling high margin players may be totally contrary to the marketing plan. Eastern European consumers may want low margin players. Also, the financial people may not be overly excited about the expense associated with the introduction of a new product when their plan calls for improving profitability.

Resource Mobilization Puts Strategy Into Motion

The futility of performing the strategic planning process without inputs from the major functional areas within the company can be quickly seen. Likewise, functional plans cannot be made without a full view of the business.

It would be an extreme coincidence if the optimum production plan was the same as the plan to meet marketing's objectives, or that of any other functional entity. Functional plans must, therefore, be vertically consistent with the firm's overall strategy and horizontally consistent with other functions of the firm.

Now it's time to span the "lesser gulf" that remains between the strategic plan (direction) and fulfillment (product). The lesser gulf can be spanned with the *implementation* of the firm's strategic plan. Implementation will be accomplished by means of resource mobilization, or, simply, the production plan.

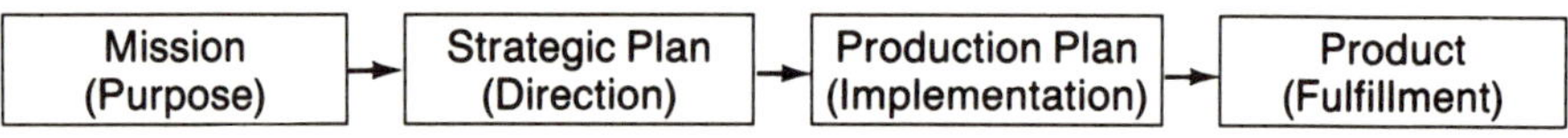

Figure 1.5. Mission completed

All Firms Have Production Plans. Be well advised that a firm does not need to be a manufacturer to have a production plan. Consider the following examples of strategic items:

- *Capture a 25% share of the world market for video game cartridges in three years.* A firm with this strategic goal may not be a manufacturer at all. It might be a distributor for several brands of video games. If, in fact, the firm is in the distribution end of the business, the production plan would involve transportation and storage facilities. Assembling and allocating resources to implement the firm's strategy is a production plan.

- *Develop composite materials to replace aluminum in commercial aircraft within five years.* This could be a strategic goal of an aircraft manufacturer, an engineering firm, the Department of Defense, or a university research department. Again, the assembling of resources to implement the strategy is the production plan.

- *Employ wide-body jets in flights to Moscow.* This could be a strategic goal of either a commercial airline or charter line. The production plan to implement this strategy would involve such measures as providing larger staging areas at the airports to be served, additional sanitation disposal service, and additional cabin service.

The above goals have one basic thing in common: They all represent a portion of a firm's strategic plan that is accomplished by means of the production plan. Without proper input from operation's executives, it would be nearly impossible for these firms to fulfill their missions.

It is confidently stated that all strategic plans are implemented and/or achieved via the production of goods and services. A production plan must exist whenever a strategic plan exists. Therefore, the production plan is perhaps the most important segment of a business entity's total system. The production plan, or implementation stage, is the only way to span the gulf between a firm's strategy and the fulfillment of its goals.

A Firm Operates as a System. The eighth step in the strategic planning process calls for a firm to operate as a system. Several key phases of the strategic planning process include:

- monitoring the environment

- constantly appraising

- willingness to change as conditions change

- reevaluating purpose, environment, and organizational capabilities

Consider that a system can be defined as:

- An array of components designed to accomplish a particular objective according to plan, or

- A regularly interacting or an interdependent group of items forming a unified whole.

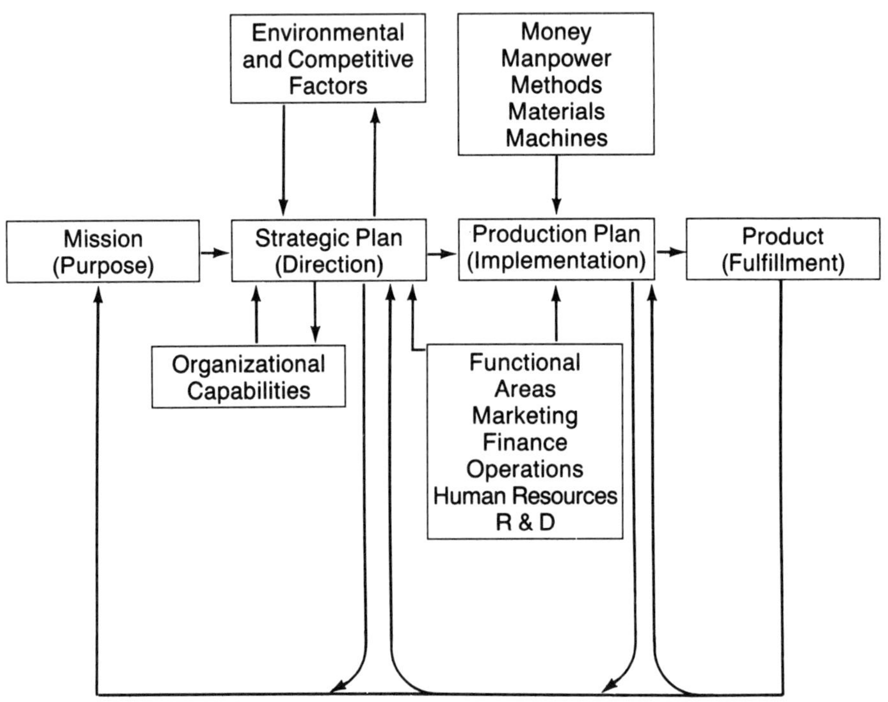

Figure 1.6. The firm as a total system

A Systems Approach

A systems approach views the organization as a whole with interacting subsets. The production plan is an element of the organizational plan. Systems thinking considers the action of each element, and that each action or reaction affects other organizational functions.

The systems approach considers that a firm operates as a dynamic organism with all parts, or subsystems, operating toward the common purpose stated in the firm's strategic plan.

The basic system in which a firm operates can be depicted as shown in Figure 1.6, which illustrates the bilateral relationship between the strategic planning process and a firm's environment as well as its organizational capabilities. This interaction was introduced earlier as Steps 2 and 3 of the strategic planning process. Notice also how the production plan "draws" from various production factors, i.e., money, labor, methods, materials, and machines as needed to carry out the strategy.

The functional areas of the firm are shown as directly affecting both the strategic plan (i.e., the direction setting process) as well as the production plan (i.e., the implementation). As previously stated, functional people, especially production executives, must be an integral part of the strategic planning process as well as the keys to the implementation stage. Perhaps this is why a *Business Week* article entitled "The Shrinking of Middle Management" stated that:

> Marketing, strategic, and financial planners are being deposed, and operations managers who not only know how to devise plans but also how to implement them are taking over.

Notice that there is extensive feedback in addition to the interactive aspects of the process.

Inasmuch as the firm operates as a system, and the definition of system includes the term "regularly interacting," it must be recognized that a firm is by definition, dynamic. Care must be taken not to draft a strategic plan and then be unwilling to make changes.

Perhaps this point can be made clear by comparing the strategic plan and strategic planning process with a firm's balance sheet and income statement. The firm's income statement depicts the continuous utilization of assets over a given *period* of time, whereas the balance sheet represents the firm's financial position at a particular *point* in time.

Likewise, the strategic planning *process* reflects the continuous influence of environmental factors and organizational capabilities over a *period* of time while the strategic *plan* portrays the chosen direction of the firm at a given *point* in time.

We can even extend this concept to include the implementation or production stage of a firm's system: The production *process* reflects the continuous assemblage and transformation of resources over a *period* of time. The production *plan* portrays the production activity at a given *point* in time.

The firm will operate optimally if the production plan reflects the strategic plan at the *same point* in time. Conversely, if the production plan lags the strategic plan, inefficiencies are certain to occur.

Section 2

PRODUCTIVITY: ENHANCING THE PRODUCTION PROCESS

Chapter 2
Productivity Is the Key
to Global Competition

Objectives

- *View U.S. productivity in comparison with Japan and other countries' productivity.*
- *Understand recent productivity problems in the U.S.*
- *Understand the American Productivity Center approach to productivity management.*
- *Know the various approaches to productivity measurement.*
- *Be able to utilize measurement results in formulating productivity-improvement strategies.*
- *Recognize the effects of productivity on profitability.*

Contents

Productivity Overview

Inasmuch as the term "productivity" is used throughout this text, it may be of value to define what we're talking about. First, let's consider several common terms and their meanings as we work our way up to the term "productivity."

- *Produce* means to give being, form or shape.

- *Product* is something produced or the expression resulting from the bringing together of two or more factors.

- *Production* is the act or process of producing; the creation of utility.

- *Productive* means being effective in bringing about a result or having the quality or power of producing in abundance.

Productivity, then, is a measure of the effectiveness with which factors are brought together to create utility. Utility, or usefulness, may be in the form of tangible products or in the form of services. Throughout this text, the expression "goods and services" is used and can be considered to be the "fulfillment" of the firm's overall strategy.

As mentioned in Chapter 1, the theme of this text is the implementation of a firm's strategy via the production process. It is one thing to understand how factors of production are brought together in the production process, but it is quite another to understand how to maximize the productivity of each of those factors.

For example, both Japanese and U.S. auto makers know how to make cars, but why are U.S. auto makers losing market share in the domestic marketplace? Why is there a push for agreements to restrict the imports of Japanese cars? Why are there major attempts by U.S. auto makers to enter into joint auto-production ventures with Japanese auto makers? The answer is simple. U.S. auto makers are not as productive with some of their available resources as are their Japanese counterparts.

Productivity Is Really a Measure of the Effectiveness of the Production Process

In the most basic terms, productivity is a ratio of the output resulting from the production process (or a portion thereof) relative to the input required to achieve the output:

$$\text{Productivity} = \frac{\text{Output}}{\text{Input}}$$

Let's say that a widget manufacturer with 200 employees produced 3,000 widgets in a given month. The basic productivity measurement is as follows:

$$\frac{\text{Output}}{\text{Input}} = \frac{3,000}{200} = 15 \text{ widgets per employee per month}$$

The 15 number is just the starting point. More information is required, specifically:

- How can productivity be improved?

- How are productivity improvements measured?

Basically, there are two ways to improve productivity in this example:

1. More output with the same input, or

2. Less input with the same output.

Productivity Is Measured in Financial Terms

The terms "output" and "input" can be expressions of many things, ranging from tangible units, units of time, or financial expressions. We'll see shortly that, ultimately, productivity is measured and expressed in financial terms. For the present example, however, the output is expressed as the number of widgets produced in a month, while the input is expressed as the number of employees required to produce the widgets.

Let's consider that there are only two options available to improve productivity in our example.

1. Increase output to 3,500 widgets per month by improving production methods; or

2. Decrease the number of employees by 12%, or by 24 employees, and work the remaining 176 employees on Saturdays.

By increasing output to 3,500 widgets, the new productivity measure becomes:

$$\frac{3,500}{200} = 17.5 \text{ widgets per month per employee}$$

By decreasing the number of employees to 176, the productivity measure becomes:

$$\frac{3,000}{176} = 17.0 \text{ widgets per month per employee}$$

It appears that it is more productive to improve production methods than it is to decrease the number of employees by 12%.

Productivity improvements are measured in terms of percent. The productivity improvements are 16.7% and 13.3% respectively.

$$\frac{17.5}{15.0} = 16.7\% \text{ and } \frac{17.0}{15.0} = 13.3\%$$

A word of caution at this point. The measure of productivity when decreasing the number of employees while working the remaining employees more hours can be very misleading. A better measurement would be "hours worked" per widget. Continuing one step further, if the additional hours worked per employee were paid at the conventional time-and-a-half rate, a better measurement might be "labor dollars" per widget.

The point is that care must be exercised when choosing productivity measurements so that meaningless objectives are not pursued at the expense of the firm's financial position.

Seven Major Aspects of Productivity

1. Productivity is a relative measure of how well we do with what we have. A widget producer employing 200 people is not expected to produce the same number of widgets over the same time as a producer employing 500 people. However, their productivity measures might be the same. In the same light, Chrysler is not expected to produce as many automobiles as General Motors. However, the number of labor hours it takes to assemble similar model cars will be close to the same for both.

2. Productivity is an absolute measure of how well we do with our total opportunity. In order to have an absolute measure of productivity, there must be a measure of the total available opportunity. In order to know the total available opportunity, there must be a constant universal benchmark. Time is that benchmark.

   Consider, for example, a father who lends money to his two sons. He lends $5,000 to one and $2,000 to the other for each of them to invest. Let's say that they both double their money. Relatively, they did equally well. But what if the one with the $5,000 had use of the money for three years, while the one with $2,000 had use of his money for just two years? In this instance, the productive opportunity is not the same. The universal benchmark to measure opportunity, then, is time.

   If, and only if, the time opportunity is the same, then the amount of other resources can be considered. In our example of the two sons, if they both had an equal time opportunity, the one with the $5,000 would naturally be expected to earn more than the one with the $2,000.

   In item 1 above, we mentioned that Chrysler would not be expected to produce as many automobiles as General Motors. Assumed in this statement was the fact that GM has more resources (net assets) than Chrysler. If, however, both Chrysler and GM have, say, $2 billion of net assets, would they not both be expected to produce the same number of cars in a year's time? Inasmuch as they had equal opportunity relative to both time and assets, the correct answer is yes.

3. Productivity is not an optional function of management. The quest to produce more for less should be intuitive for everyone involved in the production of goods and services. If one of a manager's objectives is to improve productivity, he is already behind his competitors. Sooner or later the marketplace will force the disposition of those lacking "productivity intuitiveness."

    Perhaps this point can be better understood if we consider that the term "productivity of capital" has the same meaning as "return on investment." No one would say that earning a return on assets is optional; that is the very essence of business. Consider further that productivity has been previously defined as the ratio of the input of a given resource to the output generated by that input. If a firm inputs $1 into the production process and sells a finished product for $1.10, is not the incremental 10¢ a measure of productivity of the original $1? Perhaps the original $1 was invested in the firm by an individual who purchased a share of stock for $1. If, after a given period of time, say a year, the individual who bought the stock for $1 received a dividend check for 10¢, is that not considered to be the return on investment? Therefore, ROI and productivity of capital are synonymous.

4. Productivity begins with the exchange of cash for production factors. Cash is the life blood of a business organization. It is the accepted medium of exchange by which production factors are acquired. Cash by itself kept in a wall safe, is of no value. Cash has no value and cannot be productive until it is directed into the production process. Most investors place their cash into the production process indirectly by purchasing stock, bonds, or CDs, or by depositing cash in a simple savings account.

However, the issuer of the stock, bonds, and CDs and the payer of interest on a savings account will direct the invested funds into the production of goods and services. Production factors are acquired and brought together in the production process where utility is created for someone else who is willing to pay more for the end product.

5. Productivity is relevant to all factors of production. We have said that time is the universal benchmark for the productivity measurement of capital, as evidenced by interest rates being expressed on a "per annum" basis. But how does this concept relate to other production factors? Does the opportunity clock stop when capital or cash is exchanged for labor, machines, materials, or energy? In other words, are there different benchmarks to measure the productivity of these other production factors? On a very localized level, other productivity measures may be valid. Ultimately, however, time is the measurement base for the productivity of all production factors.

Consider the labor resource. Workers are paid wages in accordance with a predetermined time period — most commonly an hour. Consider machines. The useful productive life of a machine (i.e., its depreciation cycle) is measured in years. Its day-to-day production capability is measured in cycles per time period. How about materials? If raw materials are purchased with cash, the clock continues to click off the opportunity forgone if the materials are sitting idle in inventory. And even then, energy is related to time. Homes and businesses are predominately powered by electricity. Such electricity is measured not only by the magnitude of the power (kw), but also by the magnitude per time period (kwh).

To tie the entire concept together, consider that a firm's total capacity, its total opportunity to produce goods and services, is expressed as units per time period.

Therefore, productivity is relevant to all factors of production, and they all share the common benchmark of time. In Chapter 5, we stress the importance of getting and keeping the production process rolling once cash is exchanged for production factors.

6. Productivity is ultimately measured as the increase in a firm's net assets (i.e., growth over a given period of time). A profit, which is basically an increase in net assets over a given time period, is the primary way for an ongoing business to improve its financial position, which, in turn, is required to experience growth. Growth, in essence, means increasing the capacity to produce goods and services. It can be achieved either by investing profits into more factors of production or by better utilization of existing factors. This text focuses on the latter — i.e., the productivity of production inputs. Sounds basic, doesn't it? Actually, it is.

   What have just been described are basic economic principles. They are employed on the national level by the United States as they are in the departments of individual plants. One of the measures of the productive use of resources on the national level is reflected in the amount of real economic growth attained. The primary measure of efficient resource utilization on the plant or department level is the value added to the goods or services relative to the input cost at that level.

   Federal monetary and fiscal policies may alter the total economic picture in the short run, but they cannot affect the underlying problem of inefficient resource utilization at the grass roots level. In fact, monetary and fiscal changes may prolong such underlying deficiencies and may even promote the continued inefficient use of resources. Consider, for example, an individual firm in a competitive industry that is just plodding along with, say, a 3% return on its asset base. If tax incentives are offered to the firm to increase its asset base, such as more liberal investment tax credits, the reason for the low return is not addressed — instead, additional productive resources are tied to the low productivity of capital.

Monetary and fiscal policies are, however, beyond the scope of this text. They are only mentioned as being subsidiary, and perhaps even in opposition, to the main issue, which is the productivity of inputs to the production of goods and services at the lowest manageable level. Ultimate productivity, then, is the growth per time period of an entity measured as the increase in net assets.

7. Productivity, or lack of it, results in a redistribution of wealth. In the absence of intervention in the form of monetary and fiscal incentives, capital will be attracted to the area of highest growth. In other words, capital will flow in the direction where its productivity is the greatest. Those entities that are not productive with their capital will soon lose it to those who are. We need to stress at this point that capital in this context encompasses all production factors. This is true inasmuch as capital/cash represents only the beginning and end of the production process. During the remaining portion of the cycle, the capital/cash has been exchanged for production factors, e.g., labor, machines, materials, and energy.

Productivity Is Not New

It is interesting to note that the above seven aspects of productivity have been around for several thousand years. They were originally taught as the parable of the talents found in Matthew 25:14-29. The following is an excerpt from the *Living New Testament* translation:

> For it is as a man going into another country, who called
> together his servants and loaned them money to invest
> for him while he was gone. He gave $5,000 to one,
> $2,000 to another, and $1,000 to the last . . . dividing it in
> proportion to their abilities . . . and then left on his trip.

The man who received the $5,000 began immediately to buy and sell with it and soon earned another $5,000. The man with $2,000 went right to work, too, and earned another $2,000. But the man who received the $1,000 dug a hole in the ground and hid the money for safekeeping.

After a long time their master returned from his trip and called them to him to account for his money.

The man to whom he had entrusted the $5,000 brought him $10,000. His master praised him for good work.

Next came the man who had received the $2,000, with the report, "Sir, you gave me $2,000 to use and I have doubled it." "Good work," his master said.

Then the man with the $1,000 came and said, . . . "I hid your money in the earth and here it is." But his master replied, "Wicked man! Lazy slave! You should at least have put my money into the bank so I could have some interest. Take the money from this man and give it to the man with the $10,000. For the man who uses well what is given him shall be given more, and he shall have abundance."

Productivity at the Macro Level

The United States has enjoyed the position of world leader in industrialization, technological development, and quality of life for its people for nearly 200 years. In the early 1980s, however, the U.S. economy dipped to near record lows:

- Unemployment hit a staggering 10.8%. In total numbers, there were 12 million jobless. The hardest hit segment of the economy was manufacturing, primarily the auto, steel, rubber and textiles industries.

- Inventories were at record levels. Some items, such as construction and agriculture equipment, had more than a normal year's requirement on dealers' lots. The inventory of automobiles was twice what the automakers would like. Oil field tubing inventories were measured in acres.

- Plant capacity utilization hit record low levels. The combined average for all plants was at 65%, while selected industries were operating at less than 40% capacity. Basic steel was operating at 35% capacity. Many industrial plants were mothballed for months at a time in attempts to decrease inventory levels. Many plants were closed permanently.

The Reagan administration blamed its predecessors for the economic woes while the Democrats blamed the Reagan administration. They were both wrong.

Perhaps the saddest thing about the problems of America's industrial sector was that the United States lost market share in both domestic and international markets to foreign competition in such basic products as steel, autos, and numerous consumer goods.

Two of the largest U.S. industries hard hit by the recession were the auto and steel industries. Let's consider these two very significant industries individually and try to discover whether their woes were deeper than cyclical recessionary problems. We'll also attempt to determine whether productivity, or the lack of it, played a part in their problems.

The Automobile Industry

The auto industry lost $4.2 billion in 1980 and another $1.3 billion in 1981. The total work force had been pared by more than 30% during a four-year period ending in 1982. Some 450 auto plants have been closed since 1975. This was a new twist for the domestic auto industry, which had for three decades dominated the American car market with virtually no serious competition. This dominance was primarily due to the fact that the American car buyer wanted big cars, and no other nation produced them.

The auto industry will never be the same as it was in the 1970s. Thousands of jobs are lost forever, market share is gone, and some automakers may not survive as independent companies.

Table 2.1 summarizes the plight of the automakers relative to market share. This table shows that even though total unit sales were down 24.8% in 1982 over 1972, domestic unit sales for the same time period were off 38.7%.

There had been a good demand for automobiles, especially large cars, since World War II. Competition from imports had been neither a problem nor a challenge. Consequently, productivity had not been a pressing factor.

But then along came the gasoline shortages in the early 1970s and again in the late '70s. The demand for smaller, fuel-efficient cars soared. Foreign competitors were ready to sell them; U.S. automakers were not. It was as simple as that. The big three automakers quickly sank billions of dollars into plants and equipment as they tried to match the Japanese product, but they were a day late and a dollar short. The years of riding on easy street with no serious competition in the manufacture of big cars had left its mark.

One of the biggest problems was the labor rate. In 1980, American autoworkers earned on the average $7.82 per hour *more* than their Japanese counterparts. To compound the problem, the typical Japanese subcompact car is assembled in 14 hours, while 29 hours are required for the American subcompact. The total cost advantage to the Japanese, considering all aspects of manufacturing, has been calculated at $1,677 per car.

Until recently, it didn't matter that Detroit had the highest-paid production workers in the world or that Detroit automakers used production techniques that hadn't kept pace with foreign competition. Now it does.

General Motors Chairman Roger Smith stated that GM had invested $40 billion during the four-year period ending in 1984 for new manufacturing systems for small-car production.

Table 2.1 Auto industry market share (millions of units)

Year	1972	1973	1974	1975	1976	1977	1978	1979	1980	1981	1982	1983	1984	1985	1986	1987
Units of domestic new-car sales	9.3	9.6	7.4	7.0	8.5	9.0	9.2	8.2	6.6	6.2	5.7	6.8	8.0	8.2	8.2	7.1
Units of imported new-car sales	1.6	1.8	1.4	1.6	1.5	2.1	2.0	2.3	2.4	2.3	2.2	2.4	2.4	2.8	3.2	3.2
Total U.S. new-car sales	10.9	11.4	8.8	8.6	10.0	11.1	11.2	10.5	9.0	8.5	8.2	9.2	10.4	11.0	11.4	10.3
% new-car sales that were imported	14.7	15.8	15.9	18.6	19.0	18.9	17.9	21.9	26.7	27.1	26.8	26.1	23.1	25.5	28.1	31.1

Chairman Smith went on to state that those new systems allowed GM to manufacture small cars with fewer labor hours than the Japanese. These new systems include the extensive use of robotics in the manufacturing process. GM had estimated, in fact, that it would be using 14,000-15,000 robots by 1990.

Despite these advances, auto-industry analysts have speculated that the U.S. automakers will never be able to compete with the Japanese in small-car production.

Interestingly enough, in an article reported in the *Wall Street Journal*, dated January 7, 1983 (after Smith's preceding comments), GM conceded that it needed Japanese help in its efforts to manufacture small cars. Accordingly, GM and Toyota entered into an agreement to jointly produce Toyota-designed cars in GM idle-facilities in California. U.S. automakers need to attack the costs of their cars. They need to increase productivity in the manufacturing process. Profits will be more of a factor of cost control than pricing. Labor is the first cost that must be improved relative to output. Detroit labor costs have climbed disproportionately over the last three decades. It is estimated that a 25%-30% improvement in productivity is required in labor to make Detroit automakers competitive.

The UAW has granted automakers large labor concessions, both in terms of givebacks and wage freezes. Collective bargaining in the auto industry has taken on an entirely new aspect in the past several years.

It's interesting to note that the output of autos per labor hour worked hasn't been the focal point of discussions between automakers and the UAW. However, the result of paying for less time not worked automatically improves labor productivity as measured by the Department of Labor. Labor productivity is measured by output per paid labor hour. In order to be successful, productivity improvements related to labor must penetrate substantially deeper than wage reductions.

According to industry experts, it's not just the labor-cost structure that needs to be overhauled. The entire concept of manufacturing must be renovated. The Japanese specialize in very centralized production facilities that are in close proximity to their suppliers. Major components are shipped by vendors and received directly on the production lines. As a result, inventories are measured in hours or fractions thereof instead of days or weeks. This type of inventory management greatly improves the productivity of working capital.

Another emerging trend is for automakers to form alliances with each other in an effort to reduce costs by maximizing total resources and reducing product duplication. The Big Three automakers are aggressively pursuing this course.

U.S. automakers are penetrating foreign markets, and the foreign automakers are moving with continued rapidity into domestic markets. What used to be a monopoly in the United States is now a very competitive battle. Such global competition will, it is projected, reduce the number of independent automakers by about one-half in the next 10-20 years.

Battleship or Speedboat

Like the dinosaur, it appears that America's Big Three automakers — General Motors, Ford, and Chrysler — have not adapted to change. When the rain forests shifted, some mammals and birds, such as the deer and pheasant, shifted with it. Other plants and animal life, like the lizard and cactus, adapted and survived. The dinosaur, with a small brain mass to its body weight, didn't recognize change. Dinosaurs learned the lesson that if you don't adapt, you don't survive. Read Peter Drucker's 1974 book, *Management: Tasks, Practices, and Responsibilities*. General Motors, along with Sears, are held out by Drucker as examples of excellence. There is no question that at one time these companies were dominant.

Japanese companies captured a record 26% of U.S. auto sales last year. By the mid-1990s, their combined share could top one-third of the market and exceed that of General Motors.

In the first quarter of 1990, Japanese "transplants" accounted for 22% of the cars built in America — a whopping 53% increase in just one year. The eight assembly plants that the Japanese built in the U.S. during the 1980s have put precisely that many Big Three car factories out of business in the past three years.

By the year 2000, it is predicted that Japan's gains in the United States and Europe will give its automakers 40% of global sales, up from 28% today. Detroit's share will drop to 28% from 35%. In a market free of trade restraints, a securities analyst stated, "The Japanese auto industry would over take the U.S. in about five years and assume undisputed leadership by the end of the century. The new Big Three would be Toyota, Nissan, and Honda."

As for quality, Detroit has gained ground, but is still trailing. In 1980, each Japanese car had an average of two defects, the Harbour and Associates report says, while Ford's cars averaged 6.7 defects apiece, GM's 7.4, and Chrysler's 8.1. Now, Ford has cut its defects per car to 1.5, GM to 1.7, and Chrysler to 1.8, Harbour says. But the Japanese have reduced average defects to 1.2 per car.

To Ford's credit, they have increased their share of the U.S. auto market in six of the past eight years. Sears has been in a steady decline also. It continues to lose its dominance in the market place. Who would have believed in the early 1970s that Mazda, Honda, and Walmart would be on such a roll?

The only conclusion is that management didn't recognize the changes as they were occurring. Hopefully the "brain mass" *wasn't* small like the dinosaur's. These companies have highly paid, well-educated staffs. They saw what was happening but just couldn't do anything about it. Big organizations are like battleships — any change in direction is slow and difficult. To be competitive, American companies must be more like speed boats in responding to change.

The Steel Industry

The steel industry went through an adjustment similar to the one that cut coal mining employment in half after World War II and that cut the auto industry work force by 30% during the four-year period ending in 1982.

The jobless rate in the steel industry stood at 45% in late 1981, with over 50% in some specialty mills in which imports comprise over half of domestic consumption. Total unemployment exceeded 100,000 steel workers.

During the early part of the 1980s, the industry experienced tremendous losses, which drastically curtailed capital spending to upgrade steel-making facilities. It's a vicious circle: no profits to reinvest in more efficient production processes while present facilities fall farther behind daily. Table 2.2 shows the decline of the U.S. share of world steel production.

Note that production for "all others" increased 3% in the last decade, while U.S. production fell by 50.7%. The U.S.S.R. is the largest producer of steel in the world. Its production increased 12.6% in 1982 over 1981, while U.S. production dropped 38.0%. In 1982, the steel industry was hit with a wave of financial failures and plant shutdowns. Bankruptcy claimed McLouth Steel Corp., Guteri Special Steel Corp. and Johnson Steel and Wire Co.

Steel imports to the U.S. in 1981 were over 20 million tons, which represents over 25% of total domestic consumption. At the same time, domestic output was off 38% in the first eight months of 1981, putting thousands of steelworkers on the jobless rolls.

Table 2.2 Steel production (millions of tons)

	1973	1974	1975	1976	1977	1978	1979	1980	1981	1982	1983	1984	1985	1986	1987
United States	136.9	132.2	105.8	116.1	114.7	124.0	123.3	101.7	108.8	67.5	84.6	92.5	88.3	81.6	89.2
All other	560.6	571.6	537.1	559.4	560.9	593.2	623.1	614.3	598.1	577.5	597.6	637.8	652.9	663.3	675.0
Total	697.5	703.8	642.9	675.5	675.6	717.2	746.4	716.0	706.9	645.0	682.2	730.3	741.2	744.9	764.2
% U.S.	19.6%	18.8%	16.5%	17.2%	17.0%	17.3%	16.5%	14.2%	15.4%	10.5%	12.4%	12.6%	11.9%	10.9%	11.6%

Even after the worldwide recession, which ended in 1983, the steel industry was never be the same due to permanent restructuring of the auto industry and other basic manufacturing industries.

Although in 1982 there were considerable declines in shipments, profits, employment, and capital spending, hourly wages of steelworkers increased 48¢ per hour on August 1, 1982, and another 9¢ on November 1, 1982. Those last increases took steel labor costs to more than $25 per hour, which was 95% higher than the total manufacturing average in the U.S. Labor cost per ton of steel in the U.S. was $101 higher than that of the Japanese.

Not unlike the auto industry's labor cost problems, steel labor problems built up over 40 years of collective bargaining. Of particular interest when considering the productivity of steel labor is the fact that one-third of the total wage was composed of benefits or wages paid for no production.

It was estimated that 20% of the American steel production plants that were closed beginning in the mid-1980s will be shut down permanently. Third-world steel production is increasing, which will mean even stiffer competition for American mills. Total world demand for steel will remain weak while more efficient producers will survive.

Government subsidization of several foreign nations' ailing steel producers continue to undermine any productivity gains for those producers. American steel producers don't enjoy such subsidies. A great deal of effort was expended in 1982, and will continue for several years, on establishing import quotas and other trade protection. Such activity, however, leaves the basic productivity issue untouched.

Because of the close ties, as the auto and rail industries remain weak and/or decline, so goes the steel industry. The U.S. steel industry will never be the same as it was as recently as the

1970s. And, as in the auto industry, many more mills will be eliminated — leaving fewer but more-productive and competitive producers.

Although auto and steel producers went through the greatest adjustments, America's entire manufacturing arena is in turmoil. Once again, even after the worldwide recession of the early 1980s had ended, the total industrial sector was drastically different.

Productivity: the Key in the 1990s

The 1980s were turbulent times for managers, with shifts in population dynamics, competitive forces, consumer markets, labor forces, cost control, and organization structures.

In his book *Managing in Turbulent Times*, famed management writer Peter Drucker offers several suggestions for success during unpredictable times. Companies should, says Drucker, "aim at being able to produce at least 50% more within the next 8-10 years without increasing the number of people employed." To do this, managers must (1) know where all of their money is, (2) efficiently use critical physical resources, and (3) assign people where they will produce the best results.

The other suggestions are:

- Allocate resources for results.

- Adopt a systematic abandonment policy.

- Concentrate on strength.

- Develop new personnel policies.

- Give employees more responsibility.

There needs to be a drive to produce more for less, the classic definition for productivity improvement. Robert Hayes, a business professor at Harvard, has stated that such things as foreign competition and productivity are becoming very alarming issues that are making their way to the executive suites. The new buzzword throughout industry is, in fact, "productivity."

Japan Leads in Productivity Improvements

Japan has enjoyed annual productivity gains averaging 7.2% over the last 20 years, whereas the United States has averaged just 2.2% for the same period. In fact, U.S. productivity dropped during the period 1977-1980. Government figures show service productivity — or output per hour worked — plummeted at an annual rate of 2.6% in the fourth quarter of 1986.

Why is productivity growth so poor? The answer isn't clear, but Brookings Institute economist Martin Baily believes one reason is attributable to the fact that service industries haven't learned to make the best use of their computers. In addition, the influx of younger and less-experienced workers into the service sector during the last decade and a half has probably held down productivity gains.

The struggle to become less dependent on foreign, and often unstable, oil supplies will shift to a struggle to regain dominance, or at least be able to ward off competition in several basic manufacturing industries. The U.S. has been much too quick to export technology and too slow to combat the inevitable consequences. Japan, one of the primary benefactors of U.S. technology, is very reluctant to share technology with other developing Asian countries. In finally coming to grips with the problem of the U.S. technology drain to foreign countries, the Reagan administration took a tough stance that was aimed primarily at the Soviet Union. A report compiled by a federal task force on the export of U.S. technology stressed the retention of manufacturing know-how. The report called for control on three types of technology exports:

1. Design and manufacturing data that include detailed instructions;

2. "Keystone" manufacturing, inspection or automatic test equipment that are unique and critical to a production line; and

3. Products that are accompanied by extensive information about their operation and the application of sophisticated maintenance procedures.

Of interest is the fact that the items that are felt to be of sufficient importance to control are productivity related.

So, then, U.S. industry will never again be the same as it was as recently as the '70s. Basic industry is dwindling rapidly. Much of this change is because of the expected evolution from industrialization to automation. However, much of the reason can be traced directly to industry's short-sightedness. It is a basic fact that industry, in an effort to satisfy the nearly insatiable appetite for basic big-ticket consumer goods, has priced its output at levels that the "market would bear" — with little consideration given to the cost or inefficient use of inputs. In other words, the U.S. industrial sector has not learned the management of productivity.

Productivity Helps Control Inflation and Results in Real Growth

Consider the following basic equation:

$$input = output$$

There is no profit and subsequently no growth. If, however, we alter this basic equation as shown:

$$input + value\ added = output$$

then, the difference between output value and input cost is profit to the seller and marginal utility to the buyer.

In previous years, the input-output differential was nearly exclusively a function of pricing. Now, however, the difference must come, at least in part, from increased productivity of inputs.

There are several reasons why input costs have risen at a rate that far exceeds productivity increases:

1. When business is good, management doesn't like to make waves, and so it grants labor's requests with little resistance.

2. Output prices, until very recently, grew at a pace to maintain desired (satisfactory) profit levels for the sellers.

3. Rising output prices acted as a catalyst to fuel inflation, which brought input costs up with them. (Actually the input cost/output price dilemma is analogous to the chicken and egg situation.)

Consider the previously stated equation in which input equals output. If productivity gains were tied directly to rising input costs, then as the cost of one input increased by, say, 10%, the basic premise is that one input would produce 1.1 units of output. Conversely, .91 input would produce one output. Moreover, any cost reduction in a plant, no matter how attained, increases total productivity.

These, then, are the primary objectives of productivity. The benefits are basic and obvious. In addition, prices would stabilize and real growth would result.

The approach used in this text stresses the improvement in output per unit of input for each factor of production/resource. The productivity improvement in each factor of production will improve the productivity of capital, which will, in turn, improve the firm's financial position, which will provide opportunity for growth, which will allow for more production of goods and services, which will help fulfill the American dream.

Chapter 3
Productivity Measurement
is a Function of Time

Objectives

- *Understand definition of productivity — producing more with fewer inputs.*
- *Understand relationship between production and support facilities in the overall success of a company.*
- *Learn the importance of monitoring material inputs closely.*
- *Recognize the need to control the high costs of labor and energy inputs.*
- *Know that a manager's job is to obtain maximum productivity from all production and support inputs.*
- *Realize that total inputs must be reconciled with output productivity.*
- *Be able to compare actual break-even with planned break-even.*
- *Understand how to analyze productivity.*
- *Be able to use a matrix as an aid in productivity analysis.*
- *Learn that productivity improvements can be made in various and creative ways.*

Contents

Cash: The Essential Ingredient

"Pressed to the limit by rising costs and overseas rivals, companies are investigating every path that will allow them to get more work out of employees and machines for less money." This statement was reported in *U.S. News and World Report* in an article entitled "A Drive to Produce More for Less."

Productivity finds universal applications in any activity that is engaged in the production of goods and services. True, the resources input to the production of goods and services are substantially different for an airline, dairy farm, or steel mill, but the concept to produce more for less should be the stated objective of each.

As mentioned in Chapter 2, because competition puts a lid on prices, the only other way to make a profit is to control the cost side of the equation.

The objectives of this chapter are to:

- Define various production inputs.

- Illustrate how production inputs enter the production process.

- Show how to measure production inputs.

- Illustrate how to establish priorities in controlling and/or managing production inputs.

Basic Inputs Used in the Production of Goods and Services: The Capital or Cash Input

The first input required is capital, or, more specifically, cash. In fact, cash is required in order to obtain any other inputs, i.e., labor, machines, materials, or energy. The total production process begins with cash and ends with cash. This is such an important issue that an entire chapter is included in this text entitled "Working Capital: Cash to Cash."

If the business activity in question is an airline, cash is

required initially to purchase airplanes and ground-support equipment. In order to keep providing service, cash is required continuously to purchase jet fuel, pay landing fees, pay salaries, and lease airport facilities and services. The airline cannot operate without cash.

If the business activity is a dairy farm, cash is required initially to buy cows, barns, and equipment. In order to keep producing milk, cash is required continuously to purchase feed supplies and hire help. The dairy farm cannot operate without cash.

If the business activity is a steel mill, producing products to be used in automobiles and construction, cash is required initially to purchase land, buildings, and equipment. In order to keep producing steel, cash is required continuously to pay energy bills, purchase raw materials, and pay wages. The steel mill cannot operate without cash.

In the three business activities just cited, cash was required initially to enter the business, and then cash was required continuously to sustain the business. To start the business, cash was needed to buy production equipment, namely airplanes, cows, and melting furnaces to be used in the production of goods and services. Each of the three businesses had, at that point, acquired capacity to produce different products. The individual productive capacities, whether an airplane, cow, or melting furnace, have the ability to produce many units of production over an extended period of time. A very small portion of each is consumed in the production of its respective unit of goods or service. That is, an airplane wears out a little bit with every mile flown. A cow has a lifetime capacity to produce a given number of gallons of milk. With each gallon produced, her milk-producing capacity decreases. A melting furnace wears out just a little with every ton of steel produced.

Therefore, the productivity of initial capital can be enhanced if, for the airline, for example, each mile flown has a good payload versus dead-heading. For the dairy farmer, the productivity of the cows can be enhanced if the farmer doesn't spill any milk or give too much to the cats. Likewise, the productivity of initial capital for a steel-melting furnace can be enhanced if the facility produces the optimum mix for the particular facility and keeps scrap to a minimum. Remember, each mile flown, each gallon processed, or each ton produced leaves one fewer unit of production capacity available, and once the unit is produced, the opportunity is gone or expended.

Another important point is that the airplane, cow, and melting furnace experience some deterioration over time regardless of production levels. So, not only is there an opportunity cost experienced with suboptimal use of the production capacity, i.e., mile flown, gallon processed, or ton produced, there is also a decrease in total production capability attributable to time. The productivity of the initial cash requirement is discussed in detail within the context of capital budgeting, and the continuous cash requirements are discussed within the context of the productivity of working capital.

It should be remembered that cash is the lifeblood of the business entity and, as such, all inputs should be viewed in light of their ability to be transformed into salable goods and converted back (exchanged) for cash. Cash, as the American medium for exchange, is given by a firm in exchange for resource inputs that are used in the production of its goods and services. For example, cash is exchanged for labor, materials, and/or supplies and energy. The productivity of cash is measured by the relative value added to the product by the expenditure of cash during the production process. If the goods and services are completed and sold for more cash than was consumed in the production process, the productivity of cash was positive.

Excess cash generated is the measure of the productivity of cash over a given time period.

If cash is required to obtain all other resource inputs, which in turn add value to a product or service, which in turn is sold for cash again, one would suppose that the productivity of cash could be monitored by periodically examining the cash account of a firm. That is a valid supposition. However, to maximize the productivity of cash requires that the productivity of all inputs be examined during the production process. Only by doing this can the total productivity opportunity be viewed.

Establishing Production Capacity

The first thing to be done with a portion of the cash is to acquire facilities and equipment, or, as the second section of Figure 3.1 indicates, establish capacity to produce goods and services. As per our earlier discussion, it can be in the form of airplanes, cows, steel mills, or numerous other types of facilities and/or equipment. The capacity will nearly always be in the categories of:

- Facilities and equipment used directly in the production of goods and services, and

- Facilities and equipment required to support the production process.

A specially designed high-bay manufacturing facility can house a steel-making operation, while a conventional facility can house the administrative section of the same steel company. Each is entirely different in design and purpose, but each is necessary to the overall success of the steel company.

Consider machinery and equipment. Production-type equipment may include turret lathes, melting furnaces, robots, and molding machines. Any equipment that is used directly in the manufacture of a product is classified as production equipment. On the other hand, turret lathes will also be found in the maintenance department of a plant, which is a support activity. Other types of support equipment may include cranes, fork trucks, and welding machines. These same items are also frequently used in the direct production of goods.

In any given company, there will most likely be a greater proportion of facilities and equipment used directly for the production of goods and services, but not always. Consider an airline company, for example. Its investment in support facilities, ground equipment, and maintenance facilities may easily equal its investment in aircraft.

Foolish is the manager who concentrates on the productivity of direct production facilities and equipment to the exclusion of the productivity of support facilities and equipment.

Resource Input Flow

Consider Figure 3.1 — i.e., it all begins with cash. This flow chart illustrates the conversion of cash to other resources, that are placed in the production process and then converted back to cash again when the goods and services are sold. The starting point, then, for any business entity is to have cash.

Depreciation

Depreciation is the first item in the "production input" column of Figure 3.1. Depreciation is the portion of the production facility or equipment that is expended with the production of goods or services. It can be one mile flown for an airplane, one gallon of milk for a cow, or one ton of steel for a melting furnace. However, in most cases, it is a percentage of the initial cost of the facilities and equipment recognized per time period, regardless of production levels. The important point is that time and/or use decreases the total amount of production that the equipment can be expected to provide over its remaining life.

Inasmuch as the portion of the original production capacity that is expended, either over time or per unit of production, is considered to be part of the cost of production, it will be recovered by the selling price of the goods or services. This procedure allows the firm to recover the initial cost of the production capacity as it is expended (used up), so that when it is no longer capable of producing goods and services, funds are available to replace the diminished capacity with new facilities and equipment.

The concept to be developed relative to the productivity of facilities and equipment is that as the utility of the equipment is

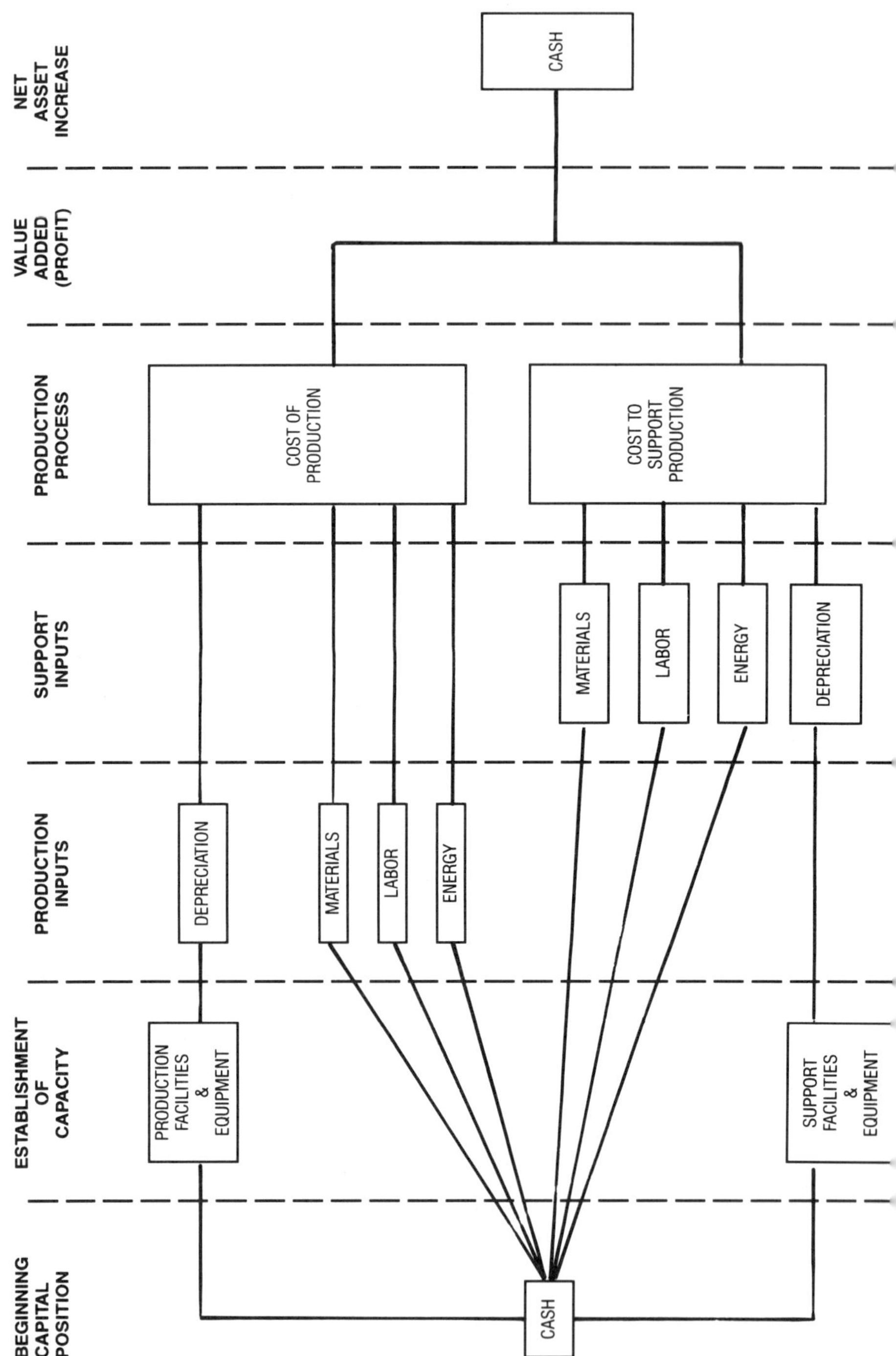

Fig. 3.1. Resource input flow chart

expended, it is done through the maximum production of goods and services. For example, if depreciation is a function of time, then maximum production per time period will enhance the productivity of the equipment. Conversely, idle capacity will have a negative effect on equipment productivity.

A comprehensive discussion relating to depreciation and cash flows can be found in Chapter 6, "Capital Planning for Production Facilities."

Production Inputs — Materials

Materials, as inputs, enter the production process in many different forms and various stages of the process. The production of goods normally begins with some kind of raw material. It might be sand, ore, raw steel, or a highly complex component. In many cases, one firm's finished product is another firm's raw material. In other cases, one firm's "throw-aways" are another firm's raw material. For example, the raw material for an iron foundry is primarily steel scrap that can be in the form of punchings, offal, or perhaps junked cars.

In assembly operations, materials can enter the production process at numerous times. It becomes a real challenge for the manager to ensure that the right materials are at the right place at the right time while minimizing inventory levels.

The point to be made is that cash is expended to purchase materials that enter the production process and are melted, forged, stamped, cut, assembled, or processed in a thousand different ways in order to end up with a product in a form that has value to a buyer.

Productivity of materials begins with the premise that all materials purchased can be accounted for. All materials purchased, it is hoped, will enter the production process, add value as they travel through the production cycle, and be sold as a part of the completed product.

Materials that are purchased but never complete the production process should be the first priority when attacking the productivity issue. Some materials never complete the production process because they are:

- Scrapped during the production process;
- Lost or misplaced;
- Spoiled because of a short shelf life; and
- Replaced by substitute materials that are introduced because of an engineering change.

Production Inputs — Labor

The labor resource/input also enters the production process at various stages and performs varied tasks. The materials that are melted, forged, stamped, cut, and assembled are handled by workers, or machines that are operated by workers. It is estimated that even today, two-thirds of the total cost of the production of goods and services is attributable to the labor input. This proportion would be substantially less if only the production of goods were considered. Undoubtedly, the proportion will steadily decrease as robotics and automated manufacturing systems continue their relentless march into the industrial sector of the economy.

When productivity statistics are compiled and reported by the Department of Labor, they are expressed as the value of goods and services per labor hour paid. Since World War II, labor unions have bargained and won more and more time off with pay while productivity of the labor force has understandably slipped. This trend drastically changed, however, with the 1981-83 recession. Companies in many industries have sought and received concessions from unions. These concessions, in many cases, are in the form of less time off with pay.

Productivity of the labor input is extremely important, because the cost of each unit of labor can be expected to increase at a faster rate than, say, materials. This is attributable to the fact that the labor input has the objective of improving quality of life in addition to keeping pace with inflation.

Recent labor contracts, in fact, spell out a separate category of increase called COLA (Cost Of Living Allowance), which is intended to automatically raise labor rates to match inflation. After the COLA, the bargaining continues for other types of increases, usually tied to employee seniority with the particular company.

Labor and Capital Productivity are Related. When a firm produces more goods and services with the same or fewer units of labor input, we say labor productivity has increased. What normally happens, however, is that there has been some degree of automation that requires less labor input to perform a given job. But, because labor hours worked is the denominator in the ratio, we say labor productivity has improved, when in fact there has been an improvement in the productivity of capital and/or equipment.

The Department of Labor reports changes in labor productivity when the time off with pay goes up or down. True improvements in labor productivity occur, however, when actual output increases per hour worked with no change in other inputs such as energy, machinery, or capital.

An interesting aspect of the labor input is that each employee is his/her own vendor who sells his/her capacity to perform work on a net Collect On Delivery (COD) basis. There is no such thing as buying labor on terms such as those that can be negotiated with a materials vendor, and then, perhaps, extending the terms unilaterally when cash is tight. Pay-day comes as steadily as the clock.

It is also interesting to note that labor input has a very direct effect on the productivity of other inputs, i.e., equipment, materials, and energy.

As in the preceding discussion on materials, it is important that all money paid to the labor input be accounted for and that a minimum is expended that does not add value to the product.

Chapters 7 and 8 address labor input in more detail.

Production Inputs — Energy

Until the 1970s, energy in general and its productivity were given very little consideration. However, because the cost of energy has increased at a rate faster than other inputs, including labor, firms are taking energy input very seriously. Energy prices have been a function of scarcity, or alleged scarcity, as is discussed in Chapter 11.

For many industries, the energy input comprises 10%-15% of their total production cost, which makes it a major input deserving close control. Energy enters the production process in a variety of ways. It may be in the form of natural gas that is burned to produce heat for manufacturing processes, or to control the temperature of the work place. It may be in the form of electricity that is supplied to a plant and distributed throughout to run electric motors to power large overhead cranes and hoists, or to pass through large inductors to melt metal.

Of primary importance in managing the energy input are the ability to:

- Measure the input; and

- Determine the energy required to do a specific job.

The energy input, as well as all other inputs, must be treated as if it were, in fact, scarce. Each British thermal unit (BTU) that enters the production process in the form of coal, gas, steam, electricity or whatever source, has the ability to do a specific amount of work. The productivity of energy focuses on the productive use of all energy delivered and consumed.

Support Inputs

Just as there are resources such as machines, labor, materials, and energy that are used directly in the production of goods and services, similar resources are consumed in support activities that do not add value directly to the product. In fact, some of the support activities may not even come in contact with the product. However, the production of goods and services cannot be carried on without certain support functions.

Support activities are classified differently by different firms. Sometimes they are classified as "overhead" or "burden." Whatever they are called, they are very necessary, and it is equally important to control the productivity of resources expended in support activities.

In many instances, more labor and energy will be required in support of the production process than in the process itself. Highly automated manufacturing processes may require very small crews to operate but very large maintenance crews. In the same light, a plant may be engaged in assembly-type production that requires more energy to control the environment of the work area than to power the limited production equipment.

Materials

Many types of materials, which do not become a part of the product itself, are required to support production processes. Management of their productivity is different, as is the method of inventory management that is employed to control them.

Consider an iron foundry. Its basic raw material is steel. Each part is cast in a mold in a medium of sand that weighs approximately 10 times as much as the product itself. The sand is a support material inasmuch as it does not become part of the product.

Every plant that has machinery and equipment carries an inventory of spare parts in the case of production equipment failure. It is not unusual for the value of these spare parts to be two or three times as much as the combined value of production inventories, i.e., raw materials, WIP (work in progress), and finished goods. Most likely, none of these spare parts will ever come into contact with the product or add value to it. Their value stems from the fact that a production machine may fail and be out of production for weeks awaiting replacement parts if the part is not carried in inventory. Because parts inventory ties up working capital, it must provide positive productivity. This is measured by comparing the carrying cost of the parts against the cost of expected lost production time awaiting repair parts.

Consider lubricants, refractories in melting or heat-treating units, hydraulic fluids, and floor-sweeping compounds. All of these are used in support of the production process. In a given plant there may well be many times more indirect (support) material items than direct. Opportunity will be missed if such items are omitted from the productivity management program.

Labor

Consider the maintenance mechanic, the fork-truck driver, the inspector, the stockroom attendant, and the janitor. None of these directly adds value to the product; however, each is absolutely necessary in the continued operation of the production process.

Workers involved in support activities for the production of goods and services are called "indirect" workers because their efforts do not directly add value to the product. However, as has been illustrated with indirect materials, the production process could not continue without them. It is not unusual for indirect laborers to outnumber direct laborers by a ratio of 2:1. Therefore, the productivity measurement of the indirect work force is at least as important as, if not more important, than that of the direct production employees.

Because measurement of direct labor activities has normally been easier to establish than indirect, more emphasis has been given to direct labor. Again, a tremendous opportunity will be missed if the productivity of the indirect labor force is ignored.

Every dollar expended on indirect labor should be accounted for, and a manager must be able to define or measure the contribution to productivity of each indirect-labor employee.

Energy

Air-conditioning units, roof exhaust fans, dust collectors and air compressors all require energy to run but they add no direct value to the product. No plant can operate without comfortable working conditions, nor can many production machines operate without compressed air. How about lights, computers, and electronic test equipment? Again, each requires energy to operate but adds no direct value to the product.

A typical assembly-type manufacturing operation may well require more energy for environmental control than to run production equipment. A manager must be able to (1) measure the energy input to the plant and (2) determine whether the energy expended for support activities is appropriate for the benefits received.

Depreciation

Just as production-related facilities and equipment decrease in utility over time, so do support facilities and equipment. Consider the equipment in the maintenance department, the test equipment in quality assurance, the computers in the administrative center, the HVAC equipment, the air compressors, and the facilities to house them. They all depreciate over time. It is not unusual for the HVAC equipment to represent 10 to 15% of the total capital invested in a given facility.

The productivity of the capital invested in support equipment is just as important as the productivity of direct production equipment.

All Support Inputs

It must be remembered at all times that the production of goods and services begins with the conversion of cash into facilities and equipment in order to establish capacity. The process continues with the conversion of cash to materials, labor, and energy. Each dollar of cash that is converted must eventually return to its original cash state, ideally with more than in the beginning. Moreover, the firm will not survive unless the initial cash generates more cash.

When goods and services are exchanged for cash after the production process, the amount received (i.e., the amount the customer is willing to pay) will not necessarily be related to the amount of input cost expended by the firm to produce the product. Simply stated, the amount of cash the customer will pay in a competitive environment is a function of what the goods or services should cost, or what the most efficient producer can do.

The problem is exemplified in the production of small cars. It costs U.S. automakers approximately $1,500 more than it does the Japanese to produce a typical small car. Therefore, even if profits are forfeited, U.S. automakers cannot expect car buyers to buy their cars, even at their cost. Even if U.S. automakers could entice car buyers to patriotically "buy American" at their cost of production, there would be no growth if there were no profits, and survival of the automakers would still be short-lived.

Input Productivity is the Measurement of Success

Each and every input, direct or support, must be considered relative to its contribution to the product or process, i.e., its productivity. Every dollar for every input must be identified and measured accordingly.

If we were to take a tour through a typical manufacturing facility we would observe machines, personnel, and materials. We would know also that energy was being consumed by seeing equipment running and lights turned on. *Everything* within view has been converted from cash. Let's say we notice an idle production machine. That machine was purchased with cash for the purpose of producing goods or services. If it is idle and not producing, it cannot be generating more cash and, therefore, the input of capital into equipment is greater than the output received. There is no productivity of equipment; in fact, there is negative productivity. Idle equipment means idle or excess capacity, which means opportunity lost, which means poor or no productivity of equipment, which means no growth or, perhaps, even no survival.

If an operator came to the machine and began to make products, we might be inclined to believe that all is well; that the productivity of the machine is positive. However, more information is required before that conclusion can be reached.

- Is the machine running at its optimum speed?

- Is it producing a part with a satisfactory price/cost relationship?

- Is the machine being underutilized by running a product that is suboptimal for the equipment?

These are very important considerations. The point to be made is that activity doesn't ensure productivity.

Perhaps as the tour continues, a machine in the maintenance department is found to be sitting idle. This may be a healthy situation. Equipment used in maintenance activities is like an insurance policy, and the period of depreciation is similar to premium payments on the policy. In fact, if the maintenance machines are operating it might be an indication that the production equipment is not operating. (The maintenance machines might be making repair parts for the production equipment.)

The productivity of machines and equipment is entirely different, depending on the intended use and purpose of the equipment. The manager must know whether the equipment is contributing in accordance with its intended purpose and design before he or she can determine productivity levels.

The same concept applies to materials. Each and every item of material that can be seen as we tour the facility has been converted from cash. If the facility is to sustain growth, the material must be converted back to cash when it is sold as a finished product. Materials are very tangible. They can be weighed, measured, handled, transported, and stored.

Reconciling Inputs with Outputs

Observing a large overhead crane place several tons of steel scrap into an electric furnace does not in itself ensure productivity. Questions similar to those asked relative to equipment productivity must be addressed:

- How much of the material melted actually ends up as the finished product?

- Is the optimum raw material being used to arrive at the desired finished product?

- How long had the steel scrap been in inventory before it was placed in the production process?

Inasmuch as materials are tangible, certain major materials, such as steel, need to be reconciled to the amount of steel placed in production, or better yet, the amount of raw steel purchased. In other words, is all the steel purchased accounted for? In simple terms, it is a matter of steel in, steel out. After the controls are established to reconcile total input to output, the problem becomes one of what *should* the output be versus the actual output levels being attained with given input.

Suppose that on the tour we discover several pallets of partially completed products, and the dust indicates they have been there for quite some time. This represents cash committed to production inputs that are not being productive. Inasmuch as the productivity of cash is a function of time, an opportunity to experience growth with the cash resource has been lost during the time the materials have been idle. All forms of materials must be examined in terms of their readiness to be converted back into cash.

As we progress through the facility, many employees are operating production machines, some are driving fork trucks transporting materials, some are repairing equipment, some are inspecting parts, and some are in the lunch room. They all have one basic thing in common: They have all contracted with the plant to sell their capacity to perform some type of productive task and they have all done so on a cash basis. Their productive capacity is also paid for as a function of time. An employee contracts to work a given number of hours per time period, typically 40 hours per week. If a machine operator must wait several hours while the machine is being repaired, that time spent waiting is part of the 40 hours, even though not productive. The point is that the clock starts on Monday and runs through Friday, and the weekly payroll checks are issued without regard to what work was actually accomplished (except under some incentive-type programs in which wages are tied to production levels). An hour purchased for an employee's services is a reduction of the cash resource, regardless of the productivity of the hour purchased. Not unlike materials, the total labor resource should be reconciled to total hours input versus total value added by labor, and recoverable through the sale of completed goods and services.

The energy input is handled slightly differently than it is for machines, labor and materials, but it is not different conceptually. As will be illustrated in Chapter 11, different energy sources have varying capacities to do work measured in Btu. If, say, coal is used in the production process, each load of coal purchased with the conversion of cash has a given productive capacity. The manager must be able to determine how the amount of work actually done with the coal compares with what amount of work should have been done. Consider, for example, that it requires a given amount of coal to melt a given number of tons of steel. The manager needs to be able to measure the amount of energy input against actual production levels to determine the productivity of the energy.

Natural gas and electricity are similar. They continuously flow through metering devices. The input consumption must be measured and then compared with calculated energy requirements that are based on some independent variable, perhaps production, time, or season of the year. Again, inputs must be compared with value added that is recoverable through the sale of completed goods and services.

As has been illustrated, all production and support inputs are the result of cash being converted to machines, labor, material, and energy. Once the cash conversion takes place, it is analogous to water passing over a dam. An hour of employee time, once worked, is irreversible; a cubic foot of gas or kwh of electricity having passed through the metering devices, is gone; an hour of machine operating time can never be repeated. The productivity of each input must be measured and managed to ensure that the output generated by each input is positive, and that the total value added equates favorably to the total input costs.

Total Cost

Now that both production and support inputs have been considered, we can move one column to the right in Figure 3.1 to the "total cost" column. This column shows that the sum total of both production and support inputs comprises the total cost for any given time period. If the sale of goods and services for any time period is just enough to cover the total cost, a break-even situation occurs, but, there is no growth. An excess of outputs over inputs is required in order to have growth.

Break Even. Every firm should have a plan as to where break-even occurs, expressed as a percentage of the capacity. Figure 3.2 illustrates a planned break-even point, or the level of capacity at which inputs equal outputs.

The most significant factor to consider when developing a break-even plan is the determination of capacity. There will be a choice of options available to express capacity. It might be sales dollars, units of products sold, tons of product produced, labor hours, or many others. The expression of capacity must be based on the limiting factor of the facility or plant. Using an incorrect expression of capacity results in major problems that are illustrated in Chapter 14. If, for example, a plant manufactures wagons and can stamp 500 per month but can assemble 700 per month, the limiting factor is the stamping function, and break-even analysis should be expressed relative to stamping capacity. Accordingly, Figure 3.2 shows the facility's capacity to be 500 wagons.

Again, using Figure 3.2, many things can be determined relative to the firm's plans to recover total input cost:

- Planned fixed cost (FC) per time period is $20,000, represented by AD.

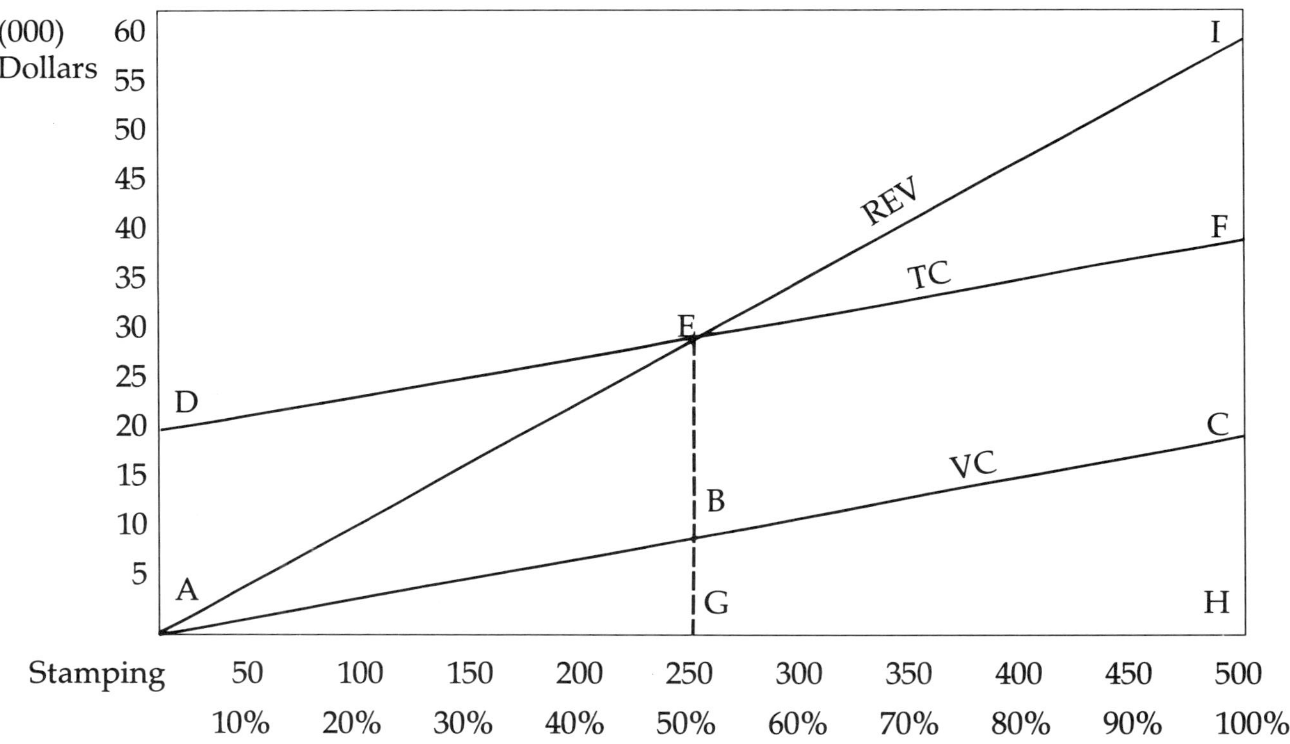

Fig. 3.2. Planned break-even

- Revenue (output value) per wagon is anticipated to be $120 ($60,000 ÷ 500 = $120).

- Variable cost per wagon is expected to be $40 ($20,000 ÷ 500 = $40).

- Contribution per wagon is calculated to be $80 ($120 - $40 = $80).

- Break-even occurs at 250 wagons, or 50% stamping capacity.

$$B/E = \frac{\$20,000}{1 - \dfrac{VC}{REV}} = \frac{\$20,000}{1 - \dfrac{\$40}{\$120}} =$$

$30,000 sales ÷ $120/wagon = 250 wagons

Looking at it another way:

Sales	250 x $120 = $30,000
Variable cost	250 x $ 40 = $10,000
Contribution @ B/E	= fixed cost = $20,000

(250 x $120) = (250 x $40) + $20,000

- Contribution at 100% stamping capacity is $40,000, represented by IC.

Sales	500 x $120 = $60,000
Variable cost	500 x $ 40 = -$20,000
Contribution	= $40,000

- Profit, or value added, at 100% stamping capacity would be $20,000.

Contribution	$40,000
Fixed cost	-$20,000
Profit	= $20,000

This takes us to the right-hand side of Figure 3.1. The value added to the production inputs at 100% stamping capacity is represented by IF and the total revenue by IH.

Break-Even: Comparing Actual and Planned

If the wagon manufacturer in the preceding example maintained the planned revenue per wagon, variable cost per wagon, and fixed cost per month, the break-even point would remain the same, regardless of actual capacity levels attained. If the firm operated at, say, 80% capacity with the same revenue and cost structure, the break-even would still be at 250 wagons per month. The only difference would be the absolute amount of contributions and profits. Break-even is a function of revenue and cost relationships; it is not a function of volume.

Let's say our wagon manufacturer operates for a year against the break-even plan and produces 3,920 wagons. According to plan, that would be operating at 65.3% capacity. Considering that selling prices remained at $120 per unit, contribution should have been $313,600 for the year, and profits $73,600.

Sales	3,920 x $120 =	$470,400
Less Variable		
Cost	3,920 x $ 40 =	156,800
Contribution		313,600
Less fixed cost		-240,000
Profit		$ 73,600

$$B/E = \cfrac{\$240,000}{1 - \cfrac{\$156,800}{\$470,400}}$$

B/E = $360,000 ÷ $120/wagon = 3,000 wagons per year = 250 wagons per month as originally planned.

Even though the selling price per wagon was unchanged at $120, the actual results were substantially different from Table 3.1.

Table 3.1. Actual operating results

Month	Wagons Sold	Revenue $120	(000) Total Cost	(000) Profit Loss
January	195	$ 23.4	$ 33.0	($9.6)
February	250	30.0	35.0	(5.0)
March	240	28.8	33.5	(4.7)
April	275	33.0	37.0	(4.0)
May	290	34.8	38.5	(3.7)
June	310	37.2	41.5	(4.3)
July	260	31.2	36.6	(5.4)
August	300	36.0	37.0	(1.0)
September	375	45.0	41.0	4.0
October	495	59.4	48.0	11.4
November	480	57.6	47.5	10.1
December	450	54.0	46.0	8.0
Total	3,920	$470.4	$474.6	($4.2)

The first thing to do in analyzing the problem is investigate why the break-even slipped. Considering that only total cost per month is known, the variable and fixed portions of the total cost must be determined. With this information, the results can be analyzed. Table 3.2 segregates the total cost into its variable and fixed components.

Table 3.2. Segregation of fixed and variable costs

Month	Wagon Production X	Total Cost (000) Y	X^2	$X{\bullet}Y$
January	195	$ 33.0	38,025	6,435
February	250	35.0	62,500	8,750
March	240	33.5	57,600	8,040
April	275	37.0	75,625	10,175
May	290	38.5	84,100	11,165
June	310	41.5	96,100	12,865
July	260	36.6	67,600	9,516
August	300	37.0	90,000	11,100
September	375	41.0	140,625	15,375
October	495	48.0	245,025	23,760
November	480	47.5	230,400	22,800
December	450	46.0	202,500	20,700
Total	3,920	$474.6	1,390,100	160,681

$\overline{X} = 326.67 \qquad \overline{Y} = \$39.55$

$$b = \frac{12\,(160,681) - (3,920)\,(474.6)}{12\,(1,390,100) - (3,920)} = .0515$$

$$a = \$39.55 - (.0515)\,(326.67) = \$22.73$$

Determining the total cost regression line in the form of $Y = a + bx$ states that total cost (Y) = fixed cost (a) + variable cost per unit (b) x number of units.

Table 3.2 determines a variable cost per unit of $.0515 (1,000) and fixed cost per month of $22.73 (1,000).

Substituting these values into the regression formula yields the following:

Total cost = ($22,730 x 12 months) + $51.50 (3,920)
= $272,760 + $201,880 = $474,640 for the year

This total matches column Y in Table 3.2.

Now, an actual break-even can be determined and graphed, using the regression line as the total cost line. Figure 3.3 illustrates this concept.

Summarizing the data from Figure 3.3, a detailed comparison can be made of the actual results versus those planned:

	Planned	Actual
• Fixed cost per month	$20,000	$22,730
• Revenue per wagon	$ 120	$ 120
• Variable cost per wagon	$40	$51.50
• Contribution per wagon	$80	$68.50
• Break-even expressed in		
1. wagons per month	250	332
2. total sales per month	$30,000	$39,816
3. percent of capacity	50%	66.4%
• Contribution per month		
• at 100% capacity	$40,000	$34,250
• Profit (value added) at		
• 100% capacity	$20,000	$11,520

Somewhere along the line, the productivity of inputs, either some or all, has drastically slipped. At this point, each input, i.e., machines, labor, materials and energy, should be examined in detail to see where the problems are.

Productivity Analysis

The first step is to consider the productivity of the capital committed to capacity, specifically in the form of production equipment. This is a good place to start, because it is the first item on the Resource Input Flow Chart, Figure 3.1. Both production and support equipment could be considered, however, if desired.

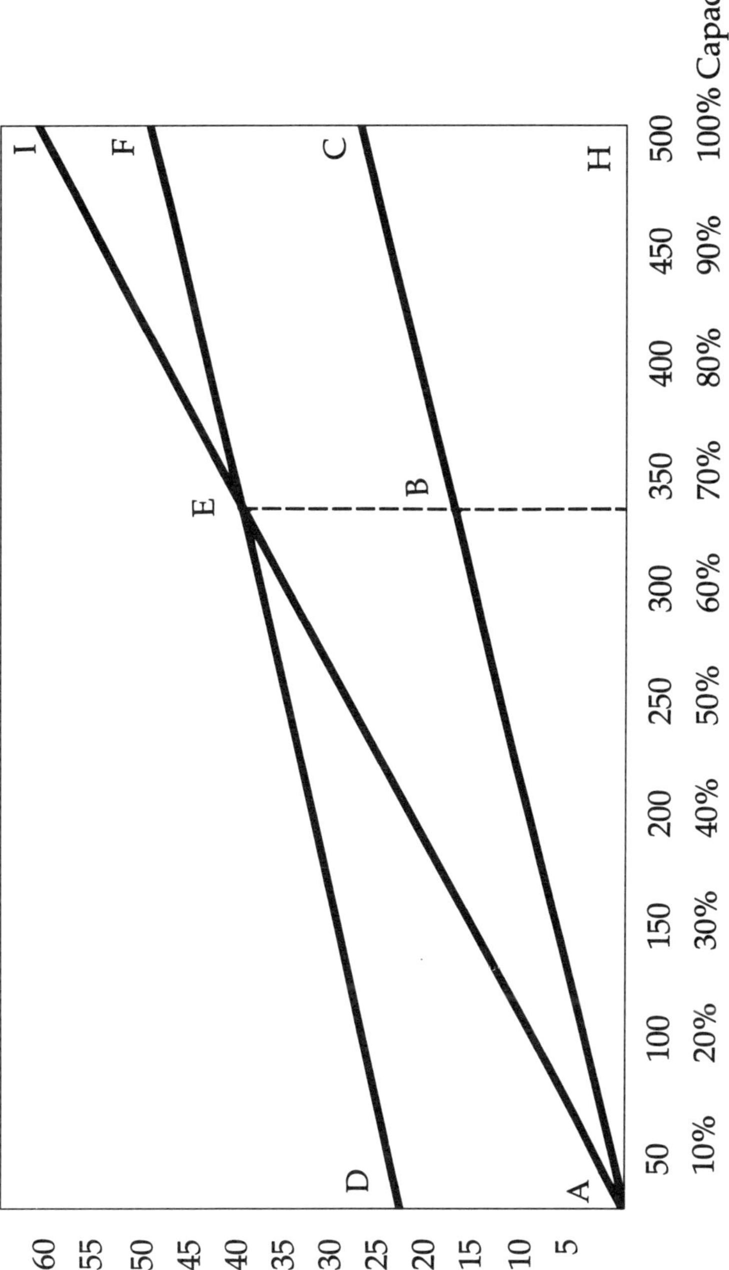

Fig. 3.3. Actual break-even

The U.S. Department of Commerce has been watching capital equipment productivity for several years. Its favored method to monitor such productivity is to plot constant dollars invested in equipment (net of depreciation) versus the value of gross domestic products of manufacturers, also in constant dollars. Table 3.3 illustrates where the U.S. stands relative to equipment productivity over the past decade. This chart indicates that more attention should be given to equipment productivity.

Table 3.3. Equipment productivity (manufacturing) (real dollars of output per real dollar of investment in net depreciated equipment in 1972 dollars)

Year	Output per $1 of Net Investment
1973	$2.55
1974	2.27
1975	2.01
1976	2.10
1977	2.12
1978	2.11
1979	2.01
1980	1.76
1981	1.66
1982	1.47

Consultant Peter F. Drucker states: "Despite its importance and payoff, not many business managers pay much attention to the productivity of capital, let alone work systematically at raising it." Another consultant states that "Direct labor may no longer be the area of opportunity for greatest productivity for U.S. companies." And finally, C. Johnson Grayson, chairman of the American Productivity Center, notes, "Productivity measures based solely on labor input are of limited value in many industries, especially those which are capital intensive."

It appears that nonlabor productivity may soon take on a more important role, both at the national policy-making level and in U.S. factories.

Productivity of capital equipment can be expressed in different ways. Remember that productivity is the ratio of some measure of input to its resultant output. Whereas, the recommended method on the macro level is to compare net capital investment dollars to gross domestic product, an individual industry or plant may devise its own particular productivity measurements on a smaller, more manageable level. There is an inherent short-fall in using the Department of Commerce method: It doesn't take into account short-run economic problems. For example, if capacity utilization is down from normal levels, as in the 1981-83 recession, productivity takes a nose dive. Productivity of equipment must reflect problems relating to capacity, utilization, and efficiency.

Consider the equipment in the stamping department in the example discussed above. It has the capability, as previously stated, to produce 500 wagons per month, or:

- 23.07 wagons per day, or

- 2.8838 wagons per hour, or

- .3468 hours per wagon (500 x 12) ÷ 260 work days per year = 23.07

Table 3.1, Actual Operating Results, showed that 3,920 wagons, or 65.33% of capacity, were produced during the year. Therefore, the productivity of equipment attributable to low capacity utilization can be shown graphically as per Figure 3.4 in which the entire shaded area represents opportunity cost generated by idle capacity.

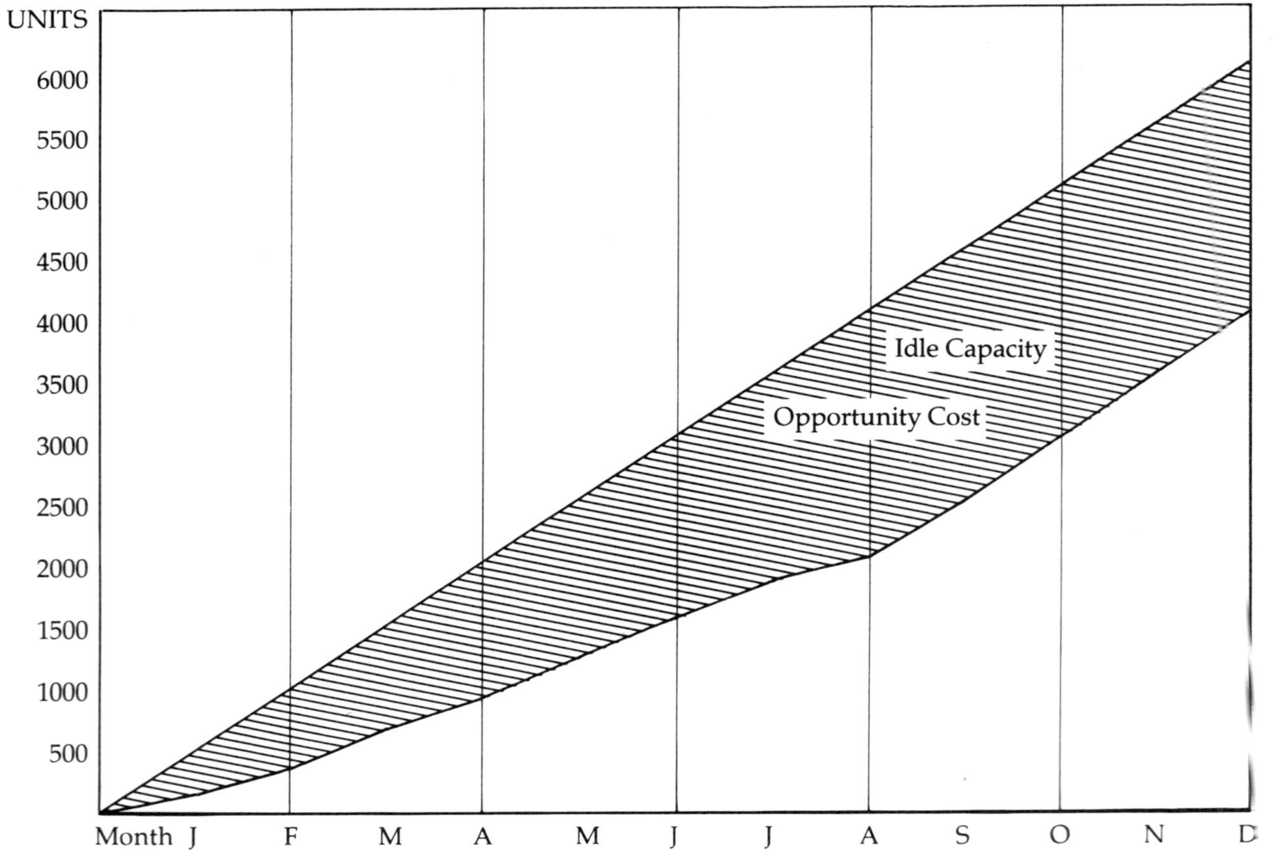

Fig. 3.4. Effects of idle capacity

To get the total picture relative to equipment productivity, we need to know how well the equipment performed while it was operating. Table 3.4 lists the actual equipment runtime hours by month.

Table 3.4. Wagon production vs. stamping hours

Month	Wagon Production	Run-time Hours
January	195	86
February	250	101
March	240	102
April	275	106
May	290	116
June	310	121
July	260	109
August	300	123
September	375	150
October	495	206
November	480	200
December	450	180
	3,920	1,600
	X = 326.07	Y = 133.33

By determining the regression line for these points, it was found that each wagon required .407 hours instead of the .3468 standard capacity. The total equation is:

Total time = .38 hr + (.407) (wagons produced)

The negligible intercept indicates that all the idle time was accounted for in Figure 3.4. In other words, the hours listed on Table 3.4 are exclusively runtime hours.

Something has happened to the equipment cycle time. Unless the problem is solved, the stamping capacity has, in effect, been reduced to 426 wagons instead of the planned 500.

$$\frac{8 \text{ hrs available}}{\begin{array}{c}.407 \text{ hrs/wagon} \\ \text{days per month}\end{array}} = \frac{19.656 \text{ wagons per day} \times 21.67}{425.9 \text{ wagons per month}}$$

Analysis of Other Inputs

There are other inputs that should not be affected by underutilization of capacity. The direct production inputs should be totally variable, and productivity problems should be limited to the efficiency of the input. Three such direct inputs are:

1. Production labor;

2. Production materials; and

3. Production energy.

In other words, there should be a direct and positive relationship between direct production labor and number of wagons produced. Accordingly, if there is no production, there should be no direct production labor expended. The same applies to production material: no production, no direct materials required. Consider, for example, that the bill of materials for a wagon calls for 4.0 lbs of steel in each. If 500 wagons are produced, 2,000 lbs of steel should be required. (Steel requirements are shown graphically in Figure 3.5.) However, once again, things don't always go as planned. Table 3.5 illustrates that a material productivity problem exits.

Regression Analysis: A Productivity Tool

Once again, a simple regression line is developed. Regression analysis is an excellent tool to use because its basic purpose is to show the relationship between two or more variables. In the present context two variables are considered, the independent variable, which is wagons, and the selected dependent variable. Remember once again the definition of productivity. It is the relationship between inputs and their resultant output; therefore, regression is one of the most appropriate tools to use in productivity analysis.

Therefore, in accordance with Table 3.5, total monthly steel consumption is calculated as follows:

Total steel = 45 lbs + 5.12 lbs/wagon x wagon production

This actual consumption pattern can be overlaid on the planned steel requirements, as per Figure 3.5.

Table 3.5. Wagon production vs. steel consumption

Month	*Wagons*	*Consumed*
January	195	1,055
February	250	1,300
March	240	1,255
April	275	1,400
May	290	1,525
June	310	1,645
July	260	1,360
August	300	1,645
September	375	1,970
October	495	2,570
November	480	2,515
December	450	2,330
Total	3,920	20,610

$\overline{X} = 326.67 \qquad \overline{Y} = 1{,}717.5$

b = 5.12 lbs per wagon

a = 45 lbs

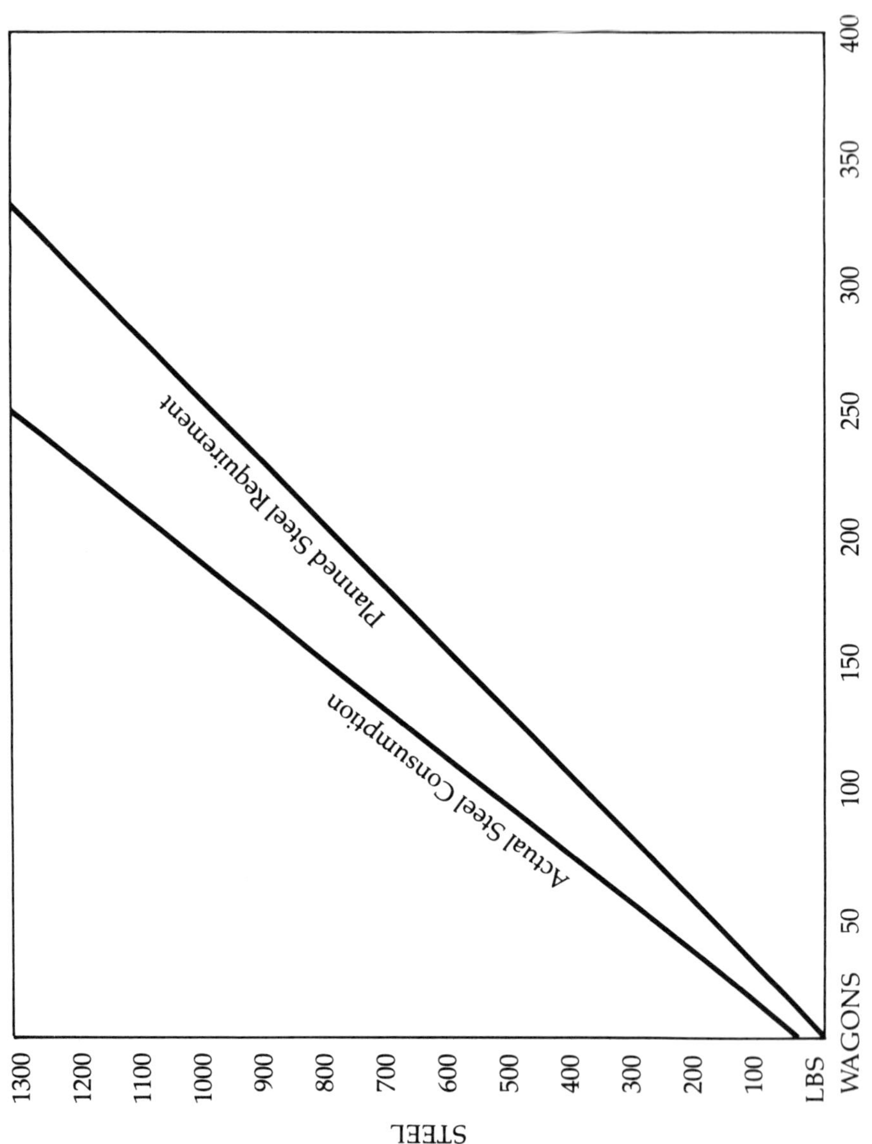

Fig. 3.5. Actual vs. planned steel consumption

The first thing to contend with is the 45 lbs consumed or lost before any wagon production. It could be lost during transit from the inventory location to the production area. For sure, 45 lbs are being paid for per month with no accompanying productivity.

Next, it is noted that each wagon produced is requiring 5.12 lbs versus the 4.0 lbs listed on the bill of materials, or 28 percent more than planned. This could be attributable to a higher scrap rate than anticipated.

When the plant is operating at 100% capacity, steel consumption should be 2,000 lbs per month. With the actual consumption patterns at full capacity, however, 2,605 lbs of steel would be required.

5.12 lbs x 500 wagons =	2,560
45 lbs per month constant	45
	2,605 lbs

This 2,605 lbs will require that cash be converted for its purchase, and then it will all be placed in the production process. However, only 2,000 lbs will end up in finished product, sold and converted back to cash. The productivity audit has uncovered this discrepancy, and it's now up to management to reconcile the difference.

Effect on Break-Even

The idle capacity experienced, the inefficient equipment runtime, and now the excess steel consumption all had a detrimental effect on the wagon manufacturer's break-even point. These items have affected both monthly fixed costs and unit variable costs.

All inputs to the production process, whether direct or support, must be analyzed.

The Productivity Matrix

Each firm or plant should determine the major part of its inputs. In other words, is the firm capital intensive, labor intensive, material intensive, or energy intensive? Most firms will be some combination of these. A basic way to determine this is to examine the relative magnitude of the different inputs in the form of a matrix such the one presented in Table 3.6. This will indicate priorities in productivity programs.

Table 3.6. Resource input matrix

Department	Material	Workers	Machine	Energy	Total
Cutting	100	70	35	145	350
Stamping	—	40	30	25	95
Fabrication	210	25	5	5	245
Assembly	—	220	30	5	255
Testing	—	140	5	5	150
Plant					
Service	—	5	50	225	280
Totals	310	500	155	410	1,375

The matrix shows the following:

- Total plant cost for a given time period is $1,375.

- The plant is primarily labor intensive.

Materials	22.6%
Labor	36.3%
Machines*	11.3%
Energy	29.8%
Total inputs	100.0%

    *Note that cost per time period attributable to machines can be depreciation for all assets within a particular department, or the repair costs required to maintain all the equipment within the department, or both.

- The cutting department is the highest cost department in the plant.

Cutting	25.5%
Stamping	6.9%
Fabrication	17.8%
Assembly	18.6%

Testing	10.9%
Plant services	20.3%
	100.0%

- The highest single category of departmental cost is energy in the plant services department.

Energy in plant services	16.4%
Labor in assembly	16.0%
Material in fabrication	15.3%
Energy in cutting	10.5%
Labor in testing	10.2%
Material in cutting	7.3%
All Other	24.3%
	100.0%

According to the matrix in Table 3.6, more than 75% of the total expenses are found in 30% of the cost categories. The purpose of matrix management is to point out areas where productivity improvements will have the greatest impact.

The matrix points out several other things. Productivity improvement plans for the cutting department will be entirely different from those of the assembly department or the fabricating department.

The first priority for the manager of the cutting department will be energy, since energy comprises 41.4% of the total department cost. The manager of the assembly department will begin his program with the labor input, since labor comprises 86.2% of his total cost. This is not to say that the assembly department isn't concerned with energy productivity. Energy should just not be the first priority. (A 10% improvement in labor productivity will reduce the total department cost by 8.6% whereas a 10% improvement in energy would reduce the total department cost by only .2%.) Likewise, the manager of the fabricating department will begin his program with the materials input, which represents 85.7% of the total cost of that department.

Many firms fall into the trap of concentrating on one category of cost input while letting the other categories slide. Sometimes, an older firm that was originally labor intensive places top priority on labor productivity. That would be entirely suboptimal for the fabricating department in the present example.

Developing Creative Productivity — Improvement Methods

It is important not only to strive for the optimum productivity from each category of input, but also to consider performing some tasks with a different input or a combination of inputs. Most jobs can, within reason, be performed with the labor input. They may just require a great amount of labor, perhaps a disproportionate amount. Consider the pyramids. They would be constructed entirely differently if they were built today. Almost any automated process in an old-line industry can be traced back to a predominantly labor-intensive operation. There have been favorable trade-offs by automating many operations. In other words, the overall productivity of capital has increased with more equipment and less labor.

Inasmuch as there are several ways to perform work and to do a specific function, it stands to reason that there is an optimum combination of inputs, i.e., labor, machines and energy, with which to do a given job or task. The concept is not new. It is being used by General Motors in the design of its renovated "Buick City" in Flint, Mich. Buick City will be fashioned after the Japanese "Toyota City." One of the main concepts is that parts plants will be built around assembly plants. This will drastically reduce inventories and will allow cars to be built with less labor.

General Motors also plans to use elaborate computer technology and new automated assembly processes. It also plans to use what it calls a "socio-technical system approach" that seeks the best combination of people and machines to complete an assembly operation. At optimum assembly capacity the technique can reduce the labor hours that a specific task takes by more than two-thirds, according to a report in the *Wall Street Journal.*

Section 3

PRODUCTIVITY:
APPLICABLE TO ALL INPUTS
TO THE PRODUCTION PROCESS

Chapter 4
Productivity of Capital:
The Initial Production Input

Objectives

- *Understand the importance of time as a factor in the productivity of capital.*

- *Recognize that "time is money."*

- *Be able to calculate the future value and present value of money.*

- *Understand that the factors of production must be productive.*

- *Understand that because productivity is a function of time, it can be an opportunity cost if not utilized.*

- *Realize that inefficiently used material may represent an opportunity cost.*

- *Comprehend the opportunity costs of poor credit use.*

- *Understand that turnover and accounts receivable are functions of time.*

Contents

The Importance of Time

Of all the various business activities that can be conceived, whether they are of an operations nature or otherwise, there is one basic, universal input: time. Its presence is not optional, it is omnipresent. That being the case, one might think that time is the most abundant input or resource. In fact, time is the most scarce of all inputs and must be handled accordingly. The assumption that time is limitless is without basis.

The general business and economic climate is extremely dynamic. Objectives, styles, and technologies are constantly changing. Change and economic growth are very closely related. Consider a popular consumer item such as a color television set. When such a product is new in the marketplace, there is a great demand for it. As each household acquires a color TV set, the market becomes saturated, demand lessens, and production facilities for making color television sets are underutilized. There is a certain length of time during the expansion of the market when the facilities are being heavily used. Later, the same facilities will gradually head toward complete idleness. Marketers label this concept the "product life cycle." In recent years, the life-cycle concept has been applied to production/operations management. The life-cycle concept, regardless of how it is applied, growth accelerates for a given time and then decelerates in accordance with changes in consumer demand.

The objective of business is to recognize the periods of growth for certain goods and services, and to then capitalize on this growth by maximizing the productivity of all inputs. This action will simultaneously maximize the productivity of time. Conversely, business must forecast declines in growth for these same goods and services in order to rechannel its inputs into other goods and services whose life cycles are on the growth side of the curve.

Time is absolutely indifferent to which portion of the life-cycle curve a particular industry or plant occupies. If a company finances a business venture with borrowed capital, the lender is not expected to change its lending cost as the company progresses along the life-cycle curve. If the company is on the declining side and the productivity of the capital is also declining, it does not affect the lending cost, because the lender could simply transfer the capital to a firm on the growth side of a similar curve.

Therefore, the opportunity for capital to be productive is a function of time, not a function of individual product life cycles. The supplier of capital has the option to direct its funds to the areas of greatest potential growth. The user of capital must recognize the supplier's opportunity by paying a constant cost for the use of the capital, regardless of his particular growth situation.

Time Is Money

A supplier of funds could expect a constant growth, or return of his funds, over any length of time. If, for example, he invested $1,000 at 15% for 20 years, he would expect his investment to grow at 15% each year for the 20-year period.

It is easy to discuss time, such as the year just mentioned, without giving thought to exactly what a year (or any period) actually is. It is a benchmark. It is not only a benchmark, but also the least changing benchmark available. When money is used as a benchmark (or productivity indicator) it must be expressed relative to its value at a particular time. Many times, we have seen financial analyses covering a space of several years, which almost always have an accompanying notation that the money values are based on constant dollars, using a given year as the base or benchmark. This type of restatement is not required for a given measure of time. A year is a year is a year. Therefore, the time period of a year is the universal benchmark to measure the growth, or productivity, of capital.

Future Value (Compounding)

Let's consider the investment of funds. If our investor simply deposited $1,000 at an interest rate of 15%, the implicit assumption is that his deposit will grow by 15% if held in deposit for a period of one year. Therefore, at the end of the year, he would expect his deposit to have grown to $1,150, or (15% x $1,000) + $1,000 = $1,150. In other words, the future value would be equal to the amount invested (principal) plus the interest rate multiplied by the principal. Simplified, it can be expressed as:

$$FV = P + P\,(IR) \text{ where}$$
$$FV = \text{future value}$$
$$P = \text{principal or present amount}$$
$$IR = \text{interest rate, expressed as a decimal}$$

It is even simpler, when a number grows by a given percent, to multiply the number by one plus the percent. Basic algebra tells us that if some number is equal to an unknown, say x plus .15 (x), then $lx + .15\% = 1.15x =$ the number. Now then, the simplified growth formula is:

$$FV = P\,(1 + IR)$$

The above future value of $1,000 invested for 1 year can be expressed as $1,000 (1.15) = $1,150.

If the investment is left on deposit for another year at the same interest rate of 15%, at the end of the second year the deposit will have grown to $1,322.50. The concept of leaving the earned interest on deposit with the original principal to earn interest on the interest is called *compounding*.

Compounding the original $1,000 for two years produces:

$$\$1,000 \times 1.15 \times 1.15 = \$1,322.50$$

Compounding the original $1,000 for three years produces:

$$\$1,000 \times 1.15 \times 1.15 \times 1.15 = \$1,520.87$$

Compounding the original $1,000 for n years produces:

$$\$1,000 \times 1.15^{n}, \text{ or } FV = P(1 + IR)^{n}$$

We can use this basic formula to determine the growth of an investment at different interest rates and over different periods. Consider the growth of $1 over time at various interest rates as illustrated in Table 4.1.

Table 4.1. Future value of $1 (compounding)

| | Interest Rates | | |
End of Year	5%	10%	15%
1	1.0500	1.1000	1.1500
2	1.1025	1.2100	1.3225
3	1.1576	1.3310	1.5209
4	1.2155	1.4641	1.7490
5	1.2763	1.6105	2.0144

If we accept this concept as valid for the growth of money deposited in a bank, then we also need to accept it as valid for any business entity with a profit (growth) objective. Inasmuch as an investor could earn 61¢ if he deposited $1 for five years at 10% interest, shouldn't he expect to do at least as well if he uses his money to buy stock in a firm? Definitely so. Otherwise, there is no incentive to withdraw from the bank and invest in a firm. The "opportunity" for the investment to grow would be greater at the bank.

If a business tries to attract investors by telling them that investment will grow (provide a return of) 10% annually, we can determine the financial position of the firm for any time in the future.

Consider a business that was new and was capitalized by 100 investors, each investing $1,000 in it.

Balance Sheet 19X0

Cash $100,000	Original stockholders equity $100,000
Total assets $100,000	Total equity $100,000

If all the earnings of the business are plowed back into the operation, the balance sheet would look like this at the end of the fifth year:

Balance Sheet 19X5

Cash	xx	Original stockholders' equity	$100,000
Inventories	xx	Profits (growth)	$ 61,050
Plant and equipment			
	xx		
Total assets	$161,050	Total equity	$161,050

The total equity requirement was determined by the basic compounding formula, using $N = 5$ years.

$$FV = P(1+IR)^5$$
$$= \$100,000 \, (1.10)^5$$
$$= \$161,050$$

(Notice also that, according to Table 4.1, the growth of $1 at 10% for 5 years is $1.6105.)

Present Value (Discounting)

Many times, it is important to know how much we would have to invest at a given rate in order to end up with a given amount at the end of a given time period. In other words, we know the future value (FV), we know the rate of interest available, and we know when we need the money. What we don't know is how much we need to invest in order for the investment to grow to meet our needs at a predetermined time. We begin with the basic compounding formula and express it in terms of the present amount (principal).

If $FV = P(1+IR)^n$, then

$$P = \frac{FV}{(1 + IR)^n}$$

If we need $10,000 for tuition in five years and our bank gives 10% interest, we can determine how much we would need to deposit presently and leave on deposit for the five-year period.

$$P = \frac{\$10,000}{1.6105}$$

$$= \$6,209.25$$

The denominator of the problem is once again found in the compounding table (Table 4.1) under the 10% column and the fifth-year row. Now, instead of compounding the growth of $1, we are discounting the $1 to its present value.

The compounding table can be expressed as a discounting table, or a present-value table, as is Table 4.2.

Table 4.2. Present value of $1 (discounting)

	Interest Rates		
End of Year	*5%*	*10%*	*15%*
1	.9524	.9091	.8696
2	.9070	.8265	.7562
3	.8638	.7514	.6576
4	.8227	.6831	.5718
5	.7835	.6210	.4972

Let's consider our previous investors once again. Let's say they wanted to own a business worth $1 million at the end of five years. They project a profit of 10% on their investment each year. How much will they need to invest now in order to reach their goal? The projected fifth-year balance sheet and the required beginning balance sheet look like this:

Balance Sheet Projected 19X5

Cash	xx	Original equity	xx
Inventories	xx	Profits (growth)	xx
Plant and equipment	xx		
Total assets	$1,000,000	Total equity	$1,000,000

Beginning Balance Sheet Required 19XO

Beginning cash	$621,000	Original equity	$621,000
Total assets	$621,000	Total equity	$621,000

Therefore, each of the 100 investors would have to currently invest $6,210 in order to end up with a $1 million equity balance at the end of five years. Annual profits for each of the five years would be as found in Table 4.3. Total profit for the five years plus the original investment equals ending equity.

$379,127 + $621,000 = $1,000,127

Notice what happens if the annual discount (present value) factors for 10% from Table 4.2, are added together.

Table 4.3. Annual profit schedule

Year	Asset Base	Growth @ 10% (Profit)
1	$621,000	$ 62,100
2	$683,100	$ 68,310
3	$751,410	$ 75,141
4	$826,551	$ 82,655
5	$909,206	$ 90,921
	Total	$379,127

	Present Value (PV) Factors
Year 1	.9091
Year 2	.8265
Year 3	.7514
Year 4	.6831
Year 5	.6210
	3.7911

Perhaps the relationship between compounding and discounting can be further illustrated by combining the present-value factors and the annual-profit schedule.

	Annual *Profits*	*PV* *Factors*
Year 1	$ 62,100	.9091
Year 2	$ 68,310	.8265
Year 3	$ 75,141	.7514
Year 4	$ 82,655	.6831
Year 5	$ 90,921	.6210
Total	$379,127	3.7911

$$\text{Then } \$62,100 \times 1.10^5 = \$100,000$$

$$\text{and}$$

$$\frac{\$1}{1.10^5} = .6210$$

The concept of the productivity of capital is built on these basic premises. The productivity of capital, measured as the growth of the original investment or the return on investment, will be discussed repeatedly throughout the remainder of the text.

Capital Investment Is a Necessity

It takes money to make money. This is another popular cliché, and we can address it appropriately on the heels of the time value of money concept.

Capital doesn't grow unless it is turned over. To be more specific, capital must be exchanged for production inputs and it must become part of the production process for goods or services. When an investor deposits funds in a bank or in the bond market, the interest earned is not for the privilege of holding the invested capital idle. Rather, the one who pays the interest will direct the capital into the production process. In essence, interest is nothing more than a modest fee for the use of capital and is normally paid to the investor who wishes minimal risk. The invested funds, however, will end up in the mainstream of production activity.

The investor who channels funds directly into production

factors stands to gain a larger return, but also faces a higher risk. The higher return is attributable to the fact that interest isn't skimmed off the top and paid to an intermediary, whereas the potentially higher risk is due to the fact that the funds may be invested in a firm experiencing less-than-anticipated growth.

If a holder of funds desires zero investment risk, he may choose to keep the funds in the form of cash locked away in a wall safe. In such a situation, the growth of the funds would equal the risk involved: zero. The only thing the owner would have is opportunity, which can't be spent. Even that is forgone for each event in which the funds are not placed in the production process. Therefore, the aforementioned cliché is entirely true and totally applicable to production and operations management.

When the holder of funds who wanted zero risk finally decides to empty his safe and invest in production factors, he creates an opportunity for growth. That is the first step, but is not an end in itself relative to the productivity of capital.

Suppose our holder of funds had considered a 12-month interest-bearing certificate of deposit (CD) at the rate of 15%. He also has a hobby of making plastic gadgets and thought that he would combine fun with making money. Consequently, he set up a small plastics manufacturing operation. (For purposes of the following illustration, the discussion will center on a manufacturing operation, but it could be any business that has a growth (profit) objective or at least the goal to sustain status quo. It could be a hospital, airline, bank, farm or janitorial service.)

Let's say the holder of funds intends to manufacture and sell ice scrapers for windshields. He enters into the following business transactions:

- Buys equipment for $1,500;

- Rents a building for $100 per month;

- Buys raw material for $1,000;

- Leases a fork truck for $50 per month; and

- Hires a helper for $5 per hour.

He originally had $10,000, but, after buying equipment and material, he had $7,500. The rent, lease, and hired help were not to be paid until month's end. After the initial purchases, the balance sheet reflected the following:

Assets:		Equity:	
Cash	$7,500		
Raw material	$1,000		
Equipment	$1,500	Original investment	$10,000
Total assets	$10,000	Total equity	$10,000

Everything looked bright. The helper began making scrapers from the raw material. During the first month of operation, the original raw material was converted to ice scrapers and $1,000 more was spent for additional raw material. The helper worked 175 hours during the month. The equipment was set up on a five-year straight-line depreciation schedule.

At the end of the first month, a friend stopped by and asked our entrepreneur, "What's going on?" He chuckled and gave the age-old answer, "The rent." Then he thought about what he had said. The rent was indeed going on, and so was the fork truck lease, equipment depreciation, and his payroll. He quickly calculated in his mind the amount of interest he would have accrued if he had invested in the CD, and realized that his $10,000 would have grown to $10,125 after one month ($10,000 x .15 ÷ 12). He quickly drafted an income statement and balance sheet and reconciled his cash statement to see whether his present position was comparable to his missed CD opportunity.

Cash Statement		Income Statement	
Beginning	+ $7,500	Sales	$ 0
Raw material	- 1,000	Rent	100
Building rent	- 100	Wages	875
Wages	- 875	Fork-truck	50
		Lease	
		Depreciation	25

		Net Loss	
Ending cash	$5,475	per month	$1,050

Balance Sheet

Assets:		Equity:	
Cash	$5,475	Original investment	$10,000
Raw material	1,000	Loss on operations	(1,050)
WIP inventory	1,000		
Equipment	1,475		
Total Assets	$8,950	Total equity	$8,950

Reviewing his financial position, our investor quickly realizes that not only did he miss the CD opportunity, but that his investment is losing ground. What if he lays off his helper until business picks up? The only thing that action will do is ensure his doom because the production process will come to a halt. The problem can be summarized very briefly: Cash was converted to production factors (i.e., inputs), but no outputs resulted. The production process implies a cycle:

Cash → production inputs → products → cash

In the present context, we want to examine the missed opportunity when the production process stops somewhere within the cycle.

Consider just three basic sets of circumstances:

1. The $10,000 kept in the vault out of circulation.

2. The $10,000 invested in a 15% CD.

3. The $10,000 channeled to production factors.
   a. Building rent at $100 per month.
   b. Fork truck lease at $50 per month.

The results are summarized in Table 4.4. If the $10,000 is locked away — in other words kept entirely out of the production process — there is absolutely no opportunity for growth. Money will not and, in fact, cannot beget money unless it is part of the production cycle. Even though it may appear that there is as much money available at the end of the year as at the beginning, the inflation phenomenon may result in the ending $10,000 having less purchasing power.

Table 4.4. Productivity opportunities

Month	$10,000 in Vault	$10,000 in 15% CD*	$10,000 in Production Factors
1	$10,000	$10,125	$9,850
2	$10,000	$10,250	$9,700
3	$10,000	$10,375	$9,550
4	$10,000	$10,500	$9,400
5	$10,000	$10,625	$9,250
6	$10,000	$10,750	$9,100
7	$10,000	$10,875	$8,950
8	$10,000	$11,000	$8,800
9	$10,000	$11,125	$8,650
10	$10,000	$11,250	$8,500
11	$10,000	$11,375	$8,350
12	$10,000	$11,500	$8,200

*Monthly accrued interest but not compounded.

If the $10,000 were invested in a 12-month, 15% CD, the $1,150 of interest would accrue to the holder. The opportunity and productivity of capital to the holder is 15%. The productivity of capital to the issuer of the CD is unknown. Only one thing is certain: The issuer didn't take the $10,000 and lock it away in some vault. The $10,000 of a surety entered the production process in some stage and was productive at a minimum of 15% for the duration of the certificate.

In the case in which our investor/entrepreneur's $10,000 is decreased monthly for the lease and rent of production factors, productivity is negative. This brings us to a critical point: After cash is converted into production factors, the factors themselves must be productive. A great deal was said in earlier chapters about the productivity of direct production factors such as labor and materials. For now, let's expand the concept that production factors that require the expenditure of cash as a function of time also need to be productive.

Thus far, it has been shown that cash, as a medium of exchange, presents continuing opportunities to grow. The opportunities are taken when cash is channeled into the production process via production factors. Every day that cash remains idle represents a lost opportunity for growth that can never be recovered. After cash is converted into production factors, the factors themselves need to be productive and complete the production process. The completion of the production process can be viewed as the transformation of factors into products or services that have value to a buyer who is willing to exchange more cash to obtain the goods and services.

Any step of the production process that stalls, for any reason, inherently produces opportunity cost and, in most cases, real cost. The latter two columns of Table 4.4 indicate, moreover, that the total cost associated with idle production factors is inversely proportional to the opportunity foregone due to their idleness.

Functions of Time

The building that our entrepreneur rented represented an actual outflow of cash. The amount of rent charged by the owner of the building is related to the opportunity that the owner had foregone by not using the building as a production factor or not selling the building and investing the proceeds elsewhere.

Just as the opportunity for the growth of capital is a function of time, so is the rent charged for the use of an asset a function of time. The difference is that instead of investing in, say, a 12%, 12-month interest-bearing security, the owner invested in a building that was suitable for some production process.

If a particular building would cost an investor $20,000 to buy, the amount that he would charge a renter can be determined relative to the opportunity forgone by not investing the $20,000 elsewhere. If the best alternative available was 12% compounded monthly, the comparable rent equivalent can be determined. (The risks associated with alternative opportunities will not be considered at this point. The exclusive point to be made centers on the time value of money concept.)

A $20,000 investment at 12% compounded monthly, yields $22,536.50 at the end of one year.

$$\$20,000 \times 1.01^{12} = \$22,536.50$$

Therefore, $2,536.50 is the opportunity to invest in interest-bearing securities compounded monthly at 12%. Accordingly, the monthly rent must provide equal opportunity for growth.

With the basic assumption that rents received could be put to work immediately earning a 12% return, we find that the rental of $200 per month is sufficient. It is known that 1/12 of the interest earned on the above $20,000 certificate is $200. That is the same requirement to be met with rent. The concept, expanded for 12 months, is summarized in Table 4.5.

Table 4.5. Reinvestment of rental income at 12%

Month	Monthly Rent	Interest Factors*	Accrued Interest	Monthly Rent and Interest
1	$ 200	$1.01^{11} = 1.1155$	$ 23.10	$ 223.10
2	$ 200	$1.01^{10} = 1.1045$	$ 20.90	$ 220.90
3	$ 200	$1.01^{9} = 1.0936$	$ 18.72	$ 218.72
4	$ 200	$1.01^{8} = 1.0828$	$ 16.56	$ 216.56
5	$ 200	$1.01^{7} = 1.0721$	$ 14.52	$ 214.52
6	$ 200	$1.01^{6} = 1.0615$	$ 12.30	$ 212.30
7	$ 200	$1.01^{5} = 1.0510$	$ 10.20	$ 210.20
8	$ 200	$1.01^{4} = 1.0406$	$ 8.12	$ 208.12
9	$ 200	$1.01^{3} = 1.0303$	$ 6.06	$ 206.06
10	$ 200	$1.01^{2} = 1.0201$	$ 4.02	$ 204.02
11	$ 200	$1.01^{1} = 1.0100$	$ 2.00	$ 202.00
12	$ 200	$1.00 = 1.0000$	—	$ 200.00
Total	$2,400		$136.50	$2,536.50

*Implied is that rent is paid at the end of the month, after the renter enjoys the use of the building. Therefore, the owner has use of the first month's rent for 11 of the 12 months.

As far as the building owner is concerned, his opportunity is being covered with monthly rental receipts. Now the productivity ball is in the court of the renter. If the facility is idle, for whatever reason, the owner is still covered because the renter is paying for his (owner's) opportunity, regardless of whether the facility is productive or not. Every single day that the facility is nonproductive, the renter forgoes a permanent opportunity. The rent goes on. Therefore, the objective of the renter is to use the facility for productive purposes at all times.

The same principle applies to the lessor/lessee of the aforementioned fork truck. The lessor has weighed his investment opportunities and determined that the most attractive is to own a fork truck and lease it to our manufacturer. His opportunity is met with monthly lease payments. Once again, it is now up to the lessee to keep the production cycle going by utilizing the fork truck in the production of goods and services.

Any time the production cycle stops, for whatever reason, opportunity to maximize productivity is lost forever. Such factors had been obtained by an exchange of cash whose productivity is a function of time, whose hourglass never stops.

Payroll: A Function of Time

Whether an employee is a production worker or a high-level manager, his/her compensation is based on a given time period. It can be by the hour, by the week, by the month, or by the year. Even production employees who are covered by some sort of incentive, or piecework, plan are governed by time. Piecework plans are designed around an estimated time period during which a given or estimated number of parts will be completed, most likely per hour.

Employee compensation points back to the concept of opportunity of production per time period. An employee can be compared to an owner of a facility. He compares the different available jobs and selects the one in which his skills provide the greatest return, measured in dollars, per time period.

The employer considers, and rightly so, the capability of the employee as a production factor and is interested in the amount of output from each time period of employee input. (This is in no way intended to limit the worth of an employee to an objective factor of production. The greater worth of the labor force will be addressed in depth in Chapter 8.)

A nonproductive employee, for whatever reason, creates a lost opportunity never that can be recovered. Once again, the payroll clock doesn't stop just because the employee does.

As described earlier in this chapter, our entrepreneur laid off hired help in an effort to curb inputs. This was a myopic action inasmuch as labor is required to operate machines, which transform materials, which adds value to goods and services. When labor is idle, so follow the other production factors.

Opportunity Costs

Idle Materials

Table 4.4 illustrated that rent or lease payments represent actual cost in addition to opportunity cost if the production factor rented or leased was nonproductive or idle. Idle material, or materials held in slow or nonmoving inventory, represent another very pronounced opportunity cost. In addition, a real cost may be incurred if there are carrying costs or deterioration costs, both of which are functions of time. Carrying cost will normally consist of, at least in part, financing charges to fund the inventory.

Material, just like all other production factors, begins with an exchange of cash, or most likely a promise of cash within a specified time period. This promise is represented by an account payable to the buyer and an account receivable to the seller. We have already seen in detail the advantage of receiving timely cash and directing it immediately into the production process, where it has the ability and opportunity to grow. Both seller and buyer accept this concept, so that it becomes the objective of the buyer to negotiate extended payment terms while the objective of the seller is to convert accounts receivable into cash. Promises to pay a bill cannot in themselves purchase additional production inputs. (Accounts receivable themselves may be sold or factored for cash, but that is beyond the basic concept of achieving liquidity as presented in the context of productivity.)

Fully recognizing that promises are not negotiable instruments, a seller may offer credit terms to the buyer, such as 2% 1ON30. Such terms are incentives for the buyer to convert his promises to pay into cash. The above terms mean that the seller will discount the purchase price of the merchandise by 2% if the buyer pays cash within 10 days from the date of invoice. The remainder of the terms indicate that the invoice is due in full (net invoice) by the 30th day, and that at any time thereafter the invoice is delinquent. The seller will usually assess a late charge, such as 1½% per month of the net amount of the invoice until paid. The 1½% per month equates to something more than 18% per year.

Earlier in this chapter, our entrepreneur purchased $1,000 worth of raw material. Let's say he bought the material on terms of 2% 30N60. Consider several possible situations:

1. The material is received but remains unused in inventory for two months. The buyer pays the invoice on day 60.

2. The material is received and is converted to product immediately. The buyer pays the invoice on day 60.

3. The material is received but remains unused in inventory for two months. The buyer pays the invoice on day 30, taking advantage of the 2% discount.

In the first instance, the seller experiences a lost opportunity for the productivity of capital. In other words, the seller had funds invested in material that was not providing a return. Moreover, if he borrowed funds to finance the material, he would experience a real loss in addition to the opportunity lost, similar to that of the renter of idle facilities in Table 4.4. The buyer also experiences an opportunity cost by not allowing the materials to enter the production process. No one gained (except perhaps the seller's bank), productivity was zero, and there was no growth. The buyer has, in essence, borrowed $1,000 from the seller but has paid no interest on it. This instance illustrates an irrevocable opportunity lost forever.

In the second set of circumstances, the seller is in no better or worse position than in the preceding example. The seller's production cycle has stopped, resulting in an opportunity cost. However, the buyer, in essence, gains by earning on an asset for which he had not committed funds. It is like earning interest on someone else's money. He gained productivity of material before exchanging cash.

In the last scenario, the loser is not quite as obvious. It would appear that the buyer suffers a double opportunity cost. He has exchanged cash on which he forgoes interest earnings, while at the same time his production factor, i.e., material, sits idle. If the buyer had to borrow funds in order to pay the invoice for the material, he would additionally experience a real cost in the form of interest expense on top of the forgone opportunities. But another factor must be contended with in this latter situation. The buyer didn't pay the total $1,000 invoice amount. He paid only $980 for the material. If a 12% return is available to both buyer and seller, how is each affected by the buyer exercising his discount privilege?

Inasmuch as capital growth is measured on an annualized basis, it becomes a question of whether the seller would rather have $1,000 earning 12% for 10 months or $980 earning 12 percent for 11 months.

- $1,000 received on day 60 (i.e., the seller has use of the $1,000 for 10 months at 12%).

$$\$1,000 \times 1.01^{10} = \underline{\$1,104.50}$$

- $980 received on day 30 (i.e., the seller has use of $980 for

11 months at 12%).

$$\$980 \times 1.01^{11} = \underline{\$1,093.19}$$

These calculations reveal basically that the future value of $1,000 invested for 10 months at 12% is $11.31 more than the future value of $980 invested for 11 months at 12%. The seller would be ahead to wait the additional 30 days for the full $1,000. (See Table 4.6 (note rounding).)

Table 4.6. Invoice discount decision

Month	$1,000 Received at End of Month 2			$980 Received at End of Month 1			
	Months Used	Interest Factor	Interest Earned	Months Used	Interest Factor	Interest Earned	Δ
1	—	—	—	—	—	—	—
2	—	—	—	11	1.1155	$ 10.932	$10.932
3	10	1.0936	$ 11.045	10	1.1045	10.824 (	.221)
4	9	1.0936	10.936	9	1.0936	10.717 (	.219)
5	8	1.0828	10.828	8	1.0828	10.611 (	.217)
6	7	1.0721	10.721	7	1.0721	10.507 (	.214)
7	6	1.0615	10.615	6	1.0615	10.403 (	.212)
8	5	1.0510	10.510	5	1.0510	10.300 (	.210)
9	4	1.0406	10.406	4	1.0406	10.198 (	.208)
10	3	1.0303	10.303	3	1.0303	10.097 (	.206)
11	2	1.0201	10.201	2	1.0201	9.997 (	.204)
12	1	1.0100	10.100	1	1.0100	9.898 (	.202)
			$ 105.665			$ 114.484	$ 8.819
	Principle		$1,000.000			$ 980.000	($20.000)
	Future Value		$1,105.665			$1,094.484	($11.181)

The buyer actually forfeited interest opportunity on $1,000 for one month, amounting to $10. However, he saved $20 by discounting the invoice for a net saving of $10. The buyer could just as easily have been a double winner if he had placed the materials in the production process upon receipt.

This discussion could be continued by determining the rate of interest of which the buyer and seller would be indifferent to the discount offered, but to pursue the issue would take the focus away from the "opportunity cost of money, a function of time" concept. The objective of assessing a late-payment penalty to an unpaid invoice is to compensate for the lost opportunity for growth of the seller's funds while the invoice remains unpaid.

This brings us to the concept that the annualized rate of return, or growth, of a particular asset is a dual function of margin and time.

Turnover and Time

Up to this point, we have focused on the lost opportunity generated by idle assets (i.e., assets that are not entered into the production process). We have noted that such forgone opportunity is a function of time.

Let us continue by considering that our entrepreneur, at the end of his first month of operations, was able to sell the inventory of ice scrapers for $2,200. In simplest terms, the $1,000 in WIP inventory is exchanged for $2,200. The revised income statement and resulting balance sheet following this transaction are as follows:

Income Statement

Sales		$2,200
Standard cost of sales	$1,000	
Payroll	875	
Depreciation	25	
Rent	100	
Lease	50	
Profit		$ 150

Balance Sheet

Assets		Equity	
Cash	$ 7,675	Original investment	$10,000
Raw material	1,000		
WIP	-0-		
Equipment	1,475	Profit	150
Total assets	$10,150	Total equity	$10,150

Therefore, in one month's time, the original investment has grown from $10,000 to $10,150 or 1.5%. A 1.5% return isn't earth-shaking. However, consider the magnitude of the annual return if the same performance is repeated every month. Ideally, the $150 earned in the first month would be reinvested in additional production factors, and subsequent monthly profits would maintain the 1.5% growth rate compounded.

The simplified annual return would be 18%: (12 x $150) ÷ $10,000 = 18%.

By applying the compounding principles illustrated in Table 4.5, the results produce an annual rate of return of 19.57%.

$$1.015^{12} \quad = 19.57\%$$

This same principle applies in determining the desirability of credit terms extended to a buyer as an inducement to liquidate invoices with cash. The previously mentioned terms of 2%, 30N60 actually allow the buyer to use the invoice amount for an additional 30 days. His cost includes the forgone 2% of the invoice amount. The period of 30 days represents annual turns of 12. In essence, it is costing the buyer an annual rate of 24% to fund the purchase for the extra month. The annualized rate should be evaluated by both seller and buyer, in view of other existing opportunities, to determine the desirability of a given set of terms.

Accounts Receivable and Time

The quality of a seller's accounts receivable is, understandably, a function of time. Each day that an invoice remains unpaid represents a day that earnings, or growth, of the capital invested in receivables is lost. The magnitude of the lost opportunity is quantified by an "aging" graph.

Consider a business that has $100,000 in outstanding accounts receivable. Of the total $100,000 outstanding:

1. $50,000 are 30 days old.
2. $25,000 are 60 days old.

3. $25,000 are 90 days old.

To calculate the opportunity lost (up to the date of the aging graph) to the seller, we need to compare the opportunity if all of the $100,000 was productive for 12 months versus:

1. $50,000 productive for 11 months;

2. $25,000 productive for 10 months; and

3. $25,000 productive for 9 months.

For illustrative purposes we will consider that the prevailing interest rate is 12%.

$$\$100,000 \times 1.01^{12} = \qquad\qquad \$112,670.00$$

1. $\$\ 50,000 \times 1.01^{11} = \$\,55,775$

2. $\$\ 25,000 \times 1.01^{10} = \$\,27,612.50$

3. $\$\ 25,000 \times 1.01^{9}\ = \underline{\$\,27,340}$ $\qquad\qquad \underline{<110,727.50>}$

$$\$ \qquad \underline{\underline{1,942.50}}$$

Although the $1,942.50 is opportunity cost to the seller, it is actual interest savings to the buyer. The magnitude of the cost of each segment of the aging graph is illustrated in Figure 4.1.

1. $(\$50,000 \times 1.01^{12}) - (\$50,000 \times 1.01^{11}) = \$\ \ 560.00$

2. $(\$25,000 \times 1.01^{12}) - (\$25,000 \times 1.01^{10}) = \$\ \ 555.00$

3. $(\$25,000 \times 1.01^{12}) - (\$25,000 \times 1.01^{9}) = \underline{\$\ \ 827.50}$

$$\$1,942.50$$

Notice the incremental cost of (3) by losing just one month's opportunity to invest $25,000 into the production process. It is little wonder why accounts receivable monitoring does (or should) receive appropriate attention.

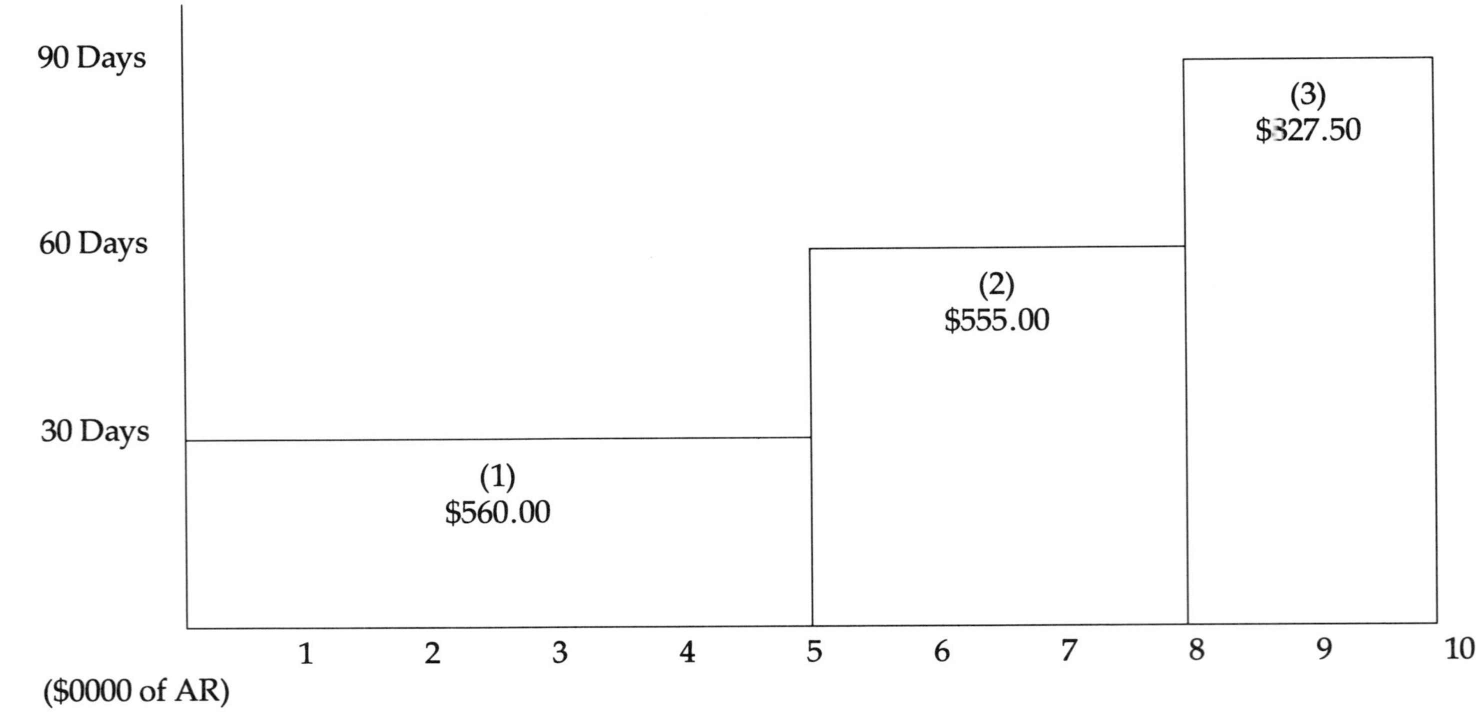

Fig. 4.1. Accounts receivable aging graph (includes cost of idle AR)

Summary

The basic premise of this chapter is that the productivity of all production factors is ultimately a function of time, either directly or indirectly. Those that are directly a function of time include the more obvious classic "fixed" costs incurred by a business, e.g., salaries, depreciation, and rents. However, all inputs that are not active in the production process, even though only temporarily (such as idle equipment or slow-moving-materials inventory), represent capital invested that is neither producing goods and/or services nor earning interest.

Given that neither the clock nor the calendar are sympathetic to production interruptions, the opportunity lost is gone forever.

Chapter 5
Working Capital: Cash to Cash

Objectives

- *Understand the necessity of closely correlating the production and accounting functions.*

- *Understand the importance of financial statements to the production manager.*

- *Be able to determine which documents (sources) should be used when planning working capital productivity and how they should be used.*

- *Appreciate that cost centers are helpful in evaluating production costs.*

- *Be able to allocate variable and fixed costs to standard product cost.*

- *Realize that actual profit results must be compared to the budget.*

- *Comprehend the flow of working capital in the production process.*

- *Realize the negative effect of idle production capacity and inefficient labor.*

- *Understand the process of inventory buildup and its potential effects.*

- *Understand why inefficient use of inputs affects the productivity of cash.*

- *Understand the concept of departmental accountability.*

Contents

Coordination of Production and Accounting Functions

Firms must recognize the inseparability of the production or operations function and the financial function. A production/operations manager who has a basic understanding of financial concepts will be more effective than one who does not have such an understanding. Conversely, the controller or plant accountant will provide better service to the firm if he has a basic understanding of the production process.

Webster provides several interesting definitions for the word "account":

- Responsible,

- Explanation,

- Give satisfactory reasons for, and

- Furnish a reckoning of money received and paid.

If we were to accept these definitions, it would be clear that the production/operations manager is every bit as much an "accountant" as the firm's controller. Typically, at the end of a fiscal period, the controller reports the actual operating results against plans or budgets. But, in order to explain the differences, the controller must consult with the production/operations manager who is responsible for ensuring that all production inputs are used efficiently. Therefore, reporting operating results in financial terms is the duty of the controller, but the responsibility for achieving the results lies with the production/operations manager.

Similarly, the preparation of plans, budgets, and strategies must also be a joint effort. Wise is the controller who feels at home on the "shop floor" or the production/operations manager who understands every item on the budget and knows what actions affect those items. While the production/operations manager may understand the flow of production inputs, as illustrated in Figure 3.1, he should further understand how the flow is expressed in conventional financial terms. He should also know and understand how his efforts are reflected in the firm's financial progress, as reported to top management.

The firm's cost-accounting system should be totally familiar to the production/operations manager. In fact, the cost system should be tailored to the particular production operation employed by the firm. While the production/operations manager may converse primarily in terms of units of production, whether they be pounds, gallons, or tons, the units must always be reconcilable to dollars on the firm's general ledger via the cost-accounting system. The production reporting system should never be independent of the firm's accounting system. Both should use the same master data base. Top management, the controller, an auditor, or anyone should, at any time, be able to take a listing of general ledger assets and go into the plant and touch them. This holds true for plant and equipment as well as inventories of any kind. Anything less is next to fraud inasmuch as the asset listing is represented to the firm's owners (shareholders) as the available resources with which to operate the business.

Balance Sheet vs. Income Statement

There are two primary financial statements that a business uses to monitor its financial progress. The balance sheet probably derives its name from the fact that the sum total of the debits (those on the left) equals the sum total of the credits (those on the right). That is not very profound, but why else? The debit side of the balance sheet is a listing of all that a firm has at a particular time. The credits simply indicate whether the firm owns the assets or owes on them. In other words:

assets = liabilities + equity

In the present context, we shall be interested primarily in the asset listing; more specifically, the listing of the typical production factors:

- Cash.

- Materials (in varied forms).

- Equipment and machines.

- Buildings and facilities.

- Land.

From Chapter 3, it was learned that cash begins the production cycle. Cash is converted to other inputs that undergo the production process, and then the resultant goods and services are sold again for cash. If the goods and services (outputs) generate more cash than was invested in their production (inputs), a profit is realized, and at the end of the fiscal period, there is more cash than at the beginning. This can also be termed an improvement in the firm's financial position. Therefore, the assets of a firm represent the firm's ability or readiness to produce goods and services.

The Income Statement

The income statement, on the other hand, tells how efficiently the production factors (inputs) have been used over a given time. The income statement lists the amount of revenue generated from the sale of goods and services (outputs) against the cost invested in their production (inputs). This sounds almost like a repeat of the preceding two paragraphs. Actually, the balance sheet and income statement work hand in hand. The difference in sales value (outputs) and cost (inputs) is profit (value added), and represents the increase in assets as just explained — resulting in an improvement in financial position that is reflected on the balance sheet. In fact, in some firms, top management just can't wait to see the "bottom line" at the end of each month. If all information required to prepare the income statement hasn't been processed, the controller will determine the increase in net assets during the fiscal period. This amount (if additional assets weren't financed by borrowing) is the firm's profit, or "bottom line," for the time period.

Many managers tend to overlook the significance of the balance sheet. It is the balance sheet that indicates the magnitude of the production opportunity. For example, consider a firm that experienced annual sales of, say, $5 million with an accompanying cost of $4 million. The 20% return on sales appears very healthy. By itself, it's not too bad. But what if the asset listing totaled $25 million? Now the return on the capital invested is just 4%. That rate of return will probably not attract too many investors when alternative opportunities provide returns that are three to four times greater.

Financial Position

The improvement of financial position, which is measured as the profitability or as the increase in productive capacity (increase in net assets), is the main theme of this text. An increase in productive capacity is required to sustain growth. This can be accomplished by raising the prices of outputs or reducing the costs of inputs. The latter is the objective of productivity management and will be the method employed in this text.

The productivity of working capital, the subject matter of this chapter, is measured not only on the absolute amount of gain but on the magnitude of the gain per time period. If a person owed $100 and the borrower repaid the debt with $120, it might appear to be a very good (if not usurious) deal for the lender. The transaction cannot be judged, however, unless the amount of time the borrower had use of the money is known. If the loan was for six months, it would be a very lucrative deal for the lender; if for three years, not so good.

The following is a comprehensive example illustrating how a firm goes about the task of planning for working capital. This will be accomplished by examining several sample planning documents for a typical operating business.

1. Beginning Balance Sheet (available production capability)

2. Sales Forecast (estimated demand for product)

3. Product Standard Cost (development of input cost)

4. Departmental Budgets (assignment of responsibility for

input cost)

5. Planned Break-Even (determining the level of production at which inputs = outputs)

6. Planned Income Statement for Time Period (summary of the expected level of efficiency of the use of the beginning production capacity per item (1) above)

7. Planned Ending Balance Sheet (the measure of the productivity of capital employed in the production of goods and services at the end of some predetermined time period, usually a year)

Planning Working-Capital Productivity

Let's consider a firm that will make skateboards. This will be a new firm financed by several individuals who deposit cash in exchange for stock or ownership in the firm that will be named Skate-Well Co. The firm is originally funded with $200,000, and the beginning balance sheet is shown in Table 5.1

Table 5.1 Beginning balance sheet for Skate-Well

Assets			*Ownership*
Cash	$200,000	$200,000	Equity
Total assets	$200,000	$200,000	Total equity

Sales Forecast

While many firms establish selling prices as a function of cost, it is more prudent to establish prices according to what the "market will bear."

Consider the three variables in the basic equation:

input + value added = output

It is a better business practice (i.e., there is more opportunity), if the output side of the equation is determined by the marketplace instead of using a predetermined percentage of the input variable.

In the present example, the Skate-Well owners feel they can sell 23,040 skateboards in their first year at $9 each. At this rate, the total planned output will be $207,360, as per Table 5.2.

Table 5.2 Sales forecast

Month	Planned Unit Sales	Planned Revenue @ $9
January	1,450	$ 13,050
February	1,500	13,500
March	1,600	14,400
April	1,850	16,650
May	1,950	17,550
June	2,000	18,000
July	1,900	17,100
August	1,800	16,200
September	2,090	18,810
October	2,100	18,900
November	2,400	21,600
December	2,400	21,600
Total	23,040	$207,360

Product Standard Cost

The standard cost of the skateboards is the expected cost of inputs if all the productive resources are utilized efficiently as per the plan. In other words, it is that level of input cost when everything goes right; it is what the skateboards *should* cost.

Skate-Well determines that the production process will require three operations that will be performed in three separate departments or cost centers. (A cost center is normally the lowest level of business activity where input cost can be defined and charged.)

1. Cutting Department — Cut boards to size.

2. Assembly Department — Assemble roller to boards.

3. Finishing Department — Sand, paint, and varnish assembled skateboards.

Cutting Department
- material $ .50 per board
- labor rate $12.00 per hour
- production rate   20 boards per hour
- labor cost per board $ .60 ($12.00 ÷ 20)
- monthly costs:

foreman's salary	$1,200
energy	240
	$1,440

Assembly Department
- material $ 3 per set of rollers
- labor rate $12 per hour
- production rate   15 boards per hour
- labor cost per board $ .80 ($12 ÷ 15)
- monthly costs:

foreman's salary	$1,144
energy	200
	$1,344

Finishing Department
- material $ .20 paint and varnish
- labor rate $13.50 per hour
- production rate   15 boards per hour
- labor cost per board $ .90 ($13.50 ÷ 15)
- monthly costs:

foreman's salary	$1,300
energy	236
	$1,536

With the preceding information, an estimated input cost can be developed for each skateboard. The labor and material portions of the costs are straightforward. These are termed "direct" expenses because they vary directly and proportionately with the number of skateboards produced. If one skateboard requires a $3 roller assembly, then rollers for 10 skateboards will cost $30.

Allocating Fixed Costs. Foremen's salaries and energy are not sensitive to production levels. These expenses (input costs) are, in fact, a function of time. They are associated with a given department and do not vary as production varies. For example, in the Cutting Department, the foreman will draw $1,200 per month in salary whether 1,200 skateboards are produced or 2,400. Input costs that are constant per time period are called fixed, overhead, burden or period expenses. The basic question, then, is how to allocate the foreman's salary, which is a monthly departmental input cost, to the product cost of each skateboard.

This is done in two basic steps:

The first step is to determine the "normal" expected production capacity, i.e., that level of capacity that can be maintained on a continuing basis. This "normal" level will be some percentage of the maximum capacity of the particular facility. In our example, the production rate in both the assembly and finishing departments is 15 boards per hour versus the cutting department's rate of 20 boards per hour. Considering 160 working hours per month, the maximum capacity for Skate-Well is 2,400 boards per month.

$$\text{Cutting } 20 \times 160 = 3,200$$
$$\text{Assembly } 15 \times 160 = 2,400$$
$$\text{Finishing } 15 \times 160 = 2,400$$

So, even though more boards can be cut than assembled and finished, it would be of no value to cut more boards than could be completed. The capacity of any facility must be determined by the limiting function.

Although maximum capacity is used to develop the break-even plan, normal ongoing capacity is used to allocate fixed departmental cost inputs to individual skateboards.

Typically, normal capacity will be 80%-90% of maximum capacity. For Skate-Well, 80% of maximum will be considered normal.

$$2,400 \times .80 = 1,920 \text{ skateboards per month} = \text{normal}$$

capacity.

Note that the sales forecast in Table 5.2 shows the annual expected unit sales to be at normal capacity: 1,920 x 12 = 23,040. This is to facilitate understanding of the example only. Estimated unit sales could have been anywhere from, say, 10,000 units to a maximum of 2,400 x 12 = 28,800.

In fact, during recessionary times, unit sales and/or capacity utilization may be 40% of maximum while normal capacity remains at 80%-90% of maximum. It will be illustrated shortly that the result produces idle capacity.

The second step comes after normal capacity is determined. The fixed cost per month is allocated to each skateboard on that basis. For example, the fixed cost per month for the Cutting Department is planned to be:

$$\begin{array}{lr}
\text{Foreman's salary} & \$1,200 \\
\text{Energy} & \underline{240} \\
& \$1,440
\end{array}$$

If, then, $1,440 per month is anticipated with a normal capacity of 1,920 skateboards per month, each skateboard will be allotted 1/1,920th of the monthly fixed cost, or 75¢. This 75¢ becomes part of the estimated, or standard, product costs. From that time on, whether 1,000 or up to 2,400 skateboards are produced per month, each carries a portion of the monthly fixed cost at the rate of 75¢ to inventory. This is commonly referred to as "overhead absorption."

At this point, the estimated/standard cost per skateboard can be determined as per Table 5.3. A great deal of information is in this table:

- Standard direct material cost per skateboard is $3.70.

- Standard direct labor cost per skateboard is $2.30.

- Total variable cost per skateboard is $6.

- Standard fixed cost per skateboard is $2.25.

- Total standard cost per skateboard is $8.25.

- Total standard input cost for cutting operation is $1.85.

- Total standard input cost for assembly operation is $4.50.

- Total standard input cost for finishing operation is $1.90.

Table 5.3 Standard product cost buildup

Department	Direct Material	Direct Labor	Fixed Overhead	Total	Cumulative Total
Cutting	$ .50	$ .60	$ .75	$1.85	$1.85
Assembly	$3.00	$ .80	$ .70	$4.50	$6.35
Finishing	$ .20	$ .90	$ .80	$1.90	$8.25
	$3.70	$2.30	$2.25	$8.25	

Departmental Budgets

With planned production/sales levels, as per Table 5.2, and standard product cost statistics, as per Table 5.3, coupled with previously estimated monthly fixed costs, departmental budgets can be developed. Tables 5.4 through 5.6 illustrate conventional budget formats. Notice that direct material and direct labor costs are a function of production levels, while monthly fixed costs remain constant for each department.

For example, the standard direct material cost for each board in the cutting department is $4.50, as per Table 5.3. Accordingly, the cutting department's budget for direct materials is $.50 times the planned units of production/sales of 1,450 units in January, resulting in a budgeted $725 for direct materials.

Table 5.4 Departmental budget (cutting)

Month	Planned Units Production	Direct Material	Direct Labor	Variable Cost	Fixed Cost	Total Cost
January	1,450	725	870	1,595	1,440	3,035
February	1,500	750	900	1,650	1,440	3,090
March	1,600	800	960	1,760	1,440	3,200
April	1,850	925	1,110	2,035	1,440	3,475

May	1,950	975	1,170	2,145	1,440	3,585
June	2,000	1,000	1,200	2,200	1,440	3,640
July	1,900	950	1,140	2,090	1,440	3,530
August	1,800	900	1,080	1,980	1,440	3,420
September	2,090	1,045	1,254	2,299	1,440	3,739
October	2,100	1,050	1,260	2,310	1,440	3,750
November	2,400	1,200	1,440	2,640	1,440	4,080
December	2,400	1,200	1,440	2,640	1,440	4,080
Total	23,040	11,520	13,824	25,344	17,380	42,624

Table 5.5 Departmental budget (assembly)

Month	Planned Unit Production	Direct Material	Direct Labor	Variable Cost	Fixed Cost	Total Cost
January	1,450	4,350	1,160	5,510	1,344	6,854
February	1,500	4,500	1,200	5,700	1,344	7,044
March	1,600	4,800	1,280	6,080	1,344	7,424
April	1,850	5,550	1,480	7,030	1,344	8,374
May	1,950	5,850	1,560	7,410	1,344	8,754
June	2,000	6,000	1,600	7,600	1,344	8,944
July	1,900	5,700	1,520	7,200	1,344	8,564
August	1,800	5,400	1,440	6,840	1,344	8,184
September	2,090	6,270	1,672	7,942	1,344	9,286
October	2,100	6,300	1,680	7,980	1,344	9,324
November	2,400	7,200	1,920	9,120	1,344	10,464
December	2,400	7,200	1,920	9,120	1,344	10,464
Total	23,040	69,120	18,432	87,552	16,128	103,680

Table 5.6 Departmental budget (finishing)

Month	Planned Unit Production	Direct Material	Direct Labor	Variable Cost	Fixed Cost	Total Cost
January	1,450	290	1,305	1,595	1,536	3,131
February	1,500	300	1,350	1,650	1,536	3,186
March	1,600	320	1,440	1,760	1,536	3,296
April	1,850	370	1,665	2,035	1,536	3,571
May	1,950	390	1,755	2,145	1,536	3,681
June	2,000	400	1,800	2,200	1,536	3,736
July	1,900	380	1,710	2,090	1,536	3,626
August	1,800	360	1,620	1,980	1,536	3,516
September	2,090	418	1,881	2,299	1,536	3,835
October	2,100	420	1,890	2,310	1,536	3,846
November	2,400	480	2,160	2,640	1,536	4,176

December	2,400	480	2,160	2,640	1,536	4,176
Total	23,040	4,608	20,736	25,344	18,432	43,776

Break Even Plan

The planned break-even is calculated in Table 5.7. The only information required for the break-even calculation are the departmental budgets (Table 5.4 - 5.6) and the sales forecast (Table 5.2).

Table 5.7 Planned break-even

Department	Planned Variable Cost	Planned Fixed Cost	Planned Total Cost
Cutting	$ 25,344	$17,280	$ 42,624
Assembly	$ 87,552	$16,128	$103,680
Finishing	$ 25,344	$18,432	$ 43,776
Total	$138,240	$51,840	$190,080

Revenue from Sales Forecast
23,040 x $9.00 = $207,360

$$B/E \quad \frac{\$\ 51,840}{1 - \dfrac{\$138,240}{\$207,360}}$$

$$= \frac{\$\ 51,840}{.3334}$$

$$= \$155,489 \div \$9.00 = 17,276 \text{ units}$$

$$= 60\% \text{ capacity } (17,276 \div 28,800)$$

Income Statement Plan

The planned (pro forma) income statement is presented in Table 5.8. It shows that sales (outputs) will exceed costs (inputs) by \$17,280, which represents profits (value added). Again, this statement can only be completed by using the sales forecast and departmental budgets.

Table 5.8 Planned income statement

Revenue		$207,360
Variable cost	$138,240	
Fixed cost	51,840	
Total cost		$190,080
Profit		$ 17,280

Ending Balance Sheet Plan

The balance sheet can now be drafted. This is the final planning document, inasmuch as it will indicate the productivity of capital over a given time. The increase in net assets at the end of a period over the beginning of the period is the productivity measure. This is usually done on an annual basis, since rates of return are commonly expressed as annual percentage rates. The planned ending balance sheet is illustrated in Table 5.9. Note that the planned productivity of capital is 8.64% ($217,280 ÷ $200,000) for the period. The planned balance sheet also indicates the firm's estimated financial position at the end of the period, which, as previously stated, indicates the productive capacity at the end of the period.

Table 5.9 Planned ending balance sheet

Assets		*Ownership*	
Cash:			
Beginning	$200,000	$200,000	Beginning equity
Profit	17,280	17,280	Profit
Ending cash	$217,280	$217,280	Ending equity

The planned balance sheet assumes that *all* other plans, as summarized in the sales forecast and departmental budgets, are achieved. The example also assumes that there is no inventory balance at the end of the period, i.e., all that was produced was sold and converted back to cash.

With detailed plans and high hopes, Skate-Well launches into production and sales of skateboards.

Comparing Actual Results with the Benefits

It is a sad fact that in the real world events do not always turn out as planned. Such was the case with Skate-Well. Actual unit sales were 21,000, as shown in Table 5.10. Let's assume, to begin with, that actual variable product costs, as per Table 5.3 were achieved along with budgeted monthly fixed costs. Consider the comparison of budgeted-to-actual costs, shown in Table 5.11.

Table 5.10 Sales analysis

Month	Actual Unit Sales	Actual Revenue @ $9.00
January	1,280	$ 11,520
February	1,330	11,970
March	1,430	12,870
April	1,680	15,120
May	1,780	16,020
June	1,830	16,470
July	1,730	15,570
August	1,630	14,670
September	1,920	17,280
October	1,930	17,370
November	2,230	20,070
December	2,230	20,070
Total	21,000	$189,000

Table 5.11 Budget vs. actual (000 $)

Dept.	Actual Units Produced	Standard Material		Standard Labor		Fixed		Total	Cost
		Budget	Actual	Budget	Actual	Budget	Actual	Budget	Actual
Cutting		10.5	10.5	12.6	12.6	17.28	17.28	40.38	40.3
Assembly		63.0	63.0	16.8	16.8	16.128	16.128	95.928	95.9
Finishing		4.2	4.2	18.9	18.9	18.432	18.432	41.532	41.5
Total	21,000	77.7	77.7	48.3	48.3	51.84	51.84	177.84	177.84

Skate-Well's actual profit turned out to be just $11,160.

Sales (Table 5.10)	$189,000
Total cost (Table 5.11)	177,840
	$ 11,160

One might erroneously assume that the profit should have been $15,750, (selling price $9 less total standard cost $8.25 x actual volume = $15,750) considering that the budgets were met even on the reduced volume. The budgets are "Flexible" because the budgeted variable expenses are based on the actual volume level achieved. Remember, however, that monthly fixed costs are exactly that, and even though the budget was achieved, an idle capacity cost will be generated whenever less-than-normal capacity is reached.

So, here is an example in which each department met its budget objectives but profit was less than when calculated using total standard product cost. Figure 5.1 illustrates how idle capacity has a real cost in addition to an opportunity cost that results in reduced productivity of working capital.

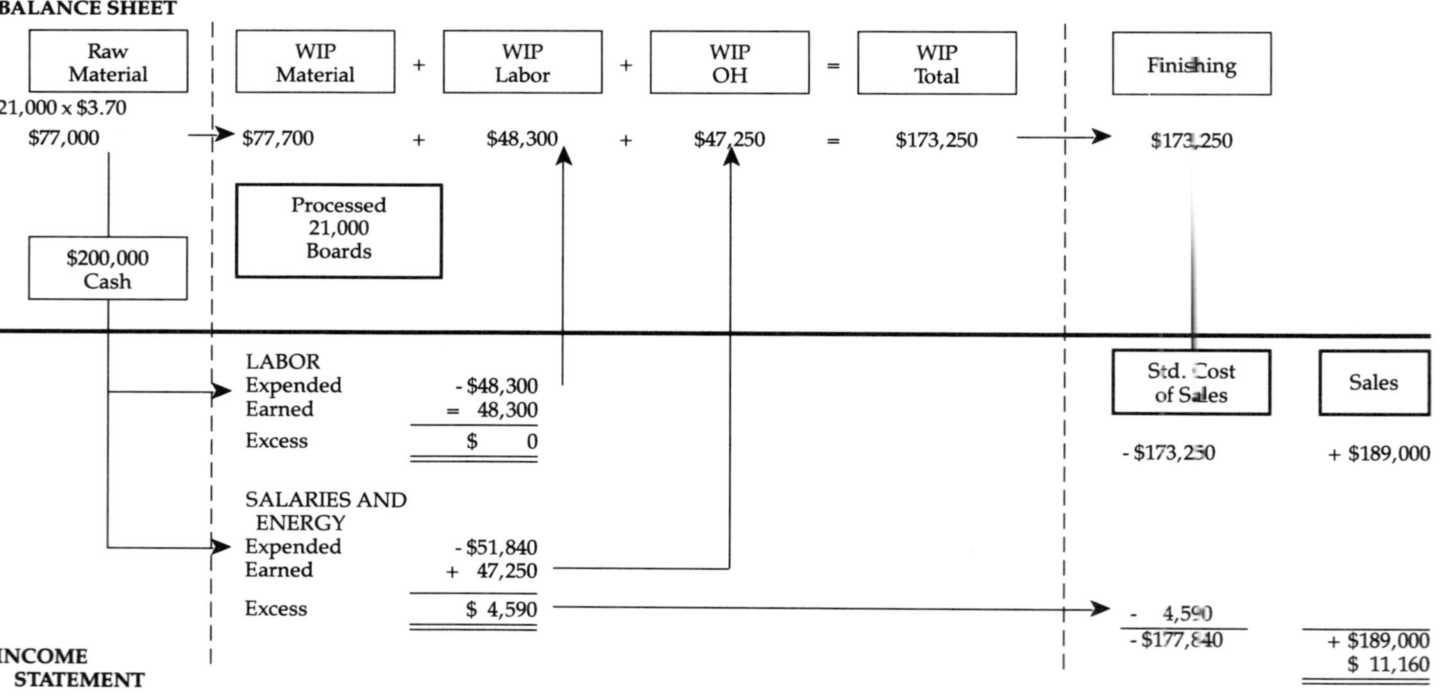

Fig. 5.1. Finishing department working capital flow
Flow expressed in financial terms

Negative Effect of Idle Capacity

Figure 5.1 illustrates the flow of working capital during the production process. This format will be used throughout the remainder of this chapter.

The first thing to note is that cash is converted to raw material. Raw material is a tangible asset. Once raw material is purchased, but prior to any other transactions, Skate-Well's balance sheet looks like this:

Assets:		*Ownership:*	
Cash	$122,300		
Raw material	77,700	$200,000	Original equity
Total assets	$200,000	$200,000	Total equity

At this point, Skate-Well's financial position has not changed. What has happened is that the company is not as liquid as it was before the purchase of raw material. Liquidity is the company's ability to pay current bills. Skate-Well cannot pay wages with $77,700 tied up in material inventory.

Effect of Inefficient Labor

Labor is different from material. It is not tangible and is not considered to be an asset. Labor is recognized as an asset when the labor effort adds standard cost to the raw material by some method of transformation — namely cutting, assembling, and finishing in the present example. The standard cost added during transformation is then transferred to WIP inventory. However, the labor force would have to be paid even if it were not productive. Consider, for example, that the payroll was $48,300, as shown as expended, but the labor wasn't productive. After paying for wages with no productivity, Skate-Well's balance sheet would look like this:

Assets:		Ownership:	
Cash	$ 74,000		
Raw material	77,700	$200,000	Original equity
		48,300	Loss on labor
Total assets	$151,700	$151,700	Total equity

Skate-Well has expended cash and received nothing in return. The raw material is still in its raw state.

If the labor effort had been productive and had performed according to the standards established as per Table 5.3, the $48,300 expended on labor would have resulted in the production of 21,000 skateboards. Then, the balance sheet would have looked like this:

Assets:		Ownership:	
Cash	$ 74,000	$200,000	Original equity
WIP material	77,700		
WIP labor	48,300		
Total assets	$200,000	$200,000	Total equity

At this point, the financial position is the same as at the beginning. Only the liquidity position continues to deteriorate.

Next, we come to salaries and energy. Cash was expended in the amount of $51,840 during the year for foremen's salaries and for energy. As was previously stated, the normal operating capacity was 1,920 units per month or 23,040 units per year. Accordingly, $2.25 ($51,840 ÷ 23,040) was allocated to each skateboard produced. Because only 21,000 skateboards were produced, the WIP inventory value could be increased by only $47,250 ($2.25 x 21,000). However, salaries and energy costs are fixed at $51,840 annually, regardless of production levels. (Cash was actually expended in the amount of $51,840.) This caused some part of the fixed cost, $4,590, to be incurred but not "absorbed" into product cost.

At this point, when all the transactions have taken place except the sale of the skateboards, the balance sheet looks like this:

Assets:		Ownership:	
Cash	$ 22,160		
WIP material	77,700		
WIP labor	48,300	$200,000	Original equity
WIP OH	47,250	4,590	Excess fixed
Total assets	$195,410	$195,410	Total equity

Skate-Well had $173,250 invested in finished skateboards, as reflected in Finished Goods Inventory in Figure 5.1. When these 21,000 units are sold at $9 each, the income statement reflects a profit in the amount of $11,160, shown in the lower right-hand corner of Figure 5.1.

The actual flow of cash during this cycle is:

Beginning cash	+ $200,000
Purchase raw materials	- 77,700
Pay wages	- 48,300
Pay salaries and energy	- 51,840
Proceeds from sale of skateboards	+ 189,000
Ending cash	$211,160

The accompanying balance sheet is as follows:

Assets:		Ownership:	
Cash	$211,160	$200,000	Original equity
		11,160	Profit on sale
			of skateboards
Total assets	$211,160	$211,160	Total equity

The productivity (return) of working capital was actually 5.58% instead of the planned 8.64%. The difference was due exclusively to idle capacity, not to the inefficiency of any other inputs.

Analysis of Inefficiently Used Production Inputs

The preceding example illustrated the reduced productivity of working capital that resulted exclusively from idle capacity. Let us expand the example and examine what happens to working-capital productivity when labor is inefficient. The expanded example assumes that labor productivity was in accordance with Table 5.12. The same actual production level of 21,000 units will be used so as not to confuse the example. Figure 5.2 illustrates the working capital flow through the production process.

The first thing to note is that the inventory value of the 21,000 skateboards is exactly the same as before. In other words, the inefficiency of the labor input has no effect on the standard cost of the skateboards. The customer is not willing to pay for either idle capacity or inefficiency. Both of these items decrease the manufacturer's profit.

After cash is expended for raw materials, labor, salaries and energy, the cash balance is $11,660.

Beginning cash	+ $200,000
Purchase raw material	- 77,700
Pay wages	- 58,800
Pay salaries and energy	- 51,840
Ending cash	$ 11,660

However, before the skateboards are sold, the balance sheet reflects both idle capacity and inefficiency.

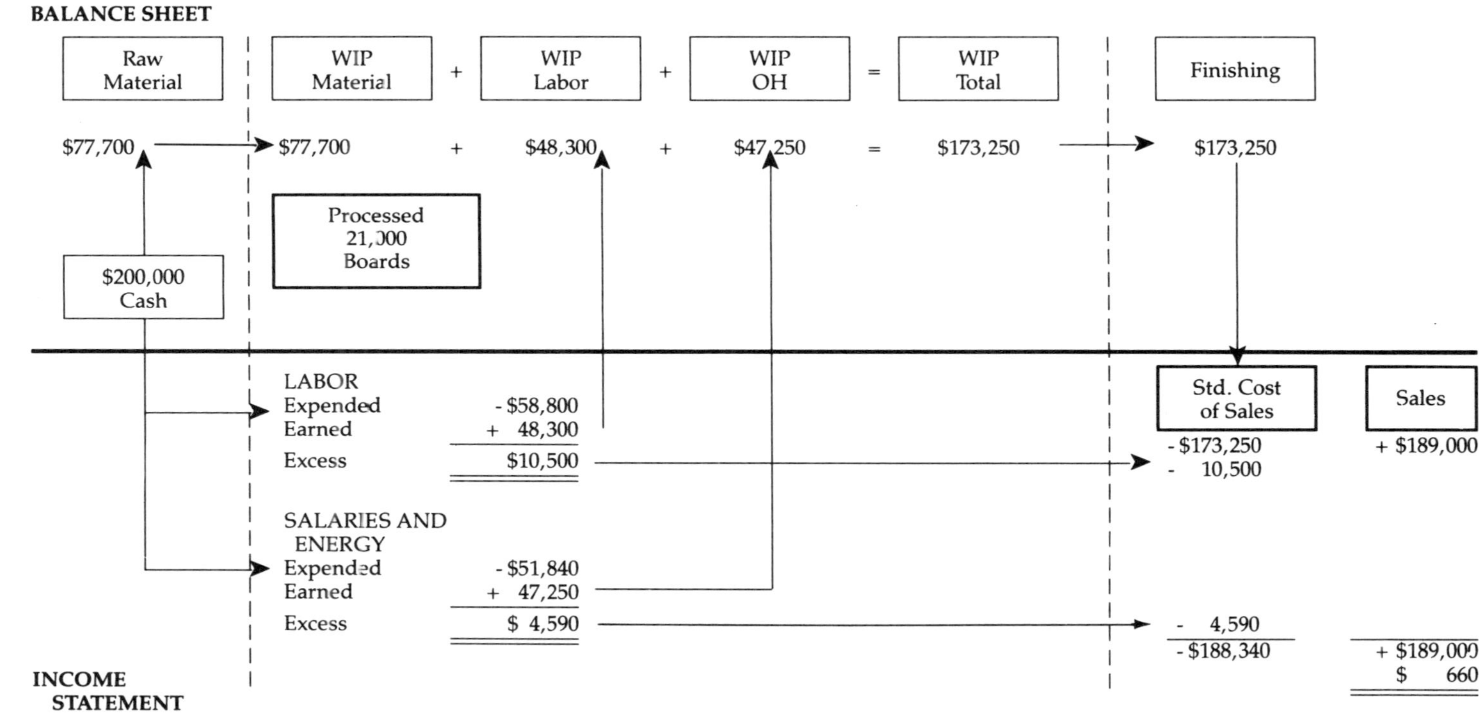

Fig. 5.2. Effects of inefficient labor

Assets:		Ownership:	
Cash	$ 11,660	$200,000	Original equity
WIP material	77,700	4,590	Idle capacity expense
WIP labor	48,300		
WIP OH	47,250	10,500	Inefficient labor
Total assets	$184,910	$184,910	Total equity

The $10,500 labor inefficiency and the idle capacity expense of $4,590 have decreased the net assets of Skate-Well.

After the skateboards are sold, which generates $189,000 in cash, the income statement, found in the lower right-hand corner of Figure 5.2, shows a meager profit of $660. The resultant balance sheet looks like this:

Assets:		Ownership:	
		$200,000	Original equity
Cash	$200,660	660	Profit
Total assets	$200,660	$200,660	Total equity

The working capital had negligible productivity, the return being substantially less than 1%. The decreases in working capital productivity are attributable to the inefficiency of the labor input. It should be noted that inefficiency will be reflected in departmental reports comparing actual to budget, whereas idle capacity is not reflected on departmental variance reports.

Inventory Build-Up

Up to now, we have considered that as many units as were started in the production process have been completed and sold. That is seldom the case in the real world. Let's consider that:

- At the beginning of the year, sufficient boards were bought to make 23,040 skateboards, as per the original sales forecast;

- 22,500 were cut; but

- Only 22,000 were transferred to the assembly department.

This becomes a little difficult. However, it is very important for the production/operations manager to understand the financial impact of having cash tied up in inventory. Idle inventory cannot generate earnings! In fact, as we shall illustrate later, idle inventory actually consumes cash.

Figure 5.3 illustrates the concept of inventory buildup for the Cutting Department. This example builds on the previous parameters of labor productivity, as per Table 5.12, and a normal capacity of 1,920 skateboards per month.

Table 5.12 Labor productivity

Department	Standard Hourly Production	Actual Labor Efficiency	Actual Hourly Production	Standard Labor Cost Per Board	Actual Labor Cost Per Board
Cutting	20	75%	15	$ .60	$ .80
Assembly	15	80%	12	$ .80	$1.00
Finishing	15	90%	13½	$ .90	$1.00
				$2.30	$2.80

After the cutting department has completed its processing, the cash account totals $153,200.

Beginning cash	+ $200,000
Purchase boards	- 11,520
Pay wages	- 18,000
Pay salaries and energy	- 17,280
Ending cash	$153,200

Assets:		Ownership:
Cash	$153,200	$200,000 Original equity
Raw material	270	405 Idle capacity
WIP (cutting)	925	expense
WIP (assembly)	40,700	4,500 Inefficient labor
Total assets	$195,095	$195,095 Total equity

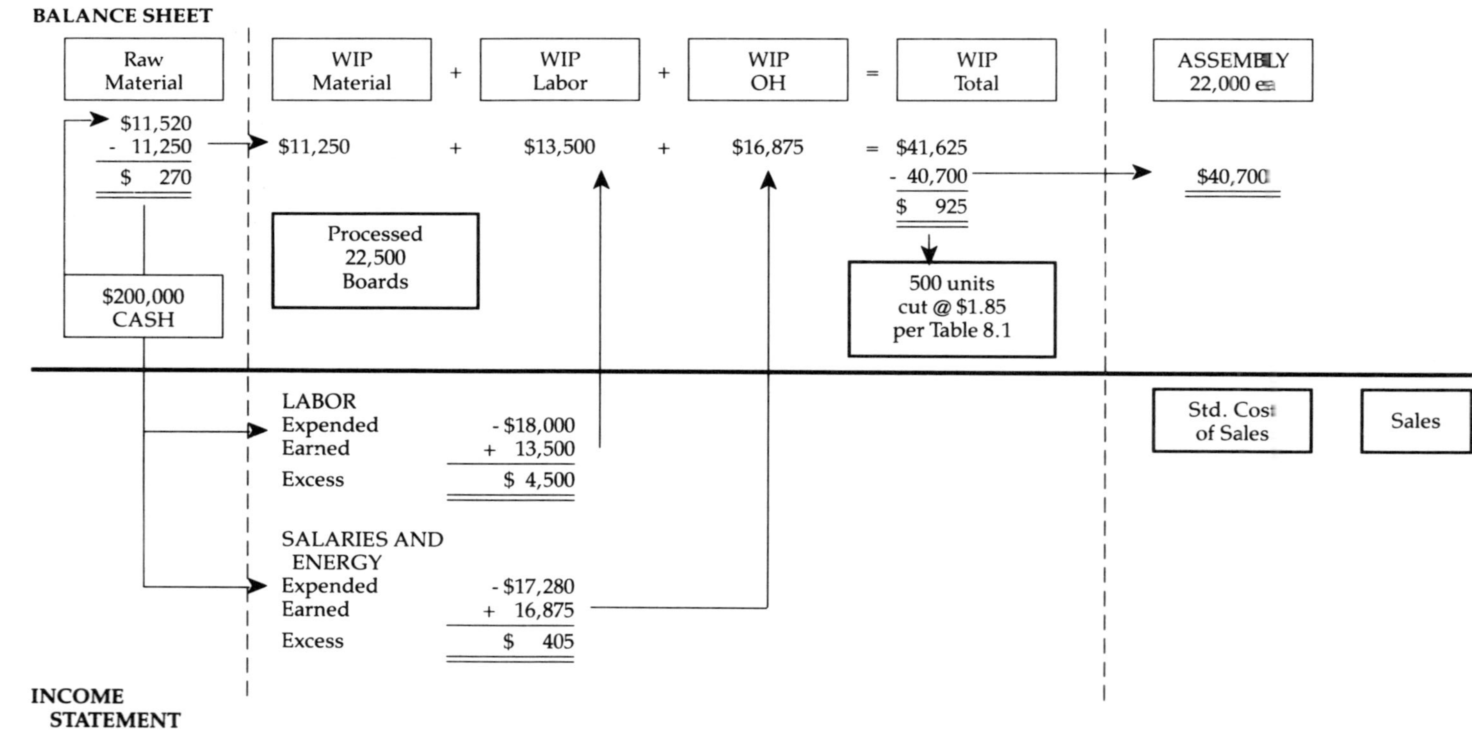

Fig. 5.3. Inventory buildup

Now let's continue the same concept for the Assembly Department. Remember, the Assembly Department begins with 22,000 cut boards with a standard cost, at that point, of $40,700. Of the 22,000 cut boards, 21,750 are assembled; however, only 21,500 are transferred to the finishing department.

Figure 5.4 shows the working-capital flow and inventory balances for the Assembly Department.

After the assembly department is finished, the cash balance and balance sheet can be analyzed.

Beginning cash	$153,200
Purchase raw material	- 66,000
Pay wages	- 21,750
Pay salaries and energy	- 16,128
Ending cash	$ 49,322

Assets:		*Ownership:*	
Cash	$ 49,322	$200,000	Original equity
Raw material	270	4,905	Loss on cutting
WIP (cutting)	925	4,350	Assembly inefficient labor
Raw material (assembly)	750		
		903	Assembly idle capacity
WIP (assembly)	2,050		
WIP (finishing)	136,525		
Total assets	$189,842	$189,842	Total equity

Production now continues on to the finishing department. From Figure 5.4, it should be noted that 21,500 skateboards have been assembled and transferred to Finishing. Of the 21,500 assembled boards, 21,250 are finished; however, only 21,000 are sold.

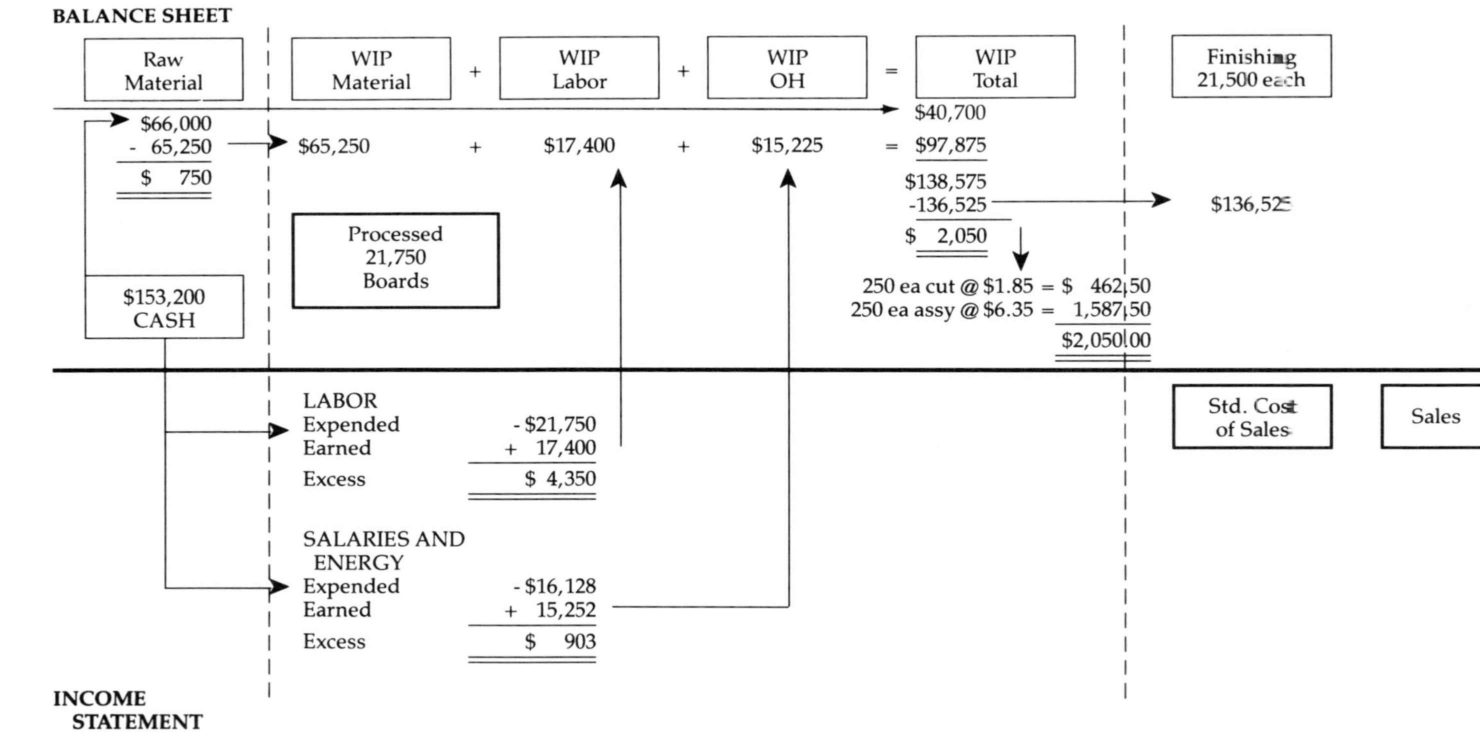

Fig. 5.4. Working-capital flow and inventory balances

Figure 5.5 completes the production cycle of skateboards. At this point, 21,000 skateboards will be sold for $9 each. The final cash analysis, income statement and balance sheet are found in Tables 5.13, 5.14, and 5.15 respectively. In addition, the actual break-even level achieved is presented in Table 5.16.

Table 5.13 Final cash analysis

Beginning Balance		+ $200,000
Raw Material Purchases		
Fig. 5.3 Cutting	$11,520	
Fig. 5.4 Assembly	66,000	
Fig. 5.5 Finishing	4,300	
		- 81,820
Wages Paid		
Fig. 5.3 Cutting	$18,000	
Fig. 5.4 Assembly	21,750	
Fig. 5.5 Finishing	21,250	
		- 61,000
Pay Salaries and Energy		
Fig. 5.3 Cutting	$17,280	
Fig. 5.4 Assembly	16,128	
Fig. 5.5 Finishing	18,432	
		- 51,840
Subtotal		+ 5,340
Proceeds from skateboard sales		+ $189,000
Ending cash balance		$194,340

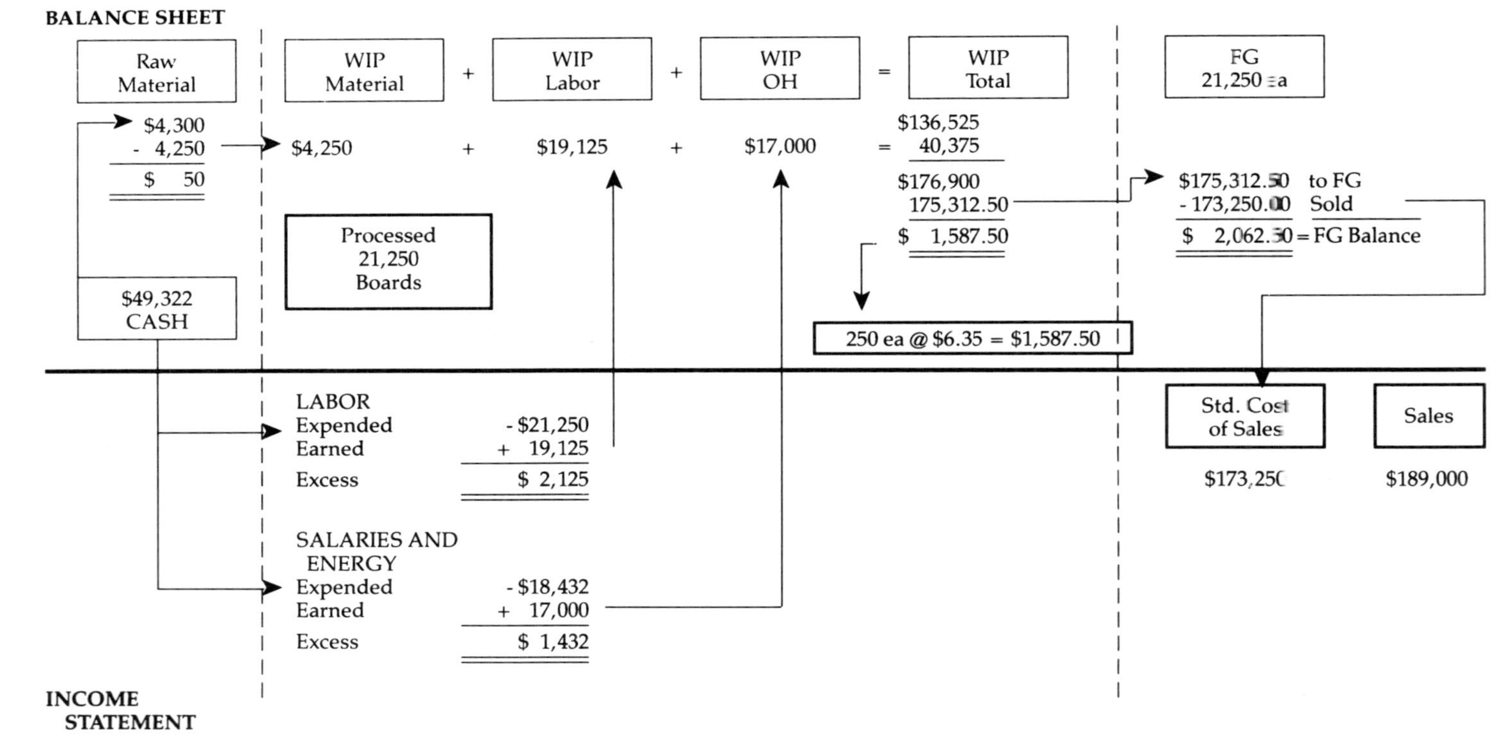

Fig. 5.5. Finishing department working capital flow

Table 5.14 Final income statement

Sales		$189,000
Standard Cost of Sales		$173,250
Gross Margin		$ 15,750
Less Labor Efficiency Variance		
Fig. 5.3 Cutting	$4,500	
Fig. 5.4 Assembly	$4,350	
Fig. 5.5 Finishing	$2,125	
		$ 10,975
Less Idle Capacity Variance		
Fig. 5.3 Cutting	$ 405	
Fig. 5.4 Assembly	$ 903	
Fig. 5.5 Finishing	$1,432	
		$ 2,740
Net Profit		$ 2,035

Table 5.15 Final balance sheet

Assets		*Ownership*
Cash	$194,340	$200,000 Beginning equity
Raw Material		
Fig. 5.3 Cutting	$ 270	
		$ 2,035 Net Profit per Table 5.12
Fig. 5.4 Assembly	$ 750	
Fig. 5.5 Finishing	$ 50	
	1,070	

WIP

  Fig. 5.3 Cutting $ 925

  Fig. 5.4 Assembly $2,050

  Fig. 5.5 Finishing $1,587.50

	4,562.50		
Finished goods	2,062.50		
Total assets	$202,035.00	$202,035	Total equity

Table 5.16 Actual break-even

Standard Material Cost	
Fig. 5.1	$ 77,700
Standard Direct Labor	
Fig. 5.1	$ 48,300
Labor Efficiency Variation	
Table 5.14	$ 10,975
Total Variable Cost	$136,975
Total Revenue	
Table 5.14	$189,000
Total Fixed Cost	
Table 5.13	$ 51,840

BE Sales = $\dfrac{\$\ 51,840}{1 \div \dfrac{\$136,975}{\$189,000}}$

= $188,304 + $9 per board

BE Volume = 20,922 boards ÷ 28,800 = 72.65% of maximum
capacity to break even

Several facts can be gleaned from final statements.

- The ending cash balance is less than in the beginning, even though a modest profit was realized. Therefore, productivity of actual cash was negative.

- Although total net assets increased in the amount of the profit, $7,695 is tied up in inventories. This amount is unavailable to purchase additional production inputs.

- The less-than-expected profit is due in part to the inefficient use of production inputs that are still tied up in inventory. In other words, only the standard product cost is inventoried. All variances associated with the production process are expenses on the income statement as they occur.

- Because of the inefficiency of the production inputs, the break-even point has slipped to the right. It now requires 72.65% of maximum capacity to recover total fixed costs. This is a far cry from the planned 60% and dangerously close to the 80% normal capacity level.

Accountability

By following the flow of inputs through the production process, it becomes evident that the primary objectives are:

- To convert all inputs to salable output; and

- To do so as quickly as possible.

In the same light, the expending of any input that does not add to the product standard costs becomes a loss on the income statement with an accompanying decrease in cash. A decrease in cash on the balance sheet has a negative effect on a firm's financial position because the firm has reduced its ability to buy more production inputs.

The customer is only interested in paying a price that reflects what the product should have cost, not what the product actually cost because of the manufacturer's inefficient use of inputs. Idle capacity or the inefficient use of any input will automatically affect the productivity of cash.

Departments — Miniature Businesses

The function of the cutting department in the present example is to cut boards to size to be used for skateboards. The cut boards represent output to the cutting department and input to the assembly department. Just as a customer won't pay for the inefficient use of production inputs, the assembly department isn't responsible for excess cutting labor or idle cutting capacity.

The assembly department receives the cut boards at their standard cost up to that point — $1.85, as shown in Table 5.3. The foreman of the assembly department is responsible for assembling rollers on the boards and transferring them to the finishing department. Any inefficient use of assembly labor remains on the assembly department's budget. All skateboards transferred to finishing are done at a unit standard cost of $6.35, as per Table 5.3.

The inputs to the assembly department are the total of the standard cost of the cut boards received plus the actual cash converted by the assembly department to perform the assembly operations. The outputs are the standard cost of assembled boards as they are transferred to finishing.

assembly department inputs = $1.85 x number of boards received + actual assembly cost incurred.

assembly department outputs = $6.35 x number of boards transferred to Finishing.

Each department's productivity can be examined. So, even though the standard product cost is a function of the skateboards themselves, inefficient input utilization becomes a function of a particular department; hence, accountability can be assigned and monitored.

Defective Products

Often, products are thought to be of satisfactory quality when, in reality, they are defective. This could happen in our example when the skateboards are inspected prior to being shipped. When defective products are discovered, several things result.

- The standard cost of their manufacture, which had been inventoried as an asset, becomes an expense, i.e., it is written off. This write-off represents a real financial loss, a decrease in cash, and a reduced ability to buy more inputs.

- The department responsible for causing the defect will be held accountable for the loss. Consider Figure 5.5, which represents the finishing department. The example stated that 21,250 skateboards were finished, but only 21,000 were sold. The 250 skateboards each have a standard cost of $8.25, as per Table 5.3, for a total standard cost of $2,062.50. If, say, 100 of these skateboards were found to have a flaw that was caused by cutting an incorrect dimension, $825 would leave the asset accounts and be expensed to the income statement via the cutting department's budget. In this case, the standard cost added by the cutting department was just $185 (100 x $1.85) for the 100 boards scrapped, but the cutting department will be charged for the total standard cost of the skateboards because it caused the defect.

- The customers will not buy the defective skateboards.

Defective parts, or scrap, have a detrimental effect on the productivity of *all* the other inputs inasmuch as all inputs contributed to the making of the skateboard. In other words, after inputs entered the production process, they produced zero output value. The firm may as well have taken the $825 and buried it.

In addition to the standard cost being written off:

- The opportunity to sell the skateboards for $9 each with a profit of $.75 has been lost.

- Each skateboard written off actually had more cost than the $8.25 standard cost invested in it, owing to idle capacity and inefficient labor, as has been illustrated.

The productivity of working capital, more specifically cash, is a function of the efficient use of production inputs. The objective is to expend as few inputs as possible to obtain a given number of outputs, and to sell them as quickly as possible to replenish the cash account. Cash productivity is, therefore, a function of both efficiency and time.

Chapter 6
Capital Planning for Production Facilities: Initial or Additions

Objectives

- *Understand how capital budgeting relates to the execution of the strategic financial plan.*

- *Examine the concept of ROI in terms of capital productivity.*

- *Understand how capital formation at the micro level affects total productivity.*

- *Build on the concept of the importance of time as it relates to capital.*

- *Consider how to make capital more productive.*

- *Understand how to counter risk in capital budgeting.*

- *Learn how to use capital-budgeting techniques.*

- *Learn how to make capital-allocation decisions.*

Contents

Capital Investments and Returns

One of the great principles of capitalism is that money flows at the discretion of the person who controls it to whatever use he sees fit. Money will normally flow in the direction where it will be the most productive to its holder, i.e., where the largest opportunity for return is. This holds true when the objective is growth, but does not necessarily hold true when the objective is security, or minimal risk.

The largest corporations in the United States are owned by individual investors who feel that this employment of their funds will provide the best possible return, based on their individual investment needs. As one would suspect, competition for available investment funds is fierce. In the end, however, it is the opportunity for the largest return and/or growth over time that attracts investors.

The term "return," in the financial sense, is synonymous with the term "productivity of capital." (Return is used to indicate the magnitude of growth or earnings of an employed asset, expressed as a percent over a time period, normally a year. The term "return on investment" is synonmous with the term "productivity of capital." Return is sometimes used interchangeably with "yield" in the context of capital budgeting.) Productivity has previously been defined as the relationship of the input of a resource to the output generated by that input. To illustrate, if a firm converts $1 to materials, workers, and machines and manufactures a product that is sold for $1.10, is that not a measure of the productivity of the original $1? And if an elderly retired schoolteacher invests $1 in the stock of a corporation and at the end of a time period, say a year, he receives a dividend check for 10¢, is not that also a measure of productivity of the $1 invested? Of course it is, but it is more commonly termed the return on investment for the teacher. It might very well have been the same $1 that was initially invested by the teacher in the stock of the corporation that purchased the materials, men, and machines to make the product.

The investor doesn't really care how the 10% return was achieved; his primary concern is that the return was higher than could be obtained with any other use of the original $1. If an investor is pleased with the rate of return, he may invest additional funds in the firm and may even talk friends into investing in the firm. This ensures the growth of the firm and provides the incentive for it to maintain or improve the productivity of the invested funds that have been entrusted to it.

If, in fact, the return to an investor is measured by the percentage growth of his invested money over a period of time (i.e., the level of funds at the end compared with that at the beginning), does it not stand to reason that the productivity of capital is also measured by the amount of resources available at the end of a period as compared with the level of resources at the beginning? Very logically, it does.

Chapter 11 of this text discusses the productivity of energy. The basic energy input is the Btu, which is defined as the capacity to do work. Similarly, a firm's total resources, measured in dollars of assets, is its capacity to do work.

It can be seen, then, that the individual investors determine the measurement of a firm's productivity, which is the growth of the asset base, over a given time period attributable to the efficient use of the assets.

We can confidently state that a firm's primary objective, and its summary productivity indicator, is the improvement in financial position, as measured by asset growth over a given time. It should be noted here that a firm can also increase its asset base by borrowing additional funds or issuing more stock. The productivity measurement, however, is based on an increase of assets through profitability, or the efficient use of the available assets, which simultaneously increases owner equity.

Capital-Labor Relationship

Chapter 3 presented the concept that economic growth, or the increase in productive capacity, is the major objective of productivity enhancements. The American Productivity Center (APC) in Houston states that growth is simply the product of the total input of resources and the efficiency with which they are applied. This statement is definitely in agreement with the premise of this text. Productivity, the Center continues, relates measured output to total resources applied to achieve it. Again, we are in total agreement.

Recent APC literature presented a schematic from the New York Stock Exchange (NYSE) Economic Research Office that interestingly relates labor productivity to economic growth. Economic growth, relative to the labor input, is a dual function of increases in both the total input and labor productivity. Increases in labor productivity are the result of:

- Increases in the proficiency of labor;

- Increases in the quantity of capital; and

- Increases in the efficiency of capital.

Increases in the efficiency of capital stem from both long- and short-term research, development, and effective dissemination of improved product and process design, as well as from more efficient machinery and equipment. Such improvements in the efficiency of capital can occur only after there have been increases in the quantity of capital investment, i.e, land, buildings, machinery, and tools.

The relationship between capital and labor can be appreciated by examining the capital/labor ratio. This ratio measures the proportions with which capital and labor are invested in the production process. The capital labor ratio is arrived at by dividing the capital input by the labor input. (For example, in 1948, 41.4 ÷ 80.9 = 51.2%. See Table 6.1, which illustrates typical input/output data for the private business economy, and use Table 6.2 to interpret Table 6.1.)

Table 6.1 Input: output for private business economy (1977 = 100)

Year	Real Output	Labor Input	Capital Input	Output/ Labor Unit	Output/ Capital Unit	Capital-to- Labor Ratio
1948	37.2	80.9	41.4	46.0	89.9	51.2
1965	67.9	86.8	66.4	78.2	102.3	76.4
1973	92.0	97.0	89.1	94.8	103.3	91.8
1979	107.7	108.4	107.2	99.4	100.4	98.9
1981	109.0	108.5	113.6	100.4	95.9	104.8

Table 6.2 Average rates of change annually total private business economy

	1948-1965	1965-1973	1973-1979	1979-1981
Real output (1972 dollar)	3.6%	3.9%	2.7%	.6%
Labor input	.4%	1.4%	1.9%	.1%
Capital input	2.8%	3.7%	3.1%	3.0%
Labor productivity	3.2%	2.4%	.8%	.5%*
Capital productivity	.8%	.1%	-.5%	-2.3%
Capital-to-labor ratio	2.4%	2.3%	1.3%	2.9%

1977	1978	1979	1980	1981
100.0	99.8	99.4	99.4	100.4

*Even though there was a .5% average annual growth rate from 1979-1981, there was an actual decrease in 1978 and 1979.

Several major deductions can be made from these two tables:

- The capital input has grown substantially faster than the labor input.

- The capital/labor ratio doubled from 1948 to 1981.

- Labor productivity, though steadily declining, has not declined as quickly as capital productivity.

- Growth rates, indicated by real output, have decreased since World War II.

Several reasons account for the growth and productivity declines. First, the heavy capital input and the resulting strong productivity growth rates of the first 15 postwar years could not be expected to continue. During the period between 1965 and 1973, growth rates slowed to a pace that was similar to those of prewar times. Pressures of rising inflation, along with growing demands for capital outlay for nonproductive environmental equipment, took their toll. By the early 1970s, the U.S. economy was in serious trouble. The problems were vastly compounded by the 1973 OPEC oil embargo.

The second "oil shock" in 1979 came on top of high interest rates and rampant inflation. This triggered the recession that began in mid-1980 and was still in progress by mid-1983. The country ended the decade of the 1970s with three straight years of declines in labor productivity. It became increasingly evident that the United States was losing ground in international marketing competition as well. Growing unemployment, layoffs, shut-downs of major factories (especially in the auto and steel industries), and foreign inroads in domestic and overseas markets of U.S. manufacturers all threatened the maintenance of this nation's high standard of living and adequate employment opportunities. (*Productivity Perspectives.* 1981 Edition. Copyright 1981, American Productivity Center.)

Capital Investment at the Micro Level

Having seen the vast implications of capital decisions at the macro level, relative to total productivity and real growth, perhaps we can better appreciate the importance of investment decisions at the micro or plant level.

Firms make capital decisions for a number of reasons. However, our discussion is limited to investment decisions that relate to the production of goods and services. Basic capital purchases can be summarized as falling into several categories: capacity increase (including existing product lines and new product lines), cost reduction, general replacement, and safety (e.g., OSHA and environmental).

Capacity Increase

When capacity is increased for existing product lines, normally more equipment of the kind presently in the plant is added to the asset base. Justification is rather straightforward. Most likely, present revenue/variable cost ratios will apply unless the added capacity will allow for economy of scale production. Although depreciation of the new equipment will add to the plant's fixed cost base, the total unit production cost from the new equipment will most likely be less than present, due to its dilution of the existing fixed-cost structure. For example, foremen's salary cost may not increase with the purchase of additional "same kind" equipment. In such instances, justification for the proposed capital expenditure is based largely on the marketing department's estimates of demand for the product to be produced on the proposed equipment.

To increase a plant's capacity by introducing new products is substantially more comprehensive. In this case, not only is a forecast of the demand for the new products required, but estimates must be made of the cost to produce the new products. New types of equipment and new processes may be required. When expansion is proposed for new products, the amount of planning is made greater than that required for increased capacity for existing products.

In either case, be it increased capacity for existing products or increased capacity for new products, the plant is striving to promote growth by increasing the amount of outputs. To promote continued growth, the incremental productivity of capital allotted to such proposals should be greater than the plant's present return on its existing asset base.

Cost Reduction

One of the primary benefits resulting from technological advances is the ability to perform a particular job either more quickly or with less input of some other resource. This type of activity results in lower production cost. As has been illustrated in previous chapters, whenever a better way of doing something provides the same or greater output in less time, the capacity of the plant has been constructively increased. This premise is a basic building block in productivity improvement.

The cost of producing goods and services can be reduced in many ways, but they all center on the reduction of one or more inputs while maintaining a given level of outputs. For example, cost reduction can be achieved by:

- Reducing the amount of time required for any step in the production process;

- Reducing the amount of energy required for each unit of output;

- Reducing the amount of material required for each unit of output;

- Reducing the amount of working capital required to support a given level of output by reducing throughput times, which in turn minimizes inventory levels; and/or

- Reducing the defect or scrap rate.

This list is certainly not intended to be all-inclusive, but all of the listed methods have one basic factor in common. Each is a way to achieve the plant's growth objective by increasing profitability through improved productivity. Whereas capital proposals to increase capacity deal with the output side of the input-output equation, all capital proposals directed toward reducing production costs deal with the input side of the equation.

From the foregoing paragraphs it can be deduced that any capital proposal for reducing costs will improve the productivity of total capital employed by the plant.

General Replacement

Both production and support equipment and facilities deteriorate with usage and time. When that happens, they need to be replaced to maintain the existing level of production. Such expenditures of capital funds are correctly termed "general replacement" projects. They are to maintain status quo of the operation, and require little justification. The cost of not replacing such equipment and facilities is obvious. Bear in mind that when a piece of equipment needs replacing, that is the best time to check the status of relevant technological improvements to see if the old equipment can be upgraded with more cost-effective equipment.

The accounting cycle has been established so that the equipment requiring replacement has been written off steadily. When the equipment is no longer capable of production, no value is shown for it on the asset side of the balance sheet. Remember, assets have been defined as the firm's ability to perform the production of goods and services. If a piece of equipment is not capable of production, it should not be listed as an asset.

Safety, Environmental, Etc.

Projects of this nature require expenditures of funds for non-productive purposes. In other words, outputs are not increased and neither are input costs reduced. In fact, safety and environmentally related capital expenditures have a negative effect on the firm's capital productivity because earnings remain the same but they are compared to a larger asset base. Although many of these types of projects are required to satisfy governmental regulations, many more are instituted voluntarily by firms to enhance the quality of the workplace, which will improve the overall productivity of the labor input.

The American Productivity Center has done some excellent work that shows a high correlation between capital investment and GNP growth rates. Quoting from its aforementioned productivity perspectives, it states:

> The significance of environmental-control expenditures is apparent in that these have constituted more than 5 percent of total business capital expenditures during recent years and have averaged more than 8 percent for the manufacturing sector. For certain manufacturing industries (especially primary metals, paper, chemicals and petroleum) this type of mandated expenditure has totaled more than 15 percent of total

capital investment. For some industries, adjustment to the regulations led to significant disruption of normal plant operation and diverted management attention from productivity improvement. It is not coincidental that these affected industries have unusually poor total-factor productivity performance during the 1973-79 span.

Growth is stunted when capital is allotted for nonproductive investments. The preceding four categories of capital projects have two basic things in common:

1. They all have a certain amount of risk associated with them.

2. They all are evaluated on the basis of estimated projections of cash flows. (Cash-flow projections are obviously much more relevant to capacity and cost reduction projects than to general replacement and/or environmental projects.)

Risk and Capital Budgeting

A discussion of capital budgeting would not be complete without mention of risk or the similar phenomenon called uncertainty. The manner in which this topic is handled by different writers varies widely. Some will devote a complete chapter to attempt to explain the difference between risk and uncertainty. Others make a simple distinction to the effect that risk is defined as those situations in which a probability distribution of the returns to a given project can be estimated, while uncertainty is defined as those situations in which insufficient evidence is available to estimate a probability distribution. Some will not differentiate between the two but will use the terms interchangeably. Inasmuch as this is a management text and capital budgeting decisions are definitely managerial in nature, we advocate the latter approach.

There is uncertainty, or risk in any decision making in which there is less-than-perfect knowledge about a given event. In capital budgeting opportunities, nearly every proposal will be accompanied by some degree of uncertainty, usually regarding expected benefits that will be realized from the proposal.

Probability distributions are inappropriate for capital budgeting decisions because probabilities are based on expected outcomes of a given event if repeated numerous times.

Consider an example in which a flood-prone town hears the following weather forecast: "There is a 10% chance that it will rain two inches, but an 85% chance that it will rain four inches. There is the slight chance — only one in 20 — that it will rain six inches or more."

Now, if the town experiences flooding problems if it rains five inches or more, how does it prepare for the rain, if at all?

$$2 \times .10 = .20$$
$$4 \times .85 = 3.40$$
$$6 \times .05 = \underline{.30}$$
$$3.90 \text{ inches}$$

In this example, the expected value of the weather forecast is 3.90 inches. However, the town will, in all likelihood, prepare for the worst — six inches of rain. It would do this because of the severe consequences associated with a six-inch rainfall, even though statistically it is not significant.

The same applies to capital-budgeting decisions. If a firm considered a proposal that had, say, a 10% chance of missing its projected cash flows by an amount that would force it into bankruptcy, it would steer clear of the proposal. In most instances, the "expected value" of the outcome of a capital investment proposal will not be one of the options. In the example above, the weather forecaster said nothing about expecting 3.90 inches of rain, while statistically that amount would be most likely.

Although it is definitely true that perfect knowledge will seldom, if ever, exist for a capital-investment opportunity, allowance should not be made by inflating the required rate of return. Risk, inflation, and the time value of money should not be pooled together in one large required return. Such practices make it difficult to evaluate the performance of a project after it has been implemented. The practice also adds uncertainty to uncertainty.

Cash-Flow Projections

The uncertainty associated with capital budgeting opportunities will most likely be related to the expected cash flows. (Cash flow represents the net increase in cash over a period of time, normally a year. It is a dynamic indicator of liquidity and reflects a firm's ability to continue the production process.) This is because that capital expenditures usually affect operations for a great length of time. In dynamic economic conditions, it may be difficult to forecast business activity for the following year, yet alone 10, 15, or even 25 years down the road. Remember that capital budgeting decisions are made based on information that is available at the time of the investment opportunity. This information may be drastically different before the project is fully implemented.

Of particular importance is the fact that cash flow is considered in a capital decision, not accounting profits or taxable income. Therefore, when any business expense does not represent an actual cash outlay, the result is taxable income less the actual net cash flow. The most common forms of noncash expenses are depreciation, depletion or amortization. These items represent a periodic recognition of the decrease in usefulness of an asset for which cash was expended at the time of acquisition.

Perhaps an example illustrating areas of uncertainty, as well as the effects of noncash expenses on cash flows, would be helpful. Consider the following capital investment opportunity:

A firm has an opportunity to add a new model skateboard to its existing product line. The production of the new model will require new equipment costing $25,000. The production rate is expected to be 2,000 per year. Each skateboard is expected to sell for $9, and each will require $2.50 in materials and a $3.50 labor cost. The new equipment will last five years, at the end of which time it will be fully depreciated. The firm pays taxes at the rate of 50% of taxable income.

Questions:

1. What is the annual profit anticipated with this opportunity?

2. What is the annual cash flow anticipated with this opportunity?

3. Which assumptions associated with this opportunity are uncertainty?

Annual Profit:

Sales		$18,000
Cost of sales		
Materials	$ 5,000	
Labor	7,000	
Depreciation	5,000	
		17,000
Profit BIT		1,000
Tax		500
Net profit		$ 500

Annual Cash Flow (not including acquisition of initial equipment)

Sales		$18,000
Cost of sales		
Materials	$ 5,000	
Labor	7,000	
Depreciation	5,000	
		17,000
Profit BIT		1,000
Tax		500
Net profit		500
Depreciation		+ 5,000
Cash flow		$ 5,500

The argument that depreciation should be left out of the calculation, because it is subtracted and then added back, is not valid. The rationale is that depreciation, although not representing an actual cash outlay, is a valid continuing business expense that reduces taxable income. The cash transaction for the equipment occurs when the equipment is originally purchased. The initial transaction is merely a realignment of assets. Because the equipment wears out, it is depreciated in value as it is used. An item of equipment has the capability to produce an estimated number of products or will last for a given period of time. Therefore, as production is experienced or time passes, the total production capability of the equipment decreases. This is the depreciation that is recognized on the income statement.

The depreciation mechanism is a means to stimulate increases in productive capacity (i.e., growth) by allowing a firm to recover a portion of the initial cash invested in production equipment through reduced income taxes. The rate of recovery is 1- tax rate. In the example above, the tax without depreciation would have been $3,000 annually ($18,000 - $12,000 x 50%). The actual tax of $500 indicates a tax saving of $2,500 per year, or $12,500 over the five-year life of the equipment. This is the same as the original investment of $25,000 x (1- .50).

The items in the original assumptions that are uncertain are annual forecasted unit sales, material cost per skateboard, labor cost per skateboard, and corporate tax rate.

Annual Forecasted Unit Sales

A high degree of uncertainty is associated with forecasting the number of skateboards that will be sold because the proposed skateboard is a new model. Forecasted consumer acceptance and subsequent demand is perhaps the most uncertain element in a proposal involving new products. Many times firms have lost millions, even hundreds of millions, by misreading the buying public's taste. Perhaps the classic example is the automobile introduced by Ford in 1957 — the ill-fated Edsel. Market researchers no doubt thought that everyone wanted a car with a grille shaped like a toilet seat. It is extremely difficult to project consumer demand, and, therefore, a great deal of uncertainty accompanies this task.

Not only are unit sales highly uncertain, the price the consumer will pay is also uncertain. Perhaps in the present case, 2,200 skateboards could be sold annually if the unit price were lowered to $8.50. It should be noted that constant dollars are used over the life of investment proposals for evaluation purposes. One of the basic reasons for this as we shall shortly see, is that, the proposal will be evaluated on the basis of its current worth, or the time of the opportunity. In addition, trying to estimate inflation factors over long periods of time is most uncertain. Earlier paragraphs noted that the concept of the time value of money should not be diluted with the inflation phenomenon.

Material Cost per Skateboard

Materials for each skateboard have been projected, based on someone's estimate of scrap and raw material availability. Both of these factors, though not nearly as uncertain as customer demand, cannot be known with total certainty.

Labor Cost per Skateboard

The labor cost per skateboard has been projected, based on someone's estimate of labor productivity in each phase of the production process. This again is subject to variation.

Corporate Tax Rate

Even the corporate tax structure is subject to change. It could increase or it could be abolished, as President Reagan suggested with tongue in cheek in January 1983.

So in reality, each factor in capital proposals, with the exception of the depreciation cycle, is clouded with uncertainty. Depreciation can be considered to be fairly certain because changes in tax laws or accounting rules will normally not affect existing depreciation schedules. There would be mass confusion if each factor involved in a capital proposal had its own probability distribution and statistical "expected" outcome.

Capital-Proposal Evaluation Techniques

To illustrate several evaluation techniques, let's consider the skateboard example, using the following factors:

- Initial outlay $25,000;

- Five-year life of project; and

- $5,500 annual net cash flow from operations.

Simple Payback Method

The simplicity of this method is one of the advantages of its use. It does not, however, consider the time value of money as discussed in Chapter 4.

In the present example, the calculation is made even simpler inasmuch as the operating cash flows are the same each year. The simple payback period, measured in years, is $25,000 ÷ $5,500 = 4.54 years.

Nondiscounted Rate of Return

This method is really an outgrowth of the above payback method, and is, in fact, its reciprocal.

$5,500 + $25,000 = .22 = 22%

In other words, if 22% of the original investment were returned/earned each year, it would require 4.54 years to recover the original investment.

22% x $25,000 = $5,500 x 4.54 = $25,000

Net Present Value

Chapter 4 pointed out that the value of money has a direct relationship to the time/timing of its possession. We learned that the growth of an investment, on the basis of periodic interest earned, is called "compounding" and that the reduced value of a future sum of money is called "discounting."

At the end of three years, the compounded value of $1,000, earning 15% per annum, is $1,520.87, while the present value (discounted value) of $1,000 that will be received at the end of the three-year period is $657.50. Of course, $1,000 in hand and not invested will still be worth $1,000 at the end of the period. (The purchasing power of the $1,000 may be less due to inflation, but that is beyond the scope of the present discussion.)

This concept is summarized in Table 6.3.

1. $1.15^1 \times \$1,000 = \$1,150$
    $1.15^2 \times \$1,000 = \$1,322$
    $1.15^3 \times \$1,000 = \$1,521$

2. $1/1.15^1 \times \$1,000 = \$870$
    $1/1.15^2 \times \$1,000 = \$756$
    $1/1.15^3 \times \$1,000 = \$658$

Table 6.3 Compounding and discounting

	$1,000 for a Three-Year Time Period *15% Opportunity*		
	Year 1	*Year 2*	*Year 3*
Compounded	$1,150	$1,322*	$1,521
Do nothing	$1,000	$1,000	$1,000
Discounted	$ 870	$ 756	$ 658

*Rounded to nearest whole dollar

The time value of money finds excellent application in the area of capital budgeting, inasmuch as capital investment opportunities usually impact a company's financial results for at least several, if not many, years.

A manager reviewing capital-investment opportunities should value investment outlays and cash inflows according to the relative timing of their occurrence. Investments in future years should appear at present to be less costly since the company has the opportunity to put such funds into profitable use until they are required for the investment. Similarly, the cost of the funds (i.e, interest) can be avoided until the funds are required. Conversely, cash flows received presently will be more valuable than if received in future time periods because the cash received presently can be employed in profitable opportunities.

An explicit assumption when using the present value method of capital-investment evaluation is that a company's opportunity cost of capital is known. If a given company earns, say, 15% on its assets, it would be feasible to use this figure in the initial evaluation process.

The present-value method, in essence, expresses the value of all future cash outlays and inflows in present dollars. If competing projects are considered simultaneously, the project with the largest absolute present value will be the most attractive. Keep in mind that all projects must be evaluated in light of the 15% opportunity. In this way, the relative timing of the outlays and inflows becomes the primary variable.

Let's consider the skateboard manufacturer. While illustrating cash-flow concepts, it was stated that sales would be constant at 2,000 units per year for the five-year period. Using the discounting concept illustrated in Table 6.3 and considering an opportunity rate of return of 15%, the present value of the project can be calculated. The annual operating cash inflow for this project was previously determined to be $5,500. (See Table 6.4.) The 15% opportunity rate is exclusively the anticipated earning rate. It does not allow for any risk associated with the project, nor is an allowance for inflation included.

Table 6.4 Net present value of skateboard expansion project (15% opportunity)

Time Period	Cash Outlay	Cash Inflows	Present-Value Factor	Net PV
Present	$25,000	—	1.000	($25,000)
Year 1	—	$5,500	.870	4,785
Year 2	—	$5,500	.756	4,158
Year 3	—	$5,500	.658	3,619
Year 4	—	$5,500	.572	3,146
Year 5	—	$5,500	.497	2,733
				($ 6,559)

Table 6.4 reveals an interesting fact. The project does not provide a 15% rate of return when the time value of money is considered. The present value of the project is negative. Moreover, the simple nondiscounted payback evaluation method indicated a 4.54-year payback period. But when discounting the cash flows to consider the opportunity cost of money, the project does not recover its initial investment by the end of its five-year life.

At this point, a myopic manager might elect to use a nondiscounted evaluation method so as to make the project look more attractive. If so, this manager would have to concede that if he had $2,733 (the present value of the $5,500 cash flow projected for the fifth year of the project discounted at 15%) and kept it for five years, it would not earn any interest, etc. Most likely he wouldn't buy that. He would probably invest in, say, certificates of deposit. If he invested in CDs with a rate of 15% for five years, he would expect to have $5,500 at the end of the five-year period, as per Table 6.5.

Table 6.5 Compounding at 15% for five years

Year	Earning Base	Interest Factor	End-of-Year Balance
1	$2,733	1.15	$3,143
2	$3,143	1.15	$3,614
3	$3,614	1.15	$4,156
4	$4,156	1.15	$4,779
5	$4,779	1.15	$5,946*

*Rounding error

Realizing, then, that the project does not, in fact, provide a 15% rate of return, it is logical to ask what the actual rate of return, or yield, for the project is.

Yield

To calculate a project's actual rate of return, or yield, requires that the interest factors chosen produce a zero present value at the end of the life of the project. In other words, the ($6,559) from Table 6.4 must be zero. If the net present value of a project is negative, as in the present case, a lower rate of return is needed to bring the net present value to zero. The converse is also true. If the net present value of a project is positive, a higher rate of return applied to the project will bring the net present value to zero.

Normally, the instructions issued to determine the rate of return are to use trial and error. However, when the cash flows are constant each year over the life of the project, there is a short cut.

In Table 6.4, the present-value factors applied to the constant annual cash flows can be added together to arrive at a single multiplier.

Year 1	.870
Year 2	.756
Year 3	.658
Year 4	.572
Year 5	.497
	3.353

Investment		$25,000
Recovery 3.353 x $5,500	=	18,441
Unrecovered @ 15%	=	$ 6,559

From this calculation, it can be determined that $5,500 (x) needs to equal $25,000 in order to have a zero net present value. Accordingly, x = $25,000 ÷ $5,500 = 4.5455. We've seen this number before. In the earlier context, it represented the number of years required for the simple payback of the project. In the present context it represents the sum of some number that, when inserted into the standard discounting formula, is equal to 1 plus the rate of return of the project.

$$\frac{1}{(x)^1} + \frac{1}{(x)^2} + \frac{1}{(x)^3} + \frac{1}{(x)^4} + \frac{1}{(x)^5} = 4.5455$$

The nearest whole percent satisfying this equation is 3%, or the rate of return for the project is approximately 3%. Table 6.6 reflects the net present value approximating zero at a 3% rate of return.

Table 6.6 Net present value of skateboard expansion project (3% rate of return)

Time Period	Cash Outlay	Cash Inflow	Present-Value Factor	Net PV
Present	$25,000	—	1.000	($25,000)
Year 1	—	$5,500	.971	5,340
Year 2	—	$5,500	.943	5,186
Year 3	—	$5,500	.915	5,032
Year 4	—	$5,500	.888	4,884
Year 5	—	$5,500	.862	4,741
				($ 183)

Options Available

If the manager determines that a 3% return is not sufficient to warrant the investment of capital funds, several other options may be considered prior to discarding the project.

- Reduce the capital outlay;

- Increase the annual cash flows;

- Alter the timing of the cash flows; or

- Any combination of the above.

Reduce the Capital Outlay. If the firm determines that a 15% return is still necessary to obtain project approval, how much could it pay for the equipment?

With all other parameters unchanged, the initial capital outlay would have to be reduced by $6,559 to obtain zero percent value at 15% return, as per Table 6.7.

Table 6.7 Net present value at 15% with $18,441 original capital investment

Time Period	Cash Outlay	Cash Inflow	Present-Value Factor	Net PV
Present	$18,441	—	1.000	($18,441)
Year 1	—	$5,500	.870	4,785
Year 2	—	$5,500	.756	4,158
Year 3	—	$5,500	.658	3,619
Year 4	—	$5,500	.572	3,146
Year 5	—	$5,500	.497	2,733
				-0-

Although it is unlikely that an equipment manufacturer will lower its quoted price for equipment by 26.2% in order to accommodate the buyer's capital evaluation criteria, any reduction in original capital will provide a return greater than the 3% calculated in Table 6.6.

Increase the Annual Cash Flows. The original estimate of production/sales for the new-model skateboard was 2,000 units per year, priced to sell at $9 each. Materials and labor were estimated at $2.50 and $3.50, respectively. After carefully reconsidering the estimates, management feels that they were conservative. It feels that a selling price of $10 is more realistic and that material cost can be limited to $2 per unit and labor cost can be held to $3 per unit. Based on the new estimates, it developed a revised cash-flow projection.

Sales		$20,000
Cost of sales		
Materials	$ 4,000	
Labor	6,000	
Depreciation	5,000	
		15,000
Profit BIT		5,000
Tax		2,500
Net profit		2,500
Depreciation		5,000

Cash flow $ 7,500

Notice that profit before income taxes increased by $4,000, while cash flow increased by just $2,000. That is because the incremental profit will be taxed at the 50% rate, leaving just half of the profit available for reinvestment in the business. The net present value of this project with a 15% required return is reflected in Table 6.8. Inasmuch as the net present value is positive, even though small, the project now returns the required 15% when discounted.

Table 6.8 Net present value at 15%; $7,500 annual cash flow

Time Period	Cash Outlay	Cash Inflow	Present-Value Factor	Net PV
Present	$25,000	—	1.000	($25,000)
Year 1	—	$7,500	.870	6,525
Year 2	—	$7,500	.756	5,670
Year 3	—	$7,500	.658	4,935
Year 4	—	$7,500	.572	4,290
Year 5	—	$7,500	.497	3,727
				$ 147

Alter the Timing of the Cash Flows. Heretofore, management has considered that the initial outlay had to be paid all at once in the beginning and that the annual operating cash flows would be constant over the life of the project. They decide to evaluate the project from another angle, i.e., delaying part of the original investment and selling more skateboards during the early years. They agree that a $10 selling price is realistic, and that material and labor costs are realistic at $2 and $3, respectively. Also, they cannot talk the equipment manufacturer into reducing the price of the equipment from the quoted $25,000. However, they are able to negotiate delaying the payment of $5,000 of the $25,000 until the beginning of Year 3 because the $5,000 was for automatic loading equipment that wasn't immediately required to manufacture the skateboards.

The marketing people still project unit sales of 10,000 units, but instead of 2,000 per year, their revised forecast reflects heavier sales in the early years, tapering off in the latter part of the project life.

Year	Unit Sales	Revenue @ $10/unit
1	3,000	$30,000
2	2,500	25,000
3	2,000	20,000
4	1,500	15,000
5	1,000	10,000

These changes will require that new annual cash-flow projections be developed, as illustrated in Table 6.9. The present value factors necessary for the 15% required return can be applied to see what effect, if any, timing of cash flows has on a project's net present value. The relevant net present value determination is reflected in Table 6.10. That table shows that the net present value is substantially positive, indicating a discounted rate of return greater than 15%. Because the annual cash flows are unequal, trial and error must be used to determine the actual rate of return.

Table 6.9 Annual operating cash-flow projection

	Year 1	Year 2	Year 3	Year 4	Year 5
Sales	$30,000	$25,000	$20,000	$15,000	$10,000
Materials	6,000	5,000	4,000	3,000	2,000
Labor	9,000	7,500	6,000	4,500	3,000
Depreciation					
original	4,000	4,000	4,000	4,000	4,000
added	—	—	1,667	1,667	1,667
Profit BIT	$11,000	$ 8,500	$ 4,333	$ 1,833	($ 667)
Tax	(5,500)	(4,250)	(2,166)	(916)	333
Net profit	$ 5,500	$ 4,250	$ 2,167	$ 917	($ 334)
Depreciation	$ 4,000	$ 4,000	$ 5,667	$ 5,667	$ 5,667
Cash Flow	$ 9,500	$ 8,250	$ 7,834	$ 6,584	$ 5,333

Table 6.10 Net present value at 15% timing of cash flows altered

| | 1 | 2 | 3 | 4 | 5 |
Time Period	Cash Outlay	Cash Inflow	Net Cash Flow	Present-Value Factor	Net Present Value
Present	($20,000)	—	($20,000)	1.000	($20,000)
Year 1	—	9,500	9,500	.870	8,265
Year 2	—	8,250	8,250	.756	6,237
Year 3	($ 5,000)	7,834	2,834	.658	1,865
Year 4	—	6,584	6,584	.572	3,766
Year 5	—	5,333	5,333	.497	2,650
		Net Present Value			$ 2,783

Yield Method. When the actual rate of return is to be determined for a given capital-investment opportunity, the process is called the yield method of evaluation. The objective of the process is to determine the rate of return that the project yields.

The yield method is similar to the preceding net present value method. Both are predicated on the discounted or time value of money concept. While the net-present-value method is used to determine if a project has a positive present value, based on a given or required rate of return, the yield method determines the exact rate of return.

In essence, the net-present-value method can be used as a forerunner to the yield method. If, as in our example illustrated in Table 6.10, the net present value is positive when applying factors for a 15% return, we know immediately that the project actually yields a return somewhat greater than 15%. Conversely, if the net present value is negative after applying 15% factors, the actual yield, or rate of return, would be less than 15%.

The actual yield for a given project is that percentage whose factors produce zero net present value. In other words, all present and future cash flows are discounted until zero net present value results. The accompanying percentage, represented by the factors, is the actual rate of return or yield of the project.

In Table 6.10, the net present value is $2,783. The problem is to determine which factors in column 4, when multiplied by the annual net cash flows in column 3 and then added, as in column

5, equal zero.

Inasmuch as the present $2,783 indicates that the project yields more than 15%, we can begin the trial-and-error method with 20% factors, as per Table 6.11. Column 7 is the product of present value factors at 20% (column 6) and annual net cash flows per column 3. As column 7 is still positive, we know the actual rate of return is somewhat greater than 20%. When present value factors for 22% are applied, however, the net present value is negative. Thus, it is determined that the project yields between 20% and 22% return.

Table 6.11 Determination of actual yield

Time Period	Cash Outlay	Cash Flow	Net Cash Flow	PV for 15%	Net PV	PV for 20%	Net PV	PV for 22%	Net PV
Present	<$20,000>	—	<$20,000>	1.000	<$20,000>	1.000	<$20,000>	1.000	<$20,000>
Year 1	—	$9,500	9,500	.870	8,265	.833	7,913	.820	7,790
Year 2	—	8,250	8,250	.756	6,237	.694	5,726	.672	5,544
Year 3	<$ 5,000>	7,834	2,834	.658	1,865	.579	1,641	.551	1,561
Year 4	—	6,584	6,584	.572	3,766	.482	3,173	.451	2,969
Year 5	—	5,333	5,333	.497	2,650	.402	2,144	.370	1,973
			Net Present Value		$2,783		$597		<$163>

The total swing in net present value from 20% to 22% is $760 ($597 + $163). The object is to find, or interpolate, the value when net present value is zero.

Therefore:

$$\frac{\$597}{\$760} = .7855 \text{ or } 78.55\%$$

$$78.55\% \times (22\% - 20\%) = 1.57\%$$

$$\text{then } 20\% + 1.57\% = 21.57\% \text{ actual rate of return}$$

Discounting the annual cash flows at 21.57% will result in zero net present value. The factors for 21.57% are as follows:

$$\text{Year 1} \quad \frac{1}{(1.2157)^1} = .8226$$

$$\text{Year 2} \quad \frac{1}{(1.2157)^2} = .6766$$

$$\text{Year 3} \quad \frac{1}{(1.2157)^3} = .5566$$

$$\text{Year 4} \quad \frac{1}{(1.2157)^4} = .4578$$

$$\text{Year 5} \quad \frac{1}{(1.2157)^5} = .3766$$

In Table 6.12 these factors are applied to the annual cash flows and the accompanying net present value.

Table 6.12 Net Present Value at 21.57%

Time Present	Cash Outlay	Cash Inflow	Net Cash Flow	PV Factors for 21.57%	Net PV
Present	($20,000)		($20,000)	1.0000	($20,000)
Year 1	—	9,500	9,500	.8226	7,815
Year 2	—	8,250	8,250	.6766	5,582
Year 3	($ 5,000)	7,834	2,834	.5566	1,577
Year 4	—	6,584	6,584	.4578	3,014
Year 5	—	5,333	5,333	.3766	2,008
Net Present Value					($4)

Of particular interest is a comparison of Tables 6.8 and 6.12. Both reflect an investment of $25,000 and a total cash inflow of $37,500 over the five-year life of the project. The basic difference in these two proposals is the relative timing of the cash flows. By delaying a portion of the original investment and accelerating sales in the earlier years, the return on invested capital increased from slightly more than 15% to more than 21%. The key is that the reduced initial investment began generating returns sooner. Also, if the additional $5,000 portion of the investment had been made currently, it would not have produced any incremental earnings for several years. As it was, management had the opportunity to invest that $5,000 in, say, short-term securities until it could be productively employed in the skateboard project.

Payback Measures Liquidity

The payback period is a measure of liquidity rather than profitability. If a project is an *infinite annuity,* then the IRR is the inverse of the payback period.

$$An = R \; \frac{1 - \dfrac{1}{(1+i)} \; n}{i}$$

$$R = \text{periodic payment}$$
$$An = \text{investment}$$
$$i = \text{interest (1RR)}$$
$$n = \text{number of years}$$

IF N = oo then $(1+i)^n$ approaches infinity if i is positive.

$1/(1+i)^n = 1/\infty = 0$

$$An = R \; \frac{1-0}{i}$$

i = R/AN

BUT An/R = payback period
i = IRR = 1/payback period

Example:

R = \$5,500 per year
An = \$25,000 initial investment
i = unknown
N = infinity

$$25,000 = 5,500 \; \frac{1 - \dfrac{1}{(1+i)^{\infty}}}{i}$$

1/i = 25,000/5,500 = 4.5455

Payback period = 4.5455 years
i = 1/payback period = 22%

Interest expenses should *not* be included in the cash flow because they have been adjusted in the calculation for the discount rate.

Other Methods for Financing Capital Equipment

This chapter has addressed the opportunity for formulating capital equipment via actual purchase, or the long-range commitment of company funds. However, when an opportunity presents itself for a profitable project but internal or borrowed funds are not available, a company may pursue avenues other than outright purchase.

Capital Lease

This basic form of equipment financing allows users to acquire productive assets with little or no cash outlay. The lender provides up to 100% of the equipment purchase price, while the borrower retains all tax benefits and ownership interests. A constant payout, coupled with flexible terms (five to seven years is typical, but up to ten years is possible), makes this a popular form of financing in the machine-tool industry.

When interest rates are volatile, a manufacturer will want to preserve the maximum degree of flexibility in whatever financing is used. Some lenders offer borrowers a float-and-fix option on their leases so that the borrower can float the cost of the lease — at an increment over the prime rate — for a period of up to one year and fix the rate any time during the period for the remaining term. In a capital lease, the equipment is listed as an asset and lease payments are deemed offsetting liabilities — an important point for some companies.

Operating Lease

This is not really a form of financing, but rather a pure lease — in effect, a rental. The user operates the equipment for a specified period of time — at a cost of less than the full purchase price — but never takes title. The fact that operating leases are off the balance sheet can be important to the user. Rental payments are shown as an operating expense. The equipment is not capitalized on the user's balance sheet. Generally, operating leases are used only for smaller-ticket items with strong residual values since the lender ends up being owner at the end of the lease period.

Operating leases provide several major benefits to users. First, the company has the use of the equipment for a stated period of time, usually two or three years. Second, because the user doesn't pay the full amount of the equipment's original cost, the company can preserve its cash for higher-yielding investments.

Vendor Leasing

In this form of leasing, a third party — generally a finance company — serves as intermediary between an equipment manufacturer (the vendor) and a user. The appeal to the manufacturer is obvious — another party handles all the details of financing, including documentation, funding, billing, and collections. Also, the equipment manufacturer's capital requirements are reduced and cash flow is accelerated.

Vendor leasing also allows the manufacturer to offer price reductions, through financing, by subsidizing the rates instead of discounting equipment cost. Tax and ownership benefits are retained by the manufacturer or the financier.

For the user, the major benefits are convenience and assured financing at a specific rate.

Tax Leasing

This type of leasing is used primarily to finance large capital assets. Tax benefits are kept by the owner/lessor. The result is a lower financing rate for the equipment user.

Summary

As we have illustrated, production facilities and equipment can be acquired in different ways. Inasmuch as facilities and equipment acquisition normally requires relatively large commitments of funds, the justification for such funding is fairly rigorous. When funds are committed for a project that has a payback period of several years, the time value of money must be considered, which takes into account the opportunity foregone by not investing in other things.

Depending on the availability of funds and individual companies' objectives, facilities and equipment may be acquired via lease or rental agreements. Whichever method of funding is chosen and for whatever reason, the overriding objective for the acquisition is the same: To maximize the productivity of capital by improving the firm's financial position in as short a time period as possible when compared to any other investment alternative.

Chapter 7
Measuring the Labor Input

Objectives

- *Learn the significance of the human aspect of the production resource called "labor."*

- *Learn the different categories of the labor resource.*

- *Learn to measure the productivity of the labor resource.*

- *Appreciate that time is, once again, the benchmark in labor measurement.*

- *Understand why labor measurement is so important and why it is used.*

Contents

The Human Element in Production is Labor

This chapter builds on the definitions of labor that were discussed in the beginning of the preceding chapter. Although the chapter's thrust is labor as a factor of production, input, resources, etc., the human element of labor cannot be dismissed. It is this attribute that makes it unique.

In a typical firm that is engaged in the production of goods, say household appliances, many levels of the human resource come into play. The chart in Figure 7.1, which illustrates layers of human resources, is sharply condensed — i.e., there could be numerous separate plants, each requiring a plant manager. Each separate plant could have its materials managers, maintenance superintendents, and facilities engineers. Each production department could have its own general foreman for each shift. Each shift may have several first-line supervisors covering work centers within each department. And within each work center there are employees who assemble components, transform materials and operate machines.

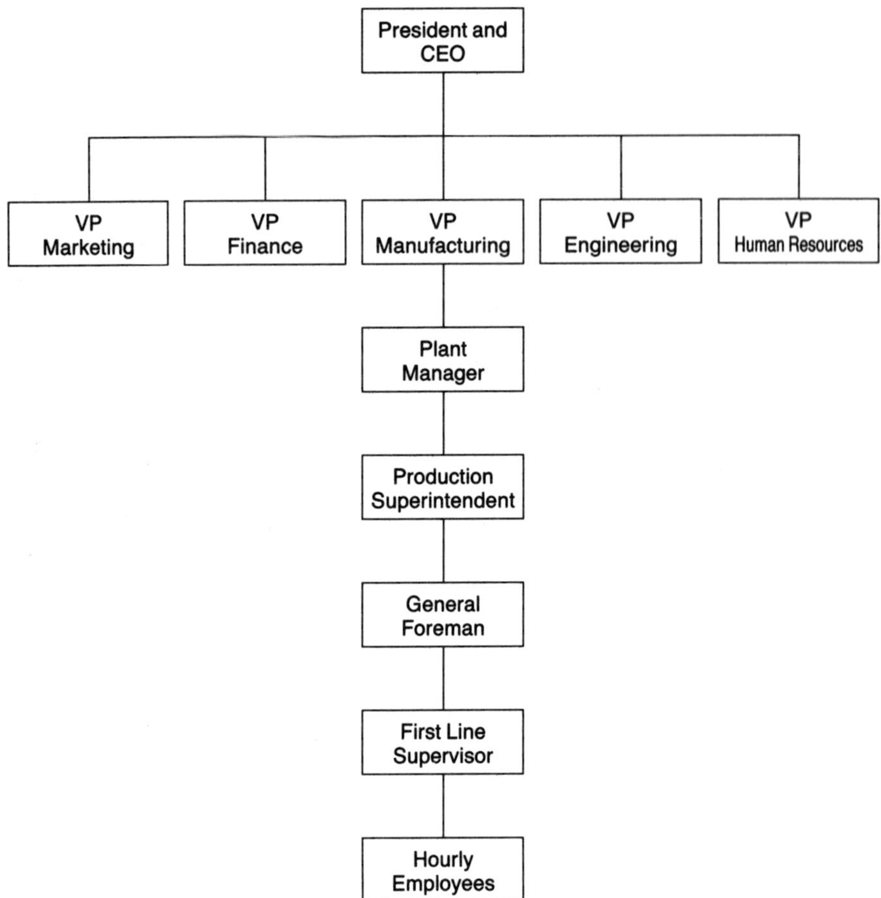

Fig. 7.1. Typical layers of the human resource in a manufacturing organization

Effective Communication Improves Productivity

Figure 7.1 shows seven layers, or tiers, of management. That means that the strategy, goals and objectives of the firm, as viewed by the president, must flow downward through five other managerial levels before they get to the hourly employees. If the strategies, goals, and objectives are communicated properly, that is, candidly and expeditiously, the firm will have obtained a head start in improved labor productivity.

In the typical firm, all managerial levels, down through first-line supervision, are staffed with salaried persons who are paid on the basis of period of time, usually monthly. Hourly employees are paid as their description implies, on the basis of actual hours worked or expended on the production of goods and services. Typically, hourly employees are required to verify the actual time worked via a time-clock system.

Effectiveness of Managers Depends on Hourly Employees

Higher up in the managerial hierarchy, the method of pay is in the form of a monthly/yearly fixed amount, plus additional amounts based on the attainment of predetermined goals and objectives. The attainment of these goals and objectives is based ultimately on the efforts expended by the hourly employees who assemble the components, transform the materials, and operate the machines. This chapter focuses on this segment of a firm's human resources.

Hourly Workers

Within the category of hourly employees there are two major divisions:

1. direct-labor employees

2. indirect-labor employees

As defined in Chapter 8, a direct-labor employee is one who directly adds value to the firm's output during the production process. A further distinction is that the direct labor expended is quantifiable and assignable to each unit of production.

Table 7.1 Resource input matrix amounts in $000

	Material	Men	Machines	Energy	Totals
Department					
Cutting	100	70	35	145	350
Stamping	—	40	30	30	25
Fabrication	210	25	5	5	245
Assembly	—	220	30	5	150
Testing	—	140	5	5	150
Plant services	—	5	50	225	280
Totals	310	500	155	410	1,375

Table 7.1 was originally introduced as Table 3.6. Reflected in this figure is the fact that labor comprises $500,000 per time period or 36.4% of the firm's total production costs. For illustrative purposes, consider the labor to be apportioned as shown relative to the number of employees:

	Direct Employees	Indirect Employees	Total Employees
Cutting	30	26	56
Stamping	12	20	32
Fabrication	5	15	20
Assembly	125	51	176
Testing	—	112	112
Plant services	—	4	4
Total	172	228	400

Direct Labor is Measured Using Production Standards

Approximately 43% of the hourly work force is considered direct and 57% of the work force is indirect. Inasmuch as our definition of direct labor includes quantifiable and assignable effort, the work of 172 employees can be evaluated with concrete production expectations. In other words, standards of performance can be established for direct-labor operations.

Within a given department, for example, Assembly, each stage of the assembly operation for each different model of the product may require a separate production standard. If the product is a wagon, there may be three distinct assembly operations:

1. Assemble bearings, wheels, axles, and hubs.

2. Assemble handle to chassis.

3. Assemble front and rear axle subassembly to chassis.

If the firm manufactures 20 different sizes and models of wagons, then as many as 60 direct-labor production standards could be required for the assembly department.

Considering five separate cutting operations, two separate stamping operations and four fabrication operations, total production standards required can be listed as per Table 7.2. It is not unusual for a manufacturing operation to have 20,000 different operations, all of which require that a predetermined production standard be established. An illustration showing the typical methodology used in establishing a production standard will follow shortly.

Table 7.2 Production standards required

Department	Different Operations	Varied Models	Total Operations
Cutting	5	20	100
Stamping	2	20	40
Fabrication	4	20	80
Assembly	3	20	60
Testing	--	20	—
Plant service	—	20	—
Total	14		280

Indirect Labor Is Not Tied to Production

An indirect-labor employee, on the other hand, is engaged in activities that are not quantifiable or assignable to a particular unit of production. Consider an employee in the Assembly

Department who delivers boxes of bearings to the assembly station with a fork truck. The movements of the fork truck may be determined and expressed in a given length of travel per minute. However, the length of travel per wagon produced may not be constant. Neither can it be expected that the driver will transport the same number of boxes of bearings each time. Therefore, even though the operation is necessary in order to support the assembly function, the activity is indirectly associated with the assembly of each particular wagon. Normally, the labor expended for material handling cannot be apportioned for each unit of production.

Other classic examples of indirect labor include equipment-setup people or custodial employees. A particular setup may require 30 minutes; however, a varying number of production units can be scheduled. A fixed time for a setup with varying production would result in varying setup times per unit produced. Any hourly employee who engages in an activity that cannot be apportioned to an individual unit of production is classified as an indirect employee.

As one would expect, the number of direct-labor employees required varies directly with production levels, while indirect-labor employees are more fixed in number. If the established production rate for assembling the handle to the chassis is ten per hour, a customer order for 200 of a given model would require 20 hours of assembly labor. If the order is increased to 300 units, the direct-labor requirement for assembling handle to chassis would be 30 hours. However, the setup people and custodians would most likely not be affected by varying production levels. Figure 7.2 illustrates typical employee requirements patterns with varying production levels.

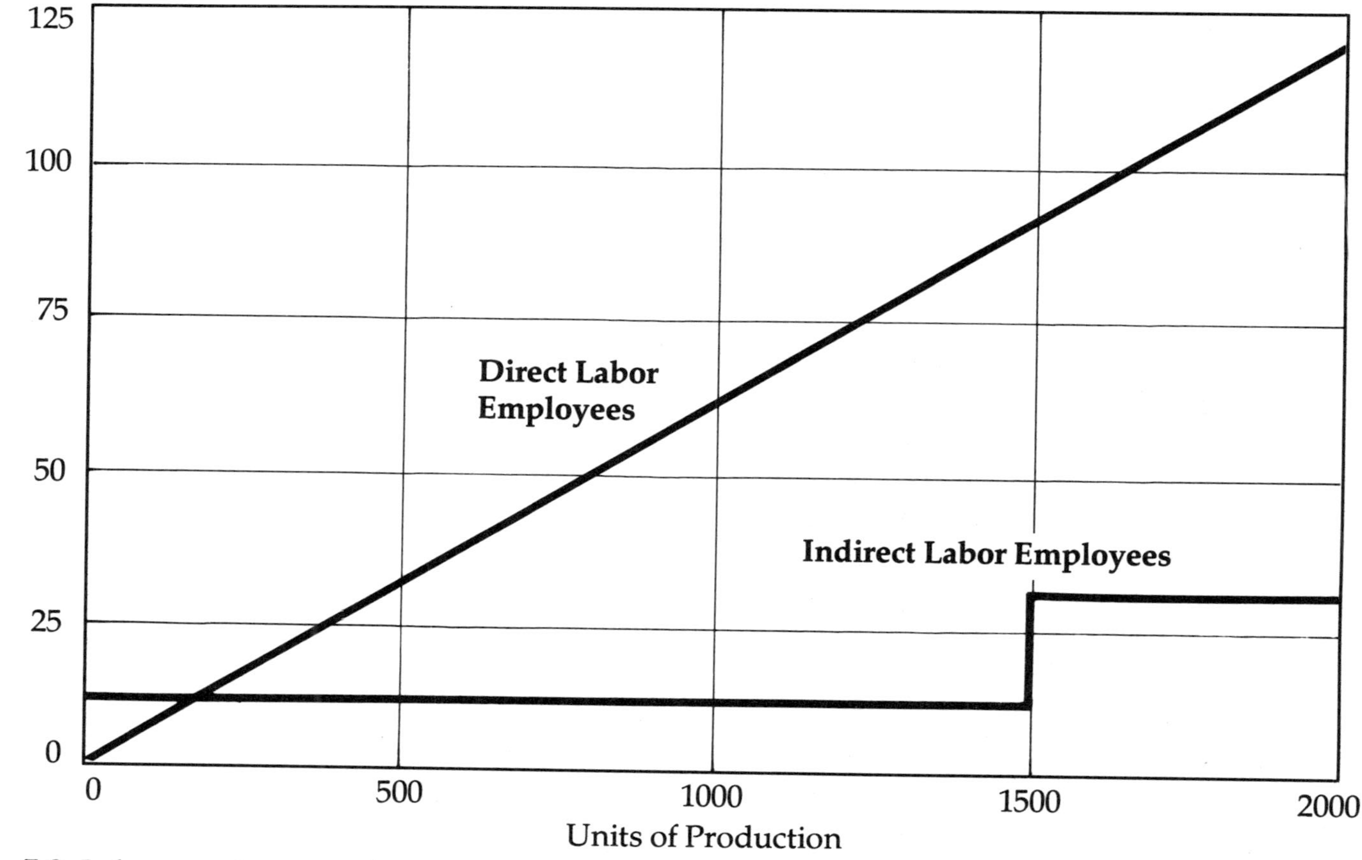

Fig. 7.2. Labor requirements for varying production levels

The Direct-Indirect Ratio May Be Misleading

Many firms still consider a fixed direct-indirect ratio to be a barometer of labor effectiveness. The ratio would vary from industry to industry and from plant to plant. For example, the desired direct-indirect ratio for a wagon manufacturer might be 3:1. The futility of this practice is noted in Figure 7.2 in which that ratio is only found at a given level of production, i.e., 1,500 wagons per time period. Above or below that point, the ratio improves down to a level of 750 units. Hiring practices that strive to maintain a given ratio are counterproductive.

As automation continues to make inroads in the production process, the direct-indirect ratio will continue to deteriorate; however, the productivity of the labor input will improve.

Table 7.3 summarizes both direct-indirect labor ratio and labor productivity from Figure 7.2. Now, suppose the manufacturer in Figure 7.2 buys a robot that reduces direct labor by 10%. Figure 7.3 reflects this improvement and Table 7.4 summarizes the results. At every level of production, the direct:indirect ratio was made worse, while simultaneously the productivity of labor improved at each production level.

Table 7.3 Direct-indirect labor ratio vs. productivity

Production Levels	Direct Employees	Indirect Employees	Direct-Indirect	Productivity (Wagons/Employees)
500	30	15	2:1	11.11
1,000	60	15	4:1	13.33
1,500	90	30	3:1	12.5
2,000	120	30	4:1	13.33
2,500	150	30	5:1	13.88

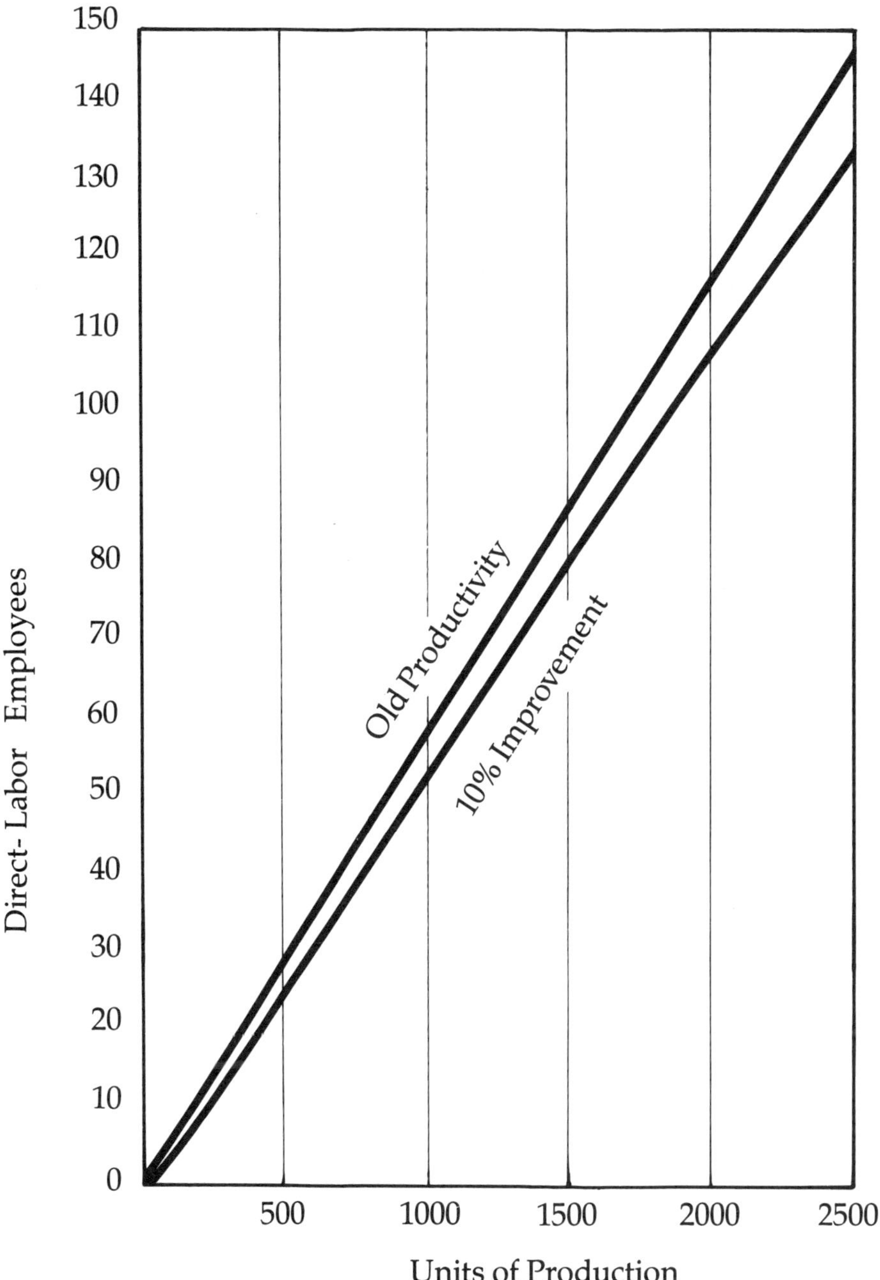

Fig. 7.3. Labor requirements for varying production levels (10% decrease in direct labor required)

Table 7.4 Direct-indirect labor ratio vs. productivity

Production Levels	Direct Employees	Indirect Employees	Direct-Indirect	Productivity (Wagons/Employees)
500	27	15	1.8:1	11.90
1,000	54	15	3.6:1	14.49
1,500	81	30	2.7:1	13.51
2,000	108	30	3.6:1	14.49
2,500	135	30	4.5:1	15.15

Measuring Labor Productivity

Numerous methods can be used to measure labor productivity. Several were listed in the preceding chapter. Consider the following two choices:

$$\frac{output}{labor\ input\ dollars} \quad vs. \quad \frac{output}{labor\ input\ hours}$$

The U.S. Department of Labor expresses labor productivity as function of labor dollars, or:

$$\frac{output}{labor\ hours\ paid}$$

At first, one tends to think that the most appropriate measure would address the labor-effort question. In other words, how much output in terms of gross domestic product does each labor-hour worked generate? However, we need also to know the productivity of the total capital paid to the labor input.

If Company A produces automobiles with 175 hours of labor and its labor rate is $15 per hour, how does it compare with Company B that produces a competitive model with 165 hours of labor? Company B's hourly labor rate is $16 per hour. (See Table 7.5.) Company B would be foolish to think that it was in a more competitive position than Company A just because fewer labor hours were required. The total cash required per car was more.

Table 7.5 Labor productivity comparisons — companies A and B

				Productivity	
	Hourly Rate	*Hours Required*	*Labor Dollars Required*	*Cars per 1,000 Hours*	*Cars per $1,000*
Company A	$15	175	$2,625	5.71	.381
Company B	16	165	2,640	6.06	.379

We can do the same with some more realistic numbers. Table 7.6 compares the United States with Japan in the manufacture of subcompact automobiles. In this case, the Japanese are slightly more than twice as productive relative to labor effort, but more than three times as productive when considering total labor costs.

Table 7.6 Labor-productivity comparisons — Japan and United States

				Productivity	
	Hourly Rate	*Hours Required*	*Labor Dollars Required*	*Cars per 1,000 Hours*	*Cars per $1,000*
Japan	*$14.68*	*14*	*$205.52*	*7.14*	*.487*
United States	*$22.50*	*29*	*$652.50*	*3.45*	*.153*

If 2,080 hours are available to work each year (52 weeks x 40 hours) and the hourly labor rate is $15, the typical employee could earn $31,200 if he worked all of the available time. Then, how about the case when Company A, because of contract obligations, pays an employee for a four-week vacation, ten holidays and five days sick leave. Now the employee still earns $31,200 for the year but is productive only 45 weeks of the available 52. Therefore, the labor cost for each hour actually worked is $17.33.

7 weeks x 40 hours x $15 = $4,200

$4,200 ÷ (45 weeks x 40 hours) = $2.33 per hour

$15.00 + $2.33 = $17.33

If Company B has the same pay policy as A, but its base rate is $16, how does it compare in labor productivity if A requires 175 hours per car and B requires just 165? The results are reflected in Table 7.7. Table 7.7 should be compared with Table 7.5 to note the difference in total labor productivity when a firm pays for hours not worked.

Table 7.7 Labor-productivity comparison — companies A and B, paying for hours not worked

	Hourly Rate	Hours Required	Labor Dollars Required	Productivity Cars per 1,000 Hours	Cars per $1,000
Company A	$17.33	175	$3,032.75	5.71	.330
Company B	$18.49*	165	$3,050.85	6.06	.328

*7 weeks x 40 hours x $16 = $4,480
$4,480 ÷ (45 weeks x 40 hours) = $2.49 per hour
$16.00 + $2.49 = $18.49

Therefore, even though it is very important to monitor labor productivity in terms of actual labor hours worked, it is absolutely necessary to monitor labor productivity relative to total labor dollars input.

Total labor productivity, then, is a function of:

- Labor efficiency;

- Labor rates; and

- Time paid for but not worked.

One can readily see the detrimental effect on total labor productivity as output per hour worked actually declined in 1979 and 1980, whereas labor rates spurred by COLA clauses increased by double-digit proportions.

Measuring Direct-Labor Effect

Painstaking care is exercised in the measurement of direct labor. This is because the total estimated cost to produce manufactured outputs is, in large part, based on the direct labor content of the outputs. This will be explained in detail in later paragraphs.

Table 7.1 indicates that the labor cost for our wagon manufacturer was only 36.4% of its total manufacturing cost. Additionally, in the early part of this chapter it was pointed out that direct labor was 43% of the total labor costs. Then, direct labor comprises just 15.6% of the total manufacturing cost. When a firm's administrative costs are also considered, the direct-labor portion of the total cost might be as low as 5%. However small this portion might be, the direct labor for a manufacturing firm remains the cornerstone of the cost-accounting system — i.e., that system that allocates a firm's total input cost to its products (outputs).

The factory of the future is heading away from the direct-labor concepts which will antiquate many traditional existing systems. However, since the existing labor force still contains approximately 25 million blue-collar employees, an illustrative example of direct-labor measurement is appropriate.

Earlier, we noted three typical assembly operations that are required by our wagon manufacturer. The first one listed was:

1. Assemble bearings, wheels, axles, and hubs. The object is to determine how much time is required to perform this particular operation. This is of importance to determine the labor content (input) required for that particular operation and to determine the capacity of the assembly facilities.

Time Is the Limiting Input

Here, we are discussing the key to productivity: time. The labor content of an input is the labor rate per time period multiplied by the time required to perform a given task. And the capacity of any facility engaged in the production of goods and services is based on output per time period. Time is the limiting input for all production factors and activities. Time cannot be expanded or contracted, only better utilized as it passes at a steadfast pace.

When establishing the time standard (measurement) for an operation, the objective is to minimize the time required to perform the operation. This is not done by requiring the assembler to perform at an excessive pace, but rather by establishing basic sound working methods. Improved labor productivity, you may recall, is not based on working faster, but working smarter. This is achieved by better time utilization.

The establishment of time standards for production operations usually rests with a firm's industrial engineering department. The actual time measurement of a particular job is the easiest part of establishing a time standard. The actual measurement is done only after care is taken to organize the work station so that minimum moves are required to perform a given task. Excessive motions require both energy and time that could better be invested in actual production. This is especially applicable to manually paced (controlled) assembly-type operations.

In-Depth Knowledge of Machines Is Often Required

Frequently, production operations are not controlled by manual effort but by machine. It may at first appear to be easier to establish a production rate based on machine cycle time than one based on manual effort. However, a machine-controlled cycle requires in-depth knowledge of the machine, the tooling used, and the material being processed. For example, the typical machine operation in hard-goods industries involves metal removal with the use of cutting tools mounted in machines. The type of metal, e.g., steel, iron, brass, determines the type of cutting tools required. In addition, for each metal type, there is an optimum cutting speed that simultaneously maximizes metal removal rates and optimizes tool life. An entire chapter could be devoted to this one aspect of "setting up" machines properly in order to maximize productivity.

The point to be made in the present context is that labor productivity begins with the establishment of proper work procedures and methods. Inefficiencies should be engineered out of the operation before it is time measured.

Also to be noted is the fact that maximum labor productivity accrues when there are no adversarial relationships between any levels of the employee hierarchy. In most instances, the most knowledgeable person about a labor operation, either machine controlled or manually controlled, is the employee performing the operation. It is a tremendous underutilization of resources when an operator's input isn't considered for whatever reason.

When the work area and work method have been established for a particular operation, the operation can then be time measured. During the process of determining the optimum work method, the particular operation will be broken down into individual steps called "elements." These elements form the basis of the time measurement. Several methods are available for work measurement: Sampling, applying predetermined time factors for each motion required, or observing several cycles of the operation and recording the elemental times with a stopwatch. Because stopwatch recordings are used extensively for manually controlled/paced operations, such as the assembly operation under present consideration, our example will employ this method.

The operation of assembling bearings, wheels, axles, and hubs can be divided into the following individual elements:

- Pick up bearing and position in wheel.

- Position wheel and bearing on axle.

- Place hub on axle and rotate assembly 180°.

- Pick up bearing and position in wheel.

- Position wheel and bearing on axle.

- Place hub on axle and set completed axle assembly on conveyor belt for transport.

Each direct-labor operation is then measured to determine the time that is required to produce one part. Figure 7.4 shows a typical time-study record illustrating how the operation of assembling bearings, wheels, axles and hubs is measured.

IND ENG DEPT TIME STUDY NUMBER 1475

DATE 7·30·1984   OBSERVER   PART NO. 90045-C
MACHINE NO.   OPERATOR SMITH   PART NAME   OPERATION NO. 31
MACHINE ASSY BENCH   OPERATION ASSEMBLE BEARING, WHEEL, &HUB TO AXLE   DEPT. NO. ASSY

DETAILED ELEMENT	1	2	3	4	5	6	7	8	9	10	Occ Pcs	Tot Obs Time	Accomp Rating	Tot Norm Min	Norm Min Per Pc	Factor	Std Min Per Pc
1. PICK UP BEARING AND	04	35	69	1.01	1.32	1.69	2.03	2.34			8						
POSITION IN WHEEL	4	4	5	6	3	4	5	4			8	.35	100	.35	.0438	1.17	.0512
2. POSITION WHEEL AND	09	40	73	1.05	1.40	1.75	2.08	2.39			8						
BEARING ON AXLE	5	5	4	4	8	6	5	5				.42	105	.4410	.0525	1.17	.0614
3. PLACE HUB ON AXLE AND	15	47	79	1.12	1.47	1.81	2.14	2.45			8						
ROTATE ASSY 180°	6	7	6	7	7	6	6	6				.51	95	.4845	.0606	1.17	.0709
4. PICK UP BEARING AND	20	51	84	1.18	1.54	1.87	2.19	2.51			8						
POSITION IN WHEEL	5	4	5	6	7	6	5	6			8	.44		.4180	.0523	1.17	.0612
5. POSITION WHEEL AND	26	58	91	1.23	1.59	1.94	2.25	2.58			8						
BEARING ON AXLE	6	7	7	5	5	7	6	7			8	.50	90	.4500	.0563	1.17	.0659
6. PLACE HUB ON AXLE AND	31	64	95	1.29	1.65	1.98	2.30	2.63			8						
SET COMPLETED ASSY ASIDE	5	6	4	6	6	4	5	5			8	.41		.4510	.0564	1.17	.0660
7. OPEN BOX OF BEARINGS AND								2.98			1						
PLACE IN BIN								35			20	.35	80	.2800	.0140	1.17	.0164
8.																	
9.																P, C, T	

NOTE: THIS STANDARD WILL BECOME OBSOLETE UPON ANY CHANGE IN STOCK, FIXTURES, JIGS, TOOLS, ETC., OR METHOD OF HANDLING.

LD RATE   NEW JOB

STANDARD HOURS PER PIECE   .0066
STANDARD HOURLY PRODUCTION   151.5
TOTAL STD. MIN PER PIECE   .3930

Fig. 7.4. Time-study record

Such a measurement, commonly called a time study, may be done for several reasons:

- A new operation or a new model may be introduced that requires an engineered time standard and the establishment of expected production rates. In this instance, the request for a time study will originate with the industrial engineering department, which is responsible for ensuring that all direct-labor operations are provided with an engineered standard. Should the job, however, be released to production/manufacturing and for some reason the industrial engineer has not initiated a time study, the department supervisor will take the initiative and request the study. Shop floor systems are designed so that no direct-labor operation may be performed without establishing a proper time standard.

- An existing operation on an existing model may have been improved by means of improved methods or a design change. Any such change requires a new standard so that the effects of the new standard can be measured and the new cost to manufacture the particular part can be determined. Such a change, which results in a lower standard time, results in a lower standard cost, which, in turn, improves the productivity of the labor input.

  In this case, the industrial engineering department will most likely initiate the time study if it initiates the improved method. However, the operators themselves initiate a great percentage of methods improvements. In such cases, the operating department will request a new time study.

- Sometimes, the operator may feel that the established time standard is unreasonable. Often, the quality of the parts received at the operator's work station deteriorates, requiring the operator to spend additional time on this particular operation. In such cases, the correct procedure begins by recognizing that the operator's performance cannot be evaluated on the basis of the existing standard.

It is important that the cause of the deterioration of quality be identified and remedied rather than altering the time standard. The latter action will automatically decrease the productivity of the labor input. In such cases, the operator will initiate corrective action because his performance will be adversely affected due to circumstances beyond his control.

When it is determined that a time study is required for any of the above reasons, the industrial engineer will complete the basic data relative to the operation to be measured or the times on the form as shown in Figure 7.4. Such basic data will include, but not be limited to, such items as:

- Part identification and operation to be studied;

- Department where operation is performed;

- Reason for study, e.g., new job or improvement of an existing job;

- Date of study and identification of the engineer performing the study;

- Type of equipment or work station on which the operation is performed;

- Setup data relevant to the particular operation to be performed, i.e., type of material, speeds and feeds of machine, fixtures used, and/or general description of workstation layout; and

- Identification of the operator to be studied and the date of study.

Once the industrial engineer, department supervisor and operator have jointly determined the proper setup, the time study can begin. Using Figure 7.4 as an example (item numbers correspond to circled items in Figure 7.4), the following steps should be taken in the time study:

1. All of the individual elements of a particular operation are listed as they occur sequentially in performing the opera-

tion. Our example shows "assemble bearing, wheel, and hub to axle." The first step, or element, of this operation is to "pick up bearing and position in wheel."

It is critical that any activity required to perform the operation be listed to ensure that its time is included in the production standard resulting from the time study. Consider element 7: open box of bearings and place in bin. Even though this element does not occur every time an axle is assembled, it does occur, as we shall shortly see, every 20th axle; therefore, the time required must be included in the production standard.

2. After the elements are listed sequentially, the time study can begin. Using a stopwatch in increments of hundredths of a minute, the industrial engineer starts the stopwatch at the beginning of the operation and records the elapsed time at the completion of each element as the stopwatch runs continuously. In the present example, 2.98 minutes elapsed during the time study.

    After the time-study observation is completed, the industrial engineer will determine the individual elemental times. This is done by comparing the elapsed time at the end of a given element with the elapsed time at the end of the immediately preceding element.

    For example, the elapsed time at the end of the fifth element (position wheel and bearing on axle) for the sixth assembly observed is 1.94 minutes. The elemental time then is .07 minutes, given that the elapsed time at the end of the preceding element is 1.87, and 1.94 - 1.87 = .07.

3. This column (Occurrences/Pieces) indicates the number of times that a given element was observed during the time study and the resulting pieces produced. The number of pieces always represents the final product. In the present example, the final product is wagons.

    Consider element number 7 (open box of bearings and place in bin). Even though this element occurred just once during the time study, each box contains enough bearings to produce 20 complete wagons.

Accordingly, 1/20 of the observed time for that element is allotted for each wagon produced.

4. This column represents the sum total of all observations for each element. The total observed time for element number 3 (place hub on axle and rotate assembly 180°) is .51 minutes.

.06 + .07 + .06 + .07 + .07 + .06 + .06 + .06 = .51

5. This column represents the industrial engineer's subjective appraisal (rating) of the level of effort expended by the operator during the performance of each element. This appraisal is based on an established "norm" or benchmark of physical effort. The norm is represented as 100%, and is compared to a person walking at a pace of two paces per second or 120 paces per minute. This is universally accepted as normal exertion or performance.

   If a particular element is rated above 100%, say element number two, the operator has actually performed at a pace that is faster than would be considered normal.

   Rating factors applied during a time study should always be discussed with the operator before the industrial engineer leaves the work station.

6. This column is simply the time that is considered to be normal to perform the listed element. Consider element number 7 again. The actual observed time for eight occurrences was .42 minutes. The industrial engineer determined that the operator was actually performing that particular element at 105% of normal. Therefore, the "normal" effort would have required more time than that taken by this operator, as the following calculation indicates: $1.05 \times .42 = .4410$ allowed for the element.

   This practice strives to "normalize" or "level" all operators. It would be unfair to expect all operators to perform at the same pace as the fastest operator. The concept is that the operation is measured, rather than the individual operator.

7. This column represents the normal time allowed per piece produced.
Element number 2 = .4410 ÷ 8 = .0525 minutes/piece.
Element number 7 = .2800 ÷ 20 = .0140 minutes/piece.

8. This column recognizes the fact that even a normal operator cannot be expected to work all day/shift without a break. An allowance is given for personal time such as restroom needs or coffee breaks. A typical personal allowance is the 17% shown in the example. More tedious jobs that require more physical effort may warrant larger allowances.

   A typical work shift is eight hours or 480 minutes per day. A 17% personal allowance provides an employee/operator 81.6 minutes or 1.36 hours per day for personal needs.

9. This column represents the "standard" time per piece. It is simply the normal time extended by the personal-allowance factor for each element.

10. The total standard minutes allowed per piece is the sum total of the standard elemental times.

   Not including element number 7, the actual elapsed/observed time to complete eight pieces was 2.63 minutes or .3288 minutes per piece. The standard allowance for the same operation (exclusive of element number 7) is .3766 minutes per piece.

11. This entry indicates the amount of time, expressed in hours, required of the assembly department's resources to complete this particular operation.
.3930 std.min. ÷ 60 min.per hr. = .0066 std. hrs. per wagon

12. The standard hourly production, expressed in pieces/units per hour, is derived as follows:

$$\frac{1 \text{ piece}}{.0066 \text{ hr.}} = \frac{x \text{ pieces}}{1.0 \text{ hr.}} = 151.5 \text{ pc/hour}$$

Work Measurement: Using Predetermined Time Factors

Another widely used approach to work measurement is based on applying predetermined time factors to a particular operation. Perhaps the most widely used method is MTM (methods — time measurement). This method was developed in the 1940s, and offshoots of the basic concepts are still widely used today in both manufacturing and service industries.

Instead of measuring an operation with a stopwatch, the industrial engineer makes a comprehensive sequential listing of all elements of the particular operation to be measured. The listing must be in much greater detail than the illustration in Figure 7.4. On completion of the detailed listing, the industrial engineer refers to published tables of predetermined time values per minute motion and determines the appropriate "normal" time. This is equivalent to item 7 in Figure 7.4.

The time factors are termed TMU (time-measurement units).

1 TMU = .00001 hours
   = .0006 minutes
   = .036 seconds

Conversely

1 hour = 100,000 TMU
1 minute = 1,666.67 TMU
1 second = 27.8 TMU

Depending on the type of work to be measured and/or the level of detail desired, the above can be expressed in thousandths of an hour instead of hundred thousandths.

Then 100 TMU = 1 TTU (thousandth time units) and:

1 TTU = .001 hours
   = .06 minutes

$$= 3.60 \text{ seconds}$$

Conversely

1 hour = 1,000 TTU
1 minute = 17 TTU
1 second = .3 TTU

Regardless of the method employed to measure the work effort, the result is the same:

- The time expressed in hours required to complete a given operation, and

- The standard expected hourly production rate expressed as units per hour.

Uses of Standard Production

The information obtained from work measurements, as illustrated in the preceding example of the wagon assembly operation, has five significant uses. It serves as a basis for:

1. Developing rates for similar operations;

2. Measuring operator performance;

3. Developing product cost;

4. Analyzing capacity and developing the master schedule; and

5. Developing incentive-pay systems.

Developing Rates for Similar Operations

One of the authors was employed as an industrial engineer with a company in Orange County, California, while attending California State, Fullerton. A newly signed labor contract gave the company authority to audit all existing production standards. This was a huge task — 31,000 separate operations required auditing, only five industrial engineers were available, and the time limitation was 18 months. The only possible way to accomplish the task was to use a statistical approach. Population

Project No.   1926-T
Operation   All Lathes
Element   Move Cross-Slide

a	b	c	d	e	f	g
Sample Point	(Inches Moved) X	(Normal Minutes) Y	$(X) +/- \overline{X}$	$(Y) +/- \overline{Y}$	$(d)^2$	$(d) \times (e)$
1	2.0	.0381	− .5	− .0351	.25	.0176
2	3.0	.0720	+ .5	− .0012	.25	.0006
3	4.0	.1078	+ 1.5	+ .0346	2.25	.0519
4	3.0	.0815	+ .5	+ .0083	.25	.0042
5	1.0	.0360	− 1.5	− .0372	2.25	.0558
6	2.0	.0605	− .5	− .0127	.25	.0064
7	1.0	.0382	− 1.5	− .0350	2.25	.0525
8	4.0	.1318	+ 1.5	+ .0586	2.25	.0879
9	3.0	.0985	+ .5	+ .0253	.25	.0127
10	1.0	.0468	− 1.5	− .0264	2.25	.0396
11	2.0	.0721	− .5	− .0011	.25	.0006
12	4.0	.0950	+ 1.5	+ .0218	2.25	.0327
Average	$\overline{X} = 2.5$	$\overline{Y} = .0732$		Totals	15.00	.3625

$B = \text{Variable Factor (Slope)} = \dfrac{g}{f}$

$A = Y \text{ Intercept When } X = 0$

$A = \overline{Y} - (B\,\overline{X})$

$B = \dfrac{.3625}{15} = .0242$

$A = .0732 - (.0242 \times 2.5)$

$A = .0127$

Fig. 7.5. Statistical method for development of standard data using least squares

parameters were estimated, based on sample points. Each sample point was the result of an individual time study. Figure 7.5 illustrates this concept.

This approach uses the least-squares method of estimation. Figure 7.5 shows the method used for estimating the time to perform a given element, knowing only the value of a predetermined independent variable. In the current example, the independent variable is the length to move the cross-slide on a common turret lathe, measured in inches, and the dependent variable is, as always, time.

The sample points in Figure 7.5 produce the regression formula:

$$Y = A + BX = .0127 + .242 (X)$$

In other words, the normal time to move the cross-slide on a turret lathe can be determined knowing only the distance the slide is to be moved, measured in inches. If, for example, an operation required a cross-slide cutting element where the slide moved 5.25 inches, the normal time required for the element would be estimated at .1398 minutes.

$$Y = .012 + .0242 (5.25)$$

Standard data development using regression analysis is very common. The regression line can actually be determined using a hand-held programmable calculator by simply inputting the corresponding X and Y sample points.

It is interesting to note that the bargaining unit at the company challenged the validity of establishing production standards that were set without an actual time study. The grievance progressed through all stages until arbitration was necessary. The arbitrator found overwhelmingly in favor of the company. The primary reason for his findings was that the statistically determined rates were both objective and consistent, and, therefore, in the best interests of the employees as well as the company.

Measuring Operator Performance

Throughout this text, the concept of productivity as a function of time has been and will be stressed. That concept is certainly relevant to this chapter. Production standards, as we have illustrated, are based on time. The labor input is paid by the hour and the expected output is measured by the hour, or some increment of time.

In Figure 7.4, the final item of data developed was the standard hourly production rate for the assembly operation. As a management tool, a supervisor can monitor the effectiveness of the labor input by comparing actual production against standard production.

Consider the standard production rate of 151.5 pieces per hour from Figure 7.4. If an operator performs at that rate during the entire eight-hour work shift, the expected production is 1,212 pieces. Conversely, from Figure 7.4 the standard allowable for each piece is .0066 hours. Therefore, the standard hours expected for the shift is also 8.0 hours (1,212 x .0066).

The productivity of labor relative to performance against standard rates is normally termed efficiency. Efficiency is, in turn, a ratio comparing outputs to inputs, or:

<u>labor output</u>
labor input

This is, in fact, the basic productivity equation that was introduced in Chapter 2. If an operator, for example, produced 970 pieces on a regular eight-hour shift, what would the labor efficiency be?

labor output = 970 x .0066 = <u>6.4</u> hours = 80%
labor input =   8.0 hours

Productivity, accordingly, is .8, and any measurement of productivity less than 1.0 indicates that inputs exceeded outputs. If, however, on the following day, the operator produces 1,394 pieces, the efficiency and productivity are substantially different.

$$\frac{\text{labor output}}{\text{labor input}} = \frac{1{,}394 \times .0066}{} = \frac{9.2}{8.0} = 115\%$$

Now the efficiency is positive as is the productivity index of 1.15.

What happens, for example, if an operator is running a machine against a production standard and the machine breaks down? Let's say that the assembly operation under discussion required a pneumatic tool to assemble the hub to the axle and the tool broke after 6.5 hours. During the 6.5 hours, the operator produced 1,083 parts. What is the efficiency and productivity? Remember that efficiency is a ratio comparing output to input while operating against standard production rates. Therefore, the efficiency is:

$$\frac{\text{labor output}}{\text{labor input}} = \frac{1{,}083 \times .0066}{} = \frac{7.15}{6.5} = 110\%$$

However, unless the operator clocked out and left the workplace, productivity would suffer. In the normal situation, the operator would be given an indirect labor task until the end of the shift. Therefore, the productivity is:

$$\frac{\text{labor output}}{\text{labor input}} = \frac{1{,}083 \times .0066}{} = \frac{7.15}{8.0} = 89\%$$

Even though the operator's efficiency was positive during the time spent performing against the standard, productivity was negative because the input included the total 8.0 hours paid, of which 1.5 hours were not productive.

Many firms also monitor the length of time a direct-labor employee spends on indirect functions; in other words, the utilization of direct-labor employees. In our present example, the utilization of the direct labor employee for the shift during which the tool broke was 81.25%. (6.5 ÷ 8.0). Direct-labor productivity can also be expressed as a function of efficiency and utilization.

81.25% utilization x 110% efficiency = .89 productivity. This is the same as the result that was obtained by dividing the total output by total input, as shown above.

Developing Standard Product Cost

Even though the direct-labor portion of a firm's total cost structure may be relatively small, direct labor remains the hub of the typical cost-accounting system.

Overhead allocation will be discussed in detail in Chapter 5. In simple terms, overhead costs (indirect costs), while collected at the department level, are transferred to product costs. This is done by allocating a given amount of overhead to each product relative to the direct-labor content of the product.

Earlier in this chapter, it was stated, for illustrative purposes, that the assembly department for our wagon manufacturer contained 125 direct-labor employees. Therefore, the number of potential direct-labor hours generated by the assembly department for a typical month would be 125 x 173.33 = 21,666. If the estimated monthly indirect, or overhead, costs for the assembly department were estimated at $500,000 monthly, the overhead rate would be approximately $23 per standard direct-labor hour. It is important to note that in the preceding example in which the tool broke and only 6.5 direct-labor hours were earned, only 6.5 x $23 was transferred to product cost, even though the actual indirect cost incurred was the same. Because the customer will only pay a price that reflects the standard value added, the excess (unallocated) indirect cost accrues to the detriment of the firm, and the total productivity of cash suffers. Remember, the productivity of cash/capital will suffer whenever the productivity of any other production factor suffers.

Many companies will consider adding new models or expanding their product lines, or, a customer will inquire as to the price of a nonstandard product. In both cases, the company will derive estimated labor standards (using such methods as the previously illustrated least-squares method) to which it will apply the established overhead rates to arrive at an estimated cost of the product. The selling price, based on the estimated cost data, can then be quoted.

Analyzing Capacity and Developing Master Schedule Input

Capacity for any given production activity is expressed as units per time period. Similarly, the productive capability of a direct-labor employee is expressed in time, while individual production standards are expressed in units per time period. Therefore, it must follow that the capacity of a facility is limited by the direct-labor resource. We find this to be true in any production activity that is paced by labor, such as an assembly-type operation or a machine operation in which the output of the machine is controlled by the effort of the employee. Capacity of a facility is not a function of labor in a highly automated process in which the output is not controlled by labor effort. In such cases the capacity, even though expressed in units per time period, is limited to the capability of the equipment.

In the example of the wagon manufacturer, the potential output of the facility, or its capacity, is a function of the labor input. Consider, for example, that it has been determined that our manufacturer's assembly department has been determined to be a bottleneck. A plant's capacity is limited to the bottleneck, or limiting department or function.

Very early in this chapter, we stated that there were three basic assembly operations and 20 different wagon models.

1. Assemble bearings, wheels, axles and hubs.

2. Assemble handle to chassis.

3. Assemble front and rear axle subassemblies to chassis.

If 125 assembly stations are in the Assembly Department setup as follows, what is the capacity of the Assembly Department?

	Assemble Bearings, Wheels, Axles and Hubs	Assemble Handle to Chassis	Assemble Axle Subassemblies to Chassis	Total
Number of work stations	5	75	45	125
Time available/month	866	13,000	7,800	21,666

The answer to the capacity question is still unknown. Table 7.9 expands the problem by listing the time requirements for each model wagon for each work center within the Assembly Department. The maximum capacity for each work center is shown below:

	Assemble Bearings, Wheels, Axles and Hubs	Assemble Handles to Chassis	Assemble Axle Subassemblies to Chassis
Wagon model requiring most time	I	L	J
Work center limit	57,733*	16,250**	17,768††

*   866 ÷ .0150 = 57,733
**13,000 ÷ .8000 = 16,250
† 7,800 ÷ .4390 = 17,768

The assembly capacity is determined to be 16,250 per month. However, capacity is greater with any other model wagon. (The capacity question is covered in much greater depth later in the text.) The point to be made at present is that the factors affecting capacity determination are the result of engineered production standards derived from work measurement techniques.

Table 7.9 Assembly-department capacity (standards expressed in hours per unit)

	Operation		
Wagon Model	*Assemble Bearings Wheels, Axles and Hubs*	*Assemble Handle to Chassis*	*Assemble Front and Rear Axle Sub-Assembly to Chassis*
A	.0066	.2000	.1500
B	.0071	.2500	.1600
C	.0089	.1800	.1560
D	.0046	.3000	.2560
E	.0062	.2600	.3000
F	.0070	.3500	.4100
G	.0069	.4000	.1690
H	.0090	.3600	.2910
I	.0150	.5600	.2700
J	.0094	.6500	.4390
K	.0086	.7100	.1750
L	.0125	.8000	.2910
M	.0140	.5600	.3010
N	.0090	.3100	.2500
0	.0095	.4600	.1750
P	.0110	.2500	.1950
Q	.0130	.4800	.3750
R	.0069	.3200	.4000
S	.0075	.2900	.3610
T	.0100	.3700	.2950

Production standards are also necessary to schedule the plant. Consider that in a given month, our wagon manufacturer receives the following orders:

Model	Quantity
A	4,000
C	2,500
F	6,000
H	6,500
P	7,500
S	3,000

The question is, how should the work centers in the assembly department be staffed? From Table 7.10, which illustrates work center loading, it can be seen that production standards are once again the key element in scheduling the plant. The present illustration shows an unbalanced condition, with work center loads ranging from 29.4% capacity to 101.1% capacity. The total assembly department will need only 96 employees to make the schedule.

Table 7.10 Work center loading

Wagon Model	Assemble Bearings, Wheels, Axles and Hubs		Assemble Handle to Chassis		Assemble Front and Rear Axle Sub Assembly to Chassis	
	Hours	*Emp.*	*Hours*	*Emp.*	*Hours*	*Emp.*
A	26.4	.15	800.0	4.62	600.0	3.46
C	22.3	.13	450.0	2.60	390.0	2.25
F	42.0	.24	2,100.0	12.12	2,460.0	14.19
H	58.5	.34	2,340.0	13.50	1,891.5	10.91
P	82.5	.48	1,875.0	10.82	1,462.5	8.44
S	22.5	.13	870.0	5.02	1,083.0	6.25
Total	254.2	1.47	8,435.0	48.68	7,887.0	45.50
Available capacity	866	5	13,000	75	7,800	45
Percent capacity	29.4%		64.9%		101.1%	

Developing Incentive-Pay Systems

The same principle of using production standards to monitor employee output is applicable to the use of incentives. When an employee who is paid on the basis of measured day work performs above standard, he has only the satisfaction of doing a good job. However, when production standards are incorporated into an incentive program, above-standard performance is rewarded with proportionately higher pay.

The standard hour plan is the most common form of individual incentive plan. It is common to refer to such a plan as a piecework plan because an employee can relate easier to units per time period than to time allowed per unit. By referring to circled items 11 and 12 on Figure 7.4, it is noted that either is a derivative of the other. In other words, the production rate can be expressed as either 151.5 pieces per hour or .0066 hours allowed for each piece. An interesting aspect of an individual incentive plan is that an employee can earn more than his regular hourly rate for superior performance, but not less than his hourly rate for substandard performance.

Using the same production standard illustrated in Figure 7.5, if an operator works the total eight-hour shift and achieves just the standard rate, the standard hours earned are 8, or:

151.5 pieces per hour x .0066 hours per piece x 8 hours per shift = 8.00.

If the employee in question earns a base wage of $15 per hour, total earnings and average hourly earnings can be calculated under varying circumstances.

Example 1

Employee works eight hours on standard and produces 970 pieces.

970 x .0066 = 6.40 standard earned hours < 8.00.

Therefore, employee is paid base rate x 8.00 or $120. No incentive pay is earned.

Example 2

Employee works eight hours on standard and produces 1,394 pieces.

1,394 x .0066 = 9.20 standard earned hours > 8.00. Therefore, employee is paid base rate x 9.20, or $138. The average hourly pay is $17.25.

Example 3

Employee works 6.50 hours on standard and produces 1,083 pieces.

Employee works 1.50 hours on indirect labor.

1,083 x .0066 7.15 standard earned hours

<u>1.50 indirect labor worked</u>

8.65 hours earned and/or worked

8.65 x $15 = $129.75.

Average hourly pay is $16.22.

In addition to individual incentive plans, there are group incentive or bonus plans. Both have obvious benefits for the employees. The benefit to the company is that even though unit labor costs are the same when an incentive plan is used, as when (the other type) is used, the total unit cost is less because production is increased while the same fixed-cost base is maintained.

Tying wages directly to productivity is another form of incentive. At its Indianapolis foundry, International Harvester and the UAW agreed to a plan under which employees' earnings are directly affected by the productivity of the total foundry operation. This implies that wages could be less if productivity slips. This is quite different from conventional incentive plans in which employees are never paid less than the base rate. International Harvester had indicated that the foundry would be closed down unless its operations could be made competitive.

The prospect of higher pay is doubtless an incentive for higher productivity. In 1914, Henry Ford said that raising the minimum daily wage from $2.34 per day to $5.00 per day was one of the most effective cost-cutting moves the company had ever made.

Labor Productivity — The Key Is the Human Aspect

The bulk of this chapter has focused on measuring the labor input, or to state it another way, the attempt to determine a reasonable expectation of labor effort. There is no question about the necessity for quantifiable production standards that are used for:

- Determining the cost of goods and services produced;

- Monitoring the efficiency/productivity of labor as a factor of production; and

- Determining the capacity of a production facility or activity.

Furthermore, the basic question regarding labor input is not whether labor productivity is important, but rather how best to attain it. It is the labor input that establishes the pace and pattern of productivity for all other inputs to the production process. The productivity of labor is not dictated by management, nor is it a function of the established production standards. Labor productivity is, rather, a matter of individual employee motivation. An employee may choose to be productive or he may choose not to be productive. An employee on a given day may far exceed the production standards, and on the following day may fall far short of the very same standards.

If an employee chooses to be productive, the productivity of all other inputs will follow accordingly. A productive employee will transform material into product and, by so doing, will make formerly idle inventory productive. During the production process, a productive employee will use equipment. The equipment will be productive as it is used to make the material productive.

Conversely, if an employee chooses not be productive for any length of time, so follows the negative productivity of the other inputs. The employee will be paid for no production, and idle material, like idle cash, will incur a lost opportunity for growth, while the depreciation cycle of the machines clicks on regardless of production or the lack thereof.

The uniqueness of the labor input, which enables it to be antagonistic and adversarial, can be rechanneled so as to be the greatest contributor to total factor productivity. Labor chooses to be nonproductive when its pursuit of the American dream is threatened or when it perceives that such a threat exists.

The labor input possesses another equally amazing attribute — ingenuity. As a rule, no one understands a particular job better than the person performing that job. If an employee's ingenuity is allowed to grow, or better yet, is nourished and fed, productivity gains are the natural result.

Consider a large midwestern manufacturer that recently installed a revised individual incentive plan. The plan was designed with the intent of improving labor productivity by placing a ceiling on employee earnings. In addition, any methods improvements resulting from employee ingenuity were incorporated into revised production standards. The result was that productive ideas that produced higher productivity actually penalized the employee. The employee was threatened with disciplinary action if the prescribed method was not followed. Additionally, if the employee improved the method, which would allow higher productivity, the incentive standard was changed so as to incorporate the employee's ingenuity. The employee's reward was that he would receive the same pay for improved productivity.

The company boasted that it annually saved millions of dollars in reduced labor costs. The truth is that employees were using their ingenuity to improve methods, but not openly. The result was that standards were exceeded while indirect time increased, which netted out to no productivity gains.

If employee ingenuity is properly channeled, production standards will not be a club or weapon, but rather a necessary tool used for accounting, scheduling and information purposes. Production standards should not be a threat to employees. If this condition exists, there will also be the adversarial relationship described in the following chapter.

The positive and unique attributes of the labor input, which are manifested in employee ingenuity, should be considered carefully before the worker is designed out of the "factory of the future."

Chapter 8
Motivation, Management, and Collective Bargaining

Objectives

- *Understand the definition of labor.*

- *Understand how labor productivity is measured at both the macro and micro levels.*

- *Realize that the growth rate of labor productivity in the United States is declining.*

- *Recognize that the United States is losing ground to other nations, especially Japan, in terms of labor productivity.*

- *Understand that labor productivity must be maximized or else severe problems such as unemployment may occur.*

- *Realize the harmful effects caused by labor costs increasing more rapidly than labor productivity.*

- *Understand collective bargaining and its indirect labor costs.*

- *Recognize that the trend for wage increases in labor contracts is downward.*

- *Be aware that an adversarial relationship between labor and man-agement exists* unnecessarily *in many companies.*

- *Understand that the quality of work life is important when improving productivity.*

- *Recognize that American management philosophies place emphasis on goals, such as short-term profits, which generate distrust and anxiety among employees.*

- *Acknowledge the trend toward high-tech industries and fully automated factories.*

- *Be aware that human considerations should not be overlooked during the rapid growth of industrial automation.*

Contents

Definition of Labor

In the present context of productivity, i.e., the relationship between inputs and outputs, we present the following definition of labor:

- Human activity that provides the goods and services in an economy, and/or

- Services performed by workers for wages, as distinguished from those rendered by entrepreneurs for profit.

The term "productivity" in itself connotes the output of an entity relative to the labor input. Such measures were adopted as benchmarks at the beginning of the industrial revolution and have survived through the decades. And even though production processes have changed drastically in recent years, firms still like to evaluate their output relative to the labor input. This practice can be better understood when we consider that as recently as 1982, wages still comprised two-thirds of total production costs for goods and services.

Labor Productivity Measurements

Several methods are available to measure labor productivity, both at the macro as well as the micro levels. Several common measurements on the macro level include:

- Gross domestic product (GDP) per hour worked;

- GDP per hour paid;

- Value added per production-worker hour;

- Output per hour of all persons employed in the private business sector;

- Output per person in the private business sector; and

- Output per direct labor hours.

Variations of the above are available, tailored to suit the particular need. Many labor productivity benchmarks are utilized at the micro level, including:

- Revenue per employee;

- Tons or units of output per hour worked or paid; and

- Value added per direct labor hour.

Once again, countless variations of these indicators exist to suit the needs of the particular industry, plant, or departments within a plant.

Care should be exercised when interpreting labor productivity data. For example, the U.S. Department of Labor reports labor productivity as a function of labor-hour paid. In this case, labor productivity can go up or down when time paid for but not worked fluctuates. In this case, there is no relation to actual labor effort or to the level of output. On the other side of the argument is the fact that ultimate labor productivity is measured by labor dollars input versus the value of outputs. Remember, the final measure of a firm's total productivity is the improvement in financial position, or an increase in net assets per time period. The point is that we need to be careful to comprehend the statistics that are being reviewed and what they tell us.

A final thought relevant here is that labor productivity measurements have their greatest value in their trends over time. Annual rates of change over several time periods are more revealing than just considering the labor input:output ratio for a single time period.

Labor Productivity Worldwide

The productivity of the American labor force is still the highest in the world, despite the fact that our growth rate is decreasing at an alarming pace.

Figure 8.1 shows that in 1960, Canada's GDP (output) per hour worked was 84% of the U.S. level. The same figure shows that Japan's output per hour was just 19% of the U.S. level.

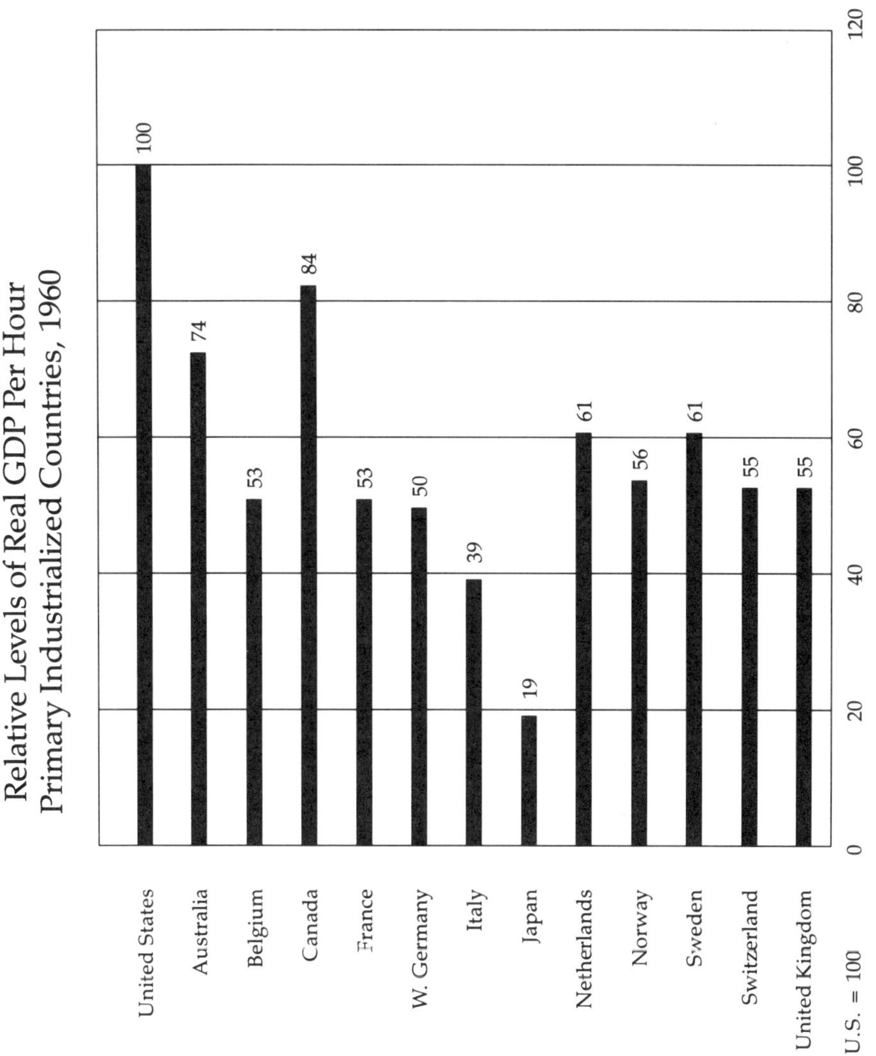

Fig. 8.1. Relative levels of real GDP per hour for primary industrialized countries, 1960

Figure 8.2 indicates that by 1973, Canada's output per hour was 88% of the U.S. level and Japan's output per hour climbed to 46% of the U.S. level. Therefore, even though the U.S. was still ahead in terms of absolute output per hour, both Canada and Japan were closing the gap. This could only mean that labor productivity in both Canada and Japan was improving at a faster rate than in the United States.

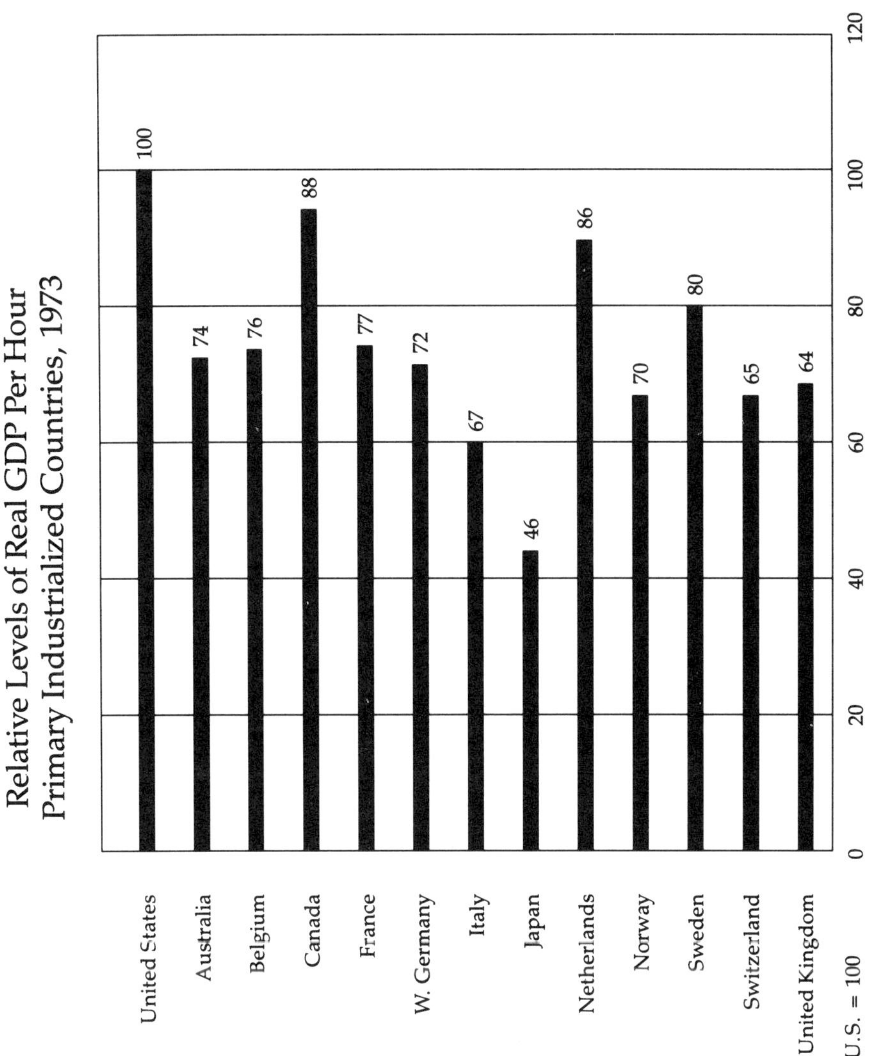

Fig. 8.2. Relative levels of real GDP per hour for primary industrialized countries, 1973

Figure 8.3 confirms this point. With the exception of Australia, the United States experienced the slowest rate of growth of labor productivity from 1960 to 1973. Figure 8.3 further reveals that Japan's improvement in labor productivity for this same period was nearly four times greater than that of the United States.

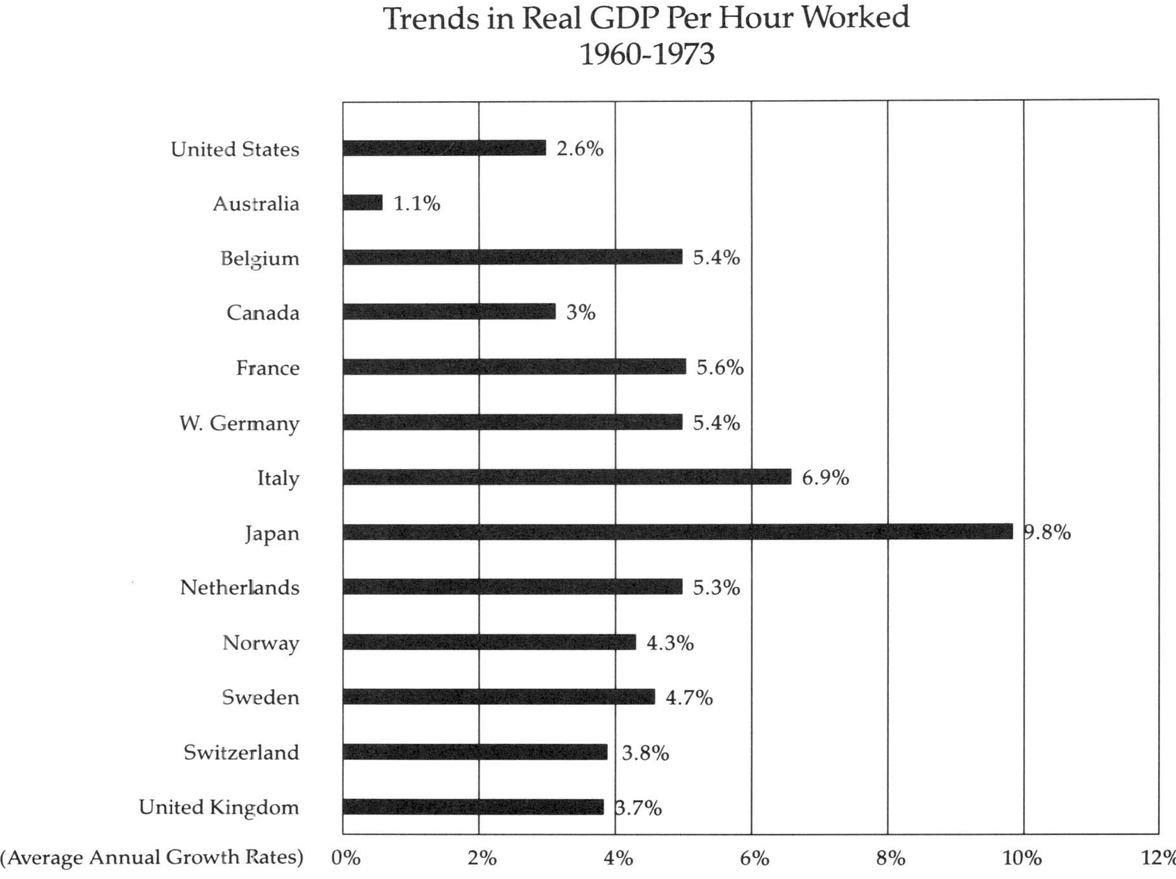

Fig. 8.3. Trends in real GDP per hour worked 1960-1973

As reflected in Figure 8.4, by 1979, all the other nations shown had closed the gap, with the lone exception of Canada. (In 1973, Canada's output was 88% of the U.S. output, but by 1979 its output per labor hour had slipped to 87% of that of the U.S.) In other words, except for Canada, all the other listed nations were growing, or improving labor productivity, at a faster pace than the United States. This fact is made abundantly clear in Figure 8.5, which shows labor productivity growth for the 1978-1981 period.

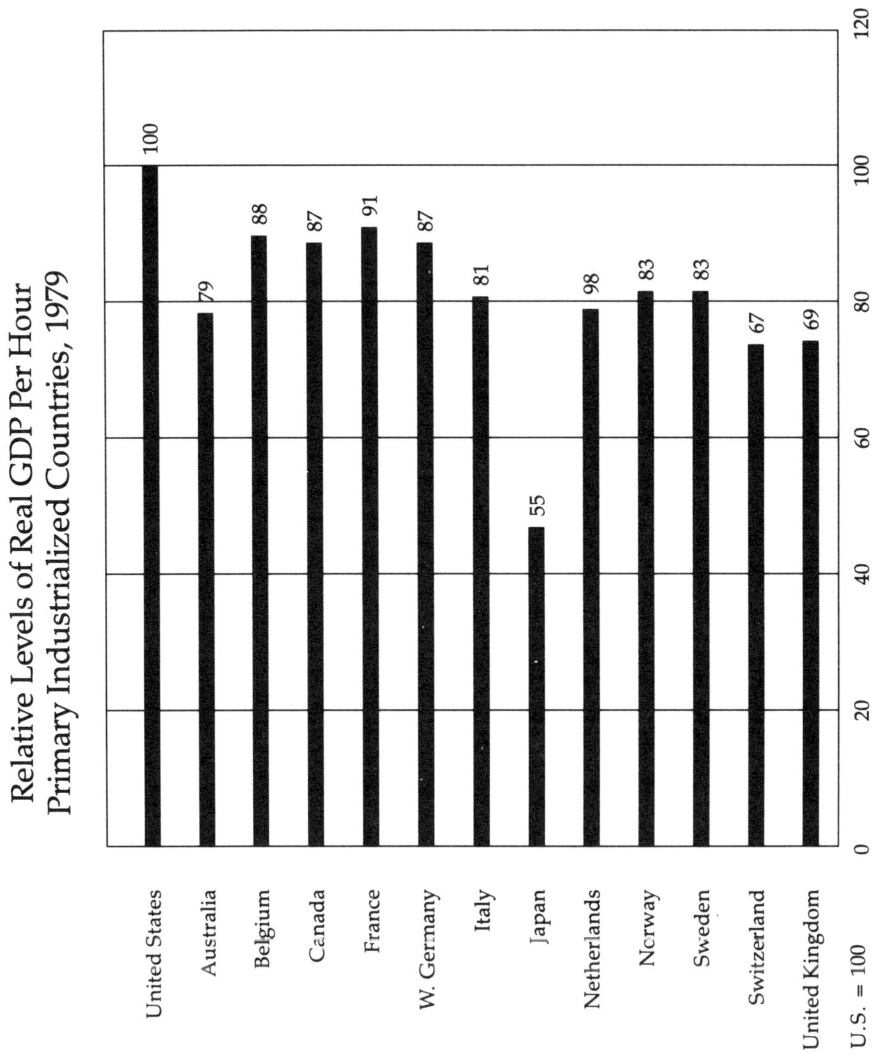

Fig. 8.4. Relative levels of real GDP per hour for primary industrialized countries, 1979

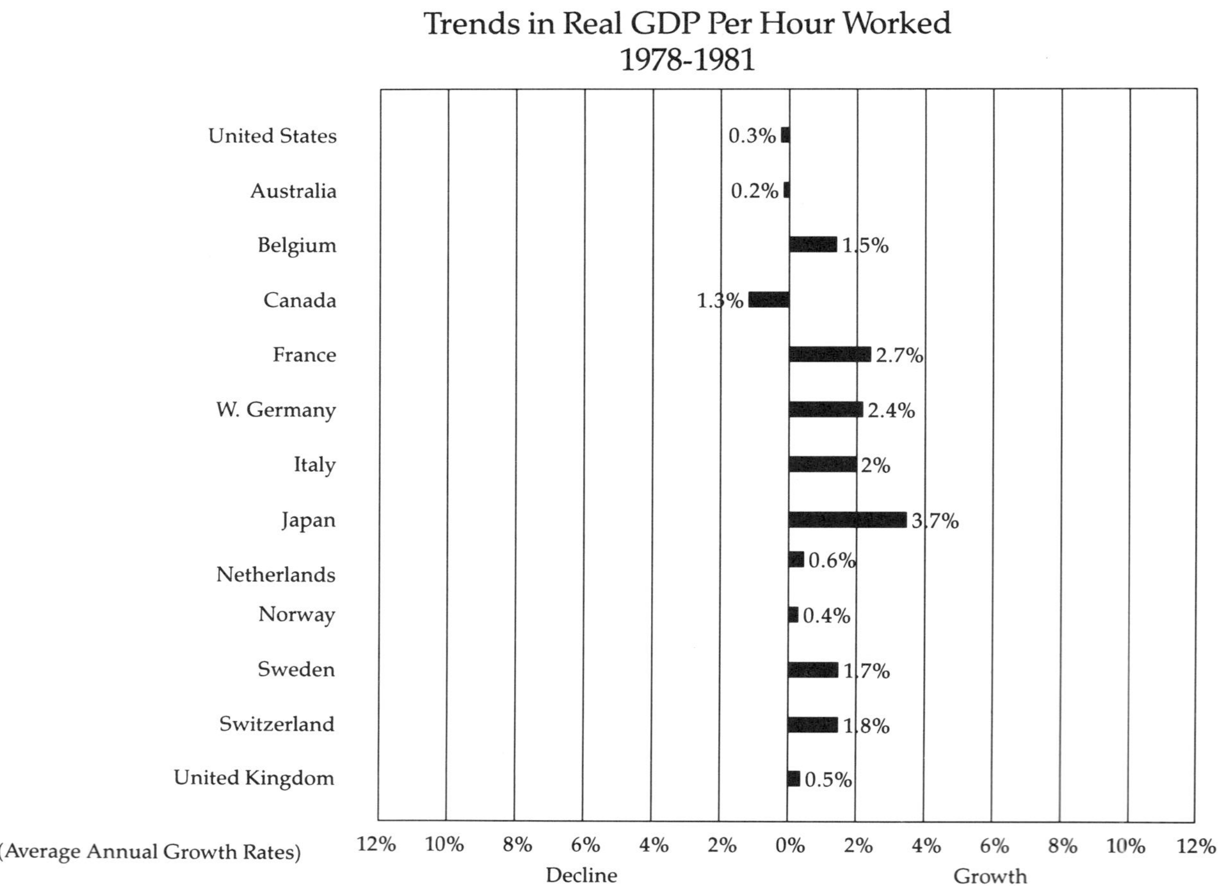

Fig. 8.5. Trends in real GDP per hour worked (1978-1981)

The data for these figures were taken from some of the excellent information published by the American Productivity Center (APC) in Houston. The selected time periods reviewed indicate without much doubt the tremendous impact of OPEC activities in 1973 and 1979. The figures indicate that the entire industrialized world reeled under OPEC's curtailments of oil. The worldwide recession of the early 1980s was due in no small part to this activity.

While most industrialized nations suffered pronounced slowdowns in their labor productivity during the period 1978-1981, Japan came through with the highest annual rate of growth — 3.7% per year. This fact is even more significant when one remembers that Japan is probably more susceptible to international problems than other countries because of its nearly exclusive dependence on oil imports.

Japan is Challenging the United States

The American Productivity Center (APC) in Houston has published several comparisons of Japanese and American labor productivity. Table 8.1 compares outputs per labor hour for 1970 and 1980. Even though this table indicates that the only area where Japanese output exceeded that of the U.S. was finance and insurance, the other categories reveal that the gap is narrowing rapidly. Despite the fact that the U.S. leads Japan in manufacturing as a total segment, three particular industries within that segment are well in Japan's favor. (See Figure 8.6.)

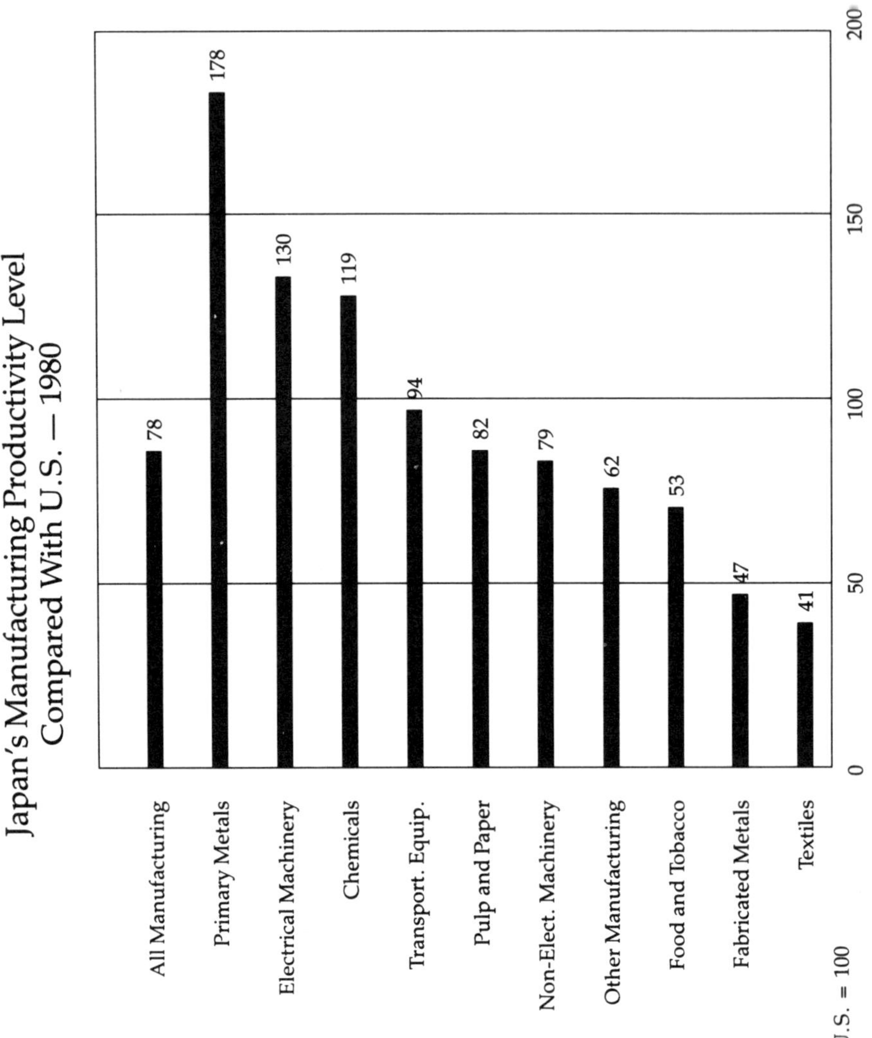

Fig. 8.6. Japan's manufacturing productivity level compared with U.S. — 1980

Table 8.1 Levels of output per hour — Japan still trails United States (1975 dollars)

	Level 1970 $/hour		Level of 1980 $/hour	
	U.S.	*Japan*	*U.S.*	*Japan*
Private Business	$ 8.27	$ 3.59	$ 9.27	$ 6.01
Goods producing sectors	8.37	3.14	9.68	5.99
Agriculture	6.17	1.37	7.21	2.38
Mining	27.57	5.07	19.25	11.67
Construction	9.45	3.85	7.43	4.13
Manufacturing	7.92	3.91	10.17	8.00
Services producing sectors	8.18	4.02	9.00	6.03
Transportation and communication	9.29	3.86	13.13	5.67
Public utilities	21.98	14.01	25.37	19.74
Trade	6.88	2.88	7.92	4.53
Finance and insurance	8.21	6.69	8.02	12.03
Business and professional services	6.79	3.39	6.70	3.60

From 1970 to 1980, the U.S. productivity growth in the total Goods Producing Sector was 15.6%, whereas the Japanese growth was a healthy 90.8%. The APC projected that U.S. labor productivity growth would reach 1.5% per year by 1985 and hold until 1990. The APC saw Japan reaching a 4.6% growth rate per year by 1984 and holding until 1990.

Present Standing of United States

It is interesting to note the switch in labor hours expended in the goods-producing vs. service-producing economic segments.

	1948	*1981*
Goods-producing industry	54.3%	40.3%
Service-producing industry	45.7%	59.7%
	100.0%	100.0%

Average annual productivity growth rates for these major segments are as follows:

	1948-1973	*1973-1978*	*1978-1981*
Goods-producing	3.6%	1.0%	.6%
Service-producing	2.3%	1.0%	-.1%
Total private business	2.9%	1.0%	.2%

A more detailed view of previous labor productivity is presented in Table 8.2. The pattern is obvious: Labor productivity, with the exception of farming, has slipped markedly since World War II. Even though a small improvement, .5%, is shown for total private business during the period 1979-1981, a negative labor productivity was recorded in 1970 and 1980. However, the slight rebound in 1981 netted a small positive growth for the three-year period.

Table 8.2 Labor productivity (output per hour worked)

	Average Annual Rate of Change (%)			
	1948-1965	1965-1973	1973-1979	1979-1981
Goods producing	4.0	2.7	.8	1.3
Service producing	2.3	2.1	.8	0.0
Farming	5.3	4.8	3.2	5.4
Manufacturing	3.0	2.8	1.5	1.5
Total private business	3.2	2.4	.8	.5

In 1989, American workers' productivity in the nonfarm portion of the nation's economy posted its worse performance since 1982 with a meager 0.9%. This was less than half of the 2.0% gain in 1988.

Meanwhile, hourly labor cost jumped by 5.4% in 1989, which was on top of a 4.7% rise in 1988. The 1989 labor cost increase was the biggest rise since the 1981-82 recession.

Uniqueness of the Labor Input

The opening sentences of this chapter included in the definition of labor the term "human activities." That by itself establishes the uniqueness of the labor input relative to any of the other inputs. Even though our original definitions included "the services performed by workers for wages as distinguished from those rendered by entrepreneurs for profit," each worker is an entrepreneur in his own right. Does not everyone classified as a worker share in the American dream to improve his standard of living? Is the desire to own a home, drive a nice car, or send the kids to college reserved for the wage payer? The answers to these questions are obvious, but the practice and the preaching may not be the same.

It is a firm's objective, in fact its responsibility, to maximize the productivity of each resource input to the production process. The labor input is no exception. The question, then, is not whether improved productivity is to be accomplished, but rather how best to go about it.

A firm's manager must recognize that each member of the labor input is very much like himself in relation to the American dream. Conversely, each member of the labor input must bear in mind that all will fall short of this dream if labor is not productive.

If any reader, on completing this chapter, feels that we are either pro-labor or pro-management, then we've failed to make our point. We are for productivity.

Consider the complexity of the situation. Business operates on the economic precept of supply and demand. In recessionary times, certain commodities may experience a lack of demand. If a commodity is elastic, prices may fall, and demand in number of units may be stimulated. Or perhaps the demand will continue to slacken. We've all seen commodity prices fluctuate. How about basic metals such as brass or aluminum? How about electricity as a production input? Rising prices have caused businesses to improve their productivity of energy so that it requires less input for given levels of production output.

Some inputs have increased in price very little or not at all (in constant dollars) in recent years, simply because of decreased or level demand.

When the demand for labor input decreases, can less of it be placed in the production process? Can less be paid for the labor input? The answers are yes, although the implications are far-reaching. To have an excess of a certain commodity causes its use to be greatly reduced, which results in no serious problem. But to have an excess amount of labor input, i.e., unemployment, causes severe problems. A firm that has to pay excess wages, or wages for idle labor, produces lower profits, which, in turn, produces a lower rate of growth. Lower growth for a particular firm causes lower growth for the entire economy.

When, on the other hand, a firm dismisses excess labor, the unemployed draw compensation from the state. If or when that ceases, they draw from their previously accumulated savings. Either way, total economic productivity is curtailed and stunted growth results. In addition, and equally important, the pursuit of the American dream is delayed.

Collective Bargaining

Collective bargaining, as its very name implies, allows individual workers to join together and negotiate, or bargain, collectively with a firm's management. If the overall aspect of collective bargaining is viewed objectively, it is recognized that a bargaining unit or labor union is, by definition, antiproductivity. Considering only the economic aspects of collective bargaining, a company's initial stand is to obtain as much production with as little cost as possible. That is square one relative to productivity. The labor force, which has joined together as a union, brings to the bargaining table an initial objective of obtaining more pay with minimum effort. Remember, workers and owners are both pursuing the American dream. The owners achieve the dream quicker by paying less for the labor input, while the workers achieve the same dream quicker by receiving more pay with the same or less production of goods and/or services. There it is in a nutshell: Owners and workers have the same goals, but for either to achieve its goals, it must be at the expense of the other.

Therefore, if the owner's original position is maximum output with minimum input, anything less than that will compromise productivity. But generally, the bargaining process will result in some relaxation of position on both sides of the table.

Many other items besides direct wages are the objects of collective bargaining, including vacation time, holidays, pension funding, insurance coverage, and COLA (cost of living adjust-ments). These items, although not in the form of direct wages, are, in essence, payments to/for the labor input with no accom-panying production of goods and services.

Vacation and holiday pay are paid to employees when they are at the place of work. Pension funding and insurance pre-miums are often paid by the owners on behalf of the employees. Such payments again add to the cost of the labor input with no production.

Then there are COLAs. This bargaining point was designed to automatically ensure that an employee would not suffer a decrease in his standard of living due to decreased purchasing power resulting from inflation. COLAs are tied predominately to the Consumer Price Index. (1967 = 100). As the consumer price index rises with inflation, an adjustment is made on the entire wage-rate structure. A typical adjustment might be that a .3 rise in the CPI produces a 1¢ per hour adjustment in the base wage rates.

One of the shortfalls of the COLA concept is that it reduces the relative spread between skilled-trades employees and non-skilled employees. If, for example, a welder's base rate is $12.50 per hour and a janitor's rate is $7.50 per hour, the welder earns 66.7% more than the janitor. If during the year the CPI increased ten points, then by using the aforementioned .3 = 1¢ formula, the ending rates are $12.83 and $7.83 respectively.

$$\frac{.3}{1¢} = \frac{10}{x} = 33¢$$

Now the welder earns only 63.8% more than the janitor. The difference in earnings, based on skill level, becomes diluted.

The biggest problem with COLAs is that they have the effect of once again increasing the cost of the labor input with no cor-responding increase in production.

The device originated with the intent of protecting employees from the effects of inflation. However, the result is that an increased cost of inputs with no corresponding increased production acts as a catalyst to inflation. The COLA concept became extremely popular as a point of collective bargaining in the 1970s when inflation reached double-digit proportions.

Collective Bargaining Issues

Other common points included in collective bargaining are seniority preservation and temporary work assignments. Both are subtle deterrents to productivity. Seniority privileges are noted most in filling job vacancies, both on the way up and on the way down. In other words, when a new job becomes available, the senior employee in the plant or department has "bidding" privileges. The job opening is not necessarily filled by the most qualified applicant, but rather the most senior applicant. And frequently, he is not the applicant who is most qualified. During a recession or curtailment of business for any reason, it may be necessary to decrease the work force by layoff. Then, the reverse of job "bidding" takes place. This is termed "bumping." Once again, jobs are filled by the most senior employees, while junior employees, even if highly qualified, are "bumped" out of their jobs into the unemployment line. This procedure requires a great deal of training, due to workers inexperienced in a given job being placed according to their seniority. An inexperienced worker cannot be expected to be as productive as his experienced junior counterpart.

The topic of temporary work assignments has also been a major bargaining issue in recent years. Especially prevalent in the ranks of skilled-trades employees, this practice hampers labor productivity by limiting what any classification of employee is allowed to do. For example, a bricklayer is not allowed to tighten bolts. The different classifications of skilled-trades employees within any given organization can be many. The net result is that perhaps three or four different employees may be required to repair a machine when one general-maintenance mechanic could do the job.

Even outside the ranks of the highly skilled, the issue of temporary work assignments can be a deterrent to productivity. For example, a molder cannot be assigned to do assembly labor. The end result is the same, i.e., more employees are required to perform the labor function that could be assigned to one employee.

The objectives of the labor force to bargain for such items centers on job security. It is labor's objective to employ as many people as possible. The problem of job security arises and productivity suffers when the firm is contractually obligated to employ excess labor. The problem becomes even more serious as firms become increasingly capital intensive and the overall requirement for the labor input decreases.

Rising Labor Costs

In recent decades, labor has bargained for and won increasingly higher base wages, plus COLAs, and a great deal of benefits that are basically payments made for no production. As long as the general economy could support the increases gained by labor by paying increasing prices for goods and services, the problem didn't really seem so serious. But suddenly, high-ticket-item markets became saturated, foreign competition appeared in full force, and OPEC activities plunged the entire industrialized world into a spiraling recession. And the walls of the house that labor built came tumbling down.

In short, the cost of the labor input has escalated at a rate exceeding the growth of productivity, for example, productivity decreased in 1978 and 1979 while the cost of labor increased at levels approaching 10% during the same two years. The collapse was inevitable and the consequences are far-reaching.

A January 31, 1983 *Wall Street Journal* article stated:

What may seem to be labor's curious preference for preserving high wages rather than more jobs isn't just a case of orneriness. It's a case of people no more eager than anyone else to take pay cuts, of holding onto what they consider hard-won gains, of retaining their traditional right to press for more pay. Even worse, generous labor settlements have, over the years, convinced them that their work is worth more than the market now is willing to pay for it.

This statement highlights a major problem: Collective bargaining tends to take the cost of the labor input out of the supply-demand arena. This creates a problem, because the output value of the goods and services will still be determined in the marketplace.

Work Rules and Productivity

Earlier, we briefly alluded to selected nonwage bargaining issues — specifically, temporary assignments. In a labor contract, such issues fall in the category of "work rules." This is a subtle area of job protection that limits a company's flexibility in assigning an employee where he will be the most productive. After years of being a stepchild issue, work rules have finally emerged to the forefront and are now a major issue. Companies have come to recognize this issue as a major cost item and productivity deterrent.

In the auto industry, about one-third of the cost disadvantage of $1,500 to $2,000 per car held by the U.S. producers compared with their Japanese rivals is attributed to high fringe benefit costs and work rules that restrict productivity. A February 14, 1983 *Business Week* article states:

> On productivity matters the UAW [at Chrysler] is prepared to play along. Restrictive work rules, such as job definitions that bar an assembler from changing a light bulb or require eight hours' pay for four hours' work, hinder management's flexibility and hurt productivity.

The following sub headline and text appeared in the *Wall Street Journal* on January 25, 1983. "Work Rule Changes Quietly Spread as Firms Try to Raise Productivity."

Until recently United Rubber Workers union members at a B. F. Goodrich Co. plant in Akron, Ohio, worked in two separate areas. Their contract specified that, under most conditions, workers in one area couldn't be required to do the same work in another area, regardless of how busy the plant was.

The rule was eliminated.

The change is part of a quiet revolution in the nation's ailing industrial sector as labor and management agree to eliminate many long-standing and costly work rules in an effort to raise productivity and profits.

Previously workers at the plant (Kaiser Aluminum Company in Ravenswood, West Virginia) were divided into 18 craft groups, such as electricians, carpenters, and certain maintenance workers. Workers in one craft couldn't do jobs in other crafts. If there wasn't specific work on a given day for, say, electricians, they remained idle but were paid. Now the 18 crafts have been reduced to 12 broader units, expanding the types of jobs each worker may do.

'With the stroke of a pen, we've corrected structural problems in our labor agreements that have built up over the years,' a Pan Am executive says about work rule changes.

Bargaining to Reduce Labor Costs

Needless to say, something had to give if the industrial sector was to recover from the pronounced slump of the early 1980s. The slump was largely aggravated by the fact that the cost of the labor input had gotten out of control relative to its value added.

The strides made in work rules were illustrated in preceding paragraphs. At this point, let's consider some of the major provisions to the master contract that was signed by the steelworkers on March 1, 1983. This contract is typical of the time period.

1. Wages — Effective March 1, 1983, wages are cut $1.25 per hour.

2. Cost of living allowance (COLA) — From February 1, 1983, through July 31, 1984, COLA payments will be deleted.

3. Vacation and holiday — One vacation week is dropped in 1983. One holiday is dropped and the 14-week extended vacation is eliminated. The vacation bonus is eliminated.

4. Work rules — There is contract language dealing with less-restrictive trade and craft job classifications.
   A worker could go from electrical to mechanical work under certain conditions.

All of these provisions will automatically reduce the cost of the labor input and/or improve labor productivity.

In total, wage concessions won from major unions in 1982 produced a marked slowdown in overall first-year pay increases in major collective-bargaining agreements reached during the year.

The Labor Department announced that pay boosts called for in 1982 settlements averaged 3.8% the first year and 3.6% per year over the life of the contract. These are the lowest average wage increases ever recorded by the Labor Department. The 1982 settlements replaced contracts that provided for an average first-year pay boost of 7.9% and a boost of 6.3% over the life of the contract.

Management-Labor Relations

Even though large strides are being made in an effort to control the cost of the labor input, the basic problem still remains, i.e., the adversarial relationship between the labor input (bargaining unit) and the management of the U.S. companies. As long as labor is considered to be no more than a factor of production, the problem will persist. The problem is exemplified every time a union and management enter into a bargaining session. The union negotiators are literally on one side of the table and the company's negotiating team is on the other side. Instead of "we," being all-inclusive of the total human factor for a given plant, it's a case of "us" versus "them." There is a common feeling of mistrust between labor and management.

It is not difficult to see why such feelings exist. Consider the steelworkers, for example. While the steel industry cried that it was in such dire straits owing to high labor costs and foreign competition, U.S. Steel Co. dropped its plan to build a multibillion-dollar mill in Ohio only to spend billions to acquire Marathon Oil Co.

The perceptions that labor and management have of each other are in need of renovations. In its booklet entitled "Mission, Activities and Services of the American Productivity Center," the APC states:

> Among the best opportunities for economic recovery in this country is changing the adversarial relationship between labor and management. The APC helps provide alternatives to this adversarial environment. From its inception, the center has maintained that productivity improvement and quality of work life are two sides of the same coin. It should not be surprising, then, to learn that the total mission of APC can be stated in a single phrase, "To improve productivity and quality of work life in the United States."

Productivity and Quality of Work Life

Several volumes could be written on the topic of quality of work life. For congruity, let's consider how the APC views the subject:

> Quality of work life is really inseparable from the productivity issue. There are a number of definitions of quality of work life. It's very easy to get lost in a lot of behavioral mumbo-jumbo or "warm and fuzzy" kinds of definitions. One simple way of looking at it is recog-

nizing that most employees like to be a meaningful part of a worthwhile organization. They like to contribute. They want to be recognized for their contributions. And most importantly, they want to have a chance to impact those decisions that are directly affecting their jobs. Quality of work life, in essence, is creating a culture, an environment to tap that great resource of the people within the organization. If you look at improving productivity without addressing the human side of the issue, you are missing a big opportunity.

An adversarial relationship cannot exist in an environment in which the quality-of-work-life concept is adopted. In general, the level of output would automatically increase if all levels of employees were participants in the goals, objectives, and performance of the total organization. However, it is definitely a two-way street. Management must recognize the human worth of the labor input, while labor must actively promote the success of the firm by producing high-quality output in an efficient manner.

Quality-of-work-life activities are springing up all over the United States. It is estimated that one quarter of the total labor force is now engaged in some type of quality-of-work-life program. Companies in virtually every industry are introducing programs aimed at tapping the experience, resources and advice of their rank-and-file employees. Firms are striving to offer workers more job satisfaction, believing that happier employees mean higher productivity.

Management Priorities

The quality circle is another greatly misunderstood popular buzzword. A quality circle is the natural end result of many years of exercising and perfecting a management philosophy. A quality circle is basically a system in which its members meet regularly to contribute their ideas on production problems.

A quality circle cannot be successfully established unless it is the result of a deeply committed participatory management philosophy. Experts agree that the productivity gains enjoyed by the Japanese in recent years were attributable primarily to their management philosophy, with perhaps as little as 10% attributable to the quality circle itself.

One of the most significant aspects of the Japanese management philosophy is its dedication to long-range goals. It views employees as vital assets rather than disposable/replaceable adversaries. The Japanese go to great lengths to avoid laying off employees. It is not unusual for production employees to become janitors, repairmen, gardeners, or even salesmen. Some Japanese employers put idle employees into training programs. Sometimes, employees are transferred among divisions of their companies or even to other companies. Sometimes, they are transferred to wholly unrelated companies. These are the lengths to which the Japanese will go to preserve their "lifetime" employment systems.

The rewards include low labor turnover, low absenteeism, and increasingly higher skill and loyalty in the employees. The quality of products or services will improve, and productivity of the organization will increase steadily.

A good example is the machine tool industry. "The strong competition in the U.S. from the Japanese machine tool industry is primarily the result of the willingness of management to invest heavily in its future, market its products aggressively throughout the world, work doggedly toward long-term goals and pay an unusual amount of attention to the training and motivation of its work force."

The American way, on the other hand, stresses short-term profit, either monthly or quarterly. Such practice requires that hundreds and even thousands of employees be laid off and recalled on short notice. This practice also causes stress and insecurity among the employees. Again, it is not difficult to see why the employer/employee adversarial relationship persists.

Automation Proliferation

The manager/union adversarial relationship has generated distrust — distrust has begotten even more distrust. Distrust also breeds stress. Employees at any level cannot function optimally under stress. Thus, the productivity of labor suffers.

In an effort to combat lagging labor productivity, firms strive towards automation and robotry. Automation, in turn, causes more anxiety among the labor force in terms of job security. As a result, while financial and work-rule concessions are being given by unions, new bargaining strategies focus on job security, i.e., the preservation of jobs or retraining for new jobs. Unions are requesting that money saved by the companies be plowed back into the plants. The irony of the situation is that many of the smokestack factories are so outdated that even a substantial infusion of funds would not ensure their survival.

Unions are also bargaining for companies not to shut down facilities. In fact, lobbying groups are promoting legislation that limits plant shutdown activities. The unions' thrust is to keep as many persons employed as possible. When a company is burdened with more labor input than necessary for its level of operation, then labor productivity continues to decline. Profits also decline, so business firms continue to replace labor with machines.

A public opinion poll conducted by Opinion Research Corp. verifies that the public view of automation and robotry is marked by fear and resistance. (See Table 8.3.)

Table 8.3 Acceptance of automation

	Would Resist a Great Deal	Feel That Employment Will Decrease
Women	53%	66%
Men	32	40
Age 60+	56	61
Less than high school education	62	61
Family income under $10,000	56	59
Family income $10,000-$15,000	46	70
Union households	50	60
Total public	44	54

High-Tech Industries

Some would say that such fears are unfounded because automation and high-tech industries will maintain employment levels. They maintain that the only change will be in the composition of the labor force. They term high-tech opportunities a panacea; however, hopes for new jobs are overly optimistic.

Consider that the Bureau of Labor Statistics has identified 92 industries that constitute high-tech industries. (An industry is determined by a separate SIC code, of which there are 977.) Here's the breakdown:

- 36   R&D expenditures and technical employees run twice as high as all U.S. manufacturing.
- 56   R&D and technical employment are above average of all U.S. manufacturing.

Included are makers of drugs, computers, electronic components, and aircraft and laboratory equipment. Also included are most of the chemical industry, petroleum refining and service industries such as computer programming, data processing and research laboratories.

And even though the growth rates of these high-tech industries are expected to exceed those of all other industries, the total number of jobs to be created in the next 10 years is modest. The absolute number of new jobs is expected to range between

750,000 and 1 million. That number is only about half of the 2 million manufacturing jobs that were lost in the three-year period that ended in 1982. The reasons for this are simple:

1. The high tech sector has a small beginning base (See Figure 8.7), and

2. The productivity of the high tech sector is growing faster (See Figure 8.8).

It was quite a shock in early 1983 when Atari, Inc., moved 1,700 jobs overseas. This company that typifies high tech transferred jobs out of the U.S. for labor-cost reasons. Hewlett-Packard Co. predicts that its overseas work force will grow faster than in the United States. It is presently building major plants in Mexico and the United Kingdom. Companies such as Hewlett-Packard are also using the very products they make to replace labor in their plants.

Products of other high-tech industries are changing the work-force composite in other industries. Robots — perhaps one of the most dramatic examples — are replacing labor in such distressed industries as steel and autos. The trend is definitely toward unmanned factories.

The W.E. Upjohn Institute for Employment Research states that robots in the auto industry will have grown to between 15,000 and 25,000 by the end of the decade of the 80s. While these robots are expected to create 3,000 to 5,000 jobs, they will be replacing up to 50,000 auto workers.

In all fairness, it needs to be brought out that the Japanese labor force is also resisting the rapid rise of industrial robots in its country. Robots were first introduced in Japan to relieve human workers of monotonous, dangerous, and/or unsanitary tasks. Initially, the displaced workers were given jobs in other expanding businesses. But the march for sophistication in robotry is relentless, and fears by Japanese workers and unions are growing that Japan's slowing economy may not be able to

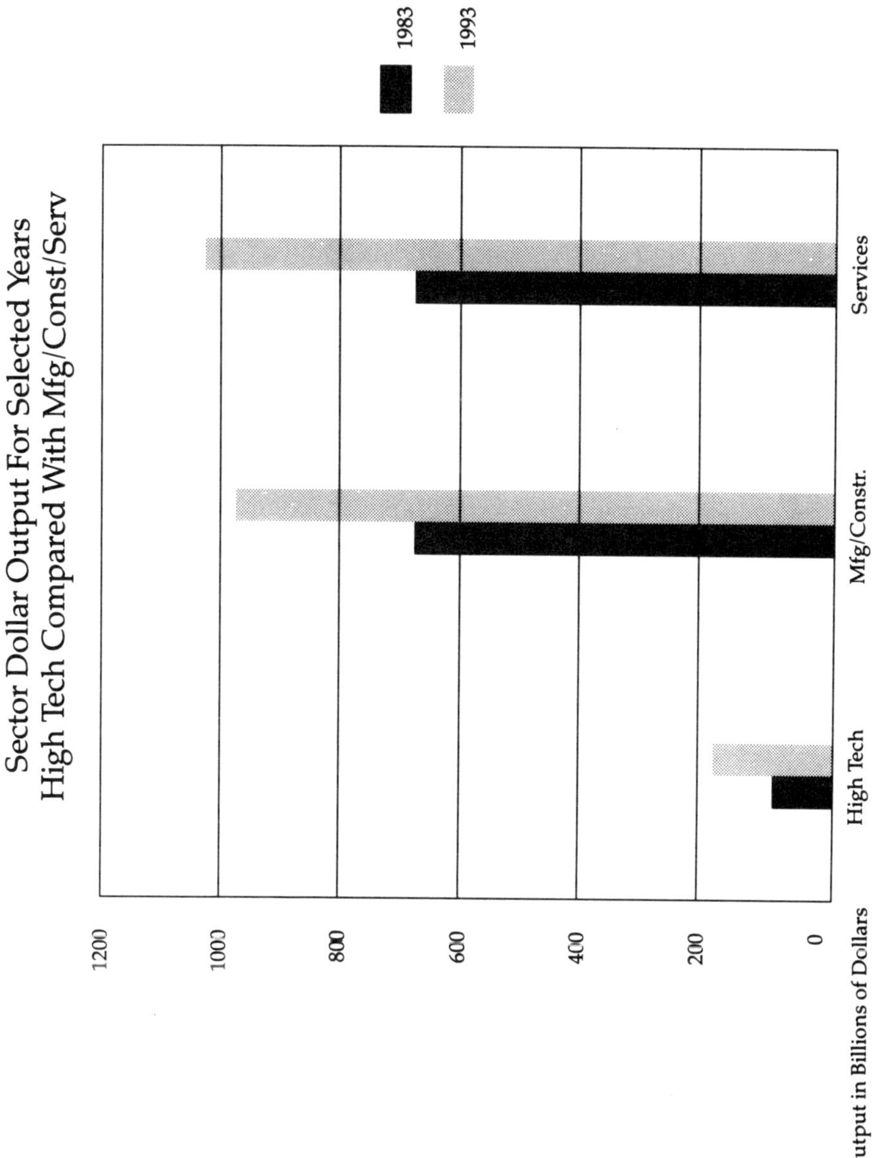

Fig. 8.7. Sector dollar output for selected years — high tech compared with mfg/const/serv

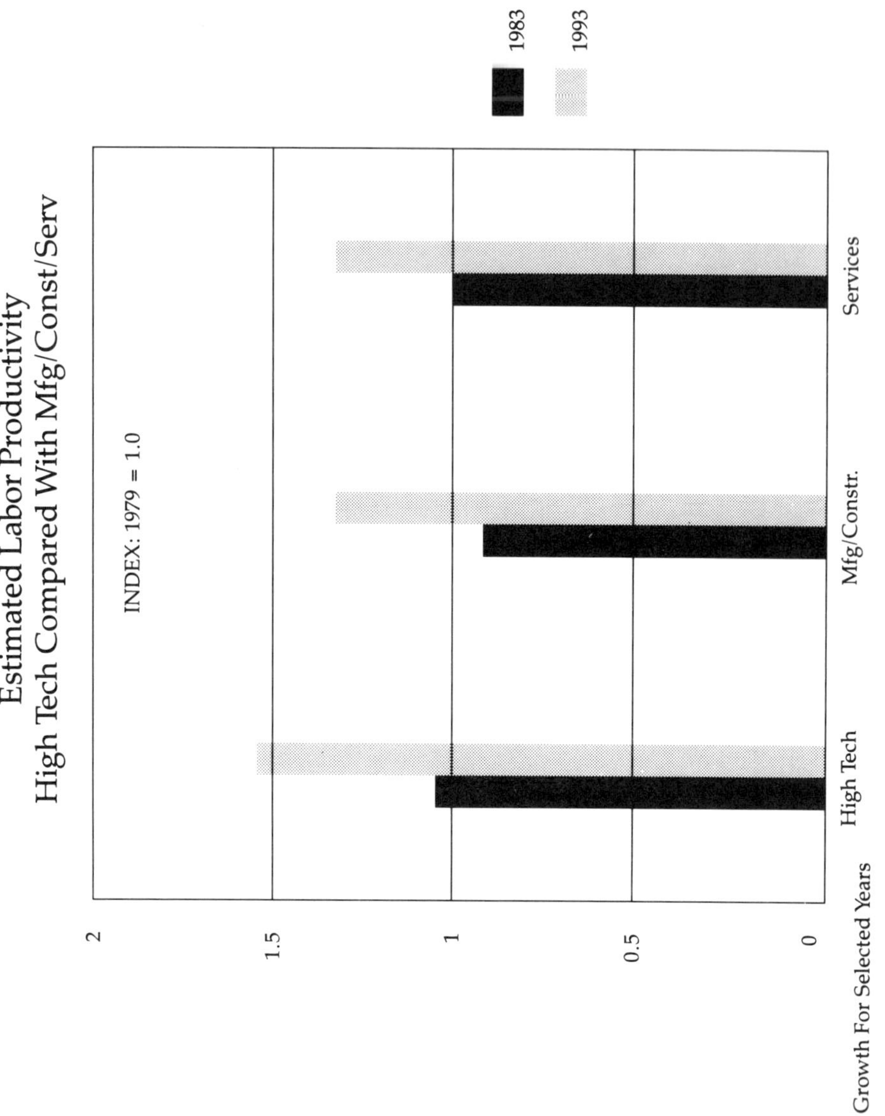

Fig. 8.8 Estimated labor productivity — high tech compared with mfg/const/serv

absorb them all. As a result, union revenues are decreasing and two actions are being taken by Japanese unions:

1. Attempt to slow the rush to robots, and

2. Attempt to change laws that would require industrial robots to carry union cards.

The Paradox Continues

Typical of a devastated smokestack town is Erie, Pennsylvania. In an effort to regain competitive status in basic industry, it is turning to automation. In the city's largest factory, a 73-year-old General Electric Co. locomotive plant, 68 skilled machinists previously spent 16 days producing a single diesel or electric motor frame. However, after extensive retooling, computer-controlled robots now complete one frame each day.

Along the same lines, automation in Detroit, for the most part, has been an effort to "design out the worker."

Despite high hopes that technology will turn Chicago, Detroit, Cleveland or Pittsburgh into enclaves of highly-paid computer scientists and engineers, no one knows yet what will happen to the blue-collar and white-collar workers who are displaced by the new machines.

Some robotics experts believe that by the year 2000, factory robots will be doing what 7 million human beings do now.

The editors of *Business Week* stated it succinctly:

The illusion that high technology alone can put the country back to work, outdistance foreign competition and restore economic vitality could generate misguided, even damaging, industrial policies. Exaggerated faith in high technology, for example, has been used to support the idea that the U.S. should adopt a policy of deliberately nurturing so-called sunrise industries while allowing sunset companies to wither away. If the haze of unreal expectations that has gathered around high-tech industry demonstrates anything, it is that nobody, especially government bureaucrats, possesses the wisdom and foresight to decide which enterprise should live and which should die. The country's industrial future must hold a place for revitalized basic industries as well. The U.S. cannot abandon steel, automobile, machinery and other basic industries to other countries and remain a viable world power.

Human Considerations

These same feelings are echoed by business leaders. Mature industries (another way of categorizing sunset industries such as steel, autos, and appliances) must continue to make major investments in productivity improvements to remain competitive. But, at the same time, business must be sensitive to the human cost of modernizing, and must demonstrate compassion for the people and communities affected by the drive to be competitive.

When factories are modernized in order to improve productivity, fewer of them will be needed. It is at that point that the human considerations have to be taken into account.

Dr. James O'Toole, professor of management at the University of Southern California, believes that "If we don't come up with some very creative ways of retraining the million or so people that are out of work today, we face the most serious challenge to our nation since the great depression." "Workers," he continues, "both union and nonunion, who for years have been well paid, even overpaid, and have enjoyed the fruits of the American system, will find technological unemployment intolerable. These people may turn and undercut that very system and create enormous social problems." As previously mentioned, Japan is already experiencing such problems, although of a lesser magnitude than those facing the U.S.

The preceding chapter focused on measuring the input/ output of the labor resource. It would have been a tremendous disservice to every reader if the vast complications surrounding the productivity of labor were not addressed. The social implications of the push for productivity are awesome.

Summary

- The push for labor productivity will most likely increase unemployment.

- So-called high-tech industries will not be the panacea that some would believe. New employment in these industries will absorb only a fraction of those unemployed by other industries.

- Basic hard-goods industries must not be allowed to die. They must modernize and absorb the labor force that is unemployed by automation in other industries.

- Labor unions perpetuate adversarial relationships between the labor input and management and are, therefore, counter-productive in the push for productivity improvements.

- Participative management is, in general, the better method to promote labor productivity improvements.

- U.S. firms must concentrate more on long-term performance rather than on short-run profit objectives. Accordingly, the labor input should be viewed as a long-term asset instead of something that is dispensable in order to achieve short-run profit goals.

- There is nothing magical about Japan's success in productivity gains, it lies in the fact that Japanese companies employ basic and sound management techniques developed by American business professionals and educators, which have, for the most part, been rejected by American industry.

Chapter 9
Materials: Composites, Substitutes, and Yield

Objectives

- *Understand that materials listed on the atomic weight charts have not been added to or deleted from for a millennia. Any new materials are just traditional materials used in varying proportions. They are often referred to as composites. And the mix may be determined by a computer utilizing a linear program.*

- *Understand that one of the greatest deterrents to material productivity is a production facility that produces items for which it was not designed.*

- *Understand that material productivity begins the design stage of any product.*

- *Understand that the total weight of physical production inputs can be accounted for either in finished product, defective products or byproducts. Regardless of the form, outbound transport and/or disposal must be provided for the total weight input to the production process.*

Contents

Major Aspects of Materials

The "materials" aspect of production/operations management is very comprehensive. Typically in POM texts, the subject is covered under the heading of "Materials Management." The heading is misleading, given that as the discussion is normally limited to the general topic of "Production/Inventory Control." However, there is much more involved in the subject of materials.

This text addresses four major aspects of materials.

1. Physical and tangible commodities:
    * research relative to new materials
    * research relative to new and innovative processes
    * material substitution

2. Efficient use:
    * yield
    * near net shape
    * defective products

3. Transport and handling:
    * inbound transport
    * in-plant handling
    * outbound transport

4. Conventional materials management:
    * demand management forecasting
    * inventory management
    * MRP and reorder point
    * capacity planning
    * the master schedule

The conventional aspect of materials management is the most popular, and rightly so. Managers are discovering that working-capital productivity can be greatly enhanced with effective production/inventory control systems. Chapter 1 of this text stated that business schools presently feel that materials management is the most relevant aspect of production/operations management. In addition, several other chapters discuss various aspects of materials management under different major concepts. For example, Chapter 5 on working-capital productivity illustrated the importance of liquidating inventories back to cash.

In this chapter, aspects of materials management other than production/inventory systems will be discussed.

Materials as Physical Commodities — Research Relative to New Materials

King Solomon wrote several thousand years ago that "there is nothing new under the sun." Applying this truism to the subject of materials, it can be said that the standard atomic-weight chart, or listing of elements, has remained unchanged for millennia. What have changed, and changed markedly, are the materials developed using different composites of existing elements. Materials developed in this manner number literally in the thousands.

Even in the last several years, we have witnessed astounding changes in materials available for home and industry. Perhaps the most vivid example is the automobile.

A new car today contains, by volume, about 40% polymeric materials or plastics. Plastic materials are popular for automobile use because they are corrosion resistant and lightweight. Designs that might not lend themselves to sheet-metal stamping can be molded from plastics. In addition, improvements in the strength and physical properties of plastic will eventually make it feasible to replace structural steel parts, and even engine components, with plastic parts.

A new fiberglass spring used on General Motor's 1984 Chevrolet Corvette was fabricated in one piece; when the spring was made from steel it required 10 pieces weighing a total of 41 lbs. The plastic counterpart weighs just 8 lbs — a weight savings of 80%.

In 1983, Honda introduced a new sports car, the Ballade

Sports CR-X, with a body that consists of 40% polymer alloys. A lighter-weight body means a reduction in engine size, which means that other components can be lighter, which further reduces the overall car weight, which improves the car's aerodynamic efficiency.

Of growing interest is the possible use of ceramic parts in gas-turbine, diesel, and gasoline engines. With ceramic parts, engines would run hotter and cooling systems could be eliminated, making the engine lighter and more energy efficient. In addition, emissions and noise would be reduced.

The Japanese are strong believers in the potential of ceramics for several reasons, among them:

- Concern about dependence on foreign supplies for most materials, while ceramic materials can be produced at home, and

- Concern about dependence on imported oil and ceramic parts for engines.

Consequently, the Japanese are strides ahead of the United States in ceramic technology. Ceramics are being defined as the "third material," following metals and plastics.

Similarly, Boeing Co. has design plans for a completely new airliner, roughly one-fourth of the weight of which is composed of graphite composite parts. Boeing Military Airplane Co. is also working on several projects that involve advanced uses of alloys and graphite composites.

Alcoa expected to have limited amounts of its new aluminum-lithium alloys available for use in the aircraft industry. The driving force behind the development of "alithalite" alloys has been the increased importance of reduced weight in aircraft. These new alloys reduce airframe weight by 10%-15%.

Reduced weight in a vehicle, automobile, ship or aircraft means less fuel required to propel that vehicle. Therefore, the productivity of energy is improved while simultaneously improving the productivity of materials. The end result is improved productivity of capital providing growth to the firm.

We need not look at the hard-goods industries to find changes in basic materials. Even the traditional ham may be turkey, or ground beef may contain nonmeat filler. Traditional wooden toothpicks can be plastic, and nearly gone are the days of TV and radio tubes.

The Need to Develop New Materials

So timely and important is the issue of material productivity that experts such as Dr. Merton Flemings, head of the Department of Materials Science and Engineering at Massachusetts Institute of Technology, testified recently before the House Committee on Science and Technology that the United States needs a comprehensive materials research-and-development policy. Dr. Flemings stated that limitations of materials and materials processing represent today's engineering limitations for a wide range of engineering structures, devices, and machines in terms of performance, cost, and reliability.

Once again, Japan is addressing such issues. For example, Japan's Ministry of International Trade and Industry has placed materials at the forefront of its development efforts in the coming years. The ministry has designated the following key areas in its next-generation industry program:

- High-performance crystalline-controlled alloys — single crystal alloys, superplastic forming, strip casting of steel;

- Composite materials — high-performance metal and polymeric matrix composites;

- High-crystalline polymers — development of new polymers comparable to metals;

- Fine ceramics — development of ceramics with improved toughness, strength, anticorrosion and antiabrasion properties;

- Electro-conductive polymers — to achieve new electrical or electronic properties; and

- Three-dimensional circuit elements — multilayer, very large-scale integrated circuits.

Japan's Honda Motor Co. increased its research-and-development budget to 5% of its projected sales as it sought to reduce engine weight and develop new materials.

The British government is also aware of the need for materials development. It has formed an advisory group to identify the areas of greatest opportunity in the United Kingdom for the development and exploitation of new materials. The advisory group will recommend how government funds might be channeled to encourage the practical application of new materials.

In all areas, the objective of developing new composite materials is to improve the productivity of capital allotted to the material resource.

Research Into New and Innovative Processes

New processes are being developed continually to enhance the productivity of existing materials. The word "process" has several meanings, one of which is "a particular method of doing something." For example, there are several ways to process an egg to make it edible. It can be boiled, fried, poached, or scrambled. Then there are several cooking processes available for each of these types of eggs. For instance, an egg can be scrambled in an electric skillet, a cast-iron skillet over an open flame, or in a microwave oven. The varied processes or combinations of processes available to prepare an egg are selected according to the taste of the person who eats the egg. Varied processes in industry, however, are selected on the basis of maximizing productivity of the production factors. In the present context we'll focus on material productivity.

Similar to the egg example, one of industry's basic processes is to form metal into desired shapes or objects. This can be done by extruding, forging, bending, or casting in a mold. There are, moreover, several processes available to melt metallics so they can be cast in a mold. Steel can be melted in furnaces with heat generated electrically, with gas, or with coke. The process chosen will be based on economic factors, i.e., the process providing the greatest productivity.

The objective of this section is to discuss several new and innovative industrial processes that improve material productivity. The processes listed below comprise a sampling of the work being done in material productivity. These have three basic factors in common:

1. The materials being processed are well-established, traditional materials;

2. The processes are state-of-the-art at the time of this writing; and

3. The benefits associated with new processes for traditional materials center on increased productivity of materials or perhaps other factors of production.

"Laser Use on Upswing for Metalworking" was the title of a recent article in a national newspaper. Following closely in a popular trend magazine was the subheadline, "Once just a curiosity, lasers are entering metalworking's mainstream."

What is a laser; what does it do; and why has Illinois Institute of Teaching Research Institute in Chicago established an Industrial Laser Center? A laser can be significantly less exotic than those laser cannons proposed by President Reagan to arm killer satellites for national-defense purposes. Perhaps one of the deterrents to widespread industrial laser acceptance is the "Star Wars" controversy.

However, the barriers to laser usage as production aids are falling quickly. For metalworking purposes, a laser can be thought of as a source of intense, finely focused heat. This scalpel of light is used principally for cutting, welding, heat treating and etching operations. Its high-energy, narrow-beam properties allow it to heat rapidly, then quickly move on. Because close tolerances can be maintained, and the metal surrounding the work area is undisturbed, it is not unusual to eliminate one entire step from the manufacturing process by using lasers.

Because the laser is only a beam of light, it can be manipulated with a mirror. This ability to easily alter the beam's path makes the laser very flexible. Systems called laser machining centers, which cut and drill on commands from computer controls, are showing up in industry in increasing quantities. Illinois Institute of Teaching Research Institute is studying the applicability of robot technology to manipulate laser beams.

At present, the primary productivity gains realized by using lasers in the production process lie in the area of machine productivity, which, in turn, enhances labor productivity. Even though lasers show marked advantages when working with traditional materials, they are very effective when used in conjunction with nontraditional materials or new composites. Some new products specify that lasers must be used in the production process.

The use of new composites, as we have seen, increases the productivity of material. Conversely, processing traditional material with lasers reduces material scrap, which increases yield, which automatically improves material productivity. Don't be astonished to see industrial laser applications grow at the same pace as robotic applications during the next two decades.

Consider the casting of traditional aluminum, i.e, the common foundry process. New casting processes have been developed to replace conventional sand-molding techniques. One such new process is called the "evaporative" or "lost foam" process. Except for Ford and General Motors, these processes were confined to low-volume prototype work. Ford's new line at its Essex plant has the capability of producing 2 million aluminum automotive parts annually. Basically, the process employs styrofoam models of the part to be produced, which are surrounded by regular foundry sand confined in a flask. The models, or patterns, are the same size and configuration as the desired finished part. As molten aluminum is poured into the styrofoam model, the styrofoam melts or evaporates as it is being replaced by the aluminum, which takes on the shape of the part.

Improvements in Productivity Improve Productivity of Capital

This innovative process increases the productivity of labor and materials since the parts produced this way are of superior quality and closer to the part's net shape (i.e., the shape considered in the early steps of the production process). Closer dimensional tolerances can be maintained with this process than with conventional foundry methods.

Of course, as the yield per ton of raw aluminum that enters the production process improves, the productivity of energy is also improved because less melting is required for each ton of finished product. Keep in mind that improvements in productivity of any production factor automatically improve the productivity of capital.

Consider another example: Traditional smelting operations. These are presently done most often with blast furnaces. Enter new "plasma technologies." (Even though plasma technology may not be a new laboratory concept, its applicability on a large scale to the production process is new.) The heart of plasma technology is the plasma generator, which uses electricity to generate intense heat in the form of gas. At 5,500° F, the atoms of the gas lose some electronics; the resultant gas is called plasma. (Basic steel melts at about 2,300° F.)

Plasma generators can use various fuels, including coal, natural gas, oil, peat, wood chips, or even charcoal made from eucalyptus trees. These powerful plasma generators can produce more heat than most industrial operations can use. The excess heat can power the entire plant, other plants nearby or surrounding municipalities.

Plasmamelt requires about half the initial capital investment of blast-furnace facilities. Also, plasmamelt plants can be much smaller in scale. To be economical, annual production at blast furnaces must reach 2 million tons; plasma-melt facilities can be economical at 250,000 annual tons.

But what about the productivity advantage of this innovative technology? Plasmamelt facilities use 25% less energy than blast furnaces. If an existing blast furnace were converted to plasma-melt, it could triple production and reduce manufacturing costs by 20%.

The list of new processes could go on and on. Sometimes a change in just part of a conventional process affects the properties and subsequent productivity of traditional materials. For example, when a metal (or metals) is melted, cast and allowed to cool at normal rates in ambient temperature, the resultant casting has certain physical properties. But if just the cooling portion of the foundry process is altered, the casting may take on entirely different physical properties. Cast aluminum may cool presently at the rate of, say, several degrees per minute or several hundred degrees per hour. Under such cooling rates, the aluminum will have predictable physical properties. There is now, however, a new technology called "rapid solidification" in which aluminum is cooled at the rate of 10,000° C per second. The result is a traditional metal with entirely different physical properties. If the altered physical properties allow new uses for aluminum as substitutes for other, more costly materials, then the productivity of materials has been improved.

Material Substitution

There are two basic ways to view material substitution. Or perhaps we should say there are two basic ways in which we will present the topic of material substitution:

1. Substituting new or traditional materials for other traditional materials to accomplish a traditional function; and

2. Developing a combination of traditional materials in such a way as to arrive at the desired ending chemical/physical properties.

In both cases, the objective is to improve the productivity of materials or the capital allocated to the material resource.

First, let's consider the substitution of new or traditional materials.

An aluminum beverage bottle has been test marketed. This event ushered in a new generation of aluminum containers and stepped up the competitive materials battle among glass, plastic, steel and aluminum. The major advantage of the aluminum bottle is its resealability, which allows it to compete with the more costly plastic bottle.

Another current example of using traditional material for a substitute in a traditional application was Ford's introduction of an all-plastic bumper for some of its 1984 subcompact models. The all-plastic bumper replaced rollformed high-strength-steel bumpers. The plastic bumpers are 8 lbs lighter than their steel counterparts and are far more corrosion resistant. In addition to the improvement in material productivity, they are also less costly to produce. Although all-plastic bumper production was new to U.S. automakers, it had been tried quite successfully in Europe.

The Cadillac Motor Division of General Motors Co. planned to bring out a redesigned limousine with plastic doors and a plastic hood. Cadillac engineers and designers believe that plastic has finally "come of age" as a first-class body material in terms of durability and appearance.

Ford introduced an all-aluminum block for its V-6 engines. Although this has partially been done with smaller four-cylinder engines, the V-6 will be innovative. A major material substitution such as this has far-reaching effects on the aluminum industry as well as the steel industry — steel being the basic raw material used in making cast-iron engine blocks and heads.

A major movement within the construction and agriculture-equipment industry is the substitution of certain grades of ductile cast iron for steel-welded fabricated parts. In this case, the steel industry will not suffer, because steel is the primary ingredient for cast iron. The productivity improvement is possible because steel fabricated parts have a great deal more labor content in them than does a casting. Consider the example of the front axle of a loader-backhoe. This part was previously fabricated from several pieces of steel; it is now cast as a single-piece ductile iron. In addition, the foundry that casts this item casts four at a time in a single mold.

The crowning irony of this example is that the steel purchased by iron foundries as their raw material is predominately steel scrap. In other words, it is someone else's throwaway. It might be in the form of shredded car bodies, punchings, scrap from dismantled bridge structures, or trimmings from a steel-fabrication shop.

This example provides a natural lead-in to the second aspect of material substitution: Developing a combination of traditional materials in such a way as to arrive at desired ending chemical/physical properties.

Consider the aforementioned front axle for the loader-backhoe. The determining criterion to evaluate if ductile iron would be a suitable substitute for fabricated steel was whether the iron casting could perform the function required of an axle equal to or better than the previous steel-fabricated axle. In other words, even if a cast-iron axle were cost-effective relative to the steel-fabricated axle, no manufacturer can afford to compromise quality. A cast-iron axle must, therefore, be of equal or superior strength when compared with a steel axle.

Let's say that the strength required of an axle, cast iron or steel, is 35,000 psi (pounds per square inch). The iron foundry determines that the ending chemistry of the iron that will provide a physical strength of 35,000 psi is as shown in Table 9.1.

Table 9.1 Chemical analysis required for axle

Element		Percent by Weight in Metallic Mix
Carbon	(C)	3.75 - 3.95
Silicon	(Si)	1.80 - 2.10
Manganese	(Mn)	.35 - .45
Copper	(Cu)	.20 - .30
Phosphorus	(p)	.04 - .06
Sulfur	(S)	.03 - .04

These elements in the listed proportions will result in an iron mix producing the required strength. If 100 lbs of this mix were prepared, the 100 lbs less the above would be the basic element iron, or Fe. It is also important to note that an alloy with the above proportions does not exist in a natural state. It must be blended. This can be done only by reducing selected raw materials to their liquid state and adding the required elements. The mixture, when frozen back to its natural solid state, will be a form of cast iron that is chemically balanced to produce the desired strength.

Consider several raw materials that are available to the foundry industry, per Table 9.2. The numbers in the matrix indicate the percentage of the elements listed on the left that are contained in each purchased material, listed across the top.

Table 9.2 Available raw material

Chemical Analysis	Pig Iron	Shredded Autos	Punch-ings	Scrap Structural	Trim-mings	Bag Carbon	Box Silicon
Carbon	3.80	.50	.25	.65	.20	100.00	—
Silicon	2.00	.10	.85	.70	1.05	—	100.00
Manganese	.40	.15	.30	.30	.20	—	—
Copper	.25	.10	.25	.20	.15	—	—
Phosphorus	.05	.03	.01	.02	.03	—	—
Sulfur	.03	.01	.01	.015	.035	—	—

Example:

Pig iron contains 2.00%, by weight, of the element silicon. In other words, each 100 lbs of pig iron contains 2 lbs of silicon. Likewise, 100 lbs of bagged carbon contains 100 lbs of the element carbon. This product contains no other element.

If the chemical analysis for pig iron is examined, it is noted that all the chemical requirements for an axle, per Table 9.1, are satisfied. This means that the foundry could purchase pig iron and no other raw material. Economics may dictate that buying just pig iron might not be a good option. Pig iron does not exist as a natural material; it is a product resulting from a production process. Some other industry had to make it by melting and mixing the required elements. Therefore, another industry has added value to the elements, plus a profit margin, resulting in a higher price for pig iron than the other available materials, such as shredded automobiles.

Another Element: Prices of Raw Materials

Now let's add another variable to the decision process, raw-material prices. Consider the pricing structure shown in Table 9.3.

Table 9.3 Raw-material prices

	Pig Iron	Shredded Autos	Punch-ings	Scrap Structural	Trim-mings	Bag Carbon	Box Silicon
Price per lb	$ .25	$ .05	$ .06	$ .08	$ .07	$ .30	$ .27
Price per 100 lbs	25.00	5.00	6.00	8.00	7.00	30.00	27.00

By this time, the astute reader recognizes a linear programming (LP) application. In fact, this very application is one of the earlier classic uses of LP in industry. It is called the "least-cost" mix. The objective is to determine the combination of available raw materials that will provide the required chemical analysis for the least cost. If we assign variables to each of the raw materials, i.e., pig iron is X_1, shredded autos is X_2, etc., then the objective function is a minimization problem represented as follows:

$$\text{minimize } \$.25X_1 + \$.05X_2 + \$.06X_3 + \$.08X_4$$
$$+ \$.07X_5 + \$.30X_6 + \$.27X_7$$

The solution is subject to the chemical constraints listed in Table 9.1. To illustrate, suppose that the limit for the amount of carbon in the resultant mix can be equal to or greater than 3.75% by weight up to an amount equal to or less than 3.95% by weight. The equation for the carbon constraint is:

$$3.75 \leq \text{carbon} \leq 3.95$$

If it is decided to satisfy the chemical requirements exclusively with the purchase of pig iron, what would a mix containing 100 lbs cost?

$.25(100) + $.05(0) + $.06(0) + $.08(0)
+ $.07(0) + $.30(0) + $.27(0) = $25.00
    (See Table 9.4)

Table 9.4 Raw material in mix (designate all pig iron)

Raw Material		Number of lbs	Cost per lb	Cost of Material
Pig iron	(X_1)	100	$ .25	$25.00
Shredded autos	(X_2)	-0-	.05	-0-
Punchings	(X_3)	-0-	.06	-0-
Scrap structural	(X_4)	-0-	.08	-0-
Trimmings	(X_5)	-0-	.07	-0-
Bag carbon	(X_6)	-0-	.30	-0-
Box silicon	(X_7)	-0-	.27	-0-
Totals		100		$25.00

However, if we turn the computer loose to choose the least-cost mix, the result is substantially different, as indicated in Table 9.5. The computer-selected minimum-cost mix saves the firm $6.37 per 100 lbs of metal. ($25.00 - $18.63) When large foundries speak in terms of hundreds of thousands of tons per year, a fraction of a cent is significant.

Table 9.5 Raw materials in mix (given table 9.2 and 9.3 subject to table 9.1)

Raw Material		Number of lbs	Cost per lb	Cost of Material
Pig iron	(X_1)	61.34	$ .25	$15.34
Shredded autos	(X_2)	4.13	.05	.21
Punchings	(X_3)	-0-	.06	-0-
Scrap structural	(X_4)	31.75	.08	2.54
Trimmings	(X_5)	1.48	.07	.10
Bag carbon	(X_6)	1.18	.30	.35
Box silicon	(X_7)	.32	.27	.09
Totals		100.20		$18.63

But now let's pose a question. (The ability to perform simulation is invaluable to this type of problem.) What if scrap structural, i.e., X_4, became more scarce, which in turn pushed the price per pound from 8¢ to 12¢? This happens frequently in the metal market. If the existing mix were maintained, per Table 9.5, the only change would be an increase per 100 lbs of the mix to $19.90.

Table 9.5 indicates scrap structural (X_4) usage to be 31.75 lbs.

X_4 present cost	31.75 lbs x $.08 = $ 2.54
X_4 price increase	31.75 lbs x $.12 = $ 3.81
increment	$ 1.27
present mix cost	$18.63
mix cost with price increase	$19.90

However, in order to arrive at the least-cost mix, all available raw materials must be evaluated again simultaneously to see whether the computer "substitutes" lower-cost materials while adhering to the desired chemistry. (See Table 9.6.) The results are:

- X_4 was eliminated;

- X_3 entered the mix;

- X_2 was eliminated; and

• All other variables experienced some change.

Table 9.6 Raw materials in mix (given tables 9.2 and 9.3 subject to table 9.1)

		X_4 price increase to $.12 per lb		
Raw Material		*Number of lbs*	*Cost per lb*	*Cost of Material*
Pig iron	(X_1)	61.17	$ .25	$16.54
Shredded autos	(X_2)	-0-	.05	-0-
Punchings	(X_3)	19.55	.06	1.17
Scrap structural	(X_4)	-0-	.12	-0-
Trimmings	(X_5)	13.14	.07	.92
Bag carbon	(X_6)	1.15	.30	.35
Box silicon	(X_7)	.16	.27	.04
Totals		100.17		$19.02

Now, what if, because of overcapacity, the price of pig iron dropped to 15¢ per pound? The obvious first impression would be that the computer would choose 100 lbs of pig iron for a total mix cost of $15. To confirm this, look at Table 9.7, which reveals that even though a total pig-iron mix of $15 per 100 lbs would be lower than any of the previous examples, the computer determined that the available materials, when evaluated simultaneously, could improve the cost to $12.30 per 100 lbs.

Table 9.7 Raw materials in mix (given tables 9.3 and 9.3 subject to table 9.1)

		X_4 reverted back to 8¢ per lb X_1 adjusted to 15¢ per lb		
Raw Material		*Number of lbs*	*Cost per lb*	*Cost of Material*
Pig iron	(X_1)	67.33	$ .15	$10.10
Shredded autos	(X_2)	8.72	.05	.44
Punchings	(X_3)	21.52	.06	1.29
Scrap structural	(X_4)	-0-	.08	-0-
Trimmings	(X_5)	1.30	.07	.09
Bag carbon	(X_6)	1.08	.30	.32
Box silicon	(X_7)	.23	.27	.06
Totals		100.18		$12.30

This program should be run whenever one of the materials experiences a price change to ensure that the "least-cost" mix is always used. It is basically a material-substitution problem. The substitution in this case doesn't involve new materials, but the relative proportions of existing ingredients for a given process.

Materials — Their Efficient Use

This aspect of the subject of materials is really basic, so basic, in fact, that many firms assume that there is little opportunity for productivity improvements in this area.

The very first consideration should be whether the firm is allotting materials to products that the firm should not be making in the first place. This is a strategic consideration. Consider the following example: *Product A* contains 10 lbs of raw material costing $15; has a total variable cost of $25; sells for $45; and provides contribution of $20. *Product B* contains 10 lbs of raw material costing $15; has a total variable cost of $25; sells for $40; and provides contribution of $15. Which of the two products has the better productivity of materials? Whether revenue or contribution is considered, the obvious answer is product A.

$$A = \frac{\text{selling price}}{\text{material cost}} = \frac{\$45}{\$15} = \$3.00$$

$$B = \frac{\text{selling price}}{\text{material cost}} = \frac{\$40}{\$15} = \$2.67$$

$$A = \frac{\text{contribution}}{\text{material cost}} = \frac{\$20}{\$15} = \$1.33$$

$$B = \frac{\text{contribution}}{\text{material cost}} = \frac{\$15}{\$15} = \$1.00$$

Granted, in many cases, certain products must be provided, regardless of productivity issues. Many times, however, there is no justification for making certain products. The initial consideration, therefore, when examining the efficient use of material, should be an evaluation of existing products and product lines. It now appears that there are as many divestitures of product lines as there are acquisitions. This is partially attributable to the push for increased productivity.

Yield

In the context of productivity, the noun form of the word "yield" is relevant: "The amount of quantity resulting, often expressed as the percentage of what is theoretically possible."

It is interesting to note the close relationship between "yield" and productivity. Both are relationships expressing:

<u>output</u>

input

It should be noted that the yield of any material cannot be greater than one. In other words, it is not possible to end up with more material, by weight, as output than was entered into the production process as inputs. The reverse is normally true, i.e., some material will normally be lost during the production process. The objective is to lose as little as possible. In an attempt to obtain the theoretical yield, each subsequent step of the production process should be examined to determine where losses occur.

Let's consider a basic example, say, the steel industry, which is one of this nation's largest industries. The raw material for the steel industry begins at the mines in iron-ore deposits. The iron ore is extracted from the earth and transported to smelting operations. (A synonym for "smelt" is "reduce.") The ore is reduced to the element iron via a deoxidation process. (Note that it is not unusual for confusion to exist about the relationship between the basic element iron and the manufactured product, steel. Steel is nothing more than iron with a given amount of carbon.)

Now then, even though iron ore may contain, say, 60% basic iron by weight, existing smelting techniques may yield only a 50% iron recovery. Accordingly, a 1,000-ton load of iron ore should produce, theoretically, 600 tons of iron. That is considered to be the input, i.e., 600 tons of iron entered the smelting, or reduction process. If, however, only 500 tons of iron are produced, which is the output, then the yield of the smelting operation is:

$$\frac{500}{600} = 83.3\%$$

Consider further that the smelter ships the 500 tons of iron/steel to a steel rolling mill in the form of large ingots, or billets. The basic function of the steel mill is to transform the ingots into usable shapes. The shapes can be ready for use, as in the case of rails for the railroad industry, or in the form of steel sheets that will be further processed by another industry. For instance, the automobile industry will purchase steel sheets that will be stamped, pressed, or punched into car components. In the present example, let's consider that the steel mill transformed the 500 tons of ingots into steel sheets. After cutting the sheets to the specified dimensions, the steel mill ends up with 480 tons of sheet steel that is forwarded to the auto industry. The yield of the steel mill is:

$$\frac{480}{500} = 96\%$$

When the auto industry processes the steel sheets by stamping, pressing or punching, additional product is lost. Consider that the 480 tons of sheet steel received by the auto industry resulted in 400 tons of completed components. The yield for the automaker, relative to steel sheet, is:

$$\frac{432}{480} = 90\%$$

So then, beginning with the original 600 tons of contained iron in the original ore, the result is 432 tons of product. The total yield is:

$$\frac{432}{600} = 72\%$$

or

600 tons x (83.3% x 96% x 90%) = 432 tons

Of course, with each additional step in this process, the decrease in yield becomes more costly because more production factors have been applied. For example, the material had been handled and transported at least four times by the time it was received by the automakers.

In the present example, the productivity of the beginning iron contained in the basic ore was considered in three stages of the production process. Each stage of a production process has its unique measure of the productivity, or yield. The common thread, however, is that the quantity of material entering production is compared with the quantity of material exiting the production process as usable product.

Productivity of a basic material is enhanced if, for example, the trimmings generated by the fabricators or auto makers can be utilized in some other manner or in some other process. Such is the case, as we have seen, with a foundry. The basic raw material for an iron foundry is steel scrap generated by other industries or production processes. Literally trainloads of punchings and trimmings are shipped from fabricators and hard-goods manufacturers to iron foundries. The foundries melt this "scrap" in giant furnaces and then produce castings, which in many cases end up as other parts for the same automakers where the trimmings were generated in other steps of the production process.

It is not unusual for a foundry to be located in the midst of scrap-generating industries in order to minimize the transportation cost for its basic raw material.

Near Net Shape

Near net shape is a concept in which the desired end shape of a product is considered in the production process, thus improving material productivity by minimizing excess material as well as production time. The idea is not new. But, due to the quest for improved productivity, it received much renewed attention in the 1980s.

Rarely can a product, part, or component be manufactured in a manner that will satisfy the dimensional accuracy required for its end use. Let's consider, for example, the case of an engine block, which using current state-of-the-art manufacturing technology, is cast in either iron or aluminum. Present casting techniques produce dimensional accuracy of $\pm$ .030 inch, at best. However, tolerances for the functioning of an engine, such as piston movement, are measured in much smaller dimensions, say $\pm$ .005 inch.

Therefore, in order to end up with the required dimensional tolerances, the basic component/part must be made "oversized" and then machined down to size. Such machining operations remove the excess material which decreases yield. This problem exists with most conventional metal-forming techniques that are currently employed by industry. Productivity can be increased either by improving basic production methods or by more efficient material-removal methods, such as with the use of lasers, as previously mentioned in this chapter.

Consider the following that was excerpted from a current trade publication:

> Fabricators and manufacturers ordering "net shape" bar and wire are seeking both cost savings and improved productivity.
>
> More specifically, they have learned that finished parts can be made more quickly, with less machining and milling, and that the yield per pound of metal purchased is far greater.
>
> Major markets for "net shapes" include machine parts, valves and pipe fittings.

The near-net-shape concept is now being pursued from a different approach. Researchers are considering material productivity in the initial design of a product/component. This new technique, termed "optimal shape generation," utilizes computer-aided design concepts to design components with required physical properties using minimum mass. Minimum mass automatically enhances material productivity.

Optimum-shape research is being done at General Motors. Its particular technique employs a mathematical optimization routine that changes the design to the shape, given minimum mass, within the required structural constraints. This integrated approach enables GM to combine the objectives of improving material productivity and meeting structural requirements in a single system.

Defective Products

Within the context of material productivity, we'll consider defective products to be materials that entered the production process as inputs, but for some reason did not maintain/achieve the required quality to be sold as finished products, or outputs.

An inverse relationship exists between yield and defective products. This is not to say that yield reacts only to the amount of defective product. Previous discussion indicated that yield is a function of output/input when a difference exists for any reason. However, the point to be made is that all defective products inversely affect yield. For example, in previous paragraphs, it was illustrated that an automaker received 480 tons of sheet steel with which to stamp, press and punch component parts. After deducting the weight of the trimmings and punchings, there were 432 tons of completed components. The yield at that point was 90%.

$$\frac{\text{output}}{\text{input}} = \frac{432}{480} = 90\%$$

Consider that during the punching operation, for instance, the die was not properly set in the press and 50 tons of components were punched which were dimensionally incorrect. These parts are called defective products, or, more simply stated, scrap. Especially for responsibility accounting purposes, care should be exercised to avoid attributing normal trim losses to scrap. There is quite a difference in product lost due to normal trimmings and product lost due to error. Normal trimmings are engineered so as to be minimized. Scrap generated, as in the present example, is the result of some slippage in the control of the production process.

In the present example, the proper calculation for the scrap should consider the input to be 432 tons. The magnitude of the scrap is calculated to be:

$$\frac{\text{input - output}}{\text{input}} = \frac{432 - (432\text{-}50)}{432} = 11.6\%$$

The total material yield, however, for the automaker has slipped from 90% to 79.6%.

Original input	+ 480 tons
Loss to trim, etc.	- 48 tons
Loss to scrap	- 50 tons
Ending output	+ 382 tons

$$\frac{382}{480} = 79.6\%$$

Scrap is one of the biggest obstacles to achieving high productivity. Scrap represents, in essence, production factors, or inputs, which never reach the output stage. When scrap is anticipated in any operation, an allowance must be made to inject more inputs to compensate for the anticipated loss.

Measuring Productivity of Material

Let's consider, for example, that our automaker had firm orders for cars that required say, 796 tons of punched component parts. The question is, how many tons of steel sheet must be ordered to end up with 796 tons, given:

- 90% primary yield from punching and normal yield; and

- 11.6% scrap rate due to anticipated die problems in the punching operative.

The proper procedure is to begin with the last known area of expected loss. In our case, it is the 11.6% loss due to die problems. In order to end up with 796 tons of punched components, the automaker must begin with 900 tons of trimmed sheets:

$$\frac{796}{1-11.6\%} = \frac{796}{.884} = 900 \text{ tons}$$

However, how many tons of purchased sheets are needed in order to end up with 900 tons of trimmed sheets?

$$\frac{900}{90\%} = \frac{900}{.90} = 1,000 \text{ tons}$$

In this case, the productivity of material is 79.6%.

$$\frac{\text{output}}{\text{input}} = \frac{796}{1,000 \text{ tons}}$$

One can readily see the compounding effect of this concept when a production process has many different steps, and each step can generate scrap losses. In the present case of the automaker, 204 tons of *excess* steel had to be purchased and inventoried in order to fulfill customer requirements.

A final thought along these lines is important. The detrimental effects of scrap may be visualized by considering that all materials purchased for use in a product appear on the firm's balance sheet as assets. As soon as any of the material is scrapped, it loses its value and is no longer a valid asset. It is not capable of generating revenue. The only recognized method to remove a useless asset from the balance sheet is to expense it via the income statement in the period in which it loses its value. It is a direct expense with no accompanying revenue; it was an input with no accompanying output. The financial consequences of scrap, or defective products, are illustrated more fully in Chapter 5, "Working Capital: Cash to Cash."

Materials: Transport and Handling

No discussion of materials would be complete without mention of logistics. Materials for a production process are of no value if they are not physically at the place of production. This truism is valid both for materials initially purchased as raw stock from another firm and for materials that are processed within a given plant. More simply stated, iron ingots at a smelter have little value to a steel mill 1,000 miles away. In the same light, steel sheets sitting on the receiving dock of an automaker's plant are of little value to the punch-press operator located 1,000 feet away. And, finally, you and I can't drive a completed automobile that is sitting in inventory in an automaker's lot in Detroit.

Inbound Transportation

Inbound transportation consists of those activities that involve delivering physical production inputs to the location of the production process.

The transportation industry is a major factor in the U.S. economy. Consider railroads, barges, supertankers, air freighters, trucks, and pipelines, just to skim the surface. Each of these modes of transportation represents industries within an industry. Their primary function is to transport production factors from one level of production to another. (Distribution of end product to consumer will be addressed separately.)

Previously, we discussed a basic example of iron ore from the mines to the smelter to the steel mill to the automaker. Let's consider the magnitude of the movement of the required materials using some realistic numbers.

- Annual domestic auto production, 7.5 million units.

- Steel content per auto 1/2 ton.

- Rail-car capacity 100 tons.

- Basic stages and yields as previously illustrated — 7.5 million x 1/2 ton = 3.75 million tons.

Automaker yield was illustrated, hypothetically, at 79.6%; therefore, required sheet to be delivered is 3.75 ÷ 79.6%, or 4.71 million tons. This movement alone would require 47,100 railcars.

Because the steel-mill yield was illustrated to be 96%, therefore, required ingot to be delivered would be 4.91 million tons. To transport this from the smelter to the steel mill would require another 49,100 railcars.

And last, it was illustrated that it required two tons of iron ore to produce one ton of iron ingot at the smelter. Therefore, 9.82 million tons of iron ore had to be delivered to the smelter. This movement from the mine to the smelter would require 98,200 railcars.

Railcar requirements

Mill to automaker	47,100
Smelter to mill	49,100
Mine to smelter	98,200
Total	194,400 railcars

This transportation project would require a train reaching from Los Angeles to Boston and back to Chicago. However, it would not be unreasonable to expect that some of the trains that delivered ore to the smelter were the same ones that delivered ingots to the steel mills and steel sheets to the automakers.

Not only does the physical movement need to be considered, but the movement must be timely and cost-effective. "Just-in-time" inventory systems are based on timely deliveries.

There are some production processes in which the cost of the transportation of the required materials exceeds the cost of the materials themselves. For example, the cost of sand for a glass plant or foundry may be less than one-third of the cost of delivering the sand.

In-plant Transportation (Material Handling)

It has been estimated that material-handling costs for firms engaged in manufacturing/production amount to between 20% and 30% of their total cost. Material handling begins at the receiving dock, whether it be rail or truck. There are as many varied methods to unload a truck or railcar as there are varied materials transported. The materials can be gaseous, liquid or solid. Materials may be transported in a state other than their normal state, which would require special handling both transporting and unloading the material. A primary example would be liquefied gas. It is no small matter to transport and unload a material that must be maintained at a temperature several hundred degrees below ambient.

Then there is the universal factor of time. Off-loading must be done quickly. The receiving plant cannot afford to tie up production factors, (e.g., labor and equipment), on this function, and the carrier certainly does not wish to have revenue-generating transportation equipment sitting idle at a customer's receiving dock. Equipment depreciates whether it is being productive or idle. An opportunity cost is generated when equipment is not being productive.

Consider a modern coal-fired power plant. Such a plant in the 500mw capacity range may easily utilize three coal trains, each in excess of 100 cars. These trains are productive when they are transporting coal. By using a rotary coupler on the cars, such a plant can unload an entire 100-car train in about an hour. The train merely stops at a certain point at the plant's unloading facility. A device clamps the car and rotates it over the center axis of the rail-car coupler. The coal dumps out and the car is never uncoupled from the train. The unloading device then automatically indexes the train so the next car is positioned to be rolled over and unloaded. Total elapsed time to unload a car and index the train is approximately 45 seconds.

The most advanced methods of handling and transporting coal are by rail. However, this is being challenged by slurry pipelines, the use of which would eliminate the need for railroads for coal transport to power plants. Factors other than economic may enter that decision.

Unloading the material from the carrier's transportation equipment is just the first step. The material, after being unloaded, is transported either to a place of inventory or directly to the production process. New inventory concepts place the material directly in the production process from the point of offloading. This eliminates at least one movement of the material and at least one accounting transaction. It also minimizes inventory carrying cost.

Once the material has entered the production process, every incremental stage of the process requires that the material be transported. (This might not be the case when the product is, for example, processed in vats to which ingredients are added.) The movement of the material or product as it takes shape is performed as a separate operation, or perhaps an interval to a series of operations, as in a flexible machining system.

Many production processes and manufacturing facilities are designed around material-handling systems. Additionally, the most promising area for robotic applications in the coming years is in the area of material handling. The material-handling function continues until the product is completed and is loaded from the shipping dock onto transportation equipment for distribution.

Outbound Transportation: Distribution

Volumes have been written on the subject of product distribution and logistics. In the present context of material productivity, we intend only to cover several very basic principles.

To begin with, the ultimate goal of a firm is to end the production in a stronger financial position than it was in at the beginning of the cycle. In the most basic terms, that means that someone must be willing to pay more for a product than the cost of the production factors that have been allotted to its manufacture. Continuing basic terms, a customer won't pay for the product until he has the use or enjoyment of the product. Therefore, any discussion on the productivity of materials (for any factor input) is not complete without mention of the absolutely necessary function of distribution.

Let's try to comprehend the magnitude of the distribution function. Consider again the 7.5 million automobiles manufactured in a typical year. A completed automobile weighs approximately one ton. Even though a railcar can transport 100 tons of weight, it cannot transport 100 cars because of volume restrictions. In other words, a one-ton car requires considerably more space than one ton of steel sheet. A railcar designed for cars can accommodate 15 automobiles. The number of railcars needed to distribute annual auto production is, therefore, 500,000.

$$7,500,000 \div 15 = 500,000$$

An over-the-road auto-transport trailer can accommodate 10 automobiles. That equates to 750,000 truck movements.

It can be stated that the weight of physical materials delivered to a production process, unless consumed in the process, will become part of the weight of the product and will be required to be transported from the production facility to the consumer. In fact, even if the material is consumed in the production process and does not become part of the product, the weight of the inbound material will still remain and will require special handling for disposition. The material has simply changed form.

A case in point is a coal-fired power-generating plant, as mentioned in earlier paragraphs. Such a plant may annually intake and consume 2 million tons of coal in the generation of electric power. The product, or output, is transported via transmission lines. The product has no weight. So then, what becomes of the 2 million tons of coal?

As it is consumed in the burning chambers, it is transformed to ash. This ash can be sold as a byproduct, disposed of as a slurry or transported and distributed over several hundred adjacent square miles by a south wind. The point remains that the 2 million tons of input are either converted to product requiring distribution or converted to refuse or byproducts requiring disposition. Transport facilities are required in either case.

Chapter 10
Facilities: Location and Installation/ Project Management

Objectives

- *Know that a facility is any object that is built, installed or established to serve a specific purpose.*

- *Understand that production facilities are capital items that establish production capacity.*

- *Recognize that facilities management involves the acquisition, installation, and maintenance of facilities.*

- *Realize that productivity improvements will increase production capacity.*

- *Understand the procedures involved in the acquisition of facilities.*

- *Understand the benefits of using PERT when installing a facility.*

- *Understand the use of Gantt Charts in PERT applications.*

- *Comprehend the use of the beta distribution when calculating expected time.*

- *Be able to determine, within a PERT network, the starting time of each project event and the critical path.*

- *Be able to calculate the probability of success of completing a project on time.*

- *Understand how to sequence a project's activities and events.*

- *Be able to analyze a PERT network.*

Contents

Defining Production Facility

In considering the production of goods and services, one normally associates a particular type of facility with a particular production process. If the production process is automobile manufacturing, the facility will include large stamping presses, long, automated assembly lines, paint lines, etc., all equipped with sophisticated machinery and controls. If, on the other hand, the end product is a service, say, providing electric power to homes, businesses, and factories, the facility will consist of large generating units powered by steam turbines driven by the burning of coal, gas, or perhaps from nuclear reactions. The generators might even be turned by mechanical means, such as water flowing over turbine blades.

A facility, then, is anything built, installed, or established to serve a specific purpose. In the present context of productivity, a facility is any tangible building or equipment that is employed to provide the means to produce goods and services. The term "facility" is an offshoot of the basic word "facilitate," which means to make some specific task easier. For example, a small amount of heat can be generated by forcing electric current through a resistance, while the task of melting steel can be facilitated by using large electric-powered melting furnaces. Therefore, if the subject production process is melting and recasting steel into varied shapes, the appropriate facility will be a foundry, and the process will be facilitated with the use of large furnaces.

In this text, production facilities are considered to be the equivalent to the establishment of capacity. This capacity includes both direct-production facilities and production-support facilities. Before production can occur, the establishment of capacity needs to take place to facilitate the particular production process.

The establishment of capacity is accomplished via the firm's capital plan, while the other factors of production, such as labor, materials, and energy are more closely associated with the firm's operating plan. The capacity of a given plant or facility is that entity's total opportunity to produce goods and services.

As such, the firm's facilities are listed on the firm's balance sheet (statement of financial position) as assets in the form of "plant and equipment." These types of assets facilitate the production process, but they are neither consumed in the process nor transformed into product.

Consider a firm that invests $500,000 for a new plant. After this initial transaction that establishes its capacity, it has the following balance sheet:

Assets		*Ownership*
Plant and equipment	$500,000	$500,000 Original equity
Total assets	$500,000	$500,000 Total equity

Let's say the company realized a profit of $80,000 during its first year of operation and ended the year with the following balance sheet:

Assets		*Ownership*
Cash	$ 25,000	$500,000 Original equity
Inventories	$ 55,000	$ 80,000 Earnings
Plant and equipment	$500,000	
Total Assets	$580,000	$580,000 Total equity

In this instance, the firm earned 16% on its original investment in facilities, which is reflected as an increase in cash and inventories. The concept of growth states that growth results in the increase of productive capacity. If this firm maintains the 16% annual pretax earnings and the same cash, inventories, and facilities, the following year the balance sheet would be as follows:

Assets		*Ownership*
Cash	$ 29,000	$500,000 Original equity
Inventories	$ 63,800	$ 80,000 Year 1 earnings
Plant and equipment	$580,000	$ 92,800 Year 2 earnings
Total assets	$672,800	$672,800 Total equity

It is not unusual for 85% of a firm's total asset base, on which it must generate earnings, to be invested in facilities. As growth continues via earnings, so grows the firm's increase in capacity. Facilities and project management are ongoing activities throughout the existence of a firm.

This chapter deals with the extremely important issue of a firm's acquisition and installation of production capacity, which is encompassed in its plant and equipment.

Facilities Management

Acquiring and installing facilities is substantially different in nature from maintaining them after they are installed. Inasmuch as they both focus on the productivity of capacity, they come together in the organizational structure of a firm.

It is typical in a company, or division of a company, especially one that is engaged in the production of goods, for the facilities manager to report to the production/operations manager. Also reporting to the production/operations manager would be the production manager and the materials manager. This, in essence, gives the production/operations manager line authority over the basic three M's of manufacturing — men, materials, and machines. Inasmuch as the facilities manager is responsible for both the acquisition/installation and maintenance of facilities, his organization will reflect this dual responsibility. (See Figure 10.1.) The plant engineer is responsible for the acquisition/ installation function, while the maintenance superintendent is responsible for the upkeep of the facilities and equipment after installation. As we might surmise, very close coordination is required between these two complementary functions to ensure continuity of the production process.

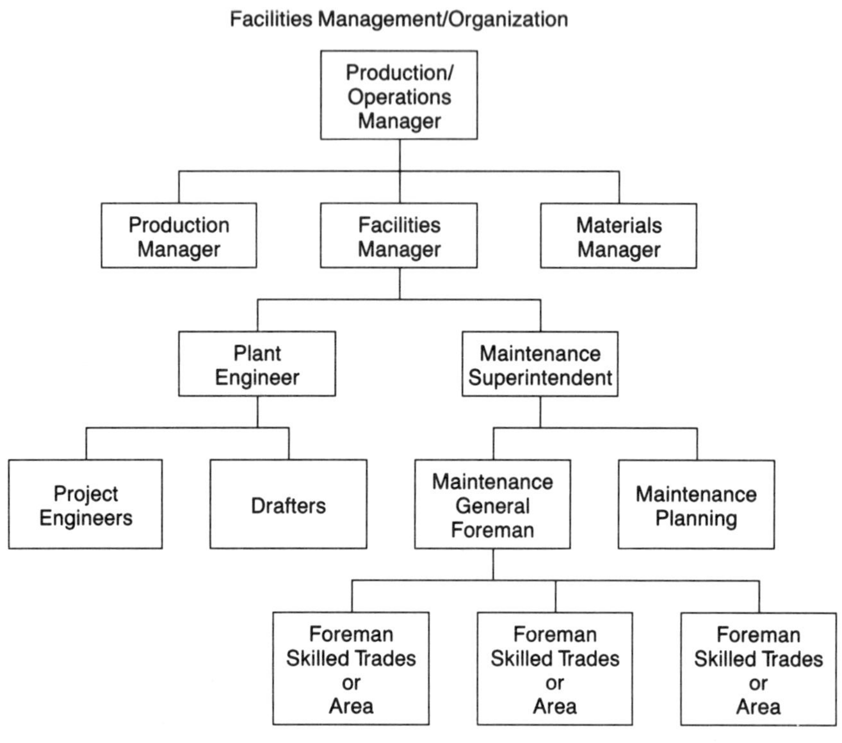

Fig. 10.1. Facilities management/organization

The vast majority of the available production/operations management texts cover the subject of facilities very slightly. The facilities function, in essence, implements the firm's capital plan and provides the capacity requirements for the strategic plan. Therefore, attention must be given to these highly visible activities.

The Acquisition/Installation Function

The design and construction of a totally new production facility is normally not the responsibility of a firm's facilities group. Rather, in such cases, the firm will retain an engineering firm that specializes in the design and construction of production facilities of a specific nature. In addition, a firm will normally not have the required depth of architectural and engineering skills that are required to handle a totally new turnkey project such as a new plant. Therefore, our discussion focuses on additions to existing capacity or general replacement-type projects.

Let's examine ae case in which a wagon manufacturer considers automating a welding operation in the fabricating department. The firm does not anticipate additional demand for wagons. However, because of heavy competition, the firm wants to increase productivity. (This type of investment proposal falls into the category of "cost reduction" and was discussed in Chapter 6.) It follows that if the productivity of the fabricating department is improved, the capacity of the fabricating department is increased.

The idea of automating the welding operation could have originated with either the manager of the fabrication department or industrial engineering. In either case, the idea is forwarded to the facilities manager to check its feasibility and to arrive at a budgeting figure in order that a capital funding request can be made. The facilities manager will communicate with several vendors of automated welding equipment and will show them the proposed application. The vendors will submit their respective proposals, including a very general cost that is to be used only for budgeting purposes. At this point, the vendors do not submit detailed installation drawings or firm bids. Rather, the proposal will consist of general conceptual schematics and approximate cost figures.

The facilities manager will compile the vendor proposals, and if the proposal indicates a favorable financial return, he will request capital funding in the vendor's approximate cost plus a generous contingency to cover the unforeseen details that most assuredly will crop up. When the request for funding is reviewed by upper management, the proposal will be reviewed to ensure that:

- Addition of automated welding equipment fits the firm's long-range strategic plan; and

- Estimated financial benefits due to increased welding productivity appear realistic.

The classic capital budgeting concepts are applied so that the proposed welding equipment can be ranked with other proposed investment opportunities. If and when the firm's top management approves the request for funding, the facilities manager's work really begins.

Facilities Manager's Role

The facilities manager, or perhaps the plant engineer, will call the vendors that submitted original conceptual proposals and arrange for a meeting at the site where the proposed equipment is to be installed. At this meeting, the plant engineer will provide detailed blueprints of the existing facility. These blueprints show in great detail the location of existing structures, such as support columns, foundations, gas, water, air lines, and elevations. These prints will be discussed and questions will be asked by the vendors concerning the existing facilities. Depending on the nature of the automated welding equipment, questions might cover such items as:

- Voltage delivered by the firm's transformers.

- Available gas, water, and air pressure.

- Available air-cleaning equipment.

In turn, the plant engineer will specify that certain criteria must be met. Such criteria might well include such items as:

- Maximum noise level that the proposed equipment can reach, measured in decibels;

- Pollutant levels allowed (both as to gas content and particulate levels); and

- Minimum safety standards.

(Some of today's modern equipment must operate in a dust-free atmosphere, which requires sophisticated filtering provisions. Also, some equipment requires very dry and moisture-free air so that air-drying equipment is required.)

Then, the plant engineer conducts a tour of the existing facilities so that the vendors, armed with detailed prints of the area, can actually examine the area where the proposed new equipment is to be installed. Such a tour is called a "walk-through." This is an appropriate term, because the vendors literally walk through the area and observe firsthand the existing facilities and available space and ask the plant engineer questions along the way.

The purpose of the above procedures is to provide each vendor who is interested in supplying the proposed welding equipment with a detailed model of existing facilities. Each vendor has an equal opportunity to view the site, ask questions and examine detailed prints, and each begins at the same starting point. After the general meeting on-site and the completion of the walk-through, each vendor will be invited by mail to "bid" on the proposed automated equipment. The bid request, termed request for quote (RFQ) will detail the criteria specified by the company and request that each vendor provide a detailed bid on the project. The bid is an extremely important document. It will be completed by each vendor and mailed directly to the firm's purchasing manager or controller. The vendor's bid includes such items as the following:

- Detailed description of proposed equipment and performance criteria;

- Detailed cost breakdown for equipment and installation;

- Amount of time required for the vendor to engineer and manufacture the equipment; and

- Certification that the firm's criteria are met or exceeded.

Any bids submitted are kept unopened until a predetermined date when all bids were to be received; then they are jointly opened by the controller, purchasing manager and the plant engineer. This procedure provides the necessary controls to maintain objectivity and to preserve integrity. Each of the three parties initials, dates, and times the bids as they are opened. The bids are summarized by the purchasing manager on a separate document, commonly referred to as a "spread sheet." The purpose of the spread sheet is to express the major points of the bids in a common format so that the facilities manager can scan one document to compare the high points of the different bids. This document will be forwarded to the facilities manager from the purchasing manager, with the latter including his recommendations based on the bid contents.

After the bids and accompanying spread sheets have been reviewed, a contract will be awarded for the acquisition and installation of the automated welding equipment.

The next challenge facing the plant engineer is how to install the equipment with minimal interruption to the existing production operations. If the project is sufficiently large in nature, the plant engineer, with the aid of the winning bidder, will establish a PERT model to both plan and monitor the progress of the installation.

Installation Monitoring Using PERT

The acronym PERT stands for Program Evaluation and Review Technique. The PERT concept, which has been around for nearly three decades, was originally developed to enhance the timely completion of the Polaris missile project. PERT concepts, which are basic and logical, find widespread application in project management, especially in normally nonrepetitive activities. Nearly all production/operations management texts address PERT in great detail.

We'll also address the concepts in detail. Keep in mind as we progress that PERT is used to plan, monitor, and improve the productivity of factors of production, specifically:

- Capital and other resources committed to the project.

- Minimum disruption of existing production activities.

- Minimum time of completion of new project so as to reap the benefits of the improved productivity (in our case) of the fabricating department.

Also, we need to remember that the concepts and applications of PERT are not mutually exclusive of other major activities of a firm. PERT finds ideal application in the installation of a facility or project. Such installation is done only after a capital decision has been made, which, in turn, is the result of implementation of a portion of the firm's strategic plan.

Some of the basic advantages of using the PERT concept are:

- PERT provides a graphic display or schematic of a total project and its individual activities.

- The PERT model displays the sensitivity to time of each individual activity as it relates to the timely completion of the total project.

PERT Is a Network Diagram

The graphic display of the PERT concept is, in essence, a network diagram made up of three primary components:

1. *Activities* are indicated by arrows. An activity requires a given amount of time to complete, and may also consume other resources.

2. *Events,* or milestones, are indicated by circles (nodes). An

event signals the completion of a given activity and the beginning of the next, following activity.

3. *Paths* connect the beginning event with the ending event. Although there may be multiple paths in a given network, all paths representing activities and events must be completed in order to satisfy the network. One of the concepts of PERT is that multiple paths may be covered concurrently.

> For example:
> A → B → C → D
> A → B, B → C, C → D are activities
> A, B, C and D are events
> A → B → C → D is a path

The concept of PERT includes the identification of the one continuous path that requires the longest time to get from the beginning to the end. This path determines the completion time of the total project, and is termed the "critical path." This aspect of PERT will be covered in more detail.

A detailed example of the basic PERT problem will quickly reveal how the PERT concept evolved. Let's use for an initial example the task of obtaining a rick of firewood. As normally is the case, the wife informs the husband that the firewood supply is low just about two hours before the Saturday football game is to begin. Therefore, time becomes a critical factor.

The first thing the husband does is list the varied activities associated with the task/project of getting the firewood. He is fortunate to have several acres of timber right behind his house so that travel time to and from the woodcutting site is not a factor. He lists the following individual activities required:

Activity	*Estimated Time Required*
1. Cut down a tree.	10 minutes
2. Trim off the branches.	20 minutes
3. Cut tree into 24-inch logs	30 minutes

4.   Split logs into firewood-size
      wedges.   40 minutes
5.   Load firewood into truck.   35 minutes
6.   Pile branches for burning.   45 minutes
                                                   180 minutes

Our woodcutter quickly realizes that he has a time problem. He lays out a simplistic form of a Gantt Chart to better analyze the situation (See Figure 10.2.) and he finds that he has three hours of work with only two hours in which to complete it.

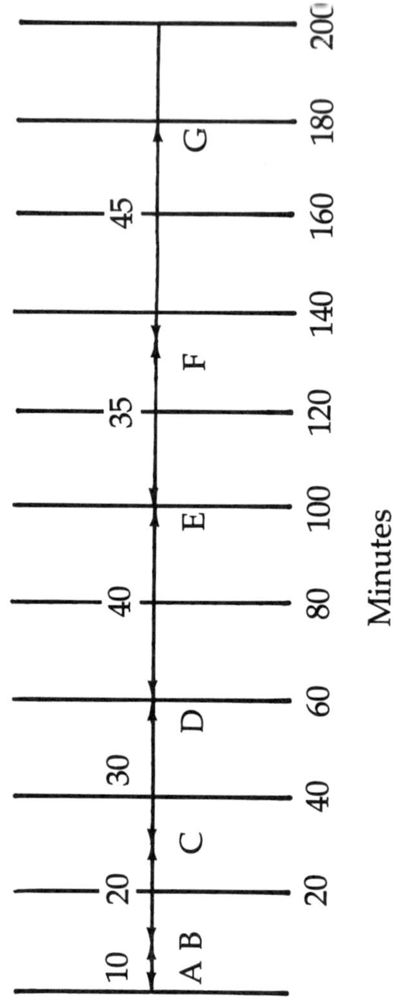

Fig. 10.2. Woodcutting Gantt chart

The thought of missing some of the football game really doesn't sound very appealing. Then he realizes that if his young son, who is presently watching Saturday morning cartoons, were to help, perhaps they could reduce the three-hour chore to something less.

As he analyzes each activity, he notes that the branches are cut off before he cuts the tree into logs, but are not piled for burning until after the rest of the activities are completed. If he were to have his son pile branches while he himself was cutting logs, how much time could he shave from the three-hour chore? He revises the horizontal chart, showing the branches being piled by his son. (See Figure 10.3.) He finds that if his son piles branches while he is cutting logs, he can reduce the elapsed time by 45 minutes. That still puts him minutes into the ball game, which is unsatisfactory.

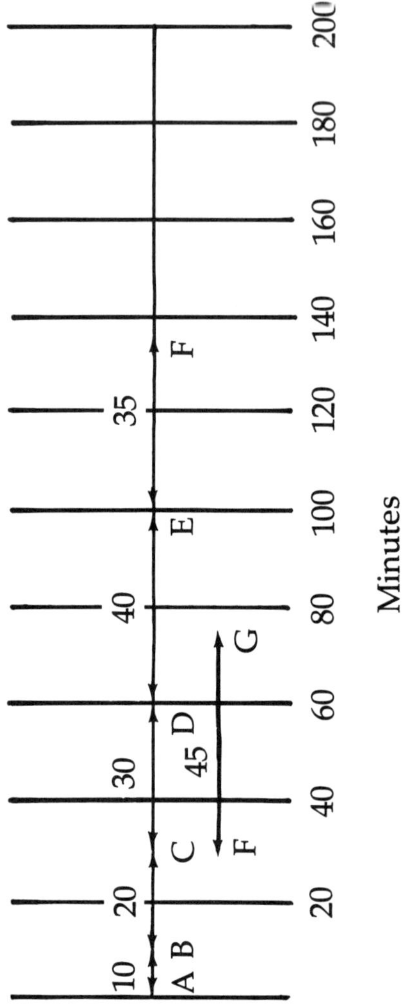

Fig. 10.3 Chart showing time saved when two activities are performed concurrently.

He notes from Figure 10.3 that when his son finishes piling branches, he (the father) has been splitting logs for 15 minutes. Another idea arises. If some wood is already split and ready to load, why not let Junior begin loading the truck as soon as the branches are piled? This would reduce the total elapsed time of the firewood project to 110 minutes. On top of that, Dad can rest for 10 minutes while he waits for Junior to finish loading. (See Figure 10.4.)

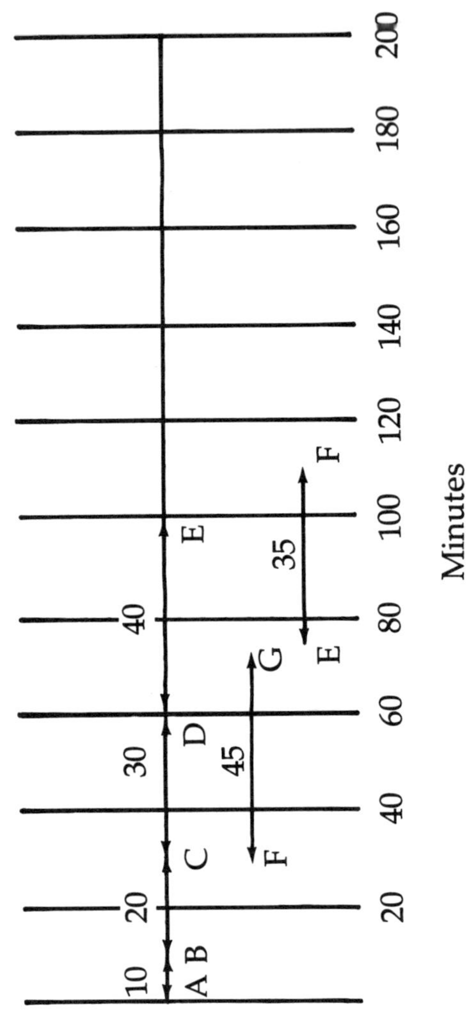

Fig. 10.4. Optimum use of time with two people.

Enthusiastically, our woodcutter grabs his chain saw, ax and son and loads them into the truck. He yells to his wife on the way past that he will be back in two hours to watch the football game. His wife asks if there is any chance that he'll be late because she wants to use the truck. He assures her that the chance of his being gone for more than two hours is less than 5%. As they leave in a cloud of dust, the son ponders the 5% and wonders if he is being dazzled by Dad's brilliance or baffled by his baloney.

The PERT Algorithm

Beginning with the same six basic steps in the preceding example, a PERT network can be depicted graphically as per Figure 10.5. Note that two different paths are available that lead to (F), the loaded truck, i.e., A → B → C → D → F or A → B → C → E → F. All solid lines represent activities that require time, resources or action. The dotted line to node (event) (E) that stems from solid line D → E indicates that activity E → F cannot begin until activity D → F has begun. A dotted line activity is termed a "dummy" activity. It requires no time or resources. Its exclusive purpose is to indicate relationships and sequencing.

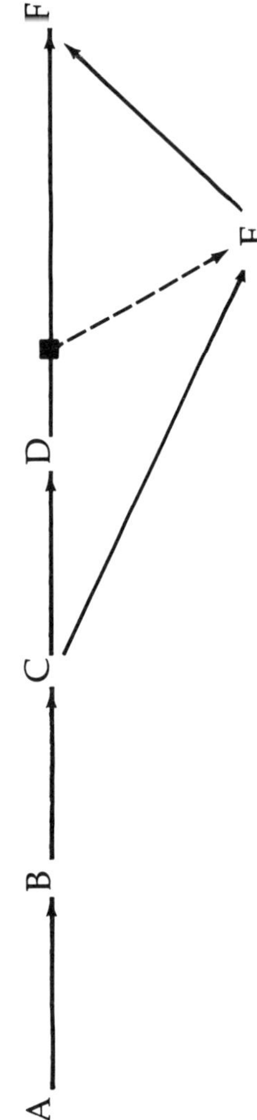

Fig. 10.5. Basic PERT network reflecting activities, events, and sequencing of woodcutting task.

The Beta Distribution

An expected time (ET) for each event is calculated using the beta distribution. Although some users of PERT are satisfied using their one best estimate of time for each activity, many feel more comfortable if they can arrive at expected times statistically. The statistical formula considers three time estimates:

1. Optimistic time = (a)
   If things progress substantially better than expected, the result would be the optimistic time for the activity. This time value has a probability of occurrence of 1% or less.

2. Average time = (m)
   If things progress as expected, the result would be the average time. (This is the one best time estimate for the activity, and was the time used by our woodcutter in the preceding paragraphs.)

3. Pessimistic time = (b)
   If things progressed substantially worse than expected, the result would be the pessimistic time. This time value has a probability of occurrence of 1% or less.

Benefits of Using Beta Distribution

From its inception, the beta distribution has been associated with PERT. Even though no concrete justification is found for the widespread use of this statistical tool, the Beta distribution does have several desirable characteristics:

- There are finite boundaries, (a) and (b), which limit the possible activity times.

- The mean, variance, and standard deviations can be readily calculated.

- The time for each activity has a standard deviation estimated at one-sixth the difference between (a) optimistic time and (b) pessimistic time. Concurrently, it is noted that nearly all of the area under a normal curve lies between

± 3 standard deviations. This is a range of six standard deviations.

- Overall, the beta distribution is flexible and easy to use.

The entries in the ET calculation are composed of the following weighting:

$$a = \text{optimistic time} \quad = 1$$
$$m = \text{realistic time} \quad = 4$$
$$b = \text{pessimistic time} \quad = \underline{1}$$
$$6$$

Therefore, the ET calculation for each activity is equal to:

$$ET = \frac{a + 4m + b}{6}$$

The corresponding variance calculation is:

$$\sigma^2 = \left(\frac{b - a}{6}\right)^2$$

and the standard deviation is:

$$\sigma = \sqrt{\sigma^2} = \frac{b - a}{6}$$

Given the earlier "best guess" times as the realistic time for the firewood project, the wood-cutter estimates the following optimistic and pessimistic times.

Activity	Description	Optimistic	Realistic	Pessimistic
A→B	cut tree	3	10	11
B→C	trim branches	12	20	28
C→D	cut into 24-inch logs	23	30	31
C→E	pile branches for burning	30	45	66
D→F	split logs into firewood size	32	40	54
E→F	load firewood into truck	28	35	36

The ET for activity A→B (cut tree) is nine minutes.

$$ET = \frac{3 + 4(10) + 11}{6} = \frac{54}{6} = 9 \text{ minutes}$$

The variance, or the amount of time an activity may require

more or less than ET, given (a) and (b) for the tree-cutting activity, is 1.78 minutes.

$$\sigma^2 = (\frac{11-3}{6})^2 = (\frac{8}{6})^2 = 1.78 \text{ minutes}$$

The ETs and variances for each activity in the project are listed in Table 10.1. At this point, even though the variance for each individual activity can be calculated, the variance for the total project cannot be determined until the critical path has been identified. Only those variances for those activities on the critical path have an effect on the variance of the total project. The critical path has been previously defined as the path requiring the longest expected time (ΣETs) to cover all the activities on the path.

Table 10.1 ETs and variance for each activity

Activity	*Description*	*ET*	*Variances (0^2)*
A → B	Cut tree	9	1.78*
B → C	Trim branches	20	7.11*
C → D	Cut into 24-inch logs	29	1.78
D → E	Pile branches for burning	46	36.00*
D → F	Split logs into firewood size	41	13.44
E → F	Load firewood into truck	36	1.78*
*Denotes critical path activity.			

The ETs and variances for each activity can now be reflected on the PERT network, as per Figure 10.6. Two paths are available to get from the beginning (A) to the ending (F).

A → B → C → D → F or
A → B → C → E → F

The first path has a combined ET of 99 minutes, while the latter option through E has a combined ET of 109 minutes. By definition, then, path A → B → C → E → F is the critical path of the firewood project.

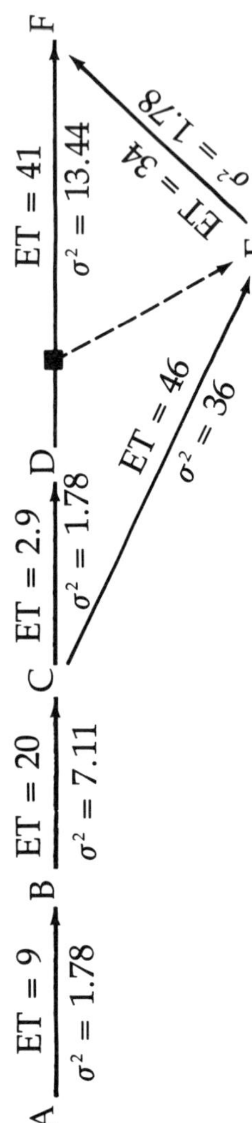

Fig. 10.6. ETs and variances for activities

In order to monitor progress along the paths of the network to provide estimates of the earliest cumulative elapsed time to reach each event or milestone, all that is required is to add the ETs for each activity along the path in question. Such estimates are designated TEs. If an event such as (F) has more than one path approaching it, the elapsed time to reach it is the sum of the ETs for the activities on the path that requires the most time.

For example, the elapsed time to reach event (C) is 29 minutes:

A → B cut tree   ET = 9 minutes
B → C trim branches   ET = <u>20</u> minutes

Therefore, the earliest time to reach

(C), or the TE for (C), is 29 minutes

Inasmuch as (F) can be reached via A → B → C → D or A → B → C → E, the TE for (F) is the longest path measured in ETs, or A → B → C → E → F, which is also, by definition, the network's critical path.

PERT Time Measurements

Similarly, we can determine the latest time that any event can be started and not miss the target completion time. An event's latest start time is designated TL. The procedure for determining an event's TL is just the opposite of that for determining an event's TE. The process starts at the end of the network with the target time and works backward toward the beginning. In the present case, the target time is 120 minutes. The latest time (TL) that any event can be started, then, is the TL for the following event, less the activity time connecting the subject event. When more than one activity approaches a given event, the one with the smallest TL value of the following event is selected.

For example, the latest time event (D) can be started without missing the completion target is 120 - 41, or 79 minutes. Therefore, TL (D) is 79. Similarly, the TL for (E) is 120 - 34 = 86. However, when considering the TL for (C) in which case two activities converge on it (i. e., D → C and E → C), the following event with the smallest TL is selected. In our case, 79<86 so (D) is the event and path chosen. Therefore, the TL for (C) is 79 - 29 — 50.

The TEs and TLs for each event are listed in Table 10.2 and reflected on the PERT network in Figure 10.7.

Table 10.2 Project time measurement and slack

Event	TE	TL	Slack
A	0	21	21 minutes
B	9	30	21 minutes
C	29	50	21 minutes
D	58	79	21 minutes
E	75	86	11 minutes
F	109	120	11 minutes

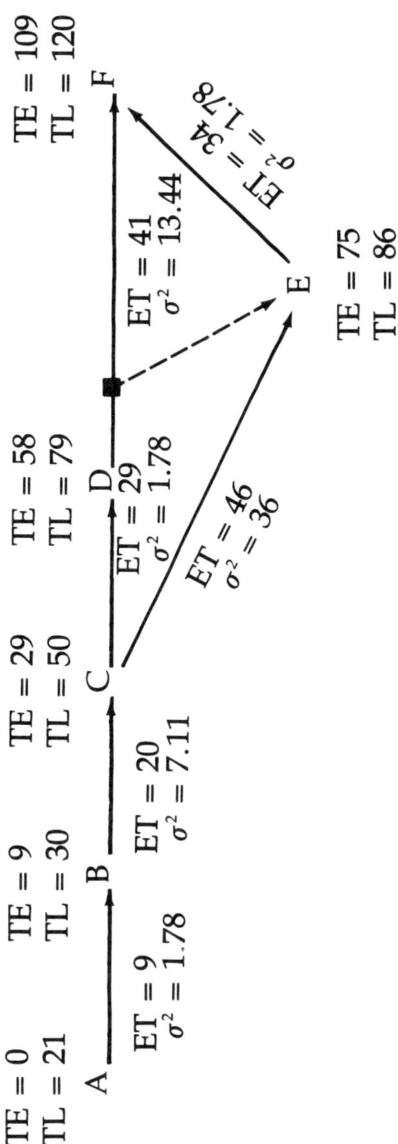

Fig. 10.7. PERT network showing TEs and TLs

Notice also the column in Table 10.2 labeled "Slack". This is an indication of the ability to meet the project-completion target of 120 minutes. If the football game begins at 3:00, the slack of 21 minutes for event (A) signifies that the project could be delayed (not begun) until 1:21 and the total project would still be completed by 3:00.

The TL column indicates the latest clock time that each event could be started and still make the 3:00 target.

Event	TL	Clock-Time Event Could Be Delayed to Without Missing Completion Target
A	21	1:21
B	30	1:30
C	50	1:50
D	79	2:19
E	86	2:26
F	120	3:00

Note from Table 10.2 that the slack decreases by 10 minutes from event (D) as compared with event (E). This is because the activity times of C→E→F are ten minutes longer than C→D→F.

Accordingly, event (D) can begin at 2:19 because D→F requires 41 minutes, which will result in a completion time of 3:00. Event (E), however, can be started at 2:26, because E→F requires just 34 minutes. (2:26 + 34 minutes = 3:00).

Calculating the Probability of Success

The probability of completing the project in the two-hour period allowed, beginning at 1:00 and finishing at 3:00, can be readily determined. The following information is required to calculate the probability includes:

- The difference between the project target time and the project estimated time.

$$TL - TE \text{ at (F)}$$

- The sum of the variances for each activity along the critical path of the network.

- Table of values for the area under the normal curve function.

The formula to calculate the Z value required to determine its respective probability is:

$$Z = \frac{TL - TE}{\Sigma \sigma^2}$$

The variance required for the formula for those activities along the critical path are:

Activity	σ^2 *(from Table 10.1)*
A → B	1.78 minutes
B → C	7.11 minutes
C → E	36.00 minutes
E → F	1.78 minutes
$\Sigma \sigma^2 =$	46.67 minutes

Therefore:

$$Z = \frac{120 - 109}{\sqrt{46.67}} = \frac{11}{6.83} = 1.6105$$

Z at 1.61 = probability of 94.5% of completing project within 120 minutes or at 3:00.

Sequencing Activities and Events

The initial requirement, as in the previous example, is to list the individual activities and events for the acquisition and installation of the proposed automated welding equipment. In actual practice, activities will fall into two categories: Those whose time is controlled by the vendor and those whose time is controlled by the plant. The listing in Table 10.3 reflects each activity in our example and its corresponding event. Also listed is the responsible party: the vendor or the plant. The listing is not intended to be in the required sequence of events. Sequencing is done after all events are identified, and is perhaps the most important element in using PERT. Remember, the monitoring aspects of PERT are used to improve the productivity of the factors of production, primarily the capital committed to the project. PERT allows the gathering of resources at the proper place at the proper time in order to minimize idle resources. In this respect, PERT is very similar to the concept of MRP (material requirements planning). This is especially true when the completion date of a project is the known parameter and the beginning date must be determined. This is the case in many companies when regular annual shutdowns are scheduled, primarily for maintenance work. Heavy manufacturers and utility power plants operate in this manner.

Table 10.3 Sequence of activities

Activity		Event		Controlled By
A-B	Evaluate Bids	A	Begin	Company
		B	Contract let	Company
B-C	Vendor manufactures Electrical controls	C	Controls shipped	Vendor
B-D	Dummy	D	Begin plant site preparation	Company
B-E	Vendor manufactures main hardware	E	Main hardware shipped	Vendor
C-L	Dummy			
E-K	Dummy			
D-F	Plant dismantle existing equipment	F	Existing equipment removed	Company
F-G	Plant excavate for foundations and install steel supports	G	Site prepared	Company
G-H	Plant route Electrical power to site	H	Power to site completed	Company
G-I	Plant provide ventilation for new equipment	I	Ventilation to site completed	Company
G-J	Plant route air lines to site from central compressor facilities	J	Compressed air to site completed	Company
H-L	Dummy			
I-K	Install main hardware	K	Main hardware set in place	Company and Vendor
J-K	Dummy			

K-L	Install electrical control and hookup to power supply	L	Electrical hookup completed	Company and Vendor
L-M	Program equipment for specific tasks	M	Programming complete	Company and Vendor
M-N	De-bug and test	N	Equipment ready for production	Company and Vendor

Responsible Party

When listing the individual activities for a given project, it is important to determine the responsible party. Very often when a firm contracts to purchase new equipment, it will prepare the site so that the vendor (supplier) can just install the equipment on the prepared site. This point is negotiable. Sometimes a general contractor is retained by the vendor if the project is to be a total turnkey project, or sometimes the general contractor is retained by the firm buying the equipment. Also, it is not unusual for the firm buying the equipment to prepare the site and to install the equipment. Whatever the combination, the important thing is to identify all activities relevant to the project and to include them in the PERT model. The model is only as valid and helpful as the identification and sequencing of the individual activities.

Developing a Total Project Network

Now, from Table 10.3, a network can be developed that depicts the total project. In our example, we will consider that the plant that is purchasing the equipment will be responsible for the site preparation work. We will also assume that the vendor will provide technical assistance for installing, programming, and testing the equipment, but that the plant will provide the actual work. This approach is typical, and provides the means for the plant to become familiar with the equipment and its operation.

Common logic is a major portion of the design of the PERT network, although all events are not clearly contingent on the completion of another event. For example, it is logically clear that the contract cannot be issued until the appropriate documents have been prepared. It is also logical that the vendor cannot ship the equipment until it has been manufactured. It is not quite so clear, however, whether the air ducting (event I), for instance, must be completed before, during, or after the routing of the power supply. These decisions must be made very carefully by the plant engineer because the project's total installation time could be affected.

Assuming that the plant engineer has carefully reviewed each activity and event, the relevant network is drafted as per Figure 10.8. It should be noted that the lengths of the arrows depicting activities is not indicative of the time required to complete the activities. The network, as shown, is to be used only for purposes of event sequencing.

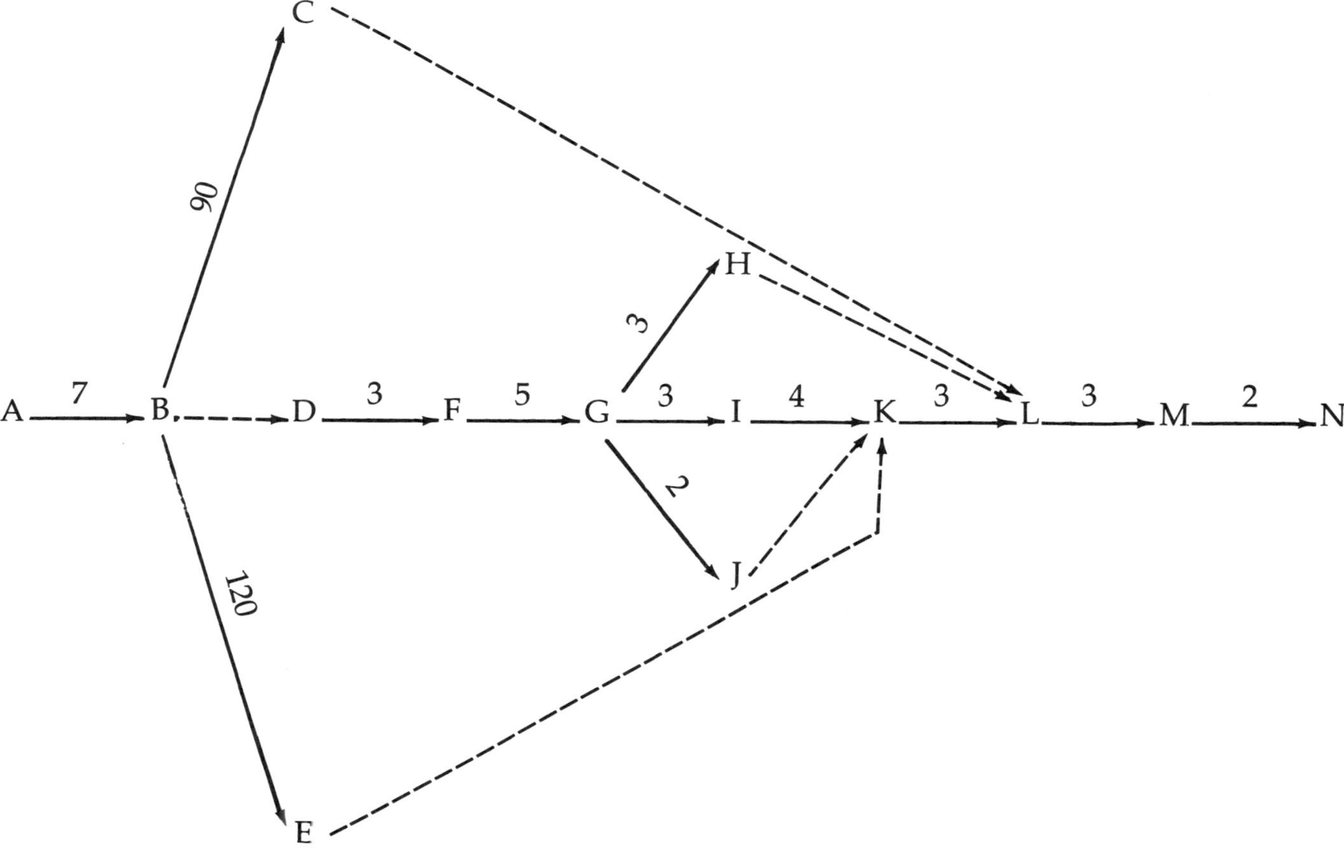

Fig. 10.8. Events sequencing network depicting project of the acquisition and installation of welding equipment.

Inject the Time Factor

Time is a significant factor in the PERT concept and its algorithm. In our example of the welding equipment, the plant will have a regularly scheduled shut-down for three weeks, beginning the first day of August. Therefore, the project will have to be completed and ready for production by the 21st day of August. From this information, we need to calculate when work on the project should begin. To do this, we must determine when the first funds will be required for the project. Remember, funds committed to the project are nonproductive until the project is complete and the equipment and/or facilities are being used in the production process. Typically, a supplier of capital equipment, especially specialized equipment, will require a partial payment upon receipt of the purchase order for the equipment and progress payments during the manufacture of the equipment. By the time the equipment is delivered to the user plant, it is not unusual for a relatively small balance (10%-25%) of the contracted purchase price to be open. Such an arrangement enhances the vendor's productivity of capital and limits the purchaser's capital productivity.

Network Analysis

The same type of analysis would be done with the network in Figure 10.8 as was done with the firewood project:

1. Determine ETs for each activity using Beta distribution.

2. Determine variance for each activity.

3. Determine earliest start times for each event (TEs).

4. Determine critical path.

5. Determine latest start times for each event (TLs).

6. Determine slack for each activity.

7. Calculate probability of completing project on target.

Inasmuch as we've previously examined the mechanics of

the PERT algorithm, it might be more beneficial to examine Figure 10.8 in light of its sequencing peculiarities. Each event is described to illustrate the variations inherent in real-world applications.

Initially, it should be noted that Figure 10.8 and the firewood project have one very significant factor in common: Both have a given completion time expressed as an absolute date/time. The firewood project had to be completed by 3:00 and the present welding equipment installation must be completed by August 21.

Project Sequence

Event A — Beginning of Project. The timing for the beginning of this project will be dictated by the critical-path time and the variances of the activities on the critical path. The beginning time will then be determined relative to the required completion date, August 21. Again, it should be stressed that the most critical aspect of this project is not the elapsed time required to complete, but rather that it be completed by a certain date.

The cost associated with missing the target date includes lost production and missed shipments.

Event B — Contract Let. After the bids have been evaluated, the company "lets" the contract, or issues a purchase order. This is the formal authorization for the vendor(s) to commit their resources to the manufacture of the equipment.

Event C and E — Main Hardware and Electrical Controls Completed and Shipped to Company Issuing Purchase Order. Several vendors may be involved in a major project. For instance, the main hardware may be manufactured by one vendor manufacturer and the electrical controls by another. Each vendor involved will not begin the manufacturing process until it has received formal authorization from the company purchasing the equipment. Or, perhaps one vendor will act as the general contractor and subcontract portions of the total order that it is not capable of fulfilling. Figure 10.8 would indicate that two separate vendors are involved in the welding equipment project.

Event D — Begin Plant Site Preparation. This is a very significant event. Although, sequentially it follows event B, its beginning time is totally independent of (B). This is why the path B → D is reflected as a dotted line, denoting a dummy activity. The start time of event D is determined by the date of the plant shutdown, which has been established as August 1. It should be noted that there is no activity time assigned to B → D.

Event F — Removal of Existing Equipment Completed. This event, similar to D above, is totally independent of the activities of the new-equipment manufacturers. It is totally dependent on the availability of the work area, which, in turn, is signaled by the start of the three-week plant shutdown.

Event G — Site Prepared Relative to Foundations and Structural Steel Supports. This event is dependent on the completion of event F. Implied in Figure 10.8 is the fact that no other preparatory work can be done until the completion of event G.

Events H, I, J — Completion of Electrical Power, Ventilation, and Compressed Air to Job Site. While no other work could occur during the excavation of foundations and the erection of structural steel, multiple events (H), (I), and (J), following event (G), can be done simultaneously.

Also not to be lost sight of is the fact that while the plant is preparing to receive the new equipment, the manufacturer is busy preparing the equipment and electrical controls for shipment.

Event K — Install Main Hardware. This is a rather peculiar event relative to the events that precede it. The activities J → K and E → K are illustrated as dummy activities. Event E could be completed days or weeks before, say, (I), but event K could not be completed until after the completion of (J). The ET of G → J < the ET of G → I, so in all likelihood, event J would be done before (I). But (I) must be completed before (K); therefore, (K) is shown to be dependent on (I) with a dummy relationship between (E) and (J).

Event L — Install Electrical Controls on New Equipment and Hook up to Plant's Power Supply. Events C and H could be done far in advance of (L), but (L) cannot be completed until (K) is completed. Therefore, like event K above, C L and H L are reflected as dummy activities only. They have no activity times; instead their value exclusively indicates a sequencing relationship.

Event M — Programming of New Equipment Complete. This event is straightforward. The activity preceding the event (L → M), cannot begin until all of the equipment is completely installed.

Event N — End of Project Installation, with Equipment Ready for Production. This event is also straightforward. No testing or debugging can precede programming of the equipment. Using the estimated time for each activity as the expected times from Figure 10.8, the system critical path and total slack can be readily determined.

Network Paths	*Time Required (Days)*
A → B → C → L → M → N	102
A → B → E → K → L → M → N	135
A → B → D → F → G → H → L → M → N	23
A → B → D → F → G → I → K → L → M → N	30
A → B → D → F → G → J → K → L → M → N	25

The critical path requires 135 days, which means that the bid evaluation procedure must begin on April 8.

April (30-8)	22 days
May	31 days
June	30 days
July	31 days
August (shutdown ends)	21 days
	135 days

Even though there is a great amount of slack in those paths that traverse the center of the network (those that don't include the vendor's manufacturing time), the plant will be in real trouble if the dismantlement, event D, does not begin on the first day of the shutdown period — August 1. This is the completion requirement date less 20 days. Even if the plant begins dismantlement on August 1, will there be a time problem? The mini-critical path is D → F → G → I → K → L → M → N = 23 days, with 21 days available. At this point, the facilities manager will review the variances for each activity on the mini-critical path to see where he can squeeze out two days from the network.

This example has actually contained a PERT chart within a PERT chart. It is typical of the types of problems that are encountered in industrial and business applications, and requires careful planning and monitoring.

Because PERT applications involve choices among alternatives and minimizations, computer assistance is not only helpful but often necessary in complex projects. Computers not only provide the optional solutions at the onset of a project, but also real-time status reports throughout the project. They also provide revised optional solutions of the algorithm, based on real-time status. Imagine the complexity of a project involving hundreds of vendors or contractors and thousands of activities requiring several years. PERT has certainly provided project and facilities managers with a useful planning and control tool, and the adoption of computer assistance has been an invaluable aid in PERT execution.

Chapter 11
Energy as a
Production Input

Objectives

- *Comprehend the recent history of energy resources.*

- *Appreciate the primary importance of energy in the industrial sector.*

- *Recognize that joint government-industry efforts are needed in the development of synthetic fuels.*

- *Understand how energy is used in production processes and environmental maintenance.*

- *Be able to list the factors used when evaluating different types of energy sources.*

- *Fully understand the two basic components of utility bills.*

- *Recognize that BTU consumption is a function of both production levels and the weather.*

- *Realize that peak power demand is a function of the time of day.*

- *Understand that energy productivity can be increased by improving the efficiency of other production inputs.*

- *Know methods of controlling both natural gas and electricity consumption.*

- *Recognize the advantages and disadvantages of operating a second shift in an attempt to decrease energy costs.*

- *Understand the advantages of using load shedding to control power demand.*

- *Understand that utility companies often implement poor policies that force individual users to conserve the energy resource.*

Contents

Energy Resources

If, under Webster's definition, energy is the capacity to do work, or potential force, it should be noted that energy abounds in inestimable proportions. Energy, in itself, is definitely not in short supply.

With restricted imports of oil from the Middle East in the early 1970s came the cry of "energy shortage." Was this actually a shortage, or was it rather a matter of resource allocation? Perhaps the point is academic, since the result was a reduction in the availability of fuel for American users, both industrial and residential. Furthermore, the reallocation process drove the price of oil to unprecedented heights. It was not unusual to see oil prices skyrocket tenfold in the decade of the 1970s.

This was a real eye-opening experience for the American populace, with a far-reaching impact on the industrial sector. For the first time, "energy" was viewed as a limited resource, owing both to decreased availability and increased price. In fact, price dictated that the amount of energy input to the production process be decreased relative to the units of output. In other words, American business realized the importance and necessity of learning how to manage the productivity of energy.

The primary importance of oil and gas to the industrial sector is not in their direct consumption in the production process, but rather in their use as sources of fuel for:

- Electric-generating facilities, which, in turn, drive the equipment used in the production process.

- Other sectors of the economy that use oil and gas directly (i.e., transportation industry and consumers).

It was interesting to note that back in 1982, the world's strongest cartel, OPEC, was teetering on the verge of collapse. Its 13 member nations could not agree on production quotas or price-level maintenance. Not much has changed. Presently, plentiful supplies of both oil and gas are available. Not only has conservation (productivity improvements) been widely implemented, but the worldwide recession of the early 1980s had markedly reduced the demand for goods and services that require energy as a production input. Wise is the energy user who realizes that the present economic state is a short-term phenomenon.

It is confidently anticipated that the basic law of supply and demand will once again dictate the outcome of OPEC's present dilemma. Those businesses that have learned the principles of managing energy productivity and can maintain those principles, along with treating energy as a scarce resource, will emerge as the winners.

Synthetic Fuels

In an effort to relieve the hold that OPEC nations had on the United States and other Western nations in 1980, President Carter established the U.S. Synthetic Fuels Corporation (SFC). The SFC was given the authority to dole out $88 billion in the subsequent 12 years as loan and price guarantees. As he signed the bill creating the SFC, President Carter said the measure would "launch the decade of the '80s with the greatest outpouring of capital investment, technology, manpower and resources since the space program."

The picture is drastically different now. In fact, the SFC has yet to spend any of its authorized funds for the development of oil and natural-gas substitutes from shale, coal and other underused energy resources. It is a case of extreme myopia on the parts of both private industry and the present administration.

The worldwide recession of the 1980s, along with productivity improvements relative to energy consumption, has created ample supplies of oil and gas. The result is termed "glut psychology." If not properly addressed, it will force the United States into worse problems than before the surplus.

Because of falling oil prices, high interest rates and construction-cost overruns, business has recently tabled several major projects:

- Ashland Oil, Inc., withdrew participation in a $3-billion coal-liquefaction plant in Kentucky.

- Standard Oil Co. of Ohio pulled out of a $2-billion coal-to-gasoline plant in Wyoming.

- Exxon Corp. withdrew from the nation's most ambitious synfuels (oil-shale) venture in Colorado.

- Panhandle Eastern Corp. canceled another multibillion-dollar coal-gasification plant in Wyoming.

Conflicting sides are taken by both congressional leaders and business. An extremely shortsighted view is expressed by Representative Tom Corcoran (R.-Ill.) who states, "There is no economic basis today for synfuels to be marketable in the next decade." An opposing view is offered by Senator Henry Jackson (D.-Wash.): "If industry is not going to go along, then the government should give serious consideration to building those (synthetic fuel) plants itself."

Perhaps the strongest twist is that some business leaders welcome government involvement in the synthetic-fuels issue. Says Ashland Oil Chairman John R. Hall, "The nation faces a dilemma in the development of a synthetic-fuels industry. If we rely on the free market with only limited government assistance, synthetic fuels may not be available in the next crisis, when they will be badly needed."

Here is a case in which both government and business acknowledge a future need of a scarce resource, but both appear unwilling to take the necessary risk. One bright spot was reported in the *Wall Street Journal*, however. Occidental Petroleum Corp. and Tenneco, Inc. said they had applied for a $1.5-billion SFC loan guarantee for an oil-shale project in Colorado. Although both companies acknowledged the "inherent economic and technical risks" in shale-oil projects, they believed "the long-term national need justifies continued development of synthetic fuels."

This voice of confidence — one of only a few — is overpowered by the pessimism accompanying the previously mentioned "glut psychology." This same psychology is also dampening other energy alternatives, such as solar, wind, and biomass.

Energy Use Production

Within each production facility, energy is used for two main purposes:

1. Production processes; and

2. Environmental maintenance (HVAC).

In addition, some industries, such as liquid fertilizer manufacturers, require large amounts of energy in the form of natural gas to manufacture their products. In such cases, the natural gas is actually part of the material input and will not be considered further in this chapter.

In order to determine where energy is consumed in the plant, reference is again directed to the basic resource input matrix (Figure 11.1) that was introduced and explained in Chapter 3. That chart indicates that 29.8% of the total input cost is energy. The chart further indicates that the energy cost charged to the plant services department is the largest single departmental expense in the entire plant. In accordance with the concept of matrix management, a large portion of effort will be directed to this area.

Fig. 11.1. Resource input matrix (amounts in $000)

	Materials	*Labor*	*Machines*	*Energy*	*Totals*
Department					
Cutting	100	70	35	145	350
Stamping	—	40	30	25	95
Fabrication	210	25	5	5	245
Assembly	—	220	30	5	255
Testing	—	140	5	5	150
Plant Service	—	5	50	225	280
Totals	310	500	155	410	1,375

Now that the matrix indicates in which department energy is being consumed, the next step is for the plant's facilities engineer to complete an energy audit, department by department. The audit is basically a comprehensive survey to determine the exact disposition of the energy delivered to each department. Before any productivity improvements can be initiated, it is necessary to know the starting point.

Evaluating Energy Sources

Different energy sources are purchased in different units of measure, and each energy source contains a different amount of "capacity to do work" per its respective unit of measure. To properly evaluate competing energy sources, a common denominator must be found. This is the British thermal unit (Btu), which is defined as the amount of energy required to raise the temperature of one pound of water from 62° F. to 63° F. Several popular energy sources and their energy content, expressed in Btu, are listed in Table 11.1.

Table 11.1 Btu equivalents for common energy sources

Energy Source	Unit of Measure	Btu per Unit of Measure
Natural Gas	cubic foot	1,031
Coal	pound	11,825
Electricity	kilowatt hour	3,413
Gasoline	gallon	124,950

Economics of Energy Substitution

By knowing the current cost of each of the competing energy sources, the trade-off points can be determined to indicate where substitution is feasible. For example, if natural gas were selling for $3.50 per M (1,000 cubic feet), and considering the Btu equivalents from Table 11.1, what would electricity have to be priced at in order to provide an equal amount of energy for the same $3.50?

1,031 cu ft × 1 M. cu ft = 1,031,000 BTU

$$\frac{1,031,000 \text{ Btu}}{3,413 \text{ Btu/kwh}} = 302 \text{ kwh}$$

$3.50 ÷ 302 kwh = $.0116/kwh

In other words, the energy costs are the same when natural gas sells for $3.50/MCF and electricity sells for $.0116/kwh. This is shown graphically in Figure 11.2 where gas, when priced at $3.50/MCF and electricity at $.0116/kwh, will result in a cost per 1,000 Btu of $3.39. Of course, this trade-off can also be determined algebraically. However, changing from one source to another is not the type of decision that can be made and changed easily. The efficiency of each energy source must be considered. Besides, the trade-off might not seem as desirable in a month's time, because energy prices are both dynamic and unstable, to say the least.

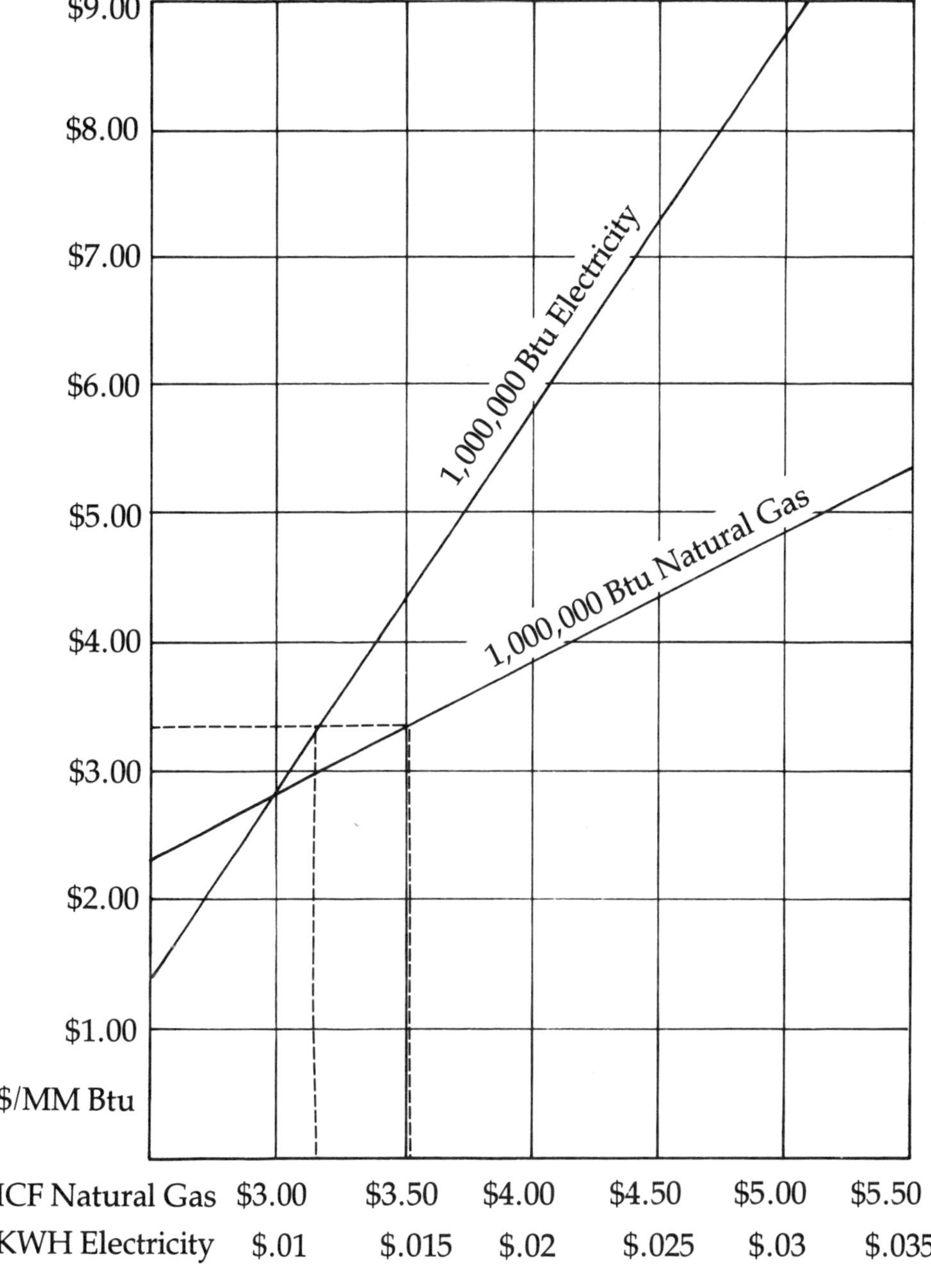

Fig. 11.2. Energy trade-off graph

As previously mentioned, the typical production facility uses energy for two primary purposes: production processes or environmental control. Even though natural gas and electricity are the most widely used energy sources in industry, there are others such as coal, diesel, oil, and steam. The principles of energy management, as presented, can be applied to other sources.

In addition to economic factors, other factors must be evaluated when choosing or considering changing energy sources:

- Availability of source.

- Suitability of a source to do a particular job.

- Capital considerations in adapting a source to a particular application.

Availability of an energy source is equally as important as the availability of raw materials and labor. Long-range availability and dependable delivery must also be considered. This becomes increasingly important if energy is used in the production process, such as heat treating and forging, and is, in fact, a key issue when choosing a site for a new facility. Many energy-intensive facilities are located in close proximity to hydrogenerating plants to ensure an economical and reliable source of electricity.

One energy source may lend itself to do a particular job more effectively than another. For example, kilns and industrial ovens are more effectively fueled with natural gas, whereas lathes and lights are more effectively powered by electricity. Some applications — for example, melting metals — may use either gas or electricity, in which case capital and operating costs become the primary considerations. As a rule of thumb, when an application can use either electricity or gas, it is more costly from the capital standpoint to install electrical facilities. If the required capital is not a major factor, then the operating cost of each alternate source becomes the primary decision factor.

The Basic Power Bill

In order to manage the energy resource, it is first necessary to understand what utility bills cover. Consider the electric bill, which is broken down into two basic components:

1. Demand charge (reserved capacity of the power company) and

2. Energy charge (actual product/service used).

The demand charge is levied by the power company to cover the amount of generating capacity it needs to reserve for each customer at any time during the billing period, which is usually a month. Inasmuch as it is a cost relative to the utilization of total generating capacity, it is fixed. The fixed-cost pool of a utility company includes its interest expense on debt financing for generating facilities. So, when a customer requires, say, 2% of a power plant's capacity to run his facility, he pays a proportionate amount of the cost of financing the power company's capacity.

For example, consider a power plant that has a generating capacity of 500 MW at any given point in time. (MW = megawatt = 1 million watts.) The fixed cost per month, or normal billing period, is $2.5 million. Therefore, each megawatt of power required by the customers generates $5,000 of revenue for the utility company before any product/service is delivered. Of particular dismay to the customer is the fact that the normal period to measure its peak power requirements for any month is relatively very small — 15 or 30 minutes. In other words, if a customer normally requires, say, 5 MW of power to run his facility, but at some time during the month he experienced a surge in the operation that required 7 MW for a half-hour period, he would receive a demand charge for the month in the amount of $35,000. (7 MW X $5,000.) Incrementally, that is a costly 30-minute period.

The advantages to the customer of being able to minimize his peak power requirements during the month becomes readily apparent. On the other hand, the utility company also has (or should have) an incentive to encourage customers to utilize generating capacity during times of the day when power requirements are relatively light — say, 1 A.M.

Consider that a 500 MW power plant operates and sells power during the popular 7 A.M. to 3 P.M. regular operating shift. At this rate of power generation, it would be providing energy, measured in megawatt hours, in the amount of 4,000 MWH during that eight-hour shift. If new customers moved into the area, bringing an additional daily energy requirement of 4,000 MWH, the power company has several options. It can:

1. Buy excess energy from another power company and use existing transmission lines to distribute added requirements to new customers. This option places the power company in the role of being an "energy broker," which is not unusual these days.

2. Build additional generating capacity to meet new customer requirements. This option, all too often chosen, results in two power plants, each operating at a meager 33% of capacity but requiring twice the original fixed cost. How futile this option is, especially if the power plant is hydroelectric and the fuel to run the turbine generators is already in place with zero incremental cost.

3. Encourage either new or existing customers to operate their facilities between 3 P.M. and 7 A.M. by offering a financial incentive called "off-shift" rates. This option requires no additional capital and utilizes existing capacity.

The second major component of an electricity bill is the energy charge. This is simply the level of power required, multiplied by the length of time it is required, measured in KWH. (Electrical energy is measured in MWH, or, more commonly, kwh. That is, 500 MW, or 500,000 kw, required for a two-hour time period, results in energy consumption of 1,000,000 kwh.)

Most power companies also have a third component of the electric bill, called "power cost adjustment." This is normally used to:

- Cover the incremental cost incurred to purchase and resell energy that they cannot themselves generate for any reason, usually owing to the lack of short-run capacity.

- Cover any increases in the cost of fuel that they buy to run the generators in the power plant.

Inasmuch as the power cost adjustment is not manageable by the customer, we will not go into it here.

Energy Consumption in the Plant

Energy consumption can be related to some form of activity. Energy is consumed when a foundry melts a ton of steel, when a machine center operates a drill press, when a heat unit is running, or when an accounting clerk switches the lights or operates a calculator.

Inasmuch as productivity is the relationship between inputs and outputs, the objective is to equate Btus consumed with some unit of output. Consider a facility that manufactures wagons. The initial objective is to determine how many units of energy input are consumed in each wagon produced and shipped. After the Btus per wagon is known, the energy management program can initiate specific actions to reduce the energy content per wagon or increase wagon output with the same level of energy input.

A good starting point in determining energy consumption patterns is to examine previous utility bills relative to production levels. Table 11.2 represents such data for a prior year.

The first thought might be to perform a simple least-squares problem, choosing wagon production as the independent variable and total Btu consumption as the dependent variable. One would suspect that this procedure would provide the behavioral pattern of energy consumption, based on production levels. Once the behavioral pattern relative to production is known, future energy requirements can be estimated, based on forecasted wagon production.

However, on examining the data in Table 11.2, it is noted that total BTU consumption is not directly related to wagon production. It is extremely important not to assume that a relationship exists between given inputs and outputs. The relationship must be tested for validity.

Further examination of Table 11.2 indicates that natural gas consumption is greatest in the winter months and least in the summer. This prompts the analyst to plot an additional piece of data called "heating degree days," as per Table 11.3. A heating degree day is defined as the temperature variance on a given day as compared with a predetermined norm or benchmark.

Table 11.3 Heating-degree days

Month	*Heating Degree Days*
January	950
February	895
March	725
April	690
May	340
June	25
July	2
August	1
September	13
October	20
November	310
December	710

Table 11.2 Energy-consumption statistics

Month	Wagons Produced	Natural Gas (MCF)	Electricity (kwh x 10^3)	Gas Btu x 10^9 (mcf x 1.031 x 10^6)	Electricity Btu x 10^9 (kwh x 3.413 x 10^6)	Total Btu x 10^6
January	650	350	139	360.85	474.41	835.26
February	720	345	147	355.70	501.71	857.41
March	705	275	146	283.53	498.30	781.83
April	830	260	159	268.06	542.67	810.73
May	980	150	163	154.65	556.86	666.03
June	1,050	70	174	72.17	593.86	710.97
July	975	—	161	—	549.49	549.49
August	950	—	162	—	552.91	552.91
September	1,250	40	180	41.24	614.34	655.58
October	900	75	158	77.33	539.25	616.58
November	875	190	161	195.89	549.49	745.38
December	640	260	141	268.06	481.23	749.29

Example

Benchmark = 65° F
Actual high temperature for a given day   51°
Actual low temperature for same day   29°
Average temperature for the day   40°

$$\frac{(51 + 29)}{2}$$

  65 benchmark
–40 actual average
  25 degree days calculated for particular day

The concept is that any time the temperature is below 65°, heating will be required and, consequently, energy will be consumed. More energy is consumed during the colder months to heat the facilities, with little or no relation to production levels.

Consider, for example, a manufacturing facility that has a 500,000-square-foot area and a 40-foot roof line. This facility would contain 20 million cu ft. of air. Some types of industries are required to recirculate the air several times, perhaps as often as 10 times per hour, in order to maintain acceptable air quality for the employees. This is accomplished with roof exhaust fans and dust-collection systems. Dust-collection systems, as their name implies, intake polluted air, clean it, and either exhaust it to the atmosphere, or, if sufficiently clean, recirculate it back into the plant.

When air is exhausted from the plant, either by roof exhaust units or dust collectors, a vacuum is created in the plant that necessitates bringing clean air in balance the pressure. In colder months, this air must also be heated as it is brought in and distributed to the work areas. It is not unusual for a medium-size facility to spend in excess of $100,000 per month during the winter just to heat and distribute "makeup" air to replace the polluted air that has been exhausted from the plant.

The data in Tables 11.2 and 11.3 indicate that total energy consumption is a function of both production levels and the weather. A formula representing total consumption, using multiple regression, will be developed shortly, but first the behavioral pattern for natural gas and electricity should be determined separately. This is important because energy management programs will be specifically tailored to gas and electricity.

Linear Regression Analysis

Consider in Figure 11.3 the relationship between electrical consumption and wagons produced. This information was taken from Table 11.2. By developing a single variable regression line, representing this relationship, in the form of $y = a + bx$, it is determined that $a = 98.64$ and $b = .0672$.

Remembering that kwh in Figure 11.3 are represented in thousands to facilitate the calculations, the equation indicates that total electrical consumption is composed of two factors:

1. 67.2 kwh are required for each wagon produced; and

2. 98,640 kwh are required per month, regardless of production levels.

Given that the annual production of wagons is 10,525, as per Table 11.4, the annual kwh requirements are summarized in their fixed and variable components.

Variable 67.2 x 10,525 =   707,280 kwh
Fixed   98,640 x 12   = <u>1,183,680</u> kwh
                          1,890,960 kwh

Table 11.4 Electrical consumption vs. wagons produced

Month	X Wagons Produced	Y Electricity (kwh x 10^3)	X^2	X
January	650	139	422,500	90,350
February	720	147	518,400	105,840
March	705	146	497,025	102,930
April	830	159	688,900	131,970
May	980	163	960,400	159,740
June	1,050	174	1,102,500	182,700
July	975	161	950,625	156,975
August	950	162	902,500	153,900
September	1,250	180	1,562,500	225,000
October	900	158	810,000	142,200
November	875	161	725,625	140,875
December	640	141	409,600	90,240
Total	10,525	1,891	9,590,575	1,682,720

$\overline{X} = 877.08 \quad \overline{Y} = 157.58$

Determine $Y = a + bx$

Where
a = intercept (fixed kwh @ zero production)
b = slope (kwh per wagon)
Y = total kwh

$$b = \frac{n\,(\Sigma X \bullet Y) - (\Sigma X)\,(\Sigma Y)}{n\,(\Sigma X^2) - (\Sigma X)^2}$$

$$a = \overline{Y} - (b)\,(\overline{X})$$

$$b = \frac{12\,(1{,}682{,}720) - (10{,}525)\,(1{,}891)}{12\,(9{,}590{,}575) - (10{,}525)^2}$$

$= .0672\text{kwh} \times 10^3 = 67.2\ \text{kwh/wagon produced}$

$a = 157.58 - (.0672)\,(877.08)$

$= 98.64\text{kwh} \times 10^3 = 98{,}640\ \text{kwh @ zero production}$

$Y = 98{,}640 + 67.2\ \text{(wagons produced)}$

Subsequent improvements in electrical consumption patterns will result in the actual consumption for a given production level being less than the consumption estimated by the formula. This is, in fact, the appropriate method to measure the effects of improvements and energy management actions relative to electrical consumption.

Similarly, as the natural-gas consumption is related to heating degree days (Table 11.5), the resultant regression equation indicates that each heating degree day requires 333.5 cu ft of gas, while 37,830 cu ft are required per month, regardless of the weather. A positive intercept with this type of problem will normally indicate that, as in this case, gas is consumed for some purpose other than heating.

Table 11.5 Natural-gas consumption vs. heating degree days

Month	Heating Degree Days X	Gas Consumption (MCF) Y
January	950	350
February	895	345
March	725	275
April	690	260
May	340	150
June	25	70
July	2	—
August	1	—
September	13	40
October	20	75
November	310	190
December	710	260
Total	4,681	2,015

a = 37.83
b = .335MCF/heating degree day

$$Y = 37,830 + 333.5 \text{ (heating degree day)}$$

The variable and fixed portions of the annual gas requirements, as reflected above, are as follows:

Variable	333.5 x 4,681	= 1,561,113
Fixed	37,830 x 12	= 453,960
		2,015,073 cu ft

As in the case of electrical consumption, conservation efforts and/or productivity improvements relative to the natural-gas

input will result in actual gas consumption being less than estimated with the formula, which is based on historical data before
improvements.

It should be noted that the dependent variables in both
examples are expressed in units of measure instead of in financial terms. This method ensures that the productivity of energy
improvements will not be diluted with inflationary factors.

It has been illustrated that total energy consumption
expressed in Btu, is a function of both production levels and the
weather. Therefore, as shown below, the behavioral pattern of
total consumption is represented by the linear equation:

$$X_{1c} = 355.16 + (.35)X_2 + (.25)X_3$$

and future energy requirements can be estimated using this formula. The two independent variables chosen provide a
correlation of 95.1%. In other words, 95.1% of the movement of
Btu consumption is attributable to production levels and temperature. Plants use other independent variables, such as number of
working days per month, which may produce a higher correlation than those obtained with two variables.

Three variables are involved in this problem:

1. X_1 is a dependent variable, total BTUs.

2. X_2 is a independent variable, wagons produced.

3. X_3 is a independent variable, heating degree day.

The first step of the equation is to solve for integer values for
the above three variables that will satisfy the linear regression
line. This is done systematically by multiplying the basic regression equation by X_2. The regression equation is again expanded
by multiplying it by X_3. The three equations as shown below are
then solved simultaneously by the conventional matrix method.

Beginning regression equation with three variables:

$$\Sigma X_1 = na + b_2\Sigma X_2 + b_3\Sigma X_3$$

$\quad$ where n = total points in the data set

Multiplying this equation by X_2 produces:

$$\Sigma X_1 X_2 = a\Sigma X_2 + b_2\Sigma X^2_2 + b_3 \Sigma(X_2 X_3)$$

Multiplying the regression equation by X_3 produces:

$$\Sigma X_1 X_3 = a\Sigma X_3 + b_2\Sigma X_2 X_3 + b_3 (\Sigma X^2_3)$$

In practice, single variable regression formulas are used to control and monitor gas and electricity separately. However, the overall measure of energy productivity will be based on total energy content per wagon produced.

The Demand Charge

After energy consumption patterns are determined, attention should be focused on the demand portion of the electric bill. Utility bills for the previous year reveal demand requirements, as is shown in Table 11.6. It should be remembered that the demand bill for any month is based on the highest level of power required at any time during that month.

Table 11.6 Demand requirements by month

Month	*Demand*
January	1,720
February	1,690
March	1,475
April	1,710
May	1,575
June	1,625
July	1,580
August	1,565
September	1,610
October	1,695
November	1,375
December	1,495

Power demand, measured in kilowatts, versus electrical energy, measured in kilowatt hours, can be compared to an ordinary garden hose. Demand in kilowatts is a rate of power delivered at a given moment. Energy consumption is the rate of power delivered continuously over a given period of time.

Total kwh, say 5,000, can be obtained in two basic ways:

1. A rate of 500 kw for a 10-hour period.

2. A rate of 250 kw for a 20-hour period.

Of course, any feasible combination of time and power levels will accomplish the same thing. The objective is to get the required amount of energy (kwh) with the lowest level of power feasible for the particular operation.

The same principle applies to the garden hose. If 500 gallons of water are required, we can turn the spigot up to deliver 100 gallons per minute (GPM) and get the 500 gallons in five minutes or, if we have the time, we can turn the spigot way down to 50 GPM and let it run for 10 minutes. If the 100 GPM option is chosen, much more is demanded of the water pump system than if the 50 GPM option were chosen.

The same concept applies to the power generating company. If a particular user/facility chooses (1) above, it is, in essence, tying up twice the generating capacity as (2). The major point is that the total monthly demand charge is based on the peak requirement, even if it is reached only one time during the month.

It is not unusual for a plant's electric bill to contain as much in demand charges as energy consumption charges. This is an important point when it is remembered that only the kilowatt hours consumed is the energy input to the plant that can accomplish some kind of "work." This concept is expanded on later when different types of specific actions that will reduce the total electric bill are discussed.

We would not necessarily expect to find a positive relationship between kilowatts of demand and units of production and/or heating degree days. The appropriate method of determining demand patterns is to plot kilowatt demand levels against time, as shown in Figure 11.3 to 11.6. Several distinct observations are noted from these Figures:

- No specific pattern is noted when monthly peaks are plotted (11.3).

- Also, no specific pattern is noted when weekly peaks are plotted (11.4).

- There is a distinct pattern when peaks are plotted daily for a week. The peaks occur on regularly scheduled operating days, and demand falls off drastically on nonoperating days (11.5).

- There is also a distinct pattern when demand peaks are plotted against specific times of normal work days (11.6).

Thus far, then, behavior patterns have been determined for natural gas consumption, electric energy (kwh) consumption, and power demand measured in kilowatts. Natural gas usage is a function of heating degree days, electric energy usage is a function of units of wagons produced and peak power requirements are predominantly a function of the time of day.

It should be noted that these patterns apply to the particular example and the data given in Table 11.2. The data are typical, but are not meant to be all-inclusive. The point is that before energy management programs can be developed and implemented, the factors affecting the movement of energy sources (i.e., their behavioral patterns) must be identified.

Managing Energy Consumption

Managing utility bills implies that a firm or plant has the ability to, at least partially, determine what its utility bills should be. Firms are annually saving hundreds of thousands of dollars, even millions in some cases, by managing the energy-input resource.

A firm that uses energy in its production process, such as a steel mill or a chemical plant, may find that energy comprises 15% or more of its total cost of doing business. Any process that

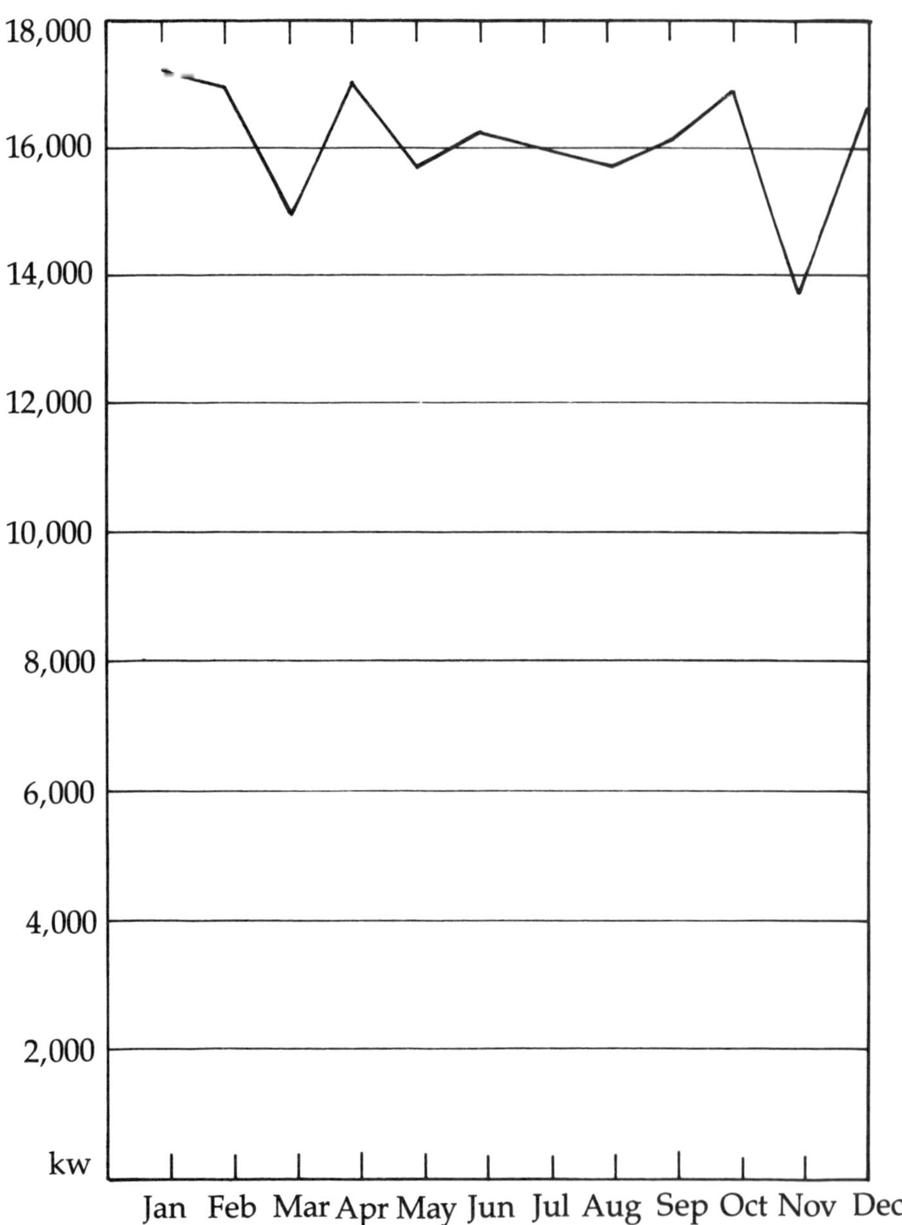

Fig. 11.3. Demand monthly for year

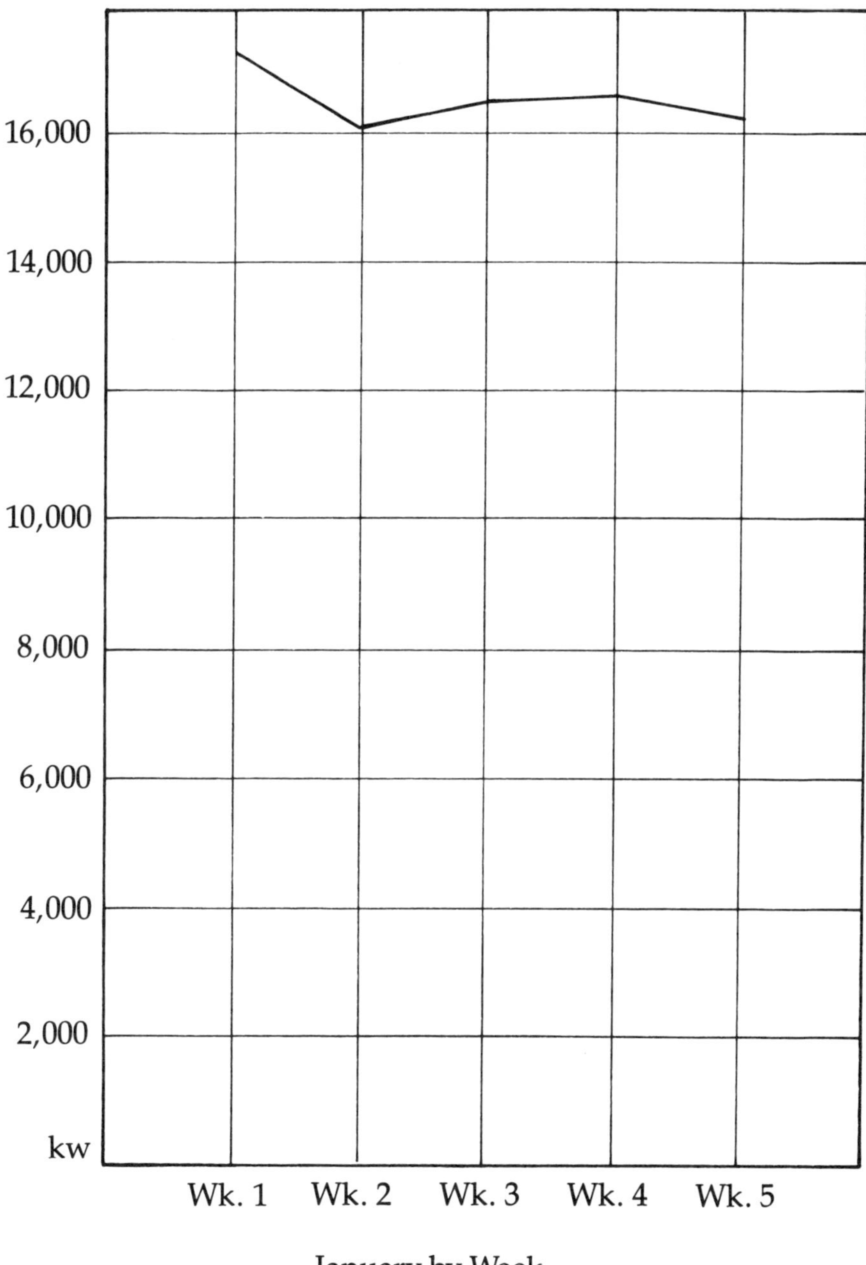

Fig. 11.4. Demand weekly for month

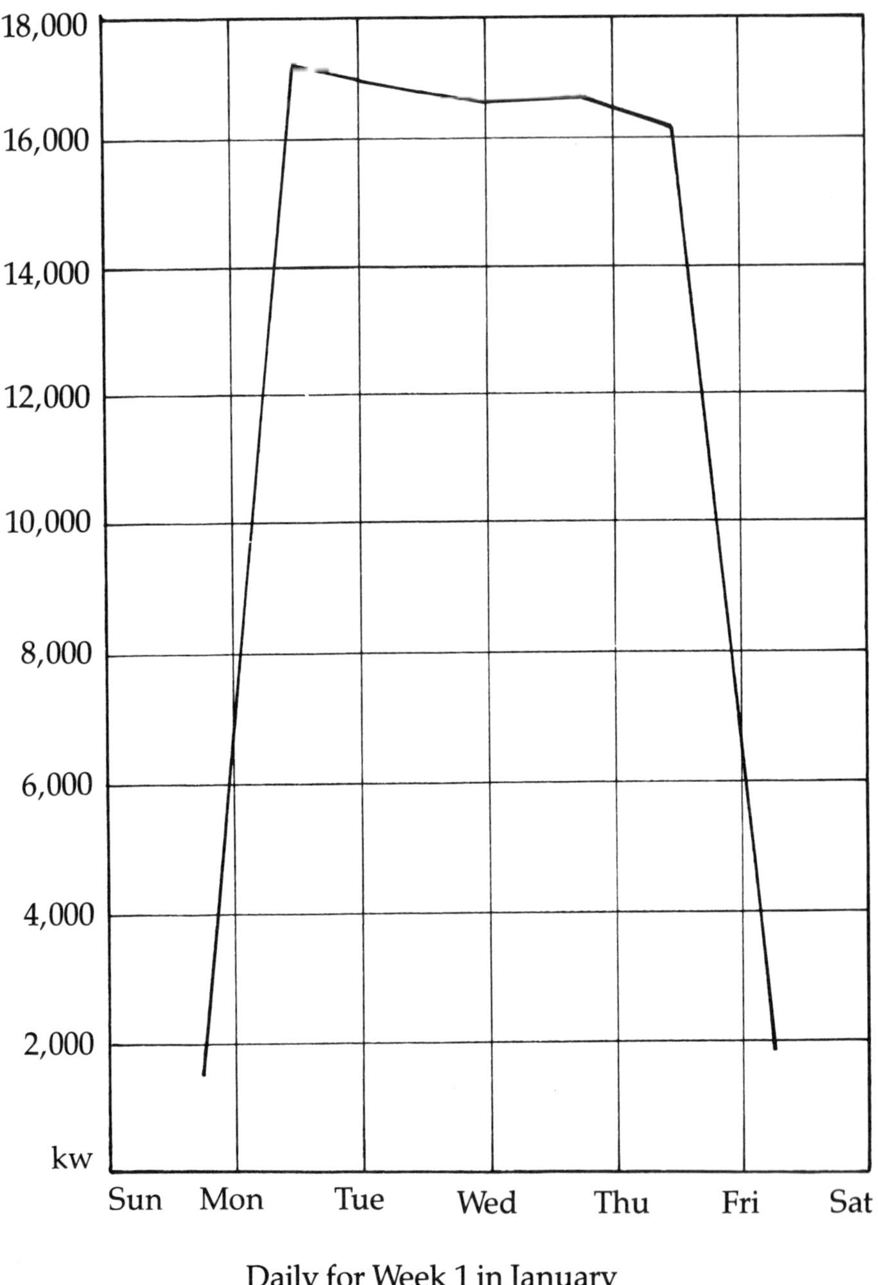

Daily for Week 1 in January

Fig. 11.5. Demand daily for week

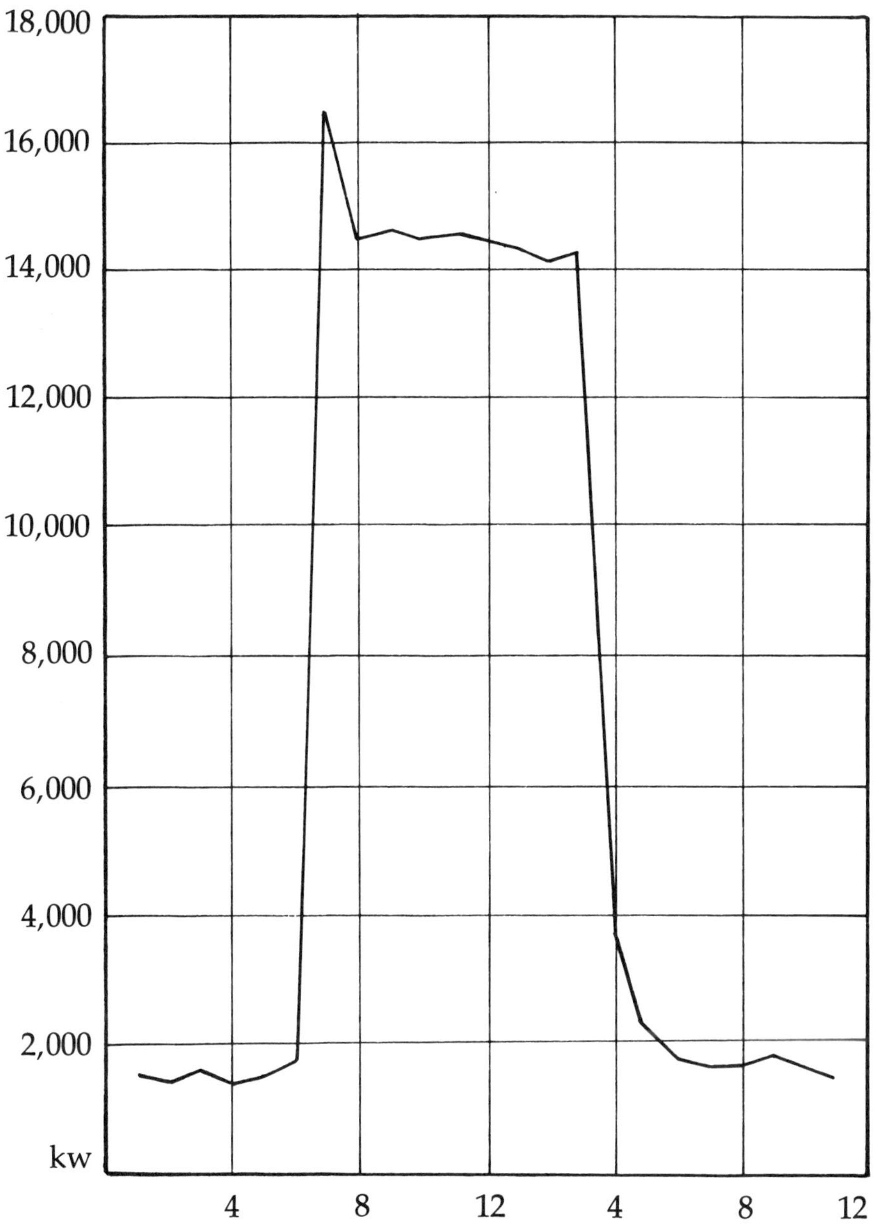

Fig. 11.6. Demand hourly for day

changes the natural state of materials, such as liquefying steel, will be a large user of energy. A typical assembly-type operation, on the other hand, may use energy primarily for lighting and HVAC, and its energy cost may not be as high a proportion of the total cost.

Productivity of the energy input can be improved in numerous ways. Normally, the most significant factor — in any case, the first step to be considered in improving energy productivity — is to improve the productivity of the other inputs. The productivity of any input is automatically improved when rejected material (scrap) is reduced.

Keeping in mind that the objective of improving energy productivity is to decrease the amount of energy in each unit of output, consider the following, based on the previously determined kwh consumption pattern from Table 11.4.

Total kwh = 98,640/month + 67.2 (wagons produced)

In January of the data set, wagon production was reported to be 650 units. The plant was experiencing a 15% reject rate but improved processes reduced the reject rate to 10%. How does this change affect the energy content per wagon shipped?

	Old Way	*New Way*
Reject rate	15%	10%
Required wagons	650	650
Wagons started in production to meet requirements	$\frac{650}{.85} = 765$	$\frac{650}{.90} = 722$
kwh required at 67.2/unit	51,408	48,518
kwh per unit shipped	79.1	74.6

There would also be some savings associated with the fixed kwh consumption of 98,640 because the electric-powered equipment and lights would not have to operate as long in order to produce the required 650 wagons. Looking at it another way, more good wagons could be produced with the same 98,640 kwh because with the new 10% reject rate, the original 765 wagons entering production would result in 688 good wagons.

The variable energy savings is 4.5 kwh per wagon, or a reduction of 5.7% per wagon shipped.

In this example, the productivity of energy was improved by improving the productivity of other inputs. Process improvements may involve labor, materials, and machines. Energy programs should not be expected to cover or compensate for sub-optimal management in other areas of plant operations. Such energy programs should follow basic improvements such as the scrap reduction cited in this example.

Controlling Natural-Gas Consumption

When natural gas consumption is a function of degree days, there are several options for improving gas pains. If the plant engineer has trouble controlling the effects of gas he may have to resort to other means to reduce gas.

As previously mentioned, gas-fired air makeup units, which replace polluted air, consume a great deal of gas in heating and distributing the replacement air during cold weather. Care should be exercised to ensure that the gas-fired burners are properly set. It is also important that proper filters are used and appropriately cleaned. These basic steps should be addressed before implementing any control program.

A basic truth that definitely finds application in energy management is that idle capacity is expensive. Idle capacity, especially if it is in a department or specific work centers within the general facility, may still require that energy be consumed to maintain temperature. Five basic premises relative to environmental controls can be summarized as follows:

It is poor practice to:

1. Heat and/or cool areas that are not in operation.

2. Exhaust air from nonpolluted areas.

3. Exhaust and makeup air more frequently than necessary.

4. Operate exhausters and makeup air units on off-shifts or weekends.

5. Maintain air temperature that is higher than necessary in cold weather or lower than necessary in warmer weather.

The most common devices that are used to control these items are minicomputers or programmable controllers. Such devices can be programmed for thermostat control and/or automatic on/off at predetermined times. This type of equipment commonly has an ROI, attributable to energy savings, of less than one year. The basic premise of these control devices is to ensure that environmental equipment is not operating when and where it is not necessary.

Electrical Energy Control

Much of the previous discussion concerning conservation is also applicable to electrical consumption, inasmuch as air exhausters are powered by electrical motors and, even though makeup air units may be gas-fired, the blowers for distribution will be electrically powered.

Defective bearings in motors and shorts in in-plant electrical distribution lines may use excess electrical power. This is an excellent application for portable infrared scanning devices that can detect areas of heat buildup caused by electrical overloads. The user simply aims at the suspect area and visually notes areas of uneven temperatures. These infrared scanners are not only useful for detecting excessive energy consumption, but for preventive-maintenance inspection and also for safety inspections.

In recent years, many firms have improved their lighting systems. Older-style, mercury vapor lights are being replaced in large numbers by high-pressure sodium lights that typically provide equivalent footcandles as the mercury vapor lights with one-half the wattage requirements. A typical installation involves replacing the older-style units with one-half the number of newer units. The result is equal lighting capacity, measured in footcandles, with one-half the energy requirements and one-half the number of lights to maintain. The typical return of capital is one-and-a-half years. A facility of 500,000 square feet can reasonably expect annual savings of $150,000 to $200,000 with this new type of lighting system. Lights are also an excellent candidate for computer-controlled on/off settings.

Electrical Demand Control. Electrical demand has been previously defined as the level of power required at a given point in time, measured in kilowatts. One may initially suppose that demand is not controllable, inasmuch that if all the motors, lights, air compressors, and other electrical devices within a facility were turned on simultaneously, a certain amount of power would be required. That is true, but remember that energy, or the capacity to do work, is measured by kilowatt hours, or a sustained level of power input, and that is what is required to maintain a production process or facility. Keep in mind the example of the garden hose. The amount of water required to do a job may be 1,000 gallons. That requirement may be met in a number of ways — for example, using a 1,000 GPM pump or a 10 GPM pump. The ability to do work is the cumulative kilowatts (unit of power) delivered over time. That being the case, one would suppose that the best method to control electrical demand is to not turn on all of the electrical devices in a facility at the same time. That is exactly the principle of demand controls. It sounds simple, doesn't it? The basic requirement is good planning and scheduling, plus recognizing the importance of capacity utilization.

Two basic options are available desiring to control power demand in a plant:

1. Operate some electrical equipment on staggered time schedules or off-shift.

2. Improve utilization in the short run, i.e., during a regular operating shift.

Any other strategies are basically offshoots of these two concepts.

Off-Shift Operation

Referring back to Figures 11.3 to 11.6, it was noted that power demand exhibited a behavioral pattern relative to the time of day. At 7 A.M. on regular operating days, the demand was at its highest point, not only for particular days but for the entire month. Therefore, the first priority is to relieve the load that occurs at the beginning of the work shift when all the equipment is turned on simultaneously. The problem is compounded by the fact that electrical motors, lights, etc., require more power to start than to maintain operation.

Typically, a plant will stagger the shift start-up by starting some of the equipment, say air-moving equipment, at 6:30 A.M. instead of 7 A.M. so that the start-up load is spread out and the total demand will not occur at the same time. The primary fact to keep in mind is that the plant's monthly demand charge will be based on the highest peak power requirement, even though it occurs only at 7 A.M. and lasts for a very short time. Any relief from the 7 o'clock peak will produce a reduction in the power bill and an automatic improvement in the productivity of energy.

After the initial actions are taken to relieve the start-up load as much as feasible, the option of operating on two shifts versus a single shift may be considered. Simply stated, the same level of production, if spread equally over two shifts instead of one, will require the same amount of energy in kilowatt hours to do the "work," while requiring just one-half the power load or demand measured in kilowatts at any given time. Again using the garden-hose example, the water supply will be turned down to half its previous flow rate but it will be run twice as long.

When a two-shift operation is considered, instead of one shift, with equal production, some incremental costs are likely to be incurred. For example:

- Some of the service departments may need to be duplicated.

- Some of the air-moving equipment may need to be operated on two shifts instead of one.

- The employees on the second shift will most likely be paid a shift premium.

- Supervision may need to be added.

These costs should be evaluated in view of the decreased peak power required by running only a portion of the equipment at the same time. The trade-off opportunity concept can be represented graphically as in Figure 11.7. Simply stated, if the reduction in power demand cost (BC) is greater than the incremental shift cost (B'C'), the trade-off by operating a two-shift operation is favorable.

If, in fact, operating two shifts reduces by one-half the amount of power required at any given time, it stands to reason that the supplying electric-utility company will have that amount of capacity to provide to some other electric user. This is an important concept. Inasmuch as the utility company has constructively increased its generating capacity with no capital additions, it will, in many cases, offer reduced energy rates for the generating capacity used during the time of the day that is not generally popular with the majority of electric users. This is called "off-shift" or "time-of-day" rates. This will be discussed further in the closing sections of this chapter.

Using Load Shedding to Conserve Energy

If staggered or two-shift operations are not feasible for any reason, or if additional power utilization is desired per shift, there is still the opportunity for demand controls by load shed-

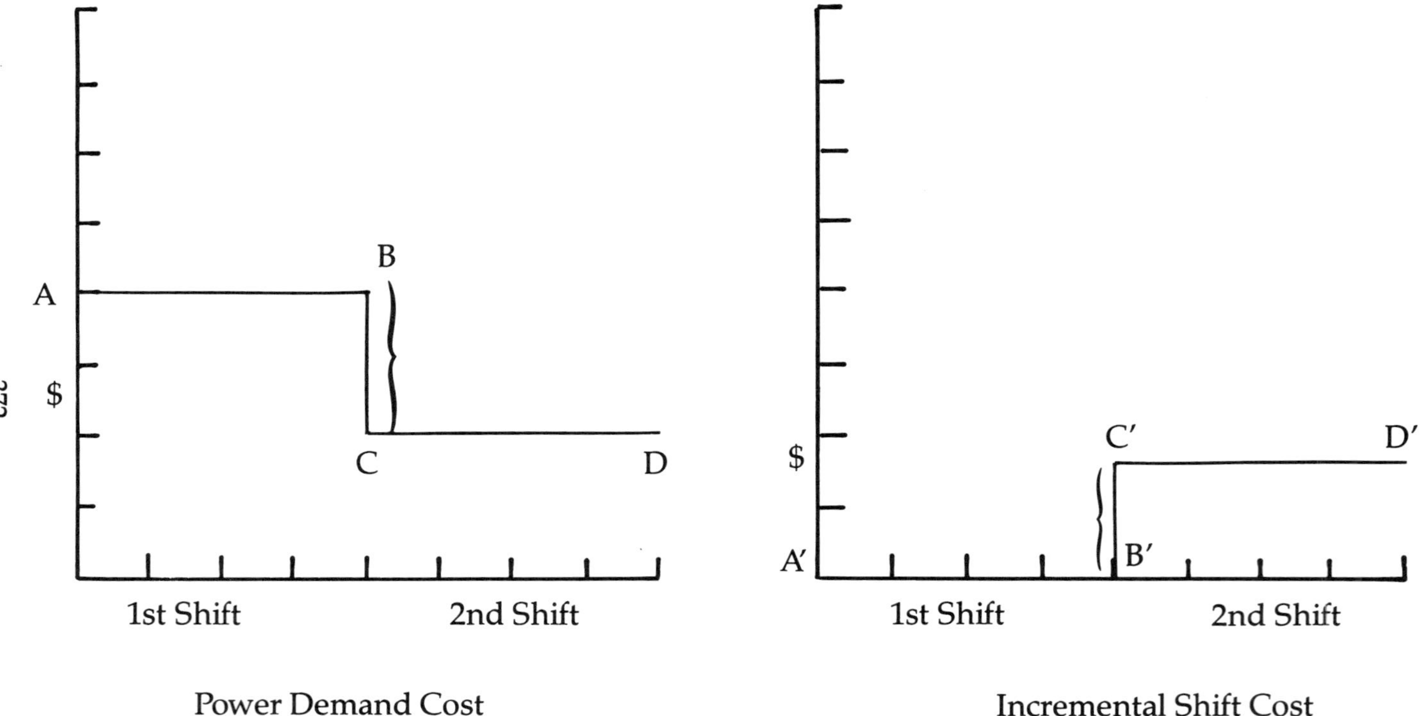

Fig. 11.7. Demand Cost Reduction Versus Shift Incremental Cost

ding. Before discussing demand-control applications, it would be advantageous to explain the concept both verbally and graphically.

In any given plant or facility, there are those items of electrical equipment that can be turned off briefly with no detrimental effect on operations. Typically, air-handling equipment qualifies for this type of operation. Of course, there is more equipment that cannot be turned off without affecting operations (e.g., production machinery). The point is that a predetermined level of power will be maintained that can be achieved only if some of the equipment is idle at all times. Or, stated another way, if all equipment were to be turned on and run at the same time, the power required would exceed the target level.

Consider a plant that has a power requirement of 10,000 kw to maintain its production equipment, which must be running at all times during the operating shift. This 10,000 kw level is termed the "base" or "noncontrollable" load. Then, consider that this plant also has 7,000 kw powering such equipment, which can be turned off for short periods without affecting the production operation. Typically, the utility company calculates the cost for power demand based on 30-minute intervals but takes a reading once every minute. Figure 11.8 illustrates a 30-minute demand interval with a target demand of 15,000 kw.

Inasmuch as a measurement of power is taken every minute (called a pulse reading), at the end of the 30-minute normal billing interval, the cumulative kilowatts for the noncontrollable load will be at the 10,000 kw level represented in Figure 11.8 by line AB. The 7,000 kw controllable load is represented by the area between AB and CD.

At any point in the 30-minute interval during which kilowatt demand exceeds the rate of 15,000, equipment must be turned off — i.e., the load is partially shed. Point E represents a point at which the target rate is reached and something is turned off.

The equipment that is turned off is typically controlled by a

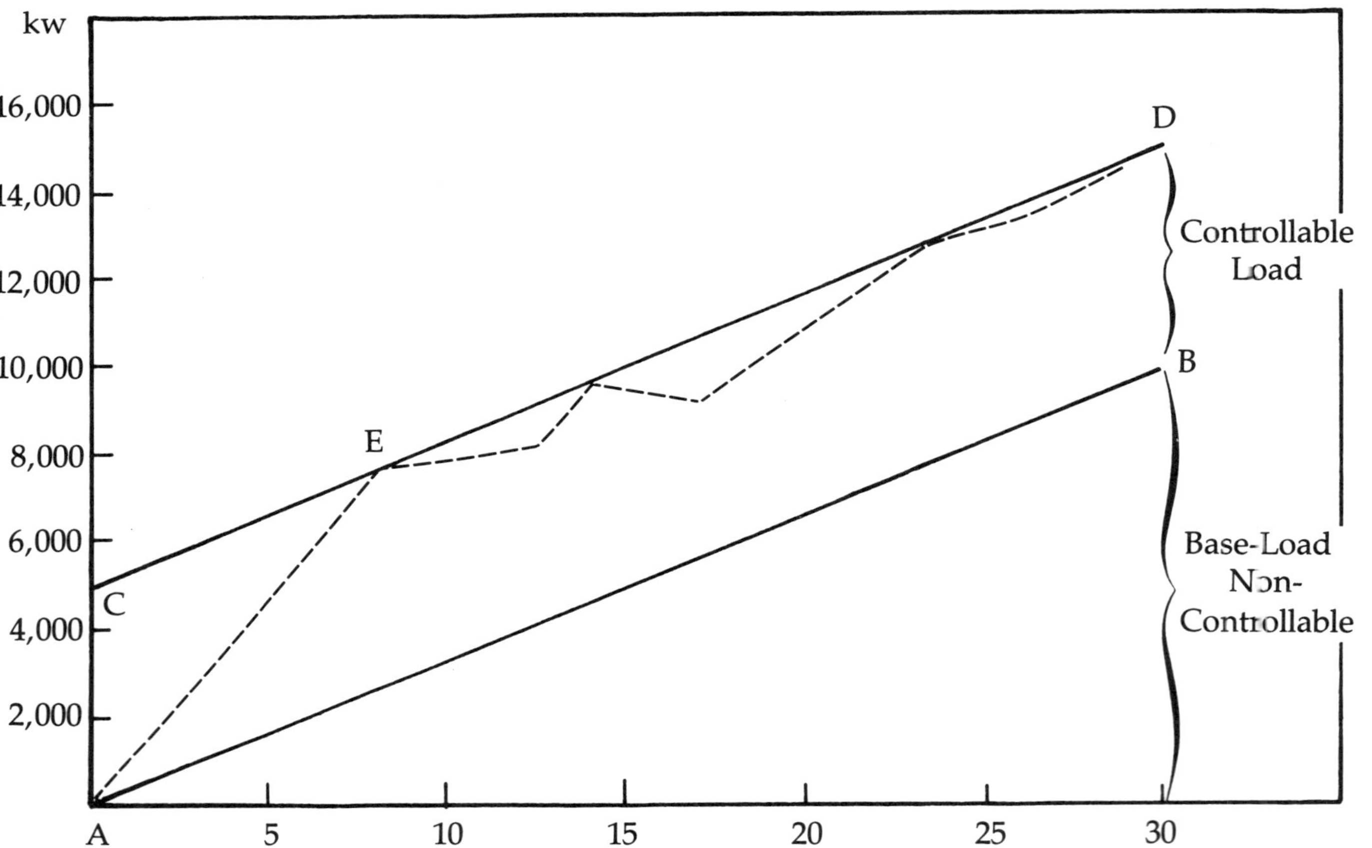

Fig. 11.8. Demand controls — conventional

374

computer that measures the demand pulses just as the utility company does. The equipment may be left off for a predetermined length of time, say two minutes, or until the target rate is again reached by other equipment cycling on/off as part of its normal operations. Either way, the turned-off equipment is turned on again, or "restored" by the computer when the targeted rate is reached or when the present turn-off time has elapsed.

Because demand controls exercised by industry have cut into the revenues of some utility companies, the latter have devised a newer method of measuring demand. Some have defined the 30-minute demand interval for billing purposes as the highest six consecutive five-minute periods in the month. This is referred to as a "floating envelope" because the search mechanism actually floats back and forth until the six highest consecutive periods are found. However, industry has met the challenge, and this type of demand billing is also being monitored and controlled by industry's computers. Throughout the entire month, the computers shed loads as required so that the average reading of any consecutive 30-minute period will not exceed the target level. Figure 11.9 illustrates this concept.

One of the most innovative systems of demand controls that has surfaced to date was developed by a sunbelt foundry that uses electric furnaces to melt its raw material, steel. Electric furnaces accounted for 65% of its power demand. Sequentially, here is how its system functions:

1. At the beginning of each billing period (month) the order backlog is reviewed.

2. The melting requirement is then leveled by dividing the tons needed during the month by the number of working days. (This eliminates the possibility of melting heavy during one day and light the next, remembering that payment would have to be made for demand in accordance with the heavy days.)

3. The energy-monitoring computer is set to turn the

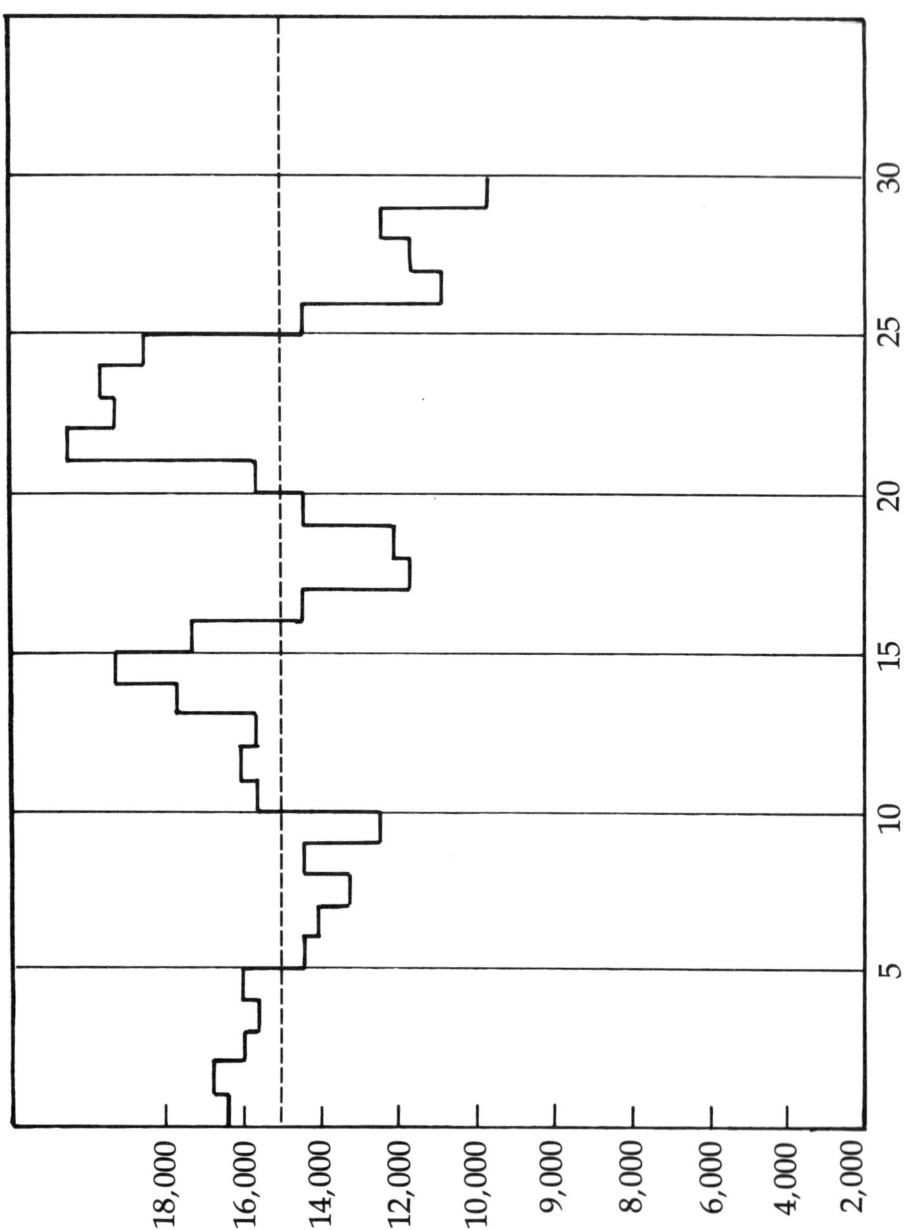

Fig. 11.9. Demand controls — floating interval

melting furnaces off for two-minute time periods when the preestablished target is reached. This action does not affect production because the average daily requirement was considered when the target was set to begin with.

4. This leveling procedure results in a demand saving of $20,000 per month. The amount of monthly production is not changed; rather, a more constant level is established and maintained.

Utility Companies

Managing The Power Factor

When a utility company contracts to deliver power to a user facility, the contract will specify that a certain level of power will be available to do the required work. Power factor is the name of the ratio of the actual power used in the facility (expressed in kilowatts) to the power apparently being used. This ratio of the actual to the apparent is, in essence, a measure of electrical efficiency. If a user facility has a power factor of, say, 70, a relatively large amount of energy is being dissipated in the distribution system, but it is neither being metered nor is the energy directly generating revenue for the utility company.

To compensate for this situation, the utility company may charge a penalty per kilowatt of demand to customers with low power factors. The user facility may offset this loss of available power by installing capacitors near the receiving point of the distribution system to raise the power factor. This discussion quickly becomes technical; however, power factor is mentioned because it is a manageable element of on the power bill. Remember, any saving in the electric bill, while maintaining a given level of production, automatically improves the productivity of energy.

Developing Sound Policies

It was previously mentioned in this chapter that some utility companies offer reduced energy rates when energy is purchased off-shift, or during times other than high-demand periods. This is really just good business for the utility company because it allows for better utilization of capacity. Incremental energy produced off-shift with otherwise idle capacity should be offered at lower rates as an incentive for the user to change its consumption patterns.

Many utility companies are actively encouraging their customers to purchase off-shift power. When this occurs, both parties benefit and the basic energy resource produces more goods and services.

However, utility companies have another side: They are the present-day monopolistic industry. During the past decade, their rates have escalated much faster than the general rate of inflation. Most deplorable are those utility companies that are classified as governmental agencies and have tax-exempt status. They have no incentive to operate within budgeting constraints, nor are they interested in optimum utilization of their existing facilities. Their philosophy leans toward building new facilities. During the past several years, business was projecting limited growth rates of 1%-3% while utility companies forged ahead with grandiose plans for growth rates of 6% and more. This was on top of tremendous gains in energy-conservation measures that have been implemented in businesses, homes, and industry. The result was exemplified by the TVA, which, in mid-1982, scrubbed four power plants that were under construction. This produced write-offs in the billions of dollars which were borne by the users. This was duplicated with at least a dozen additional power plants that were stopped during construction by other utility companies. Power companies should be much more realistic in their growth projections and much more interested in the efficient utilization of their facilities.

When it comes down to the productivity of energy, it is up to the individual industrial users who must not wait on the suppliers of energy to manage this important resource for them. The objectives of these two groups are just not the same.

Section 4

PLANNING, TRACKING, AND CONTROLLING THE PRODUCTION PROCESS

Chapter 12
Demand Management and Forecasting

Objectives

- *Understand how management tools are used to progress from planning to implementation.*

- *Realize the importance of inventory management, materials requirement planning, capacity planning and master scheduling.*

- *Know the difference between forecasting and predicting.*

- *Understand and know how to use different forecasting models.*

- *Understand how to measure forecast error.*

Contents

Forecasting Tools

Demand and forecasting topics address several concepts at a firm's planning level. They indicate projected resource requirements for planning purposes only. Progressing from the overall planning level to actual implementation requires several different types of management tools that include, but are not limited to the following:

- Inventory management

- Materials requirement planning (MRP) and reorder point

- Capacity planning

- Master schedule

Inventory Management

As inventory management is discussed in this chapter, we need to remember the overall concept of productivity, especially working capital productivity, which was discussed in detail in Chapter 5.

At one end of the inventory-management spectrum, the major concern is to never experience a stock-out. To ensure against such an occurrence, a firm may carry excess inventory of all parts, components, and subassemblies. Though this strategy may ensure that the production process will not be stopped because of material outages, it is a very expensive strategic option. While pallets of "insurance materials" gather dust in warehouses, the productivity clock continues to click off opportunity cost due to idle assets. Remember, the productivity of all factors of productivity is measured against the benchmark of time.

On the other end of the inventory-management spectrum is the fear of having idle assets. This fear begets a strategy of operating with no insurance stock. (The "just-in-time" concept is found nearer this end of the inventory management spectrum.) This strategy can produce material shortages that may have such profound consequences as:

- Idle labor or equipment waiting for material to be delivered;

- Excess cost to expedite out-of-stock material, including priority freight; and

- Interruptions of the plant's master schedule, causing missed customer shipments.

A compromise is in order that will result in overall optimum inventory levels. The optimum level will not necessarily represent the lowest inventory cost, and it certainly will not include excess inventory levels. It will, however, attempt to balance such relevant factors as:

- Working-capital productivity;

- Leveling of the production process; and

- Customer service.

The above items are typically included under the heading "inventory management."

MRP and Reorder Point

The concepts of MRP and reorder point are subservient to the major types of inventory management. They cover the front end of inventory management and address the following issues:

- What to order;

- When to order; and

- How many to order.

Perhaps the major difference between MRP and reorder point is that the latter refers to inventory items with independent demand, whereas MRP addresses items with dependent or derived demand. Independent demand refers primarily to completed items (or replacement component parts) that the customer can order directly. Such completed items progress through the production process on the plant's master schedule.

MRP, on the other hand, addresses those items whose demand is derived, or is a function of, the independent demand items.

For example, a customer orders a shipment of common snow shovels. The snow shovels are completed items and are therefore, considered independent demand items. The component parts of the snow shovels — e.g., handles, blades, and rivets — are derived demand items. The number of such component parts required is derived from the number of completed snow shovels ordered by the customer.

A typical example of items covered by the reorder-point concept might include a general purpose fastener that is used on various components and products. When the inventory of such fasteners reaches a predetermined level, the computer generates a reorder document to replenish the inventory.

Capacity Planning

Capacity planning is applicable at several levels. The total capacity for a production facility over a given time period is called its aggregate capacity. A foundry, for example, may have an aggregate capacity of 50,000 tons of castings per year. An automaker, on the other hand, may have an aggregate capacity of 3 million cars per year. Aggregate capacity relates closely to a firm's total forecast of demand.

Even though the automaker may have a given aggregate capacity per time period, the finite capacity may vary according to the mix of cars actually ordered. Similarly, with the foundry example, finite capacity may not be a perfect match for the foundry's aggregate capacity due primarily to departmental or work-center limitations.

Capacity planning, then, begins at the aggregate level, but must be reduced to departmental or work-center levels as the total demand is expressed by specific models, as in the car example, or specific castings for the foundry level. As the product mix actually materializes, the aggregate capacity and departmental capacity should approach evenness. Departmental capacities will highlight bottlenecks in the production process.

The concept of optimum product mix, which equalizes aggregate and departmental capacities, is so significant that an entire chapter (Chapter 14) is devoted to expounding on the productivity benefits provided.

The Master Schedule

The master schedule for any production facility represents the summation of all the facility's activities. All production resources are scheduled and allocated in accordance with the master schedule. The master schedule reflects the independent demand items covering the quantity and time required by the customer. It is no small thing to request a change in the master schedule. Any change in the master schedule after resources have been assembled to meet it will result in lower productivity of working capital because of idle inventory. Maximum productivity of inventory and working capital can occur only when inventory is constantly flowing.

Idleness is expensive.

Forecasting Methodology

Forecasting consumer demand for products and services is perhaps one of the least analytical aspects of the production/operations discipline. Forecasts are required for short time periods (e.g., hourly) for such entities as fast-food restaurants, video stores, or electric power plants. Forecasting consumer demand is perhaps the primary consideration when selecting the timing and site for a new production facility. This type of activity is normally covered in the firm's long-range strategic plan. The longer the forecasted period, the greater the risk of forecast errors.

The term "forecast" means in essence to cast forward present or past data in order to estimate the future. It is important to realize, then, that forecasting is a technique that is used to estimate the future, based on empirical data or history. Forecasting the future is based exclusively on the present or past.

"Predict," on the other hand, means to estimate future events based on data that may be seemingly unrelated to present or past patterns of the event/events predicted.

Short term weather forecasts are based exclusively on existing weather patterns while the prediction that George Bush would be elected president in November 1988 was based on numerous pieces of data that could not possibly be based on existing patterns because Bush had never run for president before.

Considering these definitions, the elements of both forecasting and predicting must be evaluated when estimating future consumer demand for goods and services. For ease of understanding, we use the single term "forecast" to represent such future need.

Forecasts without predictions can be and have been disastrous. If oil and gas production had been forecasted in 1985-1989 to be $30-$35 a barrel, based on price patterns experienced in 1979-1984, there would have been wide range forecast errors. The forecasts were tempered with predictions of unrest in the Middle East, and OPEC activities that resulted in the price of West Texas Crude at $12 barrel as recently as December 1988.

Consider a popular consumer item such as bicycles, which are found in every country in the world. Can an accurate forecast of the future number of bicycles be determined, based exclusively on the past history of bicycle sales? Certainly not. Such a forecast must consider predictions that are relevant to other factors. In the United States, for example, other factors might include demographic data such as population, family size, age of children in family, and average family income.

Forecasting is used for products/services that have independent demand and not dependent demand. In other words, a forecast is made for the number of completed bicycles to satisfy consumer demand for a given time period.

Basic Averaging Models

Forecasting models vary in complexity and use from the very simplistic to very comprehensive. They all have one basic thing in common — they attempt to estimate the amount of production resources that are required to meet consumer demand for future time periods.

Simple Average Forecasting. To forecast average demand, the demand for a product for all previous periods is divided by the number of periods. This provides the forecast for the succeeding periods.

Example:

Demand for bicycles (thousands)

Year	Units
1980	24
1981	23
1982	27
1983	26
1984	31
1985	29
1986	33
1987	32
1988	38
1989	40

Σ demand = 303

n = 10

Average demand = 30.3(1000) = 30,300 = forecast for 1990

The following are characteristics of simple average:

- All data points from previous time periods are used.

- All data points are equally weighted.

- No consideration is given to predictions relative to the total market.

Moving Average. The demand for a product for a given number of the *most recent* periods is divided by the number of periods selected. This provides the forecast for the succeeding period.

Example:

Demand for bicycles (hundreds)

Year	Units
1985	29
1986	33
1987	32
1988	38
1989	40

Σ demand = 172

n = 5

Moving average demand = 34.4(1000) = 34,4000 = forecast for 1990

This method produces a forecast for 1990 that is 13% more than the forecast that was determined by using the simple average method.

The following are characteristics of moving average:

- A constant number of data points are used.

- The most recent data is used.

- Each year, the oldest data point is dropped from the calculation and the current data point is entered.

Weighted Average. The demand for a product for a given number of the most recent periods is weighted. More emphasis is placed on the most recent periods. The sum of the weights = 1.00.

Example:

Demand for bicycles (hundreds)

Time Period	Actual Demand	Relative Weighting	Weighted Demand
1985	29	.10	2.90
1986	33	.15	4.95

1987	32	.20	6.40
1988	38	.25	9.50
1989	40	.30	12.00

Weighted average =   35.75(1000) =

$$35,750 = \text{forecast for 1990}$$

The following are characteristics of weighted average:

- The most recent data is used.

- Emphasis is placed on the most recent data by weighting recent data more heavily than older data.

Simple Linear Regression

A more comprehensive time series example considers the use of simple regression analysis to forecast bicycle demand for 1990 by using the previous 10 years as data points. (This model could also use as sample points just the most recent year's history.)

Example:

Year	Time Period X	Bicycle Demand (000) Y	$X\odot Y$	X^2
1980	1	24	24	1
1981	2	23	46	4
1982	3	27	81	9
1983	4	26	104	16
1984	5	31	155	25
1985	6	29	174	36
1986	7	33	231	49
1987	8	32	256	64
1988	9	38	342	81
1989	10	40	400	100
	55	303	1,813	385

$$\overline{X} = 5.5 \quad \overline{Y} = 30.3$$

Determine the linear function

$$Y = a + bx, \text{ where}$$

Y = total number of bicycles

a = intercept; constant

b = slope; increase in demand of bicycles per time period

$$b = \frac{n\,(\Sigma X \bullet Y) - (\Sigma X)(\Sigma Y)}{n\,(\Sigma X^2) - (\Sigma X)^2}$$

and

$$a = \overline{Y} - (b)(\overline{X})$$

therefore:

$$b = \frac{10(1,813) - (55)(303)}{10(385) - (3025)}$$

$$= \frac{18,130 - 16,665}{3,850 - 3,025} = \frac{1,465}{825} = 1.77$$

$$a = 30.3 - (1.77)(5.5)$$

$$= 30.3 - 9.73$$

$$= 20.57$$

Therefore, demand for 1990 would be:

$$20.57 + 1.77(11) = 40.04(1000) = 40,040$$

Similarly, demand for 1995 would be forecasted to be:

$$20.57 + 1.77(16) = 48.89(1000) = 48,890$$

The foregoing examples are all time-series based. The premise is that the future will behave in like manner as the past. Little or no consideration is given as to *why* the demand varies as time progresses. To illustrate, we will temper this most recent regression example. Let's say it was determined that bicycle demand behaved relative to average family income, as per the following:

Year	Average Family Income (000) X	Bicycle Demand (000) Y	X^2	Y^2	$X©Y$
1980	20.0	24	400.0	576	480.0
1981	23.7	23	561.1	529	545.1
1982	27.8	27	772.8	729	750.6
1983	32.6	26	1,062.8	676	847.6
1984	37.7	31	1,421.3	961	1,168.1
1985	40.0	29	1,600.0	841	1,160.0
1986	42.6	33	1,814.8	1,089	1,405.8
1987	44.1	32	1,944.8	1,024	1,411.2
1988	47.2	38	2,227.8	1,444	1,793.6
1989	49.1	40	2,410.8	1,600	1,964.0
	364.8	303	14,216.8	9,469	11,526.6

$$\overline{X} = 36.48 \qquad \overline{Y} = 30.3$$

therefore:

$$b = \frac{10(11,526.6) - (364.8)(303)}{10(14,216.8) - (133,079)}$$

$$= \frac{115,266 - 110,534}{142,168 - 133,079} = \frac{4,732}{9,089} = .52$$

$$a = 30.30 - (.52)(36.48)$$

$$= 30.30 - 18.96$$

$$= 11.34$$

$$= 11.34(1000)$$

$$= 11,340$$

If it is predicted that average family income in 1990 will increase by, say, 5% over 1989, we can readily forecast bicycle demand for 1990.

1989 average family income	= \$49,100
1990 predicted average family income	= x 1.05%
average family income	\$51,555

$$Y = \text{bicycle demand} = 11,340 + .52(\$51,555)$$

$$= 11,340 + 26,809$$
$$= 38,149 \text{ bicycles}$$

It would be of interest to know just what affect the change in family income has on bicycle demand. In other words, what percent of the variation in bicycle demand is accounted for by changes in average family income. This can be calculated handily using the correlation coefficient r =

$$\frac{n\,(\Sigma\,X\bullet Y) - (\Sigma X)(\Sigma Y)}{\sqrt{n\,(\Sigma X^2) - (\Sigma X)^2} \;\bullet\; \sqrt{n\,(\Sigma Y^2) - (\Sigma Y)^2}}$$

$$= \frac{10(11{,}526.6) - (364.8)(303}{\sqrt{10(14{,}216.8) - (133{,}079)} \;\bullet\; \sqrt{10(9{,}469) - (91{,}809)}}$$

$$= \frac{115{,}266 - 110{,}534}{\sqrt{142{,}168 - 133{,}079} \;\bullet\; \sqrt{94{,}690 - 91{,}809}}$$

$$= \frac{4{,}732}{5{,}118} = .92 = 92\%$$

Therefore, 92% of the change in bicycle demand is attributable to changes in average family income.

This most recent time series considers *why* there is variation over the time periods and is a better forecasting model than simply using time itself as the independent variable in the regression analysis.

Exponential Smoothing

Let's progress from linear relationships to relationships that vary geometrically or exponentially. The following technique is termed "exponential smoothing." Keep in mind, however, that the basic objective is still the same — to be able to forecast future consumer demand, based on historical data.

Exponential smoothing is a more sophisticated method of weighted averages. It also combines moving averages — i.e., older data points fall off as newer points are added. Additionally, the most recent time periods carry a larger weighting than the older points which weights decrease exponentially.

The exponential-smoothing model uses several components with which we need to be familiar.

α (alpha) = some factor ≤ 1 chosen to be applied to the difference between the forecasted demand and the actual demand for a given time period.

Note that the selection of the a value is extremely important. Because as it may vary from .1 to .9 at the discretion of the forecaster, it can be readily seen how the results may vary with varying a factors, commonly termed the smoothing constant.

Remember, the purpose of the exponential-smoothing model is to fit the data points and "smooth" the noise, which is defined as random variations in the data set rather than symetrical movements. Therefore, the a factor is chosen which produces a function that best fits the data points of the time series.

Other model components:

> t = current period (that which we wish to forecast)

At-1 = previous actual demand

Ft-1 = previous forecasted demand

Therefore, the forecast for period t, or current period = new forecast = old forecast + α (actual demand — old forecast)

Ft = Ft-1 + α(At-1 - Ft-1)

Suppose that in 1989 bicycle demand had been forecasted to be 39,000. The actual demand for bicycles in that year was 40,000 as we have seen from previous examples.

Using an α factor of .5, what would the forecast for 1990 be?

$$Ft\ (1990) = 39,000 + .5\ (40,000 - 39,000)$$
$$= 39,000 + .5\ (1000)$$
$$= 39,000 + 500$$
$$= 39,500$$

Notice the difference in forecasts when different a values are selected.

if $\alpha = .1$ Ft (1990) $= 39{,}000 + .1\,(40{,}000 - 39{,}000)$
$$= 39{,}000 + .1\,(1000)$$
$$= 39{,}000 + 100$$
$$= 39{,}100$$

if $\alpha = .9$ Ft (1990) $= 39{,}000 + .9\,(40{,}000 - 39{,}000)$
$$= 39{,}000 + .9\,(1{,}000)$$
$$= 39{,}000 + 900$$
$$= 39{,}900$$

To facilitate understanding of the weighting concept that is used in exponential smoothing, let's express:

Ft = Ft-1 + α(At-1 - Ft-1) as

1. Ft = αAt-1 + (1-α)Ft-1

All that has been done is to group Ft-1 terms and expand.

Subsequently:

2. Ft-1 = αAt-2 + (1-α)Ft-2, and

3. Ft-2 = αAt-3 + (1-α)Ft-3

At this point, we can substitute the equivalent of Ft-1 from Equation 2 into Equation 1 as shown below:

4. Ft = αAt-1 + (1-α)[αAt-2 + (1-α)Ft-2]

Removing brackets from Equation 4 produces:

5. Ft = αAt-1 + α(1-α)At-2 + (1-α)^{2}Ft-2

Progressing in like manner, we can substitute the equivalent of Ft-2 from Equation 3 into Equation 5 above.

6. Ft = αAt-1 + α(1-α)At-2 + (1-α)^2[αAt-3 + (1-α)Ft-3]

and by removing brackets

7. Ft = αAt-1 + α(1-α)At-2 + (1-α)^{2}At-3 + (1-α)^{3}Ft-3

if $\alpha = .4$

$$Ft = .4\ At\text{-}1 + .24At\text{-}2 + .144At\text{-}3 + \ldots.$$

if $\alpha = .2$

$$Ft = .2At\text{-}1 + .16At\text{-}2 + .128At\text{-}3 + \ldots.$$

if $\alpha = .8$

$$Ft = .8At\text{-}1 + .16At\text{-}2 + .032At\text{-}3 + \ldots.$$

The exponential decrease in weighting is readily apparent when varying α values are substituted.

Note that exponential smoothing should not be used if the time series data has a distinct upward or downward trend. Such a time series might better be fitted with a linear equation in the form:

$$Y = a + bx.$$

Remember, the objective is to as accurately as possible forecast future time periods. The fit of the time series data with a function, linear or exponential, is not the end in itself.

Measuring Forecast Error

It is important in our operations to be able to measure the effectiveness of our forecasting models. If our forecasts are not reliable and/or consistent, their value is questionable. If they do not provide an acceptable level of confidence so that decisions or strategies can be made, we might as well not bother to forecast at all.

Not only do we want to be able to measure the forecast error, but we also want to see if the errors are consistently in the same direction, i.e., high or low.

Forecast errors without regard to direction can be calculated via the error measure termed "mean absolute deviation," or MAD. A measure of forecast errors that also indicates error direction is termed BIAS.

Consider the data and resultant regression line determined in earlier paragraphs:

Y = 11.34 + (.52)(x) when (x) = average family income

By using this formula, we can determine a hypothetical fore-casted level of bicycle demand for the years 1980-89.

For example, in 1980, the average family income was $20,000. The forecasted level would have been:

Y = 11.34 + (.52)(20)
  = 11.34 + 10.4
  = 21.74

Year	Average Family Income	Forecasted Demand	Actual Demand	MAD Error	BIAS Error
1980	20.0	21.74	24	2.26	-2.26
1981	23.7	23.66	23	.66	+ .66
1982	27.8	25.79	27	1.21	-1.21
1983	32.6	28.29	26	2.29	+2.29
1984	37.7	30.94	31	.06	- .06
1985	40.0	32.14	29	3.14	+3.14
1986	42.6	33.49	33	.49	+ .49
1987	44.1	34.27	32	2.27	+2.27
1988	47.2	35.88	38	2.12	-2.12
1989	49.1	36.87	40	3.13	-3.13
		MAD Error		17.63	
		BIAS Error			.07

$$MAD = \frac{\sum_{i=1}^{n} |\text{ Forecast - Actual }|}{n}$$

$$= \frac{17.63}{10}$$

$$= 1.763$$

$$BIAS = \frac{\sum_{i=1}^{n} |\text{ Forecast - Actual }|}{n}$$

$$= \frac{.06}{10}$$

$$= .006$$

Inasmuch as we used only the sample points that were used to derive the function

$$Y = 11.34 + 52 \text{ (family income)}$$

there should in reality be no BIAS error.

The insignificant error shown for illustration is solely the result of rounding.

Summary

Forecasting consumer demand for products and/or services is an integral part of a firm's strategy. Forecasting can be employed for periods that range from several hours to several years. Forecasting methods should provide a level of confidence such that we can take action and allocate resources according to the forecast.

By its very nature, forecasting estimates the future, based on the past and present; the data points form a time series. The objective is to determine the functions that best expresses the data points so that future, or forecasted, demand may be estimated with a fair degree of confidence.

It is important to choose the method that best suits the particular operation. An incorrect method will produce unreliable results. The most appropriate forecasting method will take into account the variables that affect the data points. The most reliable forecasts will be tempered with predictions about future events that will affect the general business environment as well as the particular industry.

Chapter 13
Strategically
Managing Quality

Objectives

- *Understand how quality affects our ability to compete.*

- *Recognize the similarity and differences in the approaches of Deming, Crosby, and Juran.*

- *Recognize how quality can be strategically managed.*

- *Understand the statistical approach to inspection via sampling.*

- *Understand the concept of variability as it applies to the production process.*

- *Understand the differences in inspection vs. process control.*

Contents

Quality as It Affects the Organization

James R. Malone, former Chief Operating Officer and President of Purolator Products Company, and Dr. Joe H. Mize, Oklahoma State University professor, have important views on quality. Malone said, "If a company wants to improve the quality of its products or services, it must change its attitude." He said businesses must constantly "sell" the idea of quality improvement throughout their organizations. If you don't have a commitment to quality, then you are not going to be alive; your company won't be alive.

"If you are going to compete globally, it's not a question of whether you are going to have quality products or services — that's assumed," Malone said. "There is a high level of quality that is assumed by customers and competitors and if it isn't there, you won't be a player. The question is whether you are going to survive or not."

Malone said American business has been plagued by an attitude of "do what is necessary to get by, make it just good enough so that I don't get into trouble. Quality is an attitude of saying, 'I am not going to settle for anything other than having absolutely, positively the best.' "

Spreading this attitude throughout an organization is a difficult task for management, he said.

"You cannot assume that everybody in your organization feels as strongly about it as you do or understands it to the same extent you do. They don't. They are focused on another element of the business."

He said management must concentrate on not allowing the "getting by" atttiude to creep in. "A quality attitude is the difference between being part of an organization of which you are proud or being part of an organization of which you are drawing a salary and can't wait to find something else to do."

Mize, an author of engineering textbooks and a consultant

for manufacturers, said that the outlook for U.S. firms is not as bleak as it appears. He said "I worry more about quality than I do productivity. A few years ago it was productivity that everybody was worried about. You can be very productive, but if what you are turning out doesn't hold up out in the field or serve the customer's needs, then you can go broke."

Views of Deming, Juran, and Crosby

Every approach to quality emphasizes management commitment. The approach often begins with the approach in this book or the management philosophy of a quality expert such as Dr. W. Edwards Deming, Dr. Joseph M. Juran, or Philip B. Crosby.

To Crosby, quality is conformance to requirements. Juran defines quality as fitness for use. Deming describes quality as a predictable degree of uniformity and dependability, at low cost, and suited to the market.

Defining Quality

We define quality as meeting the perceived and real needs of a product or service in the eyes of the user.

Our approach and those of Deming, Juran, and Crosby have much in common. There are also some differences. In a sense, a study of similarity and differences is academic. All four approaches have paid off in a wide range of organizations. Author Migliore has interviewed scores of people at all organizational levels. All passionately believe that their approach is best and cite examples of success. That is a good sign for all associated with improvement of the American competitive position. We have seen improvement in quality of product and service when organizations have adapted the strategic planning and management philosophy.

Our approach views quality as a subset of the strategic planning and management process. The Deming, Crosby, and Juran approaches seem to be the driving force of many organizations. Quality as a subset is, in our view, the same as zero-based-budgeting and quality circles, etc. Some organizations use these approaches as the driving force of their planning and management systems. We know of organizations that are just as happy with zero-based budgeting as those that say they subscribe to Deming. We have no problem as long as the results are positive.

Our approach has been highly successful in the profit, non-profit, and church settings. We have seen dramatic quality improvement with all our clients.

Quality and Management Commitment

Deming, Juran, and Crosby emphasize management commitment. All 14 of Dr. Deming's points are obligations of management commitment. For example:

- Create constancy of purpose toward improvement of product and service.

- Adopt the new philosophy that poor quality is intolerable.

Dr. Juran urges all management levels to provide hands-on leadership in quality improvement by taking on their own quality projects. Upper management must ask, "Since we are asking everyone else to make a new commitment to quality, what are we going to announce as *our* part of the commitment?"

Phil Crosby's 14-step process is geared toward bringing about this breakthrough in attitude. His process also starts with management commitment. Crosby says management must understand that quality is a definable, measurable, and manageable function requiring constant attention.

Training is important in all areas of the organization. Our approach emphasizes training to improve job performance. Job performance includes quality. It appears that the other approach emphasizes training for quality, and we wonder if other needs fall through the cracks.

Tools for Measuring Quality

This text along with Crosby, Juran, and Deming all recognize the importance of measurement to track progress and assure that the plan stays on course. Although they all promote direct measures of quality performance, such as assembly line defects or billing errors, Deming places more emphasis on statistical analysis than do his counterparts. He uses statistics to understand whether the process is stable, capable, and on target.

Our approach emphasizes measurement of quality through the objective setting and review process. Quality objectives are set just like all other key result objectives. They include strategy, action, follow-up, just as with all other objectives.

Dr. W. Edwards Deming's 14 Points

1. Create constancy of purpose for improvement of product and service.

2. Adopt the new philosophy of refusing to allow defects.

3. Cease dependence on mass inspection and rely only on statistical control.

4. Require suppliers to provide statistical evidence of quality.

5. Constantly and forever improve production and service.

6. Train all employees.

7. Give all employees the proper tools to do the job right.

8. Encourage communication and productivity.

9. Encourage different departments to work together on problem solving.

10. Eliminate posters and slogans that do not teach specific improvement methods.

11. Use statistical methods to continuously improve quality and productivity.

12. Eliminate all barriers to pride in work skills.

13. Provide ongoing retraining to keep apace with changing products, methods, etc.

14. Clearly define top management's permanent commitment to quality.

Note that the approach in this text starts with Deming's 14th point. The measurement of quality is top management's responsibility and filters all the way down to the lowest organization levels.

Note that the text approach starts with Crosby's item number 10. Long- and short-term goals set the stage for Crosby's number 1, which is universally considered important — management commitment.

Philip B. Crosby's Quality Improvement Process

1. Management commitment.

2. Quality improvement team.

3. Quality measurement.

4. Cost of quality evaluation.

5. Awareness.

6. Corrective action.

7. Zero defects planning.

8. Quality education.

9. Zero defects day.

10. Goal setting.

11. Error cause removal.

12. Recognition.

13. Quality councils.

14. Do it all over again.

Crosby also developed a set of definitions called "Philip Crosby's Absolutes of Quality Management":

- Definition of quality: Conformance to requirements.

- System: Prevention.

- Performance standard: Zero defects.
- Measurement: Cost of quality.

J. M. Juran's "Journey from Symptom to Cause"

Juran developed a list of activities to achieve quality improvement.

- Assign priority to projects.
- Pareto analysis of symptoms.
- Theorize on causes of symptoms.
- Test theories; collect and analyze data.
- Narrow list of theories.
- Design experiment(s).
- Approve design; provide authority.
- Conduct experiment; establish proof of cause.
- Propose remedies.
- Test remedy.
- Action to institiute remedy; control at new level.

Quality as a Subset of the Overall Plan

Our approach emphasizes as the top priority development of an organizational strategic plan. All areas of the organization are represented in the planning process. That is the major point in Chapter One. After the overall plan is developed, then each support area develops its strategic plan. Quality objectives are set at every level of the organization.

In our approach, all objectives — quality, productivity, safety, revenue, ROI — receive equal attention and emphasis. Even though the supposedly old style MBO is not in vogue, its fundamentals still work. When objectives are set, people are involved in developing a plan to meet objectives, then there is feedback and control.

We like Deming's statistical approach. The problem is applying it at the operational level. We suspect it works in Japan because the typical Japanese worker has had better high school training in math, algebra, statistics, and calculus.

Worker Responsibility

Our approach emphasizes the workers being responsible for quality. They continually monitor and chart the quality of the process.

One company that is using an approach we recommend is T. D. Williamson, Inc., Tulsa, Oklahoma. The company defines quality as "identifying the requirements of the job, finding a way to measure whether or not they're being met, and meeting the requirements by doing things right the first time." At TDW, a growing emphasis on quality had been a focus in planning conferences for the past several years. Recently, this emphasis has taken on a concrete format as Bill Hasley, recently retired, Vice President, Director of Manufacturing Development, and Case Boshuizen, Vice-President and Director of Corporate Quality Assurance, searched for the best way to bring the message to TDW.

"We were looking for a way to bring more action to the quality emphasis," said Hasley. Initially, the objective was to investigate what various industry leaders and consultants were advising. "We read all we could find and visited some successful companies which had ongoing quality programs." One of the "gurus" of the quality movement is Philip Crosby, author of the best-selling *Quality is Free*. After attending Crosby's "Quality College," they were convinced that Crosby's message was the one most suited to TDW's needs and goals.

The plan that TDW implemented has an opening statement to the effect that TDW recognizes that everyone wants to do a good job. "Eighty-five percent of our problems are not problems of the work force — but of the system. It is management's job to work on the system to improve the system, to enable people to do what they want naturally to do — a good job.

TDW has a sophisticated strategic planning process. Migliore has been involved with them for 12 years as a consultant and adviser. The TDW example illustrates the importance of making sure you are in the right business, heading in the right direction, and *then* making sure there is an emphasis on quality. A major difference between our approach and others is that we make sure we understand the marketplace, customer needs, know what business we want to be in, and that all functional plans are coordinated. Once direction is set, make sure quality standards are met in product and service.

Statistical Quality and Process Control

Which approach fits your organizaton? It's a win-win choice. Based on interviews, research, and discussions, our approach or any of the three — Deming, Juran, or Crosby — will all pay off. Inasmuch as each of the various quality approaches requires application at the operating level, it seems appropriate to provide examples that bridge the conceptual with the practical.

This is typically done by using Deming's statistical approach. Deming's teachings fell on deaf ears in the U.S. industrial sector (e.g., automakers) shortly after World War II but were eagerly picked up by Japanese manufacturers. Now, in fact, Japan annually offers the coveted *Deming Award* to the Japanese manufacturer who has achieved the highest level of excellence in quality.

Deming's contributions to the Japanese automakers are currently having an effect on U.S. automakers who are consistently losing market share to their Japanese counterparts. One of the major reasons is that: "The quality of Japanese cars is still perceived to be better vs. U.S. vehicles, resulting in continuing increases in Japanese manufacturer's market share." (*Automotive News*, November 27, 1989, p. 1, 58).

Applications of quality concepts should be as universal as measurements of productivity. Just as there are measures for *efficiency* for each stage of the production process, there must be standards for *quality* for each stage in the production process.

Sampling Procedures for Attributes

The quality of an item begins in its design stage. A given amount of quality is designed into each product, considering such factors as end use, cosmetic appeal, cost of failure, and the competitive environment.

From the design stage, we progress to the selection of suppliers for the various materials used in the production process. We want to ensure that we minimize the likelihood of beginning the production process with nonconforming materials. To do this, there are several basic options:

- Test *all* incoming materials for quality.

- *Sample* incoming materials for quality.

- Require the *vendor to certify* that incoming materials meet or exceed quality specifications.

As a producer, we will insist that the vendors certify the quality of raw materials that we place in the production process. In like manner, we will certify the quality of our finished product prior to shipping. In reality, we can't certify the quality of each piece in a given lot without total inspection and/or testing. What is certified is that certain sampling procedures were followed that provide a probability of the status of the entire lot with a stated level of confidence.

This type of testing, or sampling, is used to determine whether the materials are accepted or rejected. They are either good or they are bad. This type of inspection is termed *attribute* inspection. At this point, there is no concern about why the part is substandard or how close it came to passing. These aspects will be covered at a later time. The immediate concern is either acceptance or rejection. This type of sampling is normally the *final* inspection prior to shipping for the *vendor* and the *initial* inspection for the *producer.* However, as indicated earlier, the vendor is also a producer and the producer is a vendor.

A word of caution at this point. It is in no way implied that a *final* inspection of outgoing products represents a total quality program. The objectives of inspection and testing are *prevention.* We inspect and test *each stage* of the production process. However, inasmuch as final inspection and the inspection for incoming material apply the same attribute sampling techniques, we'll discuss them first.

The term "sampling", implies probability. The concept is that the characteristics (attributes) of an entire lot can be estimated on the basis of random samples. Remember, however, the root of probability is *probable*, i.e., what is *likely*, but is not absolutely guaranteed.

The magnitude of estimation errors is one of the basic aspects of quality sampling. The error is that, based on probability, there is a chance that acceptable quality lots will be rejected or that defective lots will be accepted.

The probability that good quality lots will be rejected is termed the *producer risk,* designated as *alpha error,* while the probability that defective lots will be accepted is termed *consumer risk,* designated *beta error.* A good way to remember which is which is to remember that the consumer is the buyer, so that *buyer's risk* is *beta error.*

Developing Operating Characteristic Curves

No standard sampling plan is universally used. Each consumer may require a different sampling plan, with different parameters, for each product. Likewise, each different sampling plan has a unique *operating characteristic curve* (OCC) that graphically portrays these parameters. There are four parameters common to each sampling plan:

1. AQL (accepted quality level): This is the percent of defective products that a consumer specifies that it will accept as a good lot, based on sampling.

2. LTPD (lot tolerance percent defective): This is the upper level, expressed as percent defective that a consumer will

accept. Thus, the consumer would like for the lot quality to be equal to or better than the AQL, but is willing to live with the percent defective up to but not exceeding the LTPD.

3. α (alpha) or Type I Error: As mentioned briefly, this is the risk that the producer incurs that a given sampling plan will result in acceptable lots of product being rejected.

4. β (beta) or Type II Error: This is the consumer's, or buyer's, risk that a given sampling plan will result in defective product being accepted as good.

An important feature of a sampling plan and its OCC is its ability to *discriminate* between lots of high quality and lots of low quality. See Figure 13.1 in which the following parameters were chosen:

- AQL, 1% (.01)
- LTPD, 3% (.03)
- α (alpha) error or producer's risk, 5% (.05)
- β (beta) error or consumer's risk, 10% (.10)

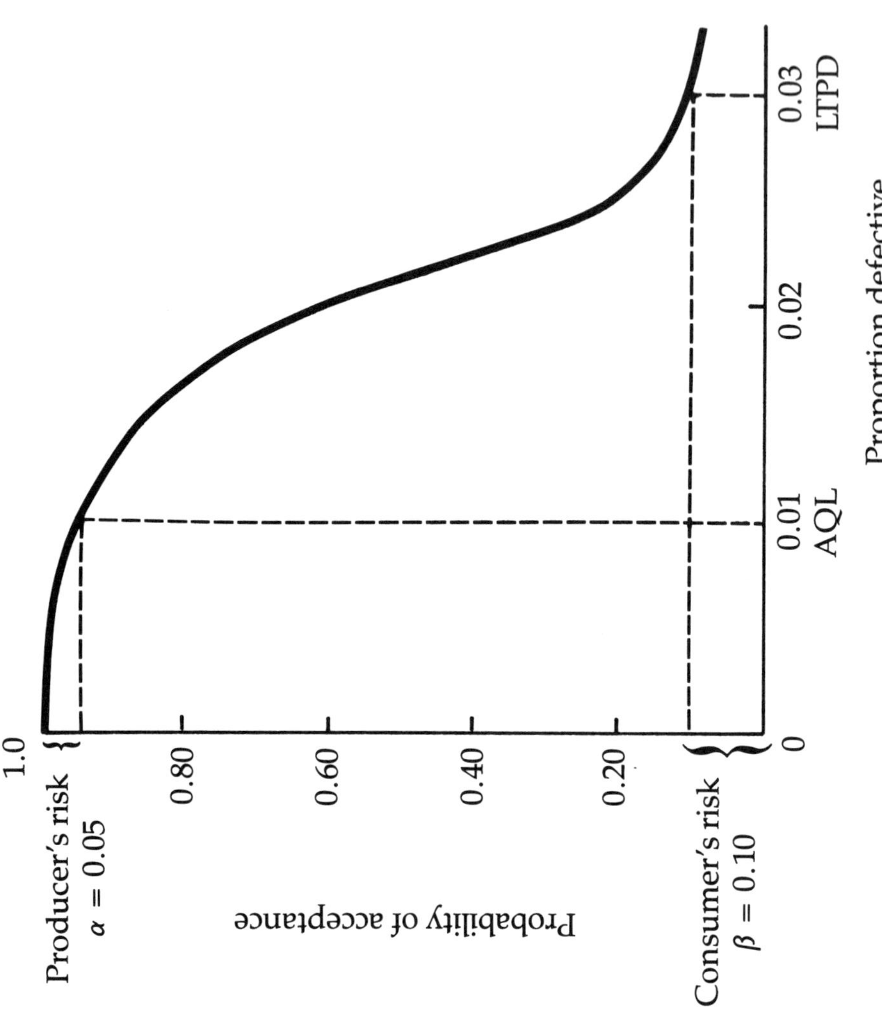

Fig. 13.1. An operating characteristic curve

Shortly, the actual construction of an OCC will be illustrated. However, at this point, let's say that the sampling parameters satisfying the desired plan parameters are:

Size of Lot (N)	Size of Sample (n)	Acceptable Defectives (c)
∞	400	7
10,000	400	7
1,000	275	5
200	125	2

Notice that the sampling plan results are a function of the *sample size* and *not* the *proportion* of the total lot to the sample size.

400/10,000 = 4%
275/ 1,000 = 27.5%
125/   200 = 62.5%

Figure 13.1 provides several important insights.

- Lots that contain 1% defectives will be *accepted* 95% of the time;

- Lots that contain 2% defectives will be *accepted* about 40% of the time;

- Lots that contain 3% defectives will be *rejected* 90% of the time; and conversely

- Lots that contain 3% defectives will be *accepted* 10% of the time.

Although operating characteristics curves are usually generated by way of computer graphics, it is beneficial to understand how they are developed.

Let's say that we have a lot with 1,000 pieces and our statistician advises that we need to pull a random sample containing 10 pieces and accept the lot if 2 or fewer defective pieces are found. Therefore:

- Total lot size N = 1,000.

- Sample size n = 10.

- Sample acceptance c = 2.

Figure 13.2 illustrates the OCC for these sample parameters. The points defining the curve are found in Table 13.1.

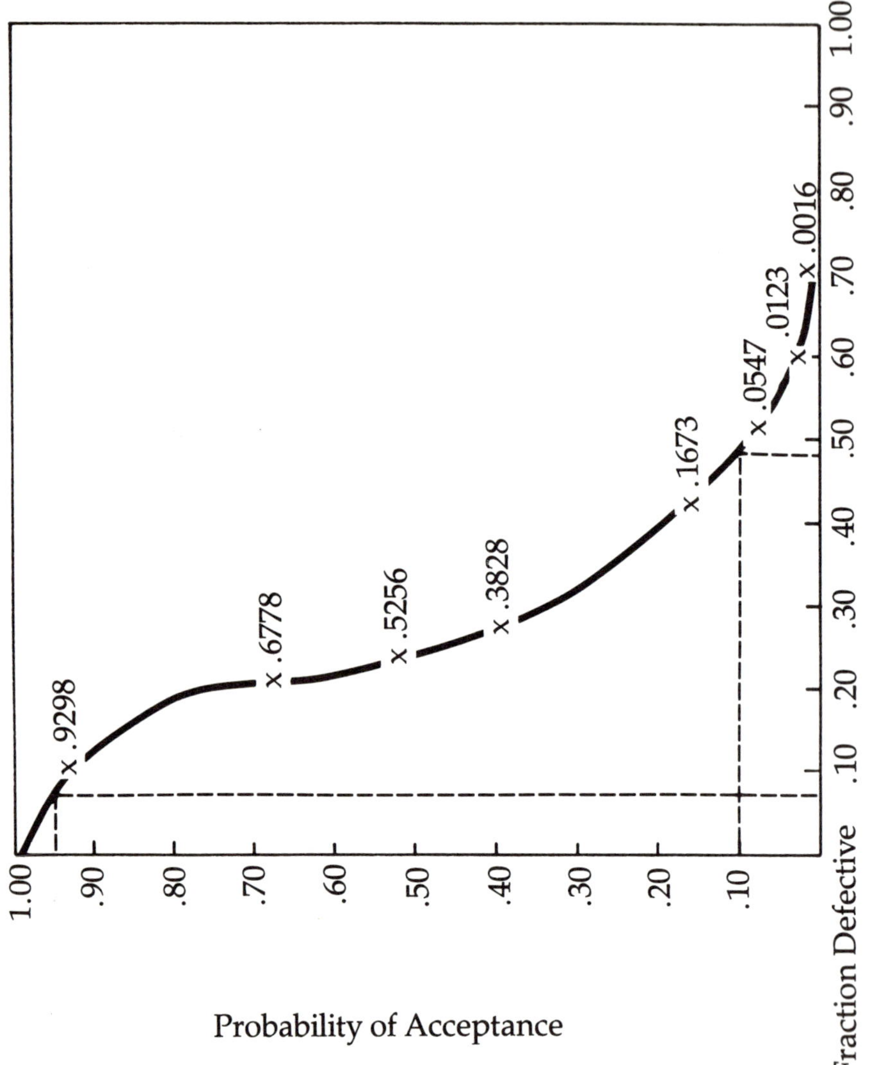

Fig. 13.2. OCC for sample parameters

Table 13.1 Binomial probability sums $\tilde{\Sigma} \, b\,(x; n, p)\; x = 0$
$$x = 0$$

		p									
n	r	0.10	0.20	0.25	0.30	0.40	0.50	0.60	0.70	0.80	0.90
5	0	0.5905	0.3277	0.2373	0.1681	0.0778	0.0312	0.0102	0.0024	0.0003	0.0000
	1	0.9185	0.7373	0.6328	0.5282	0.3370	0.1875	0.0870	0.0308	0.0067	0.0005
	2	0.9914	0.9421	0.8965	0.8369	0.6826	0.5000	0.3174	0.1631	0.0579	0.0086
	3	0.9995	0.9933	0.9844	0.9692	0.9130	0.8125	0.6630	0.4718	0.2627	0.0815
	4	1.0000	0.9997	0.9990	0.9976	0.9898	0.9688	0.9222	0.8319	0.6723	0.4095
	5	1.0000	1.0000	1.0000	1.0000	1.0000	1.0000	1.0000	1.0000	1.0000	1.0000
10	0	0.3487	0.1074	0.0563	0.0282	0.0060	0.0010	0.0001	0.0000	0.0000	0.0000
	1	0.7361	0.3758	0.2440	0.1493	0.0464	0.0107	0.0017	0.0001	0.0000	0.0000
	*2	0.9298	0.6778	0.5256	0.3828	0.1673	0.0547	0.0123	0.0016	0.0001	0.0000
	3	0.9872	0.8791	0.7759	0.6496	0.3823	0.1719	0.0548	0.0106	0.0009	0.0000
	4	0.9984	0.9672	0.9219	0.8497	0.6331	0.3770	0.1662	0.0474	0.0064	0.0002
	5	0.9999	0.9936	0.9803	0.9527	0.8338	0.6230	0.3669	0.1503	0.0328	0.0016
	6	1.0000	0.9991	0.9965	0.9894	0.9452	0.8281	0.6177	0.3504	0.1209	0.0128
	7	1.0000	0.9999	0.9996	0.9984	0.9877	0.9453	0.8327	0.6172	0.3222	0.0702
	8	1.0000	1.0000	1.0000	0.9999	0.9983	0.9893	0.9536	0.8507	0.6242	0.2639
	9	1.0000	1.0000	1.0000	1.0000	0.9999	0.9990	0.9940	0.9718	0.8926	0.6513
	10	1.0000	1.0000	1.0000	1.0000	1.0000	1.0000	1.0000	1.0000	1.0000	1.0000
15	0	0.2059	0.0352	0.0134	0.0047	0.0005	0.0000	0.0000	0.0000	0.0000	0.0000
	1	0.5490	0.1671	0.0802	0.0353	0.0052	0.0005	0.0000	0.0000	0.0000	0.0000
	2	0.8159	0.3980	0.2361	0.1268	0.0271	0.0037	0.0003	0.0000	0.0000	0.0000
	3	0.9444	0.6482	0.4613	0.2969	0.0905	0.0176	0.0019	0.0001	0.0000	0.0000
	4	0.9873	0.8358	0.6865	0.5155	0.2173	0.0592	0.0094	0.0007	0.0000	0.0000
	5	0.9978	0.9389	0.8516	0.7216	0.4032	0.1509	0.0338	0.0037	0.0001	0.0000
	6	0.9997	0.9819	0.9434	0.8689	0.6098	0.3036	0.0951	0.0152	0.0008	0.0000
	7	1.0000	0.9958	0.9827	0.9500	0.7869	0.5000	0.2131	0.0500	0.0042	0.0000
	8	1.0000	0.9992	0.9958	0.9848	0.9050	0.6964	0.3902	0.1311	0.0181	0.0003
	9	1.0000	0.9999	0.9992	0.9963	0.9662	0.8491	0.5968	0.2784	0.0611	0.0023
	10	1.0000	1.0000	0.9999	0.9993	0.9907	0.9408	0.7827	0.4845	0.1642	0.0127
	11	1.0000	1.0000	1.0000	0.9999	0.9981	0.9824	0.9095	0.7031	0.3518	0.0556
	12	1.0000	1.0000	1.0000	1.0000	0.9997	0.9963	0.9729	0.8732	0.6020	0.1841
	13	1.0000	1.0000	1.0000	1.0000	1.0000	0.9995	0.9948	0.9647	0.8329	0.4510
	14	1.0000	1.0000	1.0000	1.0000	1.0000	1.0000	0.9995	0.9953	0.9648	0.7941
	15	1.0000	1.0000	1.0000	1.0000	1.0000	1.0000	1.0000	1.0000	1.0000	1.0000
20	0	0.0216	0.0115	0.0032	0.0008	0.0000	0.0000	0.0000	0.0000	0.0000	0.0000
	1	0.3917	0.0692	0.0243	0.0076	0.0005	0.0000	0.0000	0.0000	0.0000	0.0000
	2	0.6769	0.2061	0.0913	0.0355	0.0036	0.0002	0.0000	0.0000	0.0000	0.0000
	3	0.8670	0.4114	0.2252	0.1071	0.0160	0.0013	0.0001	0.0000	0.0000	0.0000
	4	0.9568	0.6296	0.4148	0.2375	0.0510	0.0059	0.0003	0.0000	0.0000	0.0000
	5	0.9887	0.8042	0.6172	0.4164	0.1256	0.0207	0.0016	0.0000	0.0000	0.0000
	6	0.9976	0.9133	0-.7858	0.6080	0.2500	0.0577	0.0065	0.0003	0.0000	0.0000
	7	0.0996	0.9679	0.8982	0.7723	0.4159	0.1316	0.0210	0.0013	0.0000	0.0000
	8	0.9999	0.9900	0.9591	0.8867	0.5956	0.2517	0.0565	0.0051	0.0001	0.0000
	9	1.0000	0.9974	0.9861	0.9520	0.7553	0.4119	0.1275	0.0171	0.0006	0.0000
	10	1.0000	0.9994	0.9961	0.9829	0.8725	0.5881	0.2447	0.0480	0.0026	0.0000
	11	1.0000	0.9999	0.9991	0.9949	0.9435	0.7483	0.4044	0.1133	0.0100	0.0001
	12	1.0000	1.0000	0.9998	0.9987	0.9790	0.8684	0.5841	0.2277	0.0321	0.0004
	13	1.0000	1.0000	1.0000	0.9997	0.9935	0.9423	0.7500	0.3920	0.0867	0.0024
	14	1.0000	1.0000	1.0000	1.0000	0.9984	0.9793	0.8744	0.5836	0.1958	0.0113
	15	1.0000	1.0000	1.0000	1.0000	0.9997	0.9941	0.9490	0.7625	0.3704	0.0432
	16	1.0000	1.0000	1.0000	1.0000	1.0000	0.9987	0.9840	0.8929	0.5886	0.1330
	17	1.0000	1.0000	1.0000	1.0000	1.0000	0.9998	0.9964	0.9645	0.7939	0.3231
	18	1.0000	1.0000	1.0000	1.0000	1.0000	1.0000	0.9995	0.9924	0.9308	0.6083
	19	1.0000	1.0000	1.0000	1.0000	1.0000	1.0000	1.0000	0.9992	0.9885	0.8784
	20	1.0000	1.0000	1.0000	1.0000	1.0000	1.0000	1.0000	1.0000	1.0000	1.0000

Fortunately, whenever a sampling plan is needed, we can simply refer to MIL-STD tables, or several other recognized sources that satisfy our needs. We need only to know the desired values of the alpha and beta errors along with the customer's desired AQL and LTPD. The binomial distribution is appropriate to use in developing the OCC when the ratio is n/N < 5% since sampling is generally done "without replacement."

Process Controls Measure Each Phase of Production

The preceding discussion on the application of sampling dealt with "attribute" inspection, i.e., the lot was either approved or rejected. No consideration was given to "how close" a sample part came to passing. It was either good or it was bad. This type of inspection is generally done by trained inspectors at the end of the production process.

The present discussion addresses the question of how well the production process is performing relative to predetermined *process* standards. The purpose of *process control* is to minimize the generation of nonconforming material or parts. This is done by auditing process variables throughout the production process. If a given process is found to be outside the predetermined bounds established for the process, the process is stopped and the problem is corrected.

Process variables are of two basic kinds: (1) Natural or inherent variations and (2) variations that may be assigned to a specific cause. Whereas inherent variation is tolerated, specific cause variation is not. If a process or operation contains only natural (random) variation, it is said to be in control; however, when specific cause (nonrandom) variation is detected, the process or operation is out of control.

The control Chart is the tool that is used to detect process variation. Each control chart has a center line, representing the process average, or mean, and upper and lower limits defining the accepted range of the process. (See Figure 13-3.)

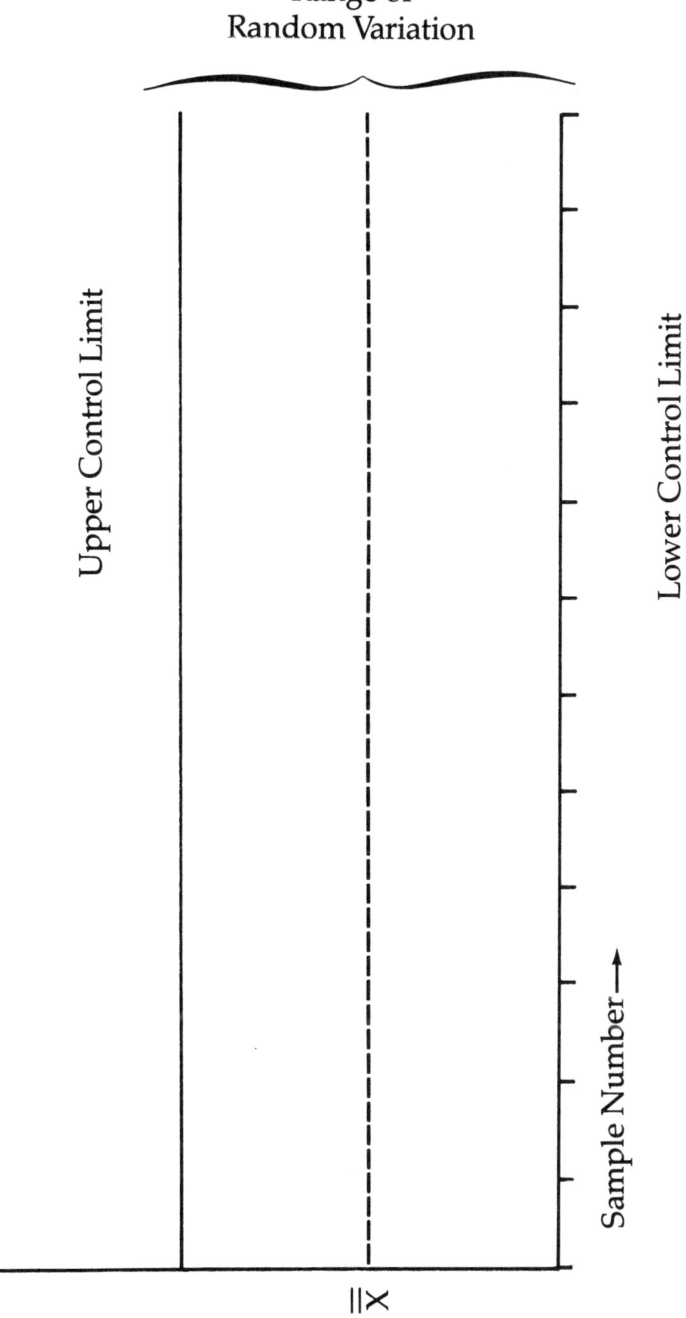

Fig. 13.3. Control chart ranges

Control chart procedure:

- Process averages and ranges are determined using empirical data.

- Periodic process samples are taken and compared to the established norms.

- Compute sample mean and/or range.

- Plot values on chart.

Every control chart is constructed according to the process distribution. Subsequent samples are then compared to the process distribution to check for movement of the process mean. Control charts for means reflect the central tendency of the process; hence, the use of the normal distribution is appropriate. Control charts for range reflect process dispersion, i.e., the extreme of the upper and lower sample means.

Example

Empirical data reflects a process for making steel shafts has a mean of 6 in. The process variability is normal and has a standard deviation of .050 in. If standard deviation is not given, it can be calculated

$$S = \sqrt{\frac{\Sigma(x-\overline{x})^2}{n-1}}$$

Determine control limits that include 99.74% (3 sigma) of sample means for a sample size of 25.

Upper control limit $\overline{\overline{x}} + Z\sigma\text{-}\overline{x}$

Lower control limit $\overline{\overline{x}} - z\sigma\text{-}\overline{x}$

$$\overline{x} = \sigma \div \sqrt{n}$$

$\sigma\overline{x}$ = standard deviation of sample means

σ = process standard deviation

n = sample size

Z = values from area under normal curve (Table 13.2)

$\bar{\bar{x}}$ = mean of sample means

$\bar{\bar{x}}$ = 6 in

σ = .050 in

Z = 3 (from Table 13.2)

$UCL = \bar{\bar{x}} + Z(\sigma \div \sqrt{n})$

$LCL = \bar{\bar{x}} - Z(\sigma \div \sqrt{n})$

UCL = 6 + 3(.050/5)   LCL = 6 - 3(.050/5)
    = 6 + 3(.01)   = 6 - 3(.01)
    = 6.03   = 5.97

We can plot mean, UCL, and LCL on a control chart as reflected in Figure 13.4.

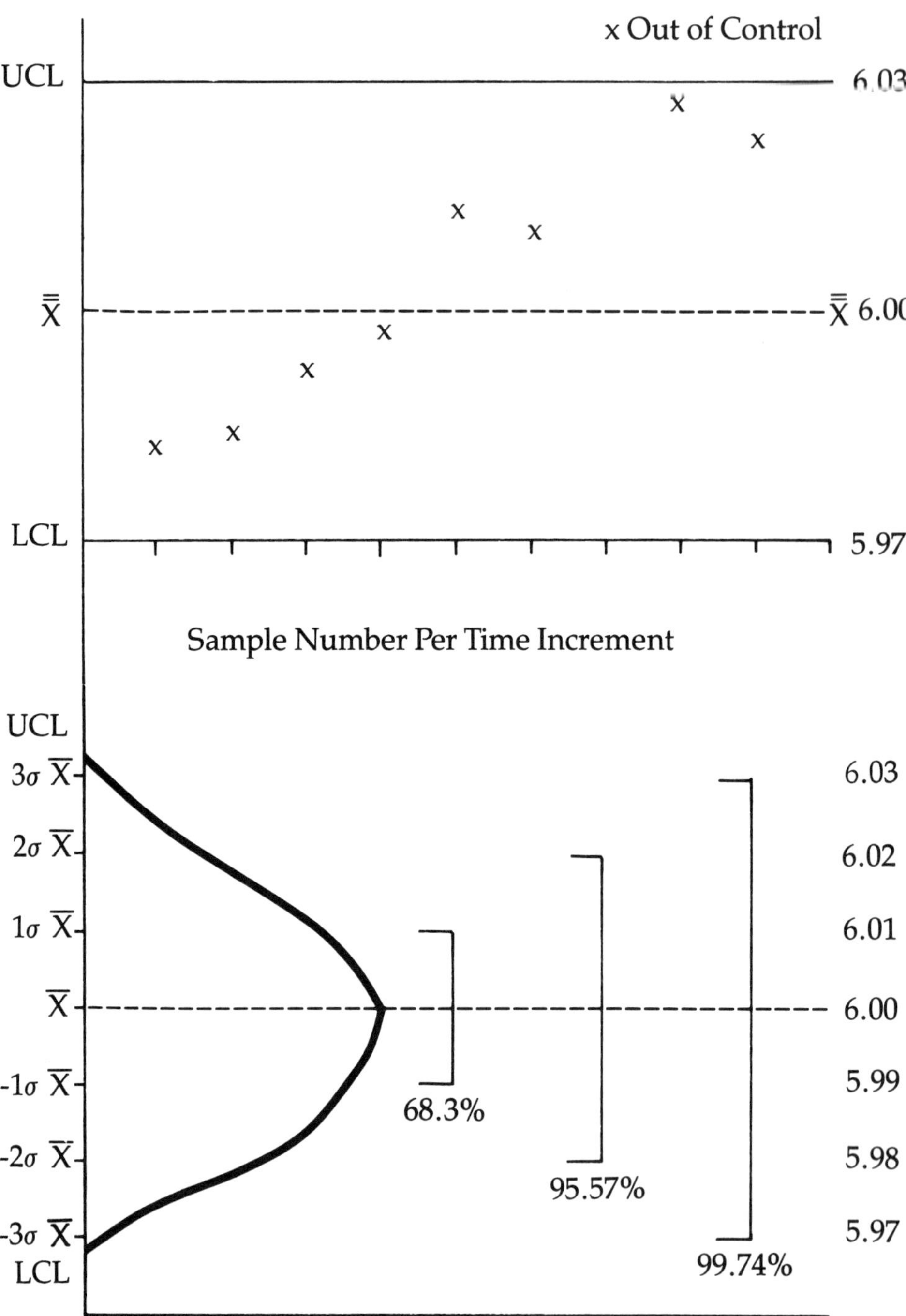

Fig. 13.4. Sample control chart

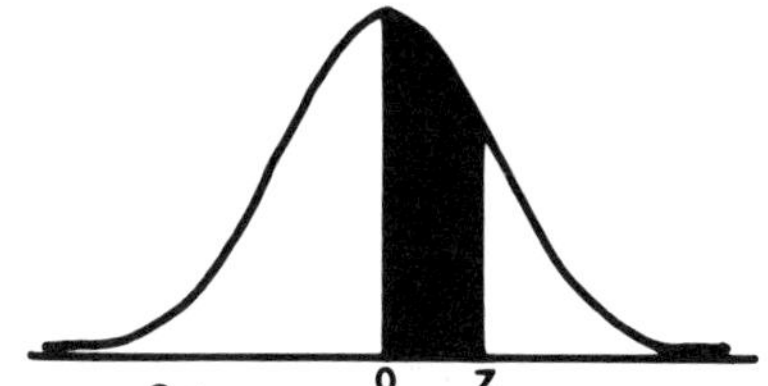

Table 13.2 Areas under the normal curve, 0 to z

z	.00	.01	.02	.03	.04	.05	.06	.07	.08	.09
0.0	.0000	.0040	.0080	.0120	.0160	.0199	.0239	.0279	.0319	.0359
0.1	.0398	.0438	.0478	.0517	.0557	.0596	.0636	.0675	.0714	.0753
0.2	.0793	.0832	.0871	.0910	.0948	.0987	.1026	.1064	.1103	.1141
0.3	.1179	.1217	.1255	.1293	.1331	.1368	.1406	.1443	.1480	.1517
0.4	.1554	.1591	.1628	.1664	.1700	.1736	.1772	.1808	.1844	.1879
0.5	.1915	.1950	.1985	.2019	.2054	.2088	.2123	.2157	.2190	.2224
0.6	.2257	.2291	.2324	.2357	.2389	.2422	.2454	.2486	.2517	.2549
0.7	.2580	.2611	.2642	.2673	.2703	.2734	.2764	.2794	.2823	.2852
0.8	.2881	.2910	.2939	.2967	.2995	.3023	.3051	.3078	.3106	.3133
0.9	.3159	.3186	.3212	.3238	.3264	.3289	.3315	.3340	.3365	.3389
1.0	.3413	.3438	.3461	.3485	.3508	.3531	.3554	.3577	.3599	.3621
1.1	.3643	.3665	.3686	.3708	.3729	.3749	.3770	.3790	.3810	.3830
1.2	.3849	.3869	.3888	.3907	.3925	.3944	.3962	.3980	.3997	.4015
1.3	.4032	.4049	.4066	.4082	.4099	.4115	.4131	.4147	.4162	.4177
1.4	.4192	.4207	.4222	.4236	.4251	.4265	.4279	.4292	.4306	.4319
1.5	.4332	.4345	.4357	.4370	.4382	.4394	.4406	.4418	.4429	.4441
1.6	.4452	.4463	.4474	.4484	.4495	.4505	.4515	.4525	.4535	.4545
1.7	.4554	.4564	.4573	.4582	.4591	.4599	.4608	.4616	.4625	.4633
1.8	.4641	.4649	.4656	.4664	.4671	.4678	.4686	.4693	.4699	.4706
1.9	.4713	.4719	.4726	.4732	.4738	.4744	.4750	.4756	.4761	.4767
2.0	.4772	.4778	.4783	.4788	.4793	.4798	.4803	.4808	.4812	.4817
2.1	.4821	.4826	.4830	.4834	.4838	.4842	.4846	.4850	.4854	.4857
2.2	.4861	.4864	.4868	.4871	.4875	.4878	.4881	.4884	.4887	.4890
2.3	.4893	.4896	.4898	.4901	.4904	.4906	.4909	.4911	.4913	.4916
2.4	.4918	.4920	.4922	.4925	.4927	.4929	.4931	.4932	.4934	.4936
2.5	.4938	.4940	.4941	.4943	.4945	.4946	.4948	.4949	.4951	.4952
2.6	.4953	.4955	.4956	.4957	.4959	.4960	.4961	.4962	.4963	.4964
2.7	.4965	.4966	.4967	.4968	.4969	.4970	.4971	.4972	.4973	.4974
2.8	.4974	.4975	.4976	.4977	.4977	.4978	.4979	.4979	.4980	.4981
2.9	.4981	.4982	.4982	.4983	.4984	.4984	.4985	.4985	.4986	.4986
3.0	.4987	.4987	.4987	.4988	.4988	.4989	.4989	.4989	.4990	.4990

The process control aspect of the quality function brings quality to the grass-roots level by involving the actual operators in the production process. This is as it should be. Operators have immediate feedback relative to the quality of their output. To be sure, the more effective the process control function, the less effort and time will be required at the final inspection stations at the end of the produution process.

Also, improved productivity of all production factors is realized because the cost of defective products is a function of the point at which it is detected. Process control attempts to prevent scrap from being created.

Section 5

BRINGING IT
ALL TOGETHER

Chapter 14
Managing Constraints

Objectives

- *Appreciate that capital planning and strategic planning cannot be separated.*

- *Understand that determining a firm's optimum mix is necessary prior to capital planning.*

- *Understand that production choices can be expressed as a linear equation.*

- *Realize that the optimum product mix provides the greatest amount of contribution.*

- *Understand that the limiting factor must be used when determining production capacity.*

- *Recognize the importance of evaluating different product mixes.*

- *Know that the highest contribution with the given facilities produces the lowest break-even point.*

- *Understand that idle capacity and inaccurate pricing policies may be due to improper product mixes.*

- *Understand the reasons for new capital expenditures and methods of capital investment evaluation.*

- *Be able to use a break-even curve and linear programming to evaluate different capital-investment alternatives.*

- *Understand the three-step strategic planning process used when maximizing asset utilization.*

Contents

Capital and Strategic Planning are Inseparable

Capital and strategic planning are rarely considered together in the same chapter. Equally unusual is the fact that they are not always considered together in the actual business environment. It is not unusual for different departments to submit their individual capital requests with little or no consideration given to the overall direction of the plant or firm. This chapter demonstrates that capital planning is inseparable in the definition and execution of a firm's total game plan.

When the topic of capital planning is presented in other texts, the discussion nearly always focuses on the concept of choosing available investment opportunities within the framework of limited funds. In other words, the thrust is toward ranking possible investments, usually in terms of the present value of money. Projects are considered to be mutually exclusive with limited consideration given to the firm's overall, continuing strategy. Granted, the ability to objectively rank investments is highly important, as is an understanding of the time value of money. These techniques, because of their classic importance, are covered in this chapter, but the initial focus is on determining where capital expenditures are most needed to enhance a firm's overall financial position. Maximum financial benefit accrues when a firm can properly define the product mix that it is designed to produce most effectively.

If a company builds a new plant to manufacture wagons, for instance, a prevailing misconception is that the plant can make all models of wagons more economically than any other plant. When a new foundry is built, it is assumed that it can make all sizes and shapes of castings better than any other foundry. Not so. In the case of the wagon plant, the new plant can make particular models more effectively than others. And in the case of a new foundry, it can produce particular types of castings more effectively than others can. Often, new plants tie up or commit manufacturing resources for the production of items that will contribute less to the improvement of the plant's financial position than items that were rejected as undesirable. It boils down to the definition of the optimum product mix for that particular plant or facility.

Optimum Mix Provides Maximum Contribution

The optimum mix for any plant is the mix that will provide the maximum contribution (revenue minus variable cost) with the existing asset base. Contribution will be emphasized, because varying the product mix with the same asset base will generally not have a significant effect on fixed cost. This approach will also allow the observance of the break-even-point movement as product mix changes.

The concepts discussed in this chapter are definitely not limited to the design of new plants. They are equally applicable to an existing facility for defining its optimum mix.

Typically, the initial step in developing an operating plan is the marketing input. From the marketing input, a firm develops its capital requirements and then the operating of operating plans and budgets. Not much is wrong with that sequence. However, if the marketing people knew the product mix that would maximize the plant's total contribution, they might alter their strategy and pursue markets heretofore left out. A firm that can determine its optimum mix may also discover that its pricing policies are inappropriate. It will most likely discover also that it existing capital budgeting priorities are suboptimal.

The optimum-mix determination can best be explained with a comprehensive example. The following step-by-step example covers a typical production-type operation. Although the example covers a foundry, the concepts are universally applicable to any manufacturing facility that produces more than one product (model) and employs multiple steps in the production process.

First, however, let's briefly explain the foundry process, with its several basic steps, so the example can be better understood.

The Foundry Process

The word "foundry" means the art of metal casting. Metal casting has been around for several thousand years. Cast objects were used in decorating Solomon's temple in 950 B.C. Today, the foundry industry produces 12 million to 15 million tons of product each year. It is a major segment of the industrial sector.

Castings are abundant in manufactured goods such as automobiles, tractors, railroad equipment, and home appliances. Engine blocks for every car, truck, tractor, and motorcycle are cast metal. Castings come in all sizes and shapes, ranging from a fraction of a pound for a brass pipe fitting up to many tons, such as a propeller for a large aircraft carrier.

A particular foundry is likely to manufacture a variety of different parts. Even the highly automated and captive foundries do not have the luxury of making one or two parts. In fact, it is not unusual for a single foundry to manufacture hundreds or even thousands of different parts. Regardless of the variety of the product mix, however, the basic foundry process is universally the same. Metals in their natural solid state are melted and recast into desired shapes with predetermined physical and chemical properties. In the typical foundry, there are four basic steps in the manufacturing process:

1. Core making: The core is used to form the interior shape of the casting.

2. Melting: Solid metals are melted, normally in large electric furnaces, into their liquid state.

3. Molding: This is the process in which the molten metal is poured into a "mold" of the shape of the desired part. When the metal cools and resumes its natural solid state, it is removed from the mold for further processing.

4. Cleaning: This process removes molding media (usually

sand) from the casting and excess metal from the part so that it will fit the tooling for the machining operations that will follow.

In our example, the core department has four different core machines. These machines will be different, depending on the requirements of individual castings. Therefore, a given job will be "tooled up" to run on a particular machine, which is to say, a job will not run on one machine one day and another machine the next.

The melting facilities are slightly different. Normally, there will be multiple furnaces and it makes absolutely no difference which furnace supplies the metal for any job. Jobs have no identity in the molten-metal stage.

The molding facility for this example will consist of one unit. Of particular significance, however, is the fact that this molding unit can make just one size mold, regardless of the size of the casting to be made within the mold. This is an inherent limitation of all automated molding equipment. In addition, an automated molding machine cycles constantly at the same speed, regardless of the casting size.

The cleaning facilities for this example will consist of six work centers. Most of the jobs will require that the part pass through two of them. The routing as to which two are assigned to a particular job depends on its properties.

The Problem

For this example, 10 different jobs are considered, as shown in Table 14.1. In actual practice, there could well be several hundred different jobs and 40 different work centers. It works exactly the same. Table 14.1 also lists the present sales volume for each of the ten parts.

Table 14.1 Existing product mix

Part	1 Casting Weight (Pounds)	2 Selling Price	3 Variable Cost	4 Contribution	5 Number Sold of Each Total Molds	6 Total Weight	7 Total Revenue	8 Total Variable Cost	9 Total Contributions
Manifold	19	$ 16	$ 13	$ 3	100	1,900	$ 1,600	$ 1,300	$ 300
Valve body	15	15	10	5	250	3,750	3,750	2,500	1,250
Lug	4	3	2	1	135	540	405	270	135
Axle housing	410	185	164	21	40	16,400	7,400	6,560	840
Gear blank	320	134	111	23	45	14,400	6,030	4,995	1,035
Differential case	360	132	105	27	25	9,000	3,300	2,625	675
Wheel hub	66	13	7	6	100	6,600	1,300	700	600
Bearing housing	20	5	3	2	25	500	125	75	50
Brake caliper	49	15	11	4	165	8,085	2,470	1,815	655
Boat anchor	13	4	2	2	75	975	300	150	150
Total					960	62,150	$26,680	$20,990	$5,690

A foundry's capacity is conventionally stated in tons per time period; even government statistics measure foundry output in tons per time. Table 14.2 expands the data for the 10 different jobs.

Table 14.2 Contribution ranked on per-pound basis

	Casting Weight	Price per lb	Contribution per lb	Ranking by Contribution
Manifold	19	.842	.158	3
Valve body	15	1.000	.333	1
Lug	4	.750	.250	2
Axle housing	410	.451	.051	10
Gear blank	320	.419	.072	9
Differential case	360	.367	.075	8
Wheel hub	66	.197	.091	6
Bearing housing	20	.250	.100	5
Brake caliper	49	.306	.082	7
Boat anchor	13	.308	.154	4

The molding unit in a foundry is considered the pacing unit because its cycle time is fixed. All other activities are considered support and are staffed to satisfy the requirements of the molding unit. Although just one molding machine is considered in our example, the concept readily handles multiple molding machines of varying sizes and production rates.

Listed below are the work centers, in addition to the molding unit, in the foundry facility.

Core department
Machine 101, 102, 103, 104

Melt department
Furnace 201

Molding department
Machine 301

Cleaning department
Machines 401, 402, 403, 404, 405, 406

To complete the data required in order to determine the

optimum product mix, given the information in Tables 14.1 and 14.2, the routing (or path through the manufacturing process) must be known for each of the 10 jobs, as well as how much of each work-center resource that each job will consume as it passes through. (Table 14.3)

Table 14.3 Routing matrix

Work Center	Manifold	Valve Body	Lug	Axle Housing	Gear Blank	Differential Case	Wheel Hub	Bearing Housing	Brake Caliper	Boat Anchor	Total WC Resource Available
101	.25				.16	10.75					480 minutes
102			.30				.41				480 minutes
103								.72		.05	480 minutes
104				.68					.41		480 minutes
201	19	15	4	410	320	360	66	20	49	13	275,000 lb
301	.50	.50	.50	.50	.50	.50	.50	.50	.50	.50	480 minutes
401	.10		.24		8.12				.18	.10	480 minutes
402		.15		2.16		.25	.30	.26			480 minutes
403			.41							.08	480 minutes
404	.65				.82	.75					480 minutes
405		.81					.71		.20		480 minutes
406				1.91				.40			480 minutes

Consider the manifold in Table 14.3.

1. It requires .25 minutes to make the core in work center 101. Work center 101 has 480 total available minutes per day, or one shift.

2. It requires 19 pounds of metal from the furnaces to make one manifold. The furnaces, work center 201, have a total daily available capacity of 275,000 pounds.

3. It requires .50 minutes of the molding unit's capacity (work center 301) of the 480 minutes available per day to make one manifold. Therefore, the molding unit's capacity is 960 per day.

4. It requires .10 minutes of work center 401 and .65 minutes of work center 404 to make one manifold. Each has 480 minutes available per day.

Linear Programming Application

It is apparent that the problem is one of choice, because each work center has limited capabilities. This presents an excellent linear programming application.

Consider that in work center 101 we could make either 1,920 manifolds or 44.65 differential cases.

$$480 \div .25 = 1,920 \qquad 480 \div 10.75 = 44.65$$

Consider that the manifold is assigned the variable X_1, the valve body X_2, lug X_3, etc. Then, work center 101 can be expressed as a linear equation.

$.25X_1 + OX_2 + OX_3 + OX_4 + .16X_5 + 10.75X_6 + 0X_7 + 0X_8 + OX_9 + OX_{10} \le 480$ min.

Accordingly, in work center 201, either 14,474 (14,473.7) manifolds or 764 (763.89) differential cases can be made, but not both.

14,473.7 manifolds x 19 lb each = 275,000

763.89 differential cases x 360 lb each = 275,000

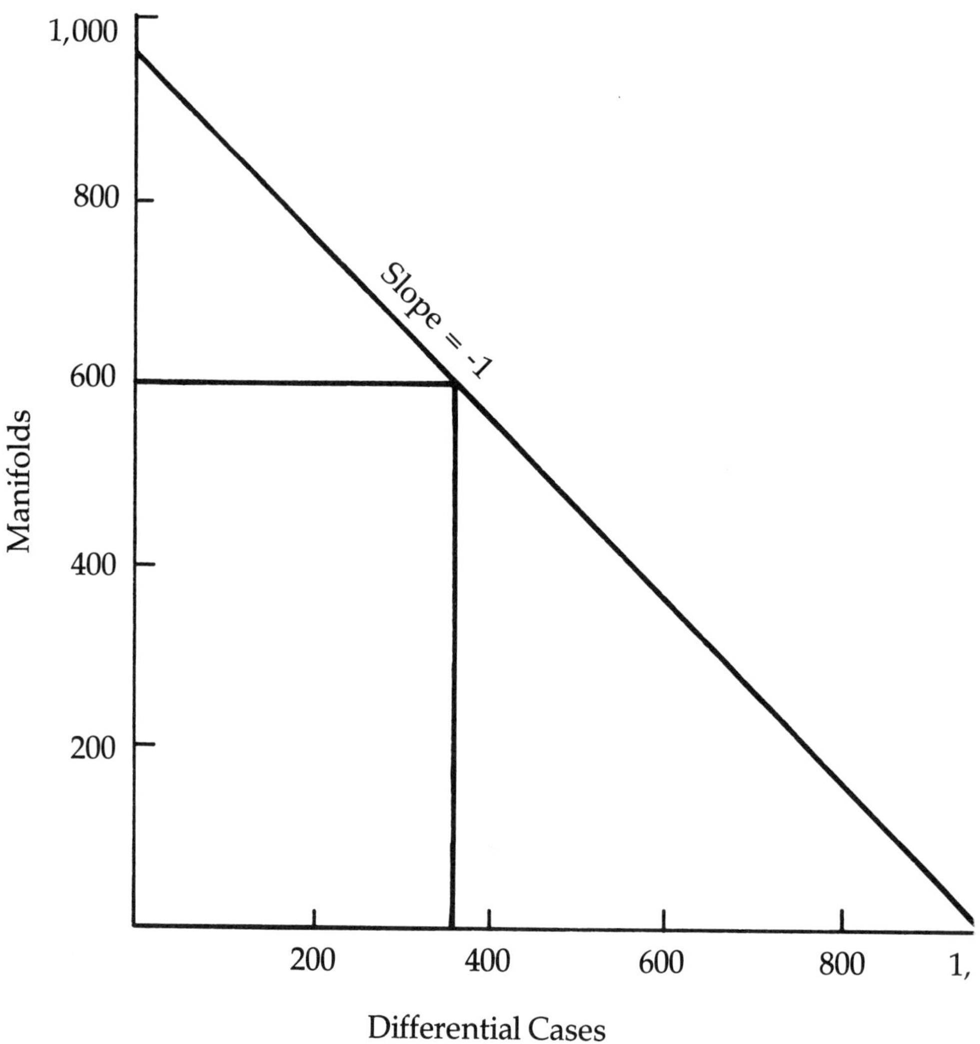

Fig. 14.1. Trade-off: manifolds vs. differential cases on work center 301

We could, however, give up one differential case weighing 360 lbs and substitute 18.95 manifolds. ($360 \div 19 = 18.95$)

Then 762.89 differential cases x 360 lb.	= 274,640 lbs
and 18.95 manifolds x 19 lb.	= 360 lbs
Total weight	275,000 lbs

The total available weight has not been exceeded. This is called the linear rate of substitution.

The total weight produced by work center 201 can be expressed as the linear equation:

$$19X_1 + 15X_2 + 4X_3 + 410X_4 + 320X_5 + 360X_6 + 66X_7 + 20X_8 + 49X_9 + 13X_{10} \leq 275,000 \text{ lbs.}$$

In work center 301, the choice between manifolds and differential cases is a bit simpler. The rate of substitution is 1. That is, if one manifold is given up, one differential case can be added. Graphically, the rate of substitution of 1 represents a line with a slope of -1. (See Figure 14.1.)

The graph illustrates that any combination of manifolds and differential cases that touches the substitution line will equal 960. The graph indicates a combination of 600 manifolds and 360 differential cases. In work center 401, the choice can be 4,800 manifolds for any level of differential case production because the differential case does not require capacity from work center 401. In work center 404, the choice is either 738 manifolds or 640 differential cases, calculated in the manner described above.

Inasmuch as the optimum mix has been previously defined as that which provides the greatest amount of contribution, the objective function can be established using the contribution data from Table 14.1 column 4. Maximize $3X_1 + 5X_2 + 1X_3 + 21X_4 + 23X_5 + 27X_6 + 6X_7 + 2X_8 + 4X_9 + 2X_{10}$ subject to the constraints listed on Table 14.3.

Production Capacity

Even though foundry capacity is traditionally expressed in tons per time period, it may not be the best measure for each foundry.

For example, if tons are the measure of capacity, then, according to Table 14.1, the foundry is operating at 22.6% capacity.

62,150 lb ÷ 275,000 lb = 22.6%

However, Table 14.3 indicates that it requires .5 minutes to make each mold, so total mold capacity is 480 ÷ .5 = 960 molds, which is the present operating level. The point is that capacity must be defined relative to the limiting factor in the individual plant, which in this case is molding.

Consider this point in light of the foundry's ability to break even on a tonnage basis with a daily fixed cost of $6,000. From data in Table 14.1, which represents current operations, the following capacity level, based on tonnage, is determined:

Revenue per ton	$26,680 ÷ (62,150/2,000) = $858.56
Variable cost per ton	$20,990 ÷ (62,150/2,000) = 675.46
Contribution per ton	$183.10

$6,000 ÷ $183.10 = 32.77 tons/day, or 23.8% of tonnage capacity to break even.

It is very evident that the wrong department has been used to determine capacity because a real loss occurred. ($5,690 present contribution - $6,000 fixed cost = -$310).

If molding is correctly used as the capacity determinator, the break-even point looks slightly different.

Revenue per mold	$26,680 ÷ 960 = $27.79
Variable cost per mold	$20,990 ÷ 960 = 21.86
Contribution per mold	$ 5.93

$6,000 ÷ $5.93 = 1,012 molds required per day to break even, or 105% of capacity.

The same result is obtained if the break-even point is calculated in terms of sales dollars.

$$BE = \frac{FC}{1 - \frac{VC}{S}} = \frac{\$6,000}{1 - \frac{\$20,990}{\$26,680}} = \$28,129 \text{ in sales}$$

But sales are $26,680 when molding is operating at full capacity, so the foundry would have to operate at 105% capacity in order to break even.

$28,129 required to break even ÷ $26,680 actual = 1.05.

It is not uncommon for a plant to incorrectly define its capacity and to work toward an unobtainable goal. It is even more serious to develop a feeling of false security by presuming the break-even point is reached at low capacity levels.

Strategic Planning is Crucial

Inasmuch as the foundry is losing money at 100% molding capacity, and break-even point is impossible, some real strategic planning is in order. The challenge is to increase the productivity of the molding operation, even though the machine speed is fixed. This will be absolutely necessary in order to stay in business.

Examining Product Mix. The biggest scapegoat of all time is to cry "product mix." This term is usually employed to cover all unexplained problems. Let's look at the 10 products presently produced and see if there is a problem area.

The question asked is: Given the present equipment, including the molding unit that is running at capacity, i.e., 960 molds per day, and the 10 available products with their respective routings, per Table 14.3, what mix would provide the largest amount of contribution?

The only factor to be changed is that there will be no limitations relative to quantities of any part that can be sold. The hope is that perhaps a break-even condition can be found with a different mix of the 10 available products.

At this point, it is wise to input all the data into a computer to solve the problem. Using this approach, a daily contribution of $9,524 is indicated with the suggested mix shown in Table 14.4.

Table 14.4 One shift with existing equipment (no market constraints)

Part	Number of Each (Total Molds)	Total Weight	Total Revenue	Total VC	Total Contribution	Rank by Contribution per Pound
Manifold	—	—	—	—	—	—
Valve body	563	8,445	$ 8,445	$ 5,630	$2,815	1
Lug	—	—	—	—	—	—
Axle housing	178	72,980	32,930	29,192	3,738	10
Gear blank	57	18,240	7,638	6,327	1,311	9
Differential case	44	15,840	5,808	4,620	1,188	8
Wheel hub	—	—	—	—	—	—
Bearing housing	—	—	—	—	—	—
Brake caliper	118	5,782	1,770	1,298	472	7
Boat anchor	—	—	—	—	—	—
Total	960	121,287	$56,591	$47,067	$9,524	

First, let's determine whether a break-even point is now attainable.

Revenue per mold	$56,591 ÷ 960 = $58.95
Variable cost per mold	$47,067 ÷ 960 = 49.03
Contribution per mold	$ 9.92

$6,000 ÷ $9.92 = 605 molds required per day to break even, or 63% of molding capacity.

There is a tremendous difference with the computer-selected mix. (Compare Table 14.1 with Table 14.4)

- With the same total molds:
  1. Total casting weight increased   95%
  2. Total revenue increased   112%
  3. Total contribution increased   67%
  4. Break-even point reduced   40%

(1,012 molds to 605 molds)

- Only five of the available parts were selected. Furthermore, 4 of the 5 selected (axle housing, gear blank, differential case, and brake caliper) were ranked as the lowest out of the 10 for contribution *per pound* of casting. The reason for this is that even though a particular part may have a relatively low contribution *per pound*, such as the axle housing with a contribution of only $.051/lb, the product weight may be relatively large.

Consider, for example:

	Part Weight	Contribution/lb	Contribution/mold
Valve body	15 lb	$.333	$ 5.00
Axle Housing	410 lb	$.051	$20.91
			(rounded to
			$21.00)

It is clear, therefore, that the contribution per mold is a superior indicator and should be the criterion for selecting parts to produce at this foundry.

Produce Maximum Amount in Each Cycle. The above concept is applicable to any industry or plant in which any portion of the process is fixed as to cycle time and resources required per cycle, without regard to the quantity of product processed per cycle. The objective is to get as much product as possible into each cycle of the operation. It is really very similar to a fixed-cost work center. The cost in a fixed-cost work center is fixed over time, regardless of the level of production. The cost per cycle of an automated piece of equipment, such as the molding machine presently being discussed, is also fixed regardless of the size part within the mold.

Let's consider all 10 parts relative to contribution per mold:

Selected Parts

	Part Weight	Contribution/lb	Contribution/Mold
Valve body	15 lb	$.333	$ 5.00
Axle housing	410	.051	21.00
Gear blank	320	.072	23.00
Differential case	360	.075	27.00
Brake caliper	49	.082	4.00

Rejected Parts

Manifold	19 lb	.158	3.00
Lug	4	.250	1.00
Wheel hub	66	.091	6.00
Bearing housing	20	.100	2.00
Boat anchor	13	.154	2.00

Maximize Total Contribution. The reason that a part, say the valve body, with a contribution of $5 per mold, would be selected over the wheel hub with a $6 per mold contribution, is that each part was competing for available work-center capacity. The objective of the linear program is to maximize total contribution, so if there is any available capacity in any work center that will increase the total contribution, the part will be selected. It can, however, be confidently accepted that no other combination of the 10 available parts and existing work-center routings will provide a higher contribution than the $9,524 reflected in Table 14.4.

It is little wonder that the lug was rejected. It contributes only $1 per mold, which is not a very good tradeoff when more than $20 is available with the axle housing, gear blank, and differential case.

It is understood that the most desirable parts to maximize total contribution are those with a relatively high mold contribution. Then, if there were no support work-center constraints, one would expect the mold line to run 960 differential cases. Table 14.5 confirms this premise. Therefore, the maximum contribution available to this particular foundry, produced with 960 molds, is $25,920 per day. It should be noted from Table 14.5, however, that melting capacity would need to be increased by 25.7% to accommodate this many differential cases. (345,600 lb required ÷ 275,000 lb available).

Table 14.5 One-shift molding: no other constraints

Part	Number of Each (Total Molds)	Total Weight	Total Revenue	Total VC	Total Contribution	Rank by Contribution per Pound
Manifold	—	—	—	—	—	—
Valve body	—	—	—	—	—	—
Lug	—	—	—	—	—	—
Axle housing	—	—	—	—	—	—
Gear blank	—	—	—	—	—	—
Differential case	960	345,600	$126,720	$100,800	$25,920	8
Wheel hub	—	—	—	—	—	—
Bearing housing	—	—	—	—	—	—
Brake caliper	—	—	—	—	—	—
Boat anchor	—	—	—	—	—	—
Total	960	345,600	$126,720	$100,800	$25,920	

The resultant break-even point shifts even farther to the left.

Revenue per mold	$126,720 ÷ 960 = $132.00
Variable cost per mold	$100,800 ÷ 960 = 105.00
Contribution per mold	$ 27.00

$6,000 ÷ $27.00 = 222 molds required to break-even, or 23% of capacity.

It should be noted here that the highest possible contribution with given facilities produces the lowest possible break-even point.

Heretofore, our subject foundry had been aggressively pursuing more valve bodies and similar business. In accordance with Table 14.1, 26% of the mold capacity had been allotted to the manufacture of valve bodies. The reasoning was based on high contribution per pound.

Idle Capacity and Poor Pricing Policies

The basic fact that was overlooked, and is in many firms, was that even though the mold line was operating at 100% capacity, every mold made, which contained less product than the machine could accommodate, was generating idle capacity.

Another important point, related to the preceding one, which also catches many firms off guard is pricing. The valve body, by itself, looked attractive. However, continuation of this type of work should initiate new pricing policies. If a low-weight part ties up resources, such as the mold line in the present example, the price should cover the opportunity cost generated by the making of each mold. For example, if there is sufficient large work available which produces a significant mold contribution, the lower-weight job should be priced to match what the heavier mold would generate. In many (if not most) cases, this pricing policy would price the job out of the reach of the particular foundry. That is not unhealthy.

Consider, for example, that a good job will generate $20 per mold in contribution. If the job weighs 360 lbs, as does the differential case, the contribution would be $.056 per lb. If the molding unit is committed to run parts weighing, say, 50 lbs, then the 50-lb job should still provide $20 per mold, or $.40 per lb. If that price can't be obtained, then the part most likely does not fit the particular facility. Other molding units in the marketplace provide maximum contribution with parts in the 50-lb range. It goes back to a much earlier statement that all parts cannot economically be manufactured in all foundries, even if the facility is new.

"If we quote all jobs at 10% markup on cost, then the total plant will be profitable." That popular statement can be misleading. As has been illustrated, idle capacity generated by running low-weight parts was not covered by the contribution provided.

Another important point is that even though individual parts may appear to be desirable to run, they must be evaluated in the context of *all* the parts presently run in the plant. What may happen is that even though an individual part has a high contribution per pound, or maybe even a high contribution per mold, it may tie up support-department resources that could be used for more-desirable parts. The entire product mix must be examined simultaneously. Linear programming provides an excellent tool to do this.

Firms are reevaluating their entire strategies relative to capacity analysis. To increase the contribution by 67% (Table 14.1 to Table 14.4) with existing facilities just by analyzing the products they manufacture is no small thing. This is just good business, and is a way to fine-tune a manufacturing operation.

Evaluating Capital Investments

It's time now for a new concept. From Table 14.4, it was learned that $9,524 contribution per day is attainable with existing equipment and present price/cost ratios for the available parts. Knowing that molding capacity is reached with 960 molds per day, the following questions can then be asked: If capital money were invested to buy another molding machine with the same capacity, what would be the financial advantage? What, in fact, would be the cash flow relative to this investment decision?

There are several classic techniques that can be used to evaluate the relative merits of competing capital projects. The most popular are:

- simple payback

- nondiscounted rate of return

- discounted rate of return

- net present value

- yield

These five methods have one important factor in common: The answers that they provide are based on the estimated cash flow associated with the project. The initial cash outlay required is usually a definite amount, but the cash benefits generated from improved operations are, at best, someone's estimate. The most sophisticated evaluation methods provide answers that are only as valid as the parameters used — in the present discussion, the operating benefits resulting from making a capital decision. This is especially applicable in discretionary-type projects.

Reasons for Capital Expenditures

Capital expenditures may be required for a number of purposes:

1. General replacement

2. Safety, OSHA, environmental

3. Cost reduction

4. Capacity increase/expansion

5. Facility maintenance

Categories 1, 2 and 5 above are normally considered nondiscretionary. In other words, they are required either to comply with company or external directives, as in the case of (2) above, or they are required just to maintain present production capability. Normally, these types do not require rigorous financial justification; they are just accepted as necessary to keep the business going.

On the other hand, when funds are requested to reduce operating costs and/or increase capacity, such projects are normally competing with other, similar types of projects for which limited funds are available. This necessitates the use of some kind of ranking system.

Better Asset Use Increases Productivity

Thus far in this chapter the focus has been on capacity utilization and optimum product mix definition. These items, especially the latter, are strategy related and are part of the firm's overall game plan. So far, in the foundry example, tremendous gains in the productivity of capital have been realized just by minimizing idle capacity in existing work centers. It would be incorrect to say that capacity was increased. It would be more precise to say that existing facilities were better utilized. The same number of molds were made before and after, the only difference being that each mold contained more product. True, nearly twice the amount of metal was required of the melting department, but, this was once again satisfied by better utilizing the existing melting capacity.

The optimum mix with existing facilities (Table 14.4) required the full 480 minutes (960 molds) available. A closer examination reveals that work center 101 was fully utilized. This is illustrated in Table 14.6, which is compiled from data shown in Table 14.3 and 14.4.

Table 14.6 Work center 101 utilization

Parts Using Work Center 101 (Table 14.3)	Time Required per Part (Table 14.3)	Number of Parts Produced in Optimum Mix (Table 14.4)	Work Center 101 Time Used
Gear blank	.16	57	9.12 minutes
Differential case	10.75	44	473.00 minutes
			482.12*

*Error due to rounding. Computer selected mix not in whole number. In reality, however, partial parts cannot be produced.

At this point, there are two investment opportunities: (1) increase the capacity of work center 101 or (2) that of another molding unit, work center 301. Because that there are limited funds, only one of the projects can be completed. It becomes a matter of choice.

First, there was a choice as to products to manufacture, and now the choice is among investment alternatives. Is this not what the management process is based on — i.e., choosing among different alternatives? The concepts in this chapter are intended to provide objective inputs for the decision-making process.

Determine Cash Flows First

The first step in evaluating these competing alternatives is to determine the cash flows relative to each. What will happen if a new 101 machine is installed, to double existing capacity to 960 available minutes, if molding capacity is not also increased? It might be initially assumed that the capacities of both work centers should be increased, inasmuch as both are fully utilized. In other words, if more molds can't be made, why make more cores? Conversely, why make more molds if core capacity to support the added molds is lacking? The answer lies in the fact that the addition of capacity in just one work center will require a reevaluation of the product mix.

The procedure is to run the linear program again; the only change being the addition of available time in the individual work center. To evaluate the benefits of adding 101 core capacity requires one minor change in Table 14.3. Instead of 480 minutes being available, now 960 minutes will be available. All other parameters and constraints remain the same.

The computer reexamines the parameters and selects a different mix, as reflected in Table 14.7. The major difference between the optimum mix with existing facilities (Table 14.4) and the new recommended mix, with an additional 101 core machine, is found primarily in the number of differential cases and brake calipers produced. The molds previously allotted to brake calipers are now allotted to differential cases. This could be anticipated, because each mold containing a differential case contributes $27, as compared to a mold containing a brake caliper that contributes just $4. Previously, however, capacity in work center 101 was insufficient to make more than 44 differential cases. The brake calipers were previously selected in the mix because they utilized a core work center other than 101 while providing some amount of incremental contribution.

Table 14.7 Buy additional core machine WC 101; all other equipment one shift; one shift with existing equipment (no market constraints)

Part	Number of Each (Total Molds)	Total Weight	Total Revenue	Total VC	Total Contribution	Rank by Contribution per Pound
Manifold	—	—	—	—	—	—
Valve body	576	8,640	$ 8,640	$ 5,760	$ 2,880	1
Lug	—	—	—	—	—	—
Axle housing	172	70,520	31,820	28,808	3,612	10
Gear blank	58	18,560	7,772	6,438	1,334	9
Differential case	89	32,040	11,748	9,345	2,403	8
Wheel hub	—	—	—	—	—	—
Bearing housing	—	—	—	—	—	—
Brake caliper	65	3,185	975	715	260	7
Boat anchor	—	—	—	—	—	—
Total	960	132,945	$60,955	$50,466	$10,489	

How do the total new contribution and associated break-even statistics resulting from with the addition of one 101 machine compare with the contribution and break-even data with existing facilities?

Revenue per mold	$60,955 ÷ 960 = $63.49
Variable cost per mold	$50,466 ÷ 960 = 52.57
Contribution per mold	$10.92

$6,000 ÷ $10.92 = 549 molds required per day to break-even point, or 57% of molding capacity.

Once again, a significant difference exists in contribution and break-even point, with a relatively minor change in the plant's equipment. The productivity of capital has greatly improved, as evidenced by the continued movement of the break-even level to the left.

Using Break-Even Curves

Inasmuch as the break-even points in Tables 14.4, 14.5, and 14.7 have been expressed as a percentage of one-shift mold capacity, this function can be graphed as shown in Figure 14.2.

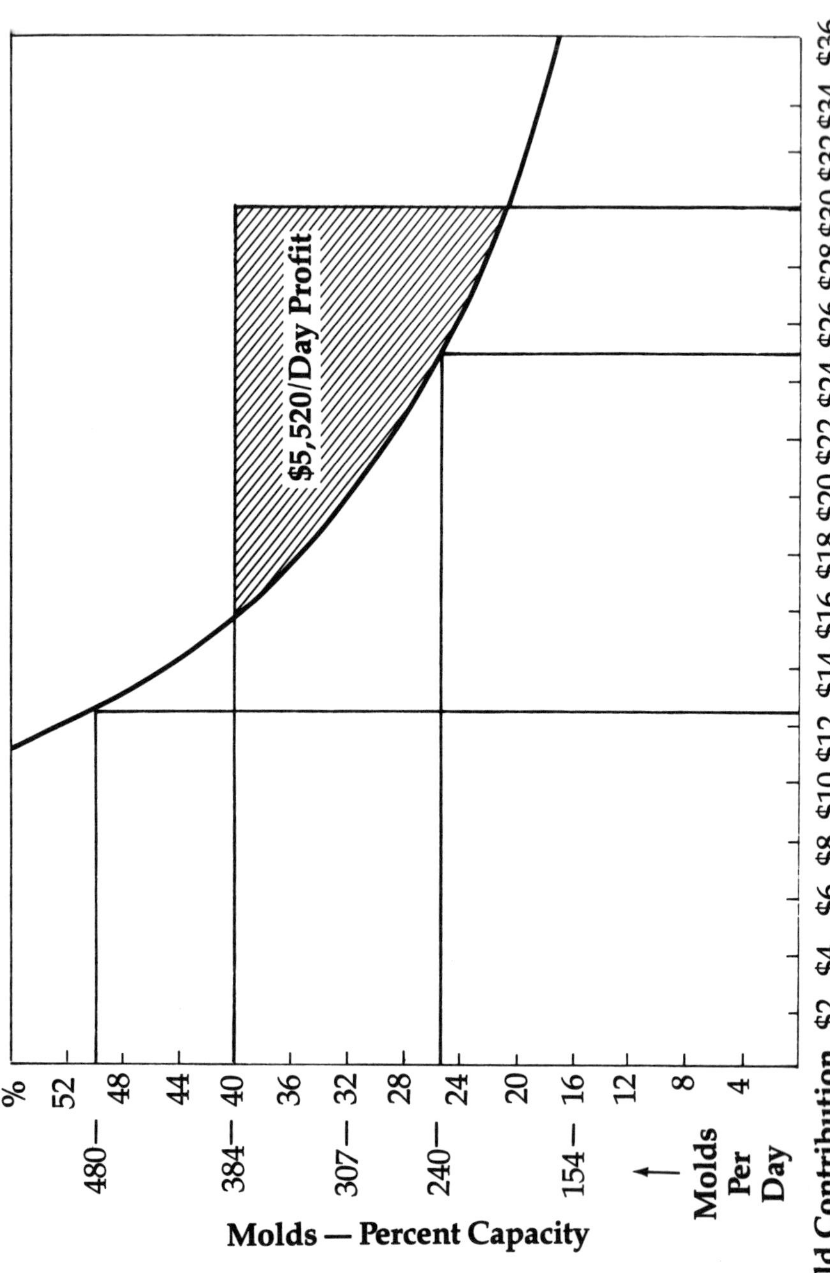

Fig. 14.2. Break-even curve

Listed on the Y axis are daily mold-production rates with the accompanying percent capacity that the production level represents. The three points used to plot this break-even function are as shown:

	Mold Contribution X Value	Daily Mold Rate and Percent Capacity Y Value
Table 14.4 (optimum mix with existing equipment)	$ 9.92	605 @ 63% capacity
Table 14.5 (one-shift molding; no other constraints)	27.00	222 @ 23% capacity
Table 14.7 (add one machine to WC 101; all other parameters unchanged)	10.92	549 @ 57% capacity

In using Figure 14.2, let's say that a production rate of 480 molds per day is expected. Follow this point on the Y axis horizontally until the curve is reached, and then drop down to intercept the X axis. The X axis intercept represents the required contribution per mold to break-even point. In this instance, a production rate of 480 molds per day requires a contribution of $12.50 per mold. To check, simply multiply the rate of 480 x $12.50 = $6,000, which is the fixed cost to recover.

Conversely, if marketing feels that it can sell products with a contribution of $25, the break-even point will be achieved at a daily production rate of 240 molds, or 25% of mold-line capacity.

This graph can also be viewed in another way. Inasmuch as the curve represents the break-even point at varying levels of production and mold contribution, any combination of mold contribution and production that intersects above or to the right of the curve, the area to the right represents profit. For example, consider a contribution of $30 per mold with the plant operating at 40% capacity (384 molds per day). The profit would be $5,520 per day.

($30.00 x 384) - $6,000 = $5,520.

Cash-Flow Determination

Perhaps the most astounding benefit from using linear programming to determine maximum contribution under varying equipment constraints is the ability to determine the cash flow associated with a given investment proposal. The formerly very tedious exercise of trying to estimate such cash flow is virtually eliminated by comparing the contribution with existing circumstances, and then again as provided with the proposed equipment addition.

Here's how it works:

	Optimum Mix with Existing Equipment (Table 14.4)	Optimum Mix by Adding WC 101 Capacity (Table 14.7)	Incremental Contribution
Contribution per day	$9,524	$10,489	$965

Therefore, the decision to invest in a new work center 101 core machine provides operating cash flows in the amount of $965 per day, or, considering 250 operating days per year, $241,250 annually. This amount is then used in the conventional project-evaluation techniques.

Let's consider the other option of adding another molding unit. This time, work center 301 is increased to 960 available minutes, or 1,920 daily molds. All other parameters remain the same. Also, remember to revert work center 101 back to the original 480 minutes available.

The linear program is run again, producing a mix with the maximum possible contribution by adding another work center 301 molding unit. Once again, as illustrated in Table 14.8, there is a substantial change in mix when compared with the optimum mix with existing equipment shown in Table 14.4. The greatest amount of movement is found in manifolds and brake calipers. These seemingly less-desirable parts were included because there is now additional molding capacity and neither of these parts requires a large amount of support equipment, as per Table 14.3.

Table 14.8 Buy additional molding machine; all other equipment one shift

Part	Number of Each (Total Molds)	Total Weight	Total Revenue	Total VC	Total Contribution	Rank by Contribution per Pound
Manifold	424	8,056	$ 6,784	$ 5,512	$ 1,272	3
Valve body	382	5,730	5,730	3,820	1,910	1
Lug	—	—	—	—	—	—
Axle housing	192	78,720	35,520	31,488	4,032	10
Gear blank	35	11,200	4,690	3,885	805	9
Differential case	34	12,240	4,488	3,570	918	8
Wheel hub	—	—	—	—	—	—
Bearing housing	—	—	—	—	—	—
Brake caliper	853	41,797	12,795	9,383	3,412	7
Boat anchor	—	—	—	—	—	—
Total	1,920	157,743	$70,007	$57,658	$12,349	

Contribution per mold = $12,349 ÷ 1,920 = $6.43

The total contribution, as compared with Table 14.4 and Table 14.7, is as follows:

	Optimum Mix with Existing Equipment (Table 14.4)	Optimum Mix by Adding WC 101 Capacity (Table 14.7)	Optimum Mix by Adding WC 301 Capacity (Table 14.8)
Contribution per day	$9,524	$10,489	$12,349

Now it can be seen that adding a new molding unit (WC 301) provides more operating cash flow than adding a new core machine (WC 101).

$$\$12,349 - \$9,524 = \$2,825 \times 250 = \$706,250$$
$$\$10,489 - \$9,524 = 965 \times 250 = \underline{\$241,250}$$
$$\underline{\$465,000}$$

Remember, only the operating cash flow has been determined. Conventional capital-evaluation techniques should now be employed. The original outlay for each machine still has not been determined. All that has been done is to determine the operating cash flow associated with each option.

Before entering into a summary discussion about the concept of integrating capital and strategic planning, several important items relative to Table 14.8 should be noted. The contribution per mold in Table 14.8 drops off rather drastically, owing to the fact that the parts providing high mold contribution do not have adequate core support. Although total contribution is increased, care should be taken not to load the plant with suboptimal types of work. Table 14.5 shows that maximum contribution is attained with heavy-type parts, and this should be the continuing strategy.

This will increase the overall capacity of the plant in terms of *contribution*. Firms are now beginning to speak of capacity in these terms. It becomes of primary importance to maximize the existing assets. The strategy for our example includes increasing the work-center capacity that supports such jobs as the axle housing, gear blank, and differential case. The firm should not be making lugs or boat anchors.

It is interesting to note that the parts originally thought to be desirable, owing to their high contribution on a *weight* basis, are, in reality, less profitable than the higher-weight parts that have a high mold contribution. This becomes evident by ranking the parts by their contribution per mold, which has been determined to be the most appropriate criterion when the objective is maximizing total plant contribution. (See Table 14.9.)

Table 14.9 Contribution ranked on per-mold basis

Part	Weight	Contribution per Pound	Rank	Contribution per Mold	Rank
Manifold	19	.158	3	3	7
Valve body	15	.333	1	5	5
Lug	4	.250	2	1	9
Axle housing	410	.051	10	21	3
Gear blank	320	.072	9	23	2
Differential case	360	.075	8	27	1
Wheel hub	66	.091	6	6	4
Bearing housing	20	.100	5	2	8
Brake caliper	49	.082	7	4	6
Boat anchor	13	.154	4	2	8

The strategic process to maximize asset utilization is basically accomplished in three steps:

1. Define all bottlenecks that surface when present available parts are mixed for maximum contribution as per Table 14.4.

2. Relieve each bottleneck systematically with computer simulation.

3. After each bottleneck is relieved, a new one will appear. Increase the available time on the next bottleneck that surfaces. Proceed until equipment additions are no longer feasible within the existing physical plant *or* until the incremental contribution generated does not equate favorably with the required cash outlay to relieve the bottleneck.

Implied in the presentation of these concepts is that the marketing people can sell the computer-generated product mix that provides the maximum contribution for the particular plant. That is rarely the case. However, to include marketing constraints in the model would not enhance the basic understanding of the concepts. In practice, the marketing people will provide realistic sales constraints, not unlike production constraints. For example, if a maximum of 50 axle housings could be sold per day for any reason, then a restricting equation is established in the form of:

axle housing $\leq$ 50 per day

The model will readily handle numerous other "what if" questions. Examples include:

- What if the plant in question operated with two hours overtime each day?

- What if the industrial engineers devised better methods on WC 101 so that it required only five minutes, instead of the present 10.75 minutes, to process a differential case?

- What if two manifolds could be made in a single mold instead of the present one?

- What if the price of bearing housings was lowered by 10%?

- What if a design change resulted in a decrease in the weight of the axle housing to 375 lbs instead of its present 410 lbs?

- What if the scrap rate on the brake caliper were cut in half, resulting in a variable cost of $10 instead of the present $11?

- What if the molding unit could be speeded up to a 25-second cycle instead of the present 30 seconds?

These items are just a sampling, but each of them has a direct impact on the definition of the optimum product mix.

Summary

One of the primary objectives of this chapter was to illustrate the futility of trying to formulate capital or strategic plans without considering them simultaneously.

Capital planning should be considered as a function to support a firm's strategic plan. The strategic plan should define overall direction, including product-mix determination. Few plant managers realize that their plants can do some things much more effectively than other things.

This concept, when applied on a macro level, implies, for example, that the United States should produce a great amount of foodstuffs because we are so efficient at it, while third-world nations might best concentrate on high-labor-content consumer goods.

Optimum-mix definition for a plant will provide the greatest contribution with a given asset base. A plant's optimum mix will also result in the lowest possible break-even point, as well as minimize idle capacity. Idle capacity generates opportunity cost.

A plant should define its capacity relative to its limiting factors, which may not be the conventional method for the particular industry. Improper capacity definition may result in incorrect break-even projection.

A plant's pricing policy should be structured to cover, or recover, the amount of resources consumed in the manufacturing process. Idle capacity caused by the underutilization of equipment, such as the molding-machine example, should be borne by the customer. A plant cannot evaluate the financial desirability of a given part solely on its merits. It must be considered as part of the total product mix to see what effect it has on total plant contribution.

The most accurate projections of operating cash flows associated with a proposed capital expenditure are obtained by examining the incremental contribution that results from the addition of the proposed equipment. Just as a single part (job) cannot be considered mutually exclusive when considering its contribution, neither can a proposed new machine that alters plant capacity in any work center.

Chapter 15
Developing the
Production Plan

Objectives

- *Understand that there are three primary levels of productivity.*

- *Understand the concepts underlying the unending time span.*

- *Understand the relationship of time and opportunity in the development and execution of the production plan.*

- *Understand the concepts of "when" and "how long."*

- *Understand that each major resource included in the production plan must have an accompanying information support system.*

- *Understand the concepts of measurement and evaluation of production resources.*

- *Understand that process controls are preventive functions.*

Contents

Productivity Begins with Comparative Advantage

As this book is brought to completion, it is paramount that the readers have a grasp of "where and how" production and productivity fit into the overall scheme of things.

Productivity can be viewed in terms of three levels:

1. Macro

2. Micro

3. Mini

Macro level productivity involves the application of the comparative advantage principle. If, in fact, the United States produced, consumed, and/or exported items that could be produced with fewer production resources than any competitor nation, we would be practicing comparative advantage. In other words, if we focused our productive efforts on those items in which we were the most productive, we would maximize our resources. Conversely, if a competitor nation is more productive with different items than we, they should be the producer and consumer and we should be an importer and consumer. The application of this concept would result in the maximization of productivity at the gobal level as well as among each participating nation. Benefits to each participating nation would also include the highest standard of living that could be attainable for its citizens.

Comparative advantage is limited in application for numerous reasons, not the least of which is the concern that each nation has for its own people. Nonproductive industries may be subsidized in an attempt to bolster local economies. Political ambitions may overshadow economic considerations. Cultural issues and constraints may have an inordinate influence on a nation's goals and ambitions.

Comparative Advantage Requires Free Enterprise

Inherent in the concept of comparative advantage is that each participating nation operate in the arena of free enterprise where supply and demand, rather than the State, defines production. Pricing is also established on the basis of supply and demand. There can be no restraint of trade due to tariffs, import quotas, or other trade restrictions.

Whatever the barriers and for whatever reasons the barriers exist, it is doubtful that global and national productivity will be maximized because of them. However, the last decade of the 20th century is seeing major barriers and walls come tumbling down. Of particular significance is the fact that several major nations have abandoned central planning of their economies. Until such time, that each global participant can ask, in the presence of all other players, "What is right for me to produce?" macro productivity will be less than it could be.

Now then, accepting that national, or macro productivity, is less than perfect, let's progress to the second level — micro productivity.

Matching Production with Facility Design

Micro productivity occurs within a particular industry. The concept is very similar to macro productivity in that it also addresses the basic question: "Are we producing the right things?" The preceding chapter dealt with defining a producer's optimum product mix, which is the application of micro level productivity.

Every production facility can do some things better than it can do others. A production facility is typically designed with a particular product mix in mind. The proposed product mix dictates equipment sizing, tooling, processes, and other constraints/limitations. If the facility is designed for a particular range of products, relative to size and nomenclature, it stands to reason that those are the products that will maximize resource productivity for that firm. When the firm attempts to produce items that are outside the range for which it was designed, productivity will suffer.

Implied in the application of micro productivity is that any given facility has some choice in the items it produces. Granted, a jobbing facility may have more freedom of choice than a captive facility, however, even in the captive situation, such as a vertically integrated manufacturer, each producing level must be assertive at its level. No level should acquiesce to producing everything and anything that is channeled in its direction if it is not economically advantageous.

It is a popular misconception that a new facility can produce the total range of sizes within a product line and/or mix more economically than any competitor just because it is a new facility and employs state-of-the-art technology. When a facility attempts to produce products for which it was not designed, several things are likely to occur. There will be:

- Imbalance in the production process.

- Idle capacity or underutilization of equipment.

- Less than optimum use of working capital.

Whenever a production facility produces items for which it was not designed, less than optimum productivity will result and less than optimum financial performance will be achieved. More than likely, there will be a competitive production facility designed to produce those items to fill that gap.

Care and judgment must be exercised in the pursuit of this concept. A production facility may be designed and tooled for too narrow a mix. Such was the case with Ford's Flatrock Foundry in Michigan. This impressive facility was idled when the demand for large horsepower engines dwindled and the cost to retool for smaller engines was prohibitive.

Production Implementation

As we progress to the next level — mini productivity — it

must be realized that the preceding two levels were strategic considerations. This final level is tactical, in that it deals with implementation of the strategic decision about "what" to produce. This final level involves the determination of the optimum sociotechnical system for each phase of the production process.

In order to place this final level of productivity in proper perspective, let's reconsider the four basic stages of a firm.

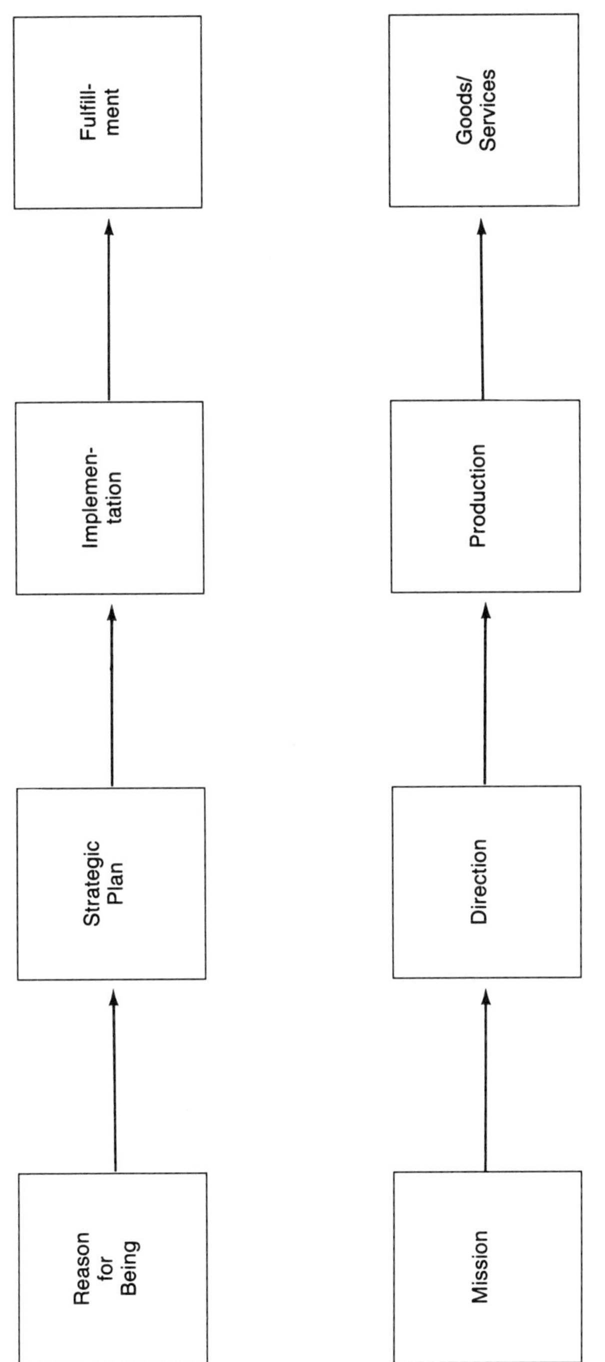

Fig. 15.1. Four stages of the total firm

The production function is, therefore, the implementation of the firm's strategy and the application of mini productivity. In other words, the decision has been made about "what" the firm will produce; the remaining choice is to determine "how" to produce it in order to maximize the firm's resources.

The production function (implementation of the firm's strategy) can also be segmented into four stages.

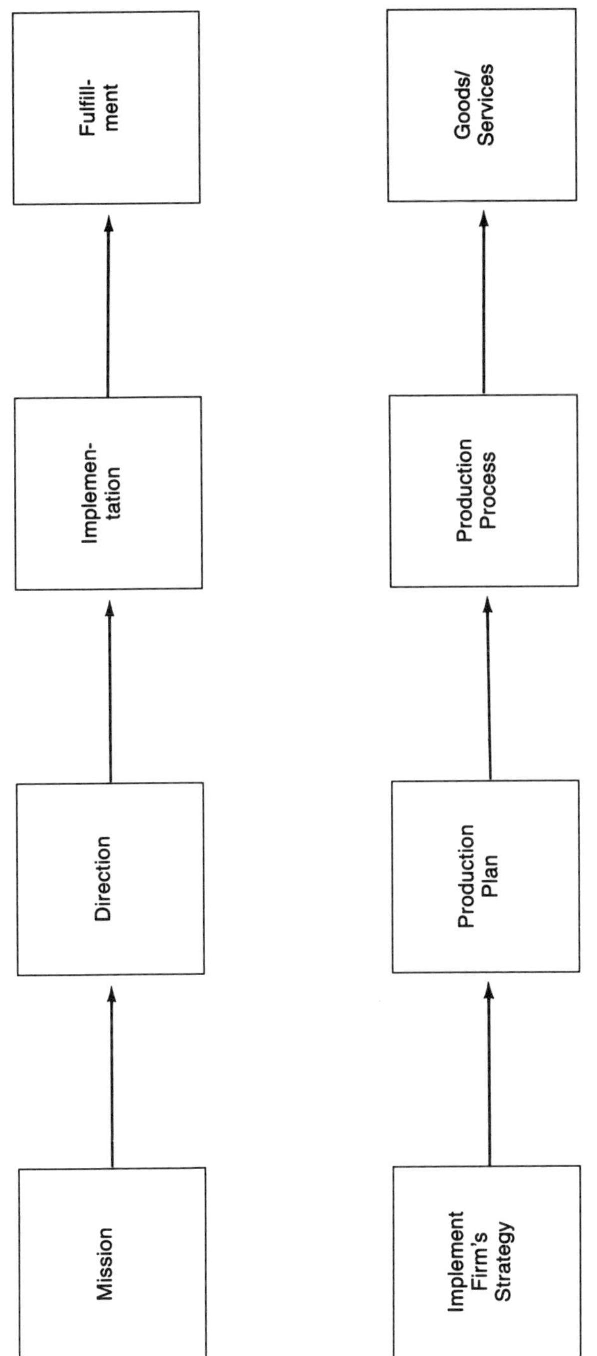

Fig. 15.2. Four stages of the production function

Note:

- The mission, or reason for being, for the production func-tion is to implement the firm's strategy.

- The production function's direction is contained in the production plan.

- Implementation is the production process.

- Fulfillment is expressed, once again, in terms of goods/services.

Now then, let's consider the four stages representing the total firm in conjunction with the four stages of the production function. The resultant combination is reflected below.

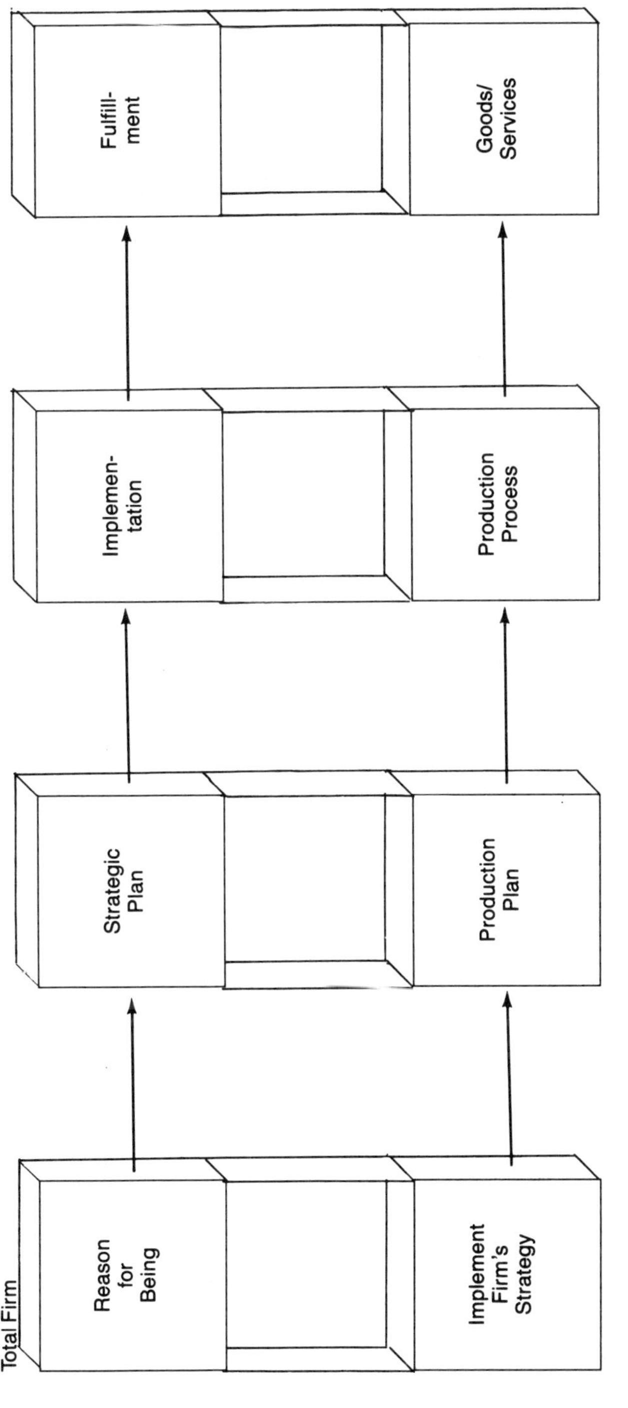

Fig. 15.3. Four stages the total firm/production function

Notice the alignment of the four stages representing both the total firm and its production function. This alignment is significant and will be explained shortly.

Time as the Universal Benchmark

As we progress in the development of a production plan, we must pass from concept to application, from strategy to tactics, and from plans to quantifiable goals. In order to establish and subsequently evaluate quantifiable goals there must be benchmarks. In the area of production, time is the universal benchmark. All who study and apply the exciting discipline of production must be intimately familiar with the uniqueness of *time*.

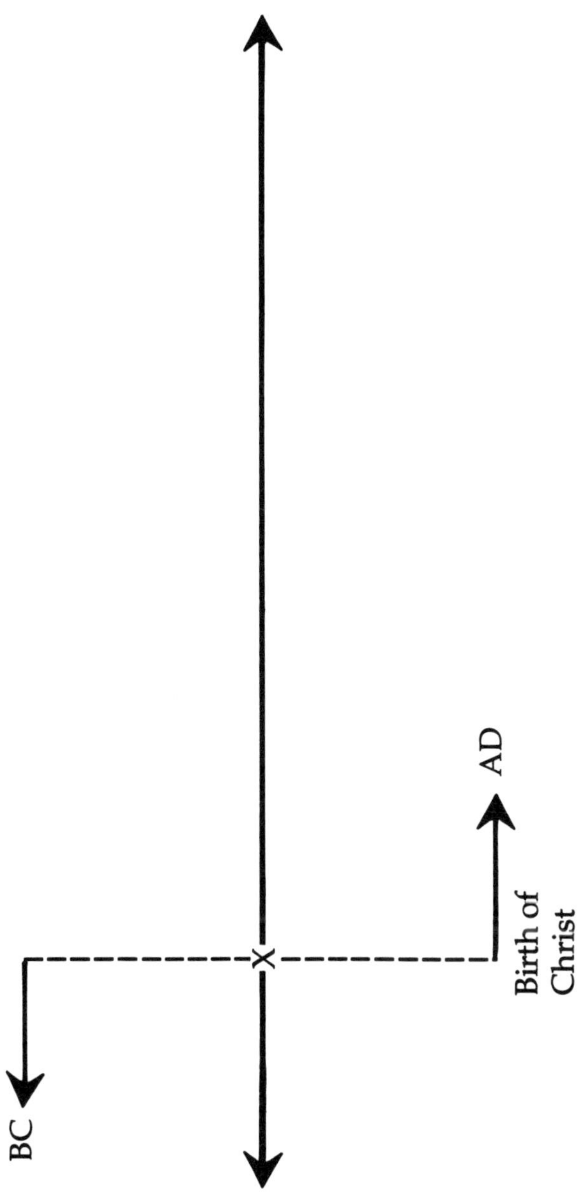

Fig. 15.4. Time span & reference point

On the unending time span is a reference point, the birth of Christ, which forms the basis of the Gregorian calendar that we use daily. From this reference point we can progress to the right to the present or to the future.

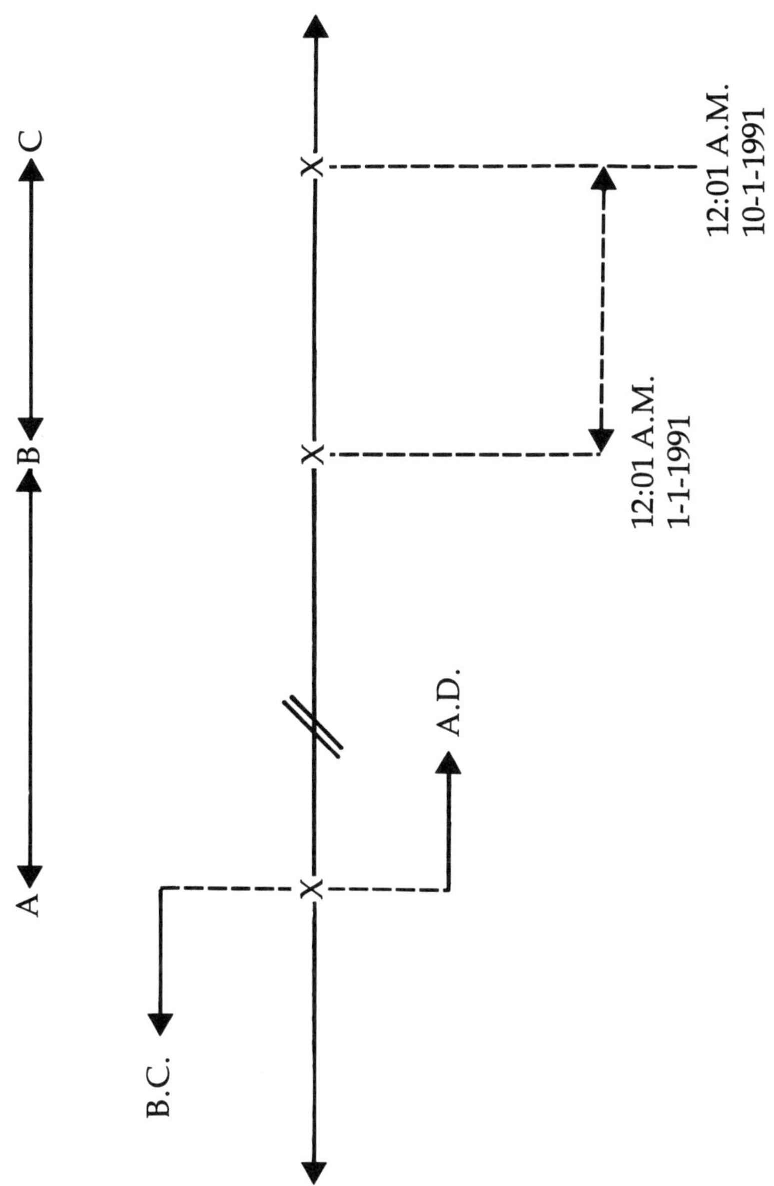

Fig. 15.5. Time span: when and how long

When points A, B, and C are examined individually, i.e., mutually exclusive of each other, the "when" aspect of time is considered. The "when" aspect occurs at a particular *point* on the unending span. Such a point is valid for an instant and then becomes history never to repeat itself nor reappear. Consider, however, the segments on the span determined by A ← → B and B ← → C. Even though the length of the segments may vary substantially, the *rate* at which the segments increase in length is exactly the same.

Example

A strategic goal for an Iron Foundry is to enter the market with a Ductile iron gear housing by 1-1-91. The company expects to capture a 5% share of the gear housing market by 10-1-1991.

When do they plan to enter the market? 1-1-1991

How long do they think it will take to capture 5% of the market? 9 months

Let's add the time dimensions to the basic model depicting a firm and its production functions.

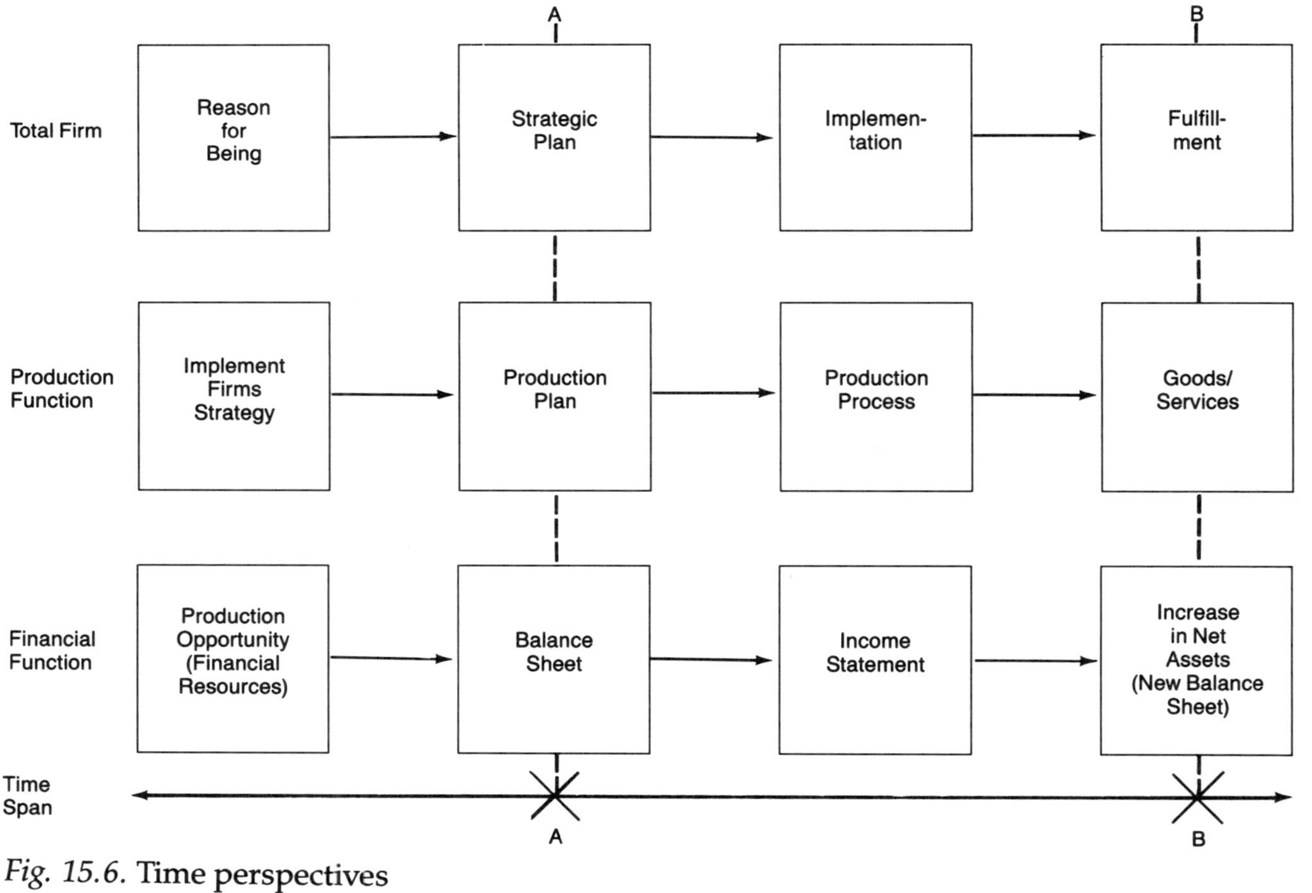

Fig. 15.6. Time perspectives

Figure 15.6 represents relationships that inherently exist in all firms. An examination of the relationships will readily indicate the firm's relative productivity.

The Production Plan Must Reflect the Strategic Plan

Consider point A on the time span. It signifies:

- The strategic *plan* for the firm at a particular *point* in time, based on current knowledge of all factors that influence the firm's direction that was established to fulfill its purpose.

- The production plan, or the amount and nature of resources required to implement the strategic plan at the *same point* in time.

- The *financial readiness* (in terms of the firm's balance sheet) to fulfill the strategic plan by listing the required production resources in financial terms.

Key Points:

- Whenever the firm's strategy shifts, for whatever reason, the production plan must respond immediately.

- Optimum financial performance, measured as the increase in net assets, the ultimate productivity indicator, occurs when the production plan exactly reflects the strategic plan.

- Care must be exercised not to *drive* the strategic plan and production plan with the balance sheet. The balance sheet should be a *reflection* and not the genesis. As long as the proper relationship between a dog and his tail is maintained, there should not be a problem.

Consider now the segment A ← → B on the time span in Figure 15.6. This span allows time for the production process — i.e., implementation of the firm's strategy. It can be compared to a firm's capacity. What is capacity?

4 Ships
40 Drilling rigs
400 Airplanes
4,000 Engines
40,000 Tons
400,000 CD players
4,000,000 Filters
40,000,000 Cassettes
400,000,000 Cigarettes
4,000,000,000 Hamburgers

These units of measure have no meaning without knowing the appropriate time segment required for their production. Therefore, capacity of any production function is measured in units per time period, most generally a year. The *rate* that time passes from A to B is known with certainty; hence, it is the *universal benchmark* with which to measure *productive opportunity* (capacity).

The production process is continuous — new orders are received daily and placed in the production system. Therefore, even though point B *ends* the segment A ← → B, it also *begins* the segments B ← → C, B ← → D, etc. Therefore, point B also signifies the same items that point A did in previous paragraphs. Any such *point* on the time span addresses the question "when" and any *segment* addresses the question "how long."

Production Resources and Subsidiary Information Systems

Now armed with a firm grasp of the time concept, we can progress to finite measures of other production resources that are required in the production plan to fulfill our strategy.

The following listings of resources and subsidiary monitoring/support systems is not intended to be all inclusive. It is intended to highlight the concept of measurement of the major resources required to successfully implement a firm's strategy via the production function.

Major Production Resources

- labor

- materials

- equipment

- energy

- working capital

Subsidiary Monitoring/Support Systems

- labor productivity/utilization reports

- production/inventory control systems

- equipment utilization/downtime reports

- energy requirements/utilization reports

- operating budgets for planning/control

- quality measurement/monitoring systems

As each major production resource, or factor, is discussed, its accompanying monitoring/support system will also be discussed.

The production function operates within an environment of standards and measures. The primary standard to which productivity is compared is found in the "never-ending hourglass." The productivity opportunity of all production factors is either directly or indirectly a function of time. Perhaps this point can be made more clear by considering that a bank loans money (the medium of exchange for all other production factors) on the basis of the time period the borrower will have the money. It is not based on *how well* the time opportunity is used, but the *length* of the time opportunity.

As we walk through a production facility, we might hear a variety of sounds such as motors or blowers. Above the sounds of production, we should be able to hear a faint ticking of the opportunity clock. And, if production slows and/or stops for whatever reason, the ticking will get louder because the opportunity clock doesn't stop even if production does.

Labor

Consider the labor resource. This is the most important resource in the production process, not necessarily because of the high ratio of labor cost in the products, but because of the profound effect labor (human resources) has on the productivity of all other production resources. Two entire chapters (7 and 8) were devoted to this resource.

Once the capacity of a production facility is established — after the strategically determined product mix and volume have been determined for a planning time segment (normally a year) — the labor resource for the production plan can be developed.

The next step is to divide the year into smaller time segments. Interim financial reports, operating budgets, and the Master Schedule typically cover a month's activity. Chapter 7, "Measuring the Labor Input," indicated that production standards were expressed as standard hours/piece or standard pieces/hour. In either case, the labor standard is contained in the data base for each part or product. When the master schedule is "exploded" for each month, the direct labor requirements are listed. This is the basis for the direct labor portion of the production plan. The indirect or support portion of the labor resource must then be considered. It requires intimate knowledge of the production process to properly define the indirect effort to support the production process for varying levels of activity.

In keeping with the common thread of time, it is quickly realized that the labor resource is planned, controlled, and paid as a function of time. With proper shop-floor reporting systems, it is not necessary to wait for interim, or monthly, reports to track the productivity/utilization of the labor resource. Daily reports should reveal the effectiveness of labor by work center, individual, and product, expressed in terms of efficiency, utilization, and total labor productivity.

At the end of the planning segment, the product mix that actually ran will be "exploded" to indicate how much labor *should have* been required for that particular mix.

A primary concern at this point is the difference between the product mix and capacity utilization actually achieved vs. that which was planned. Will this difference cause a change in strategy or was the difference caused by a change in strategy? In either case, whenever the production plan does not match the strategic plan, less than optimum financial performance will result, as per Figure 15.6.

Material

The material resource is also a function of the Master Schedule. Not unlike the labor resource, when the master schedule's subset, called the bill of materials, is exploded, the materials requirements are listed. The MRP (materials requirements planning) module will indicate "when" the raw material or component parts are needed in order to meet the completed product requirement listed on the Master Schedule. The "when" aspect of time is critical to successfully plan and control the material resource. This aspect of time, relative to materials, gave birth to the "just in time" concepts. There has been perhaps more study and writings about this production resource than any of the others.

Two major categories of materials planning and control must be considered in the establishment and subsequent control of the production plan:

1. Logistical — The tracking of the material component of the end product from the acquisition of raw material to the distribution of the finished product. This aspect also includes the tracking of the materials as they flow through the production process.

2. Physical — The attributes of products relative to their mass and other physical and/or chemical characteristics.

One of the major differences between planning for labor vs. materials is that the labor resource is typically within the firm's control. Labor effort can be assigned where needed on short notice. The material resource, on the other hand, is typically something that a firm depends on others to supply. Therefore, materials requirements planning is a major effort for any production function.

The control of the logistics aspect of materials is straight forward. Production and inventory-control systems will reveal such problems as production downtime, work center imbalance, missed shipments, and inventory fluxuations, to mention a few related items. Such items should not be included in the production plan. If these items appear, they should be viewed as "variations" due to the production process being out of synchronization with the production plan. Any of the items mentioned will result in less than optimal financial performance.

Chapter 9, "Materials: Composites, Substitutes and, Yield," addressed the second major category of materials planning and control listed above. It stressed the physical aspects of materials such as reconciling "mass in vs. mass out." This unique aspect of materials allows a firm to monitor the total weight of raw materials and account for it by mass. The total mass input to the production process represents the productivity opportunity. The output is termed "yield," which represents the quantity resulting as percentage of what is theoretically possible. This aspect of materials has significant advantages to process type production functions.

Equipment

The equipment resource, as it applies to the development of the production plan, considers utilization, not acquisition which was covered in Chapters 6 and 10 relative to capital planning.

Once again, the master schedule is the key. Just as labor and materials requirements are determined by the master schedule, so is machine loading. Finite loading and machine line balance result from the Master Schedule. Finite loading addresses the reality that a given machine can operate just so many hours in a time segment. The production plan must take this reality into consideration. Continued line imbalances and/or equipment limitations revealed by the finite loading module of the master schedule may result in additions to the capital plan. It should be noted that the reaction time to relieve such a bottleneck is typically longer than a material or labor resource imbalance. Line balancing should be an integral part of the production plan for the equipment resource.

There are two major categories of planning and control for the equipment resource.

1. Effectiveness while operating; and

2. Downtime or reason for not operating.

The first category deals with machine productivity or efficiency. Production standards, as reflected in the production plan, are engineered for each item of equipment and each operation it performs. Any deviation from production standards will cause an imbalance in work center or machine loading.

The second category is primarily a control device inasmuch as downtime should not be reflected in the production plan. Downtime is a variance, just as defective materials or inefficient labor are. Downtime is a subtle deterrent to productivity, moreover, it can cost thousands of dollars per minute. Equipment downtime should be monitored as to duration and cause as surely as any other production resource. Machine downtime is a major pulse point signaling trouble in the production process and must be given due consideration.

Energy

The next major production resource to be included in the production plan is energy. Depending on the production function, energy may become part of the product (e.g., natural gas in a fertilizer plant), used in the production process (e.g., fuel furnaces to melt steel) or consumed in support activities (e.g., HVAC equipment).

A key point to keep in mind is that the amount of energy required to do any job can be defined. Energy may not be a significant part of the cost of many light or assembly type production functions, or it may represent 25% of total cost to an industry that changes the natural state of material (i.e., a foundry). For energy intensive industries, the required energy to do a given job may be part of the product data base, similar to the product's bill of materials or routing sequence. In such cases, the consideration of energy in the production plan is fairly routine.

Energy requirements are typically expressed in common units such as Btu and then translated into the unit of measure in which the energy is delivered to the production process (e.g., kwh for electricity or cubic feet for natural gas).

The control aspects of the energy resource necessitate localized metering systems so that consumption patterns can be monitored. Not unlike labor, materials, and machines, the energy consumed per time segment must be compared with the actual product mix ran in order to determine meaningful energy variances. A comprehensive discussion on energy relative to the production function is found in Chapter 11, "Energy as a Production Input."

Working Capital

Working capital must be included as a major production resource. Working capital in the form of cash is the medium of exchange that is used to purchase all other production resources except time. Cash, therefore, is the first production resource or input. Two entire chapters are included in this text covering the aspects of cash. Chapter 4 deals with how it all begins with cash, while Chapter 5 explains that the production process not only begins with cash but must also end with cash. In fact, the production process is not complete until the goods and services are translated into the liquid state of cash. Additional production factors to sustain growth for the firm cannot be purchased with non-liquid assets.

It should be intuitive for every manager, especially the production manager, to feel a sense of urgency to complete the production process. The "never-ending hour glass," as the term implies, doesn't rest. *Idle* production resources in the form of labor, materials, equipment, energy, or cash itself represent an opportunity lost forever while the time span continues at its incessant pace.

Every production plan should have provisions for the measure of the time resource required to complete the production process. There is ample research done on the aspect of idle raw material in the form of JIT, but little study has been done on the aspect of the detrimental affect of idle work-in-process or finished goods inventory. Idle inventories are dollars waiting to happen so as to begin the production process again! There is no virtue in providing a "bank" of work-in-process inventory for insurance against shutting down a production line if it's never used. Meanwhile the hour glass continues to flow.

The monitoring of the "return to cash" state may begin with goals for inventory turnover. However, a linear program that minimizes time as the objective function would be appropriate.

The primary control tool to measure working capital effectiveness is the variable operating budget. When budgets are used for planning purposes, the process begins by reducing the master schedule to production resources, expressed in dollars. The logic is that the firm's strategy is reduced to monthly sales forecasts that are reduced to the master schedule, which is, in turn, reduced to individual production resources that form the basis of the production plan. The production plan reduced to dollars, becomes the operating budget.

When operating budgets are used as control tools, there is a basic difference. Instead of keying from the Master Schedule to determine the level of resources required, the input is the actual product mix processed. Variances are reflected by comparing actual expenses, or resources consumed, vs. what *should have been* consumed for the actual product mix processed.

The differences between the master schedule and actual product mix must be examined separately. Such differences may be extremely important because they reflect a difference between the strategy and implementation. Once again, when this occurs, less than optimum financial performance results.

Budgets as a control tool should not produce surprises at the end of the time segment covered. Each production function has its peculiar "pulse points" or vital signs that provide an excellent continuous view of the general health of the production process. These pulse points are generally taken no less than daily. Such a pulse point may be in the form of excess scrap or an increase in the cycle time of a major item of equipment. Each production manager will quickly establish appropriate pulse points, which, when properly read and interpreted, will result in an operating budget at the end of a time segment that is primarily confirmatory.

There may be additional production resources for particular industries or firms, however, the five discussed, (labor, materials, equipment, energy, and working capital) are generic in nature and will find applicability in most firms.

Quality Control for Products and Processes

There remains the topic of quality measurement/monitoring systems. This is another control tool that is used to check on how well, or effectively, the *production resources* are being used. It is also a measure of the effectiveness of the production *process*. There are two general phases of a basic quality program:

1. Final inspection

2. Process controls

They are very closely related, and are, in fact, functions of one another. For example, a firm's final inspection results may spur more process controls. Likewise, process control results may lessen or increase the need for final inspection.

Chapter 13, "Strategically Managing Quality," deals with the concepts and statistical application of both of these phases. The first phase dealing with final inspection is a tool to determine the overall level of quality resulting from the production process. It is determined statistically through sampling. These sampling procedures produce a given confidence level that the total production run is acceptable or not, based on a desired percentage of defective parts contained therein.

The need for a comprehensive final inspection function is greatly reduced if the second phase, i.e., process control, is effective. Consider, for example, that a firm desires an overall defect rate of less than 4%. Consider further that the final inspection reveals a 6% defect rate. What does the firm do? Well, process control should determine the areas of process variation, or the *causes* for defective products and eliminate or minimize them before making scrap.

Consider that there were 60,000 deaths last year on the nation's highways. The 60,000 is the magnitude of the problem, just as 6% is the magnitude of the problem in the preceding paragraph. Nothing is said, however, about the *cause* of the highway deaths.

Well, the 60,000 number can't be wished away any easier than the 6% defective product rate. What if, however:

- It was announced that every state adopted a seatbelt law with rigorous enforcement, such as fines for offenders?

- It was mandated in each state that first-time DWI offenders would lose their licenses for a year?

- All major insurance companies announced that they would reduce automobile insurance premiums by 10% for every year a person drove accident free?

Does wearing seatbelts reduce highway deaths? Do drunken drivers cause highway deaths? Would people drive more safely if it meant money in their pockets?

These questions are easy to answer. The idea is that the causes of highway death must be identified and pursued in order to reduce the magnitude of the problem. The same principle applies to process controls as a means to lower the rate of defective products. In fact, it is a bit easier to reduce defective products with process control because each and every step of the production process is capable of causing defects. The concept is that if every step of the production process were within prescribed limits, there would be no defective products. Although the concept is valid, employees get tired and machine tools wear so that total consistency is difficult if not nearly impossible to maintain.

Because defective products are perhaps the single largest deterrent to productivity, process control should have a high priority with any firm.

Summary

A firm's production plan is the implementation of its strategy. To have planned a strategy to get from its purposes, or mission, to its fulfillment without a production plan is like trying to cross the Pacific Ocean in a sailboat without a sail. The production plan addresses the concept of mini productivity by defining the sociotechnical system in the production process that optimizes resource utilization.

Finally, there are three levels of productivity:

1. *Macro:* This nation produces, consumes, and exports those items in which we are competitive. We import and consume those items in which we are not competitive.

2. *Micro:* Each industrial entity examines its strengths and produces the size and mix of products that maximizes their contribution. Those products that fall outside a firm's optimum product mix should be produced at facilities that were designed for such production.

3. *Mini:* Each production function defines the sociotechnical systems that optimizes its resources in the production process. This is basic efficiency.

If a firm has previously incorporated the first two items above, it will be efficient at the "right things," which results in effectiveness.

If the United States will address productivity at all three of the levels listed, we will develop World Class (Stage IV companies, as defined by Hayes and Wheelright) competitors that will be able to make their marks in the global marketplace.

Appendix A

Improving Worker Productivity by Communicating Knowledge of Work Results

Behavior can be viewed as a response to human needs, the motive being the desire for need fulfillment. Human behavior is, thus, behavior toward a goal. When a worker receives the "knowledge of results" of his behavior in relation to goal attainment, it registers in his mind, and the behavior is either positively or negatively reinforced. The brain and the nervous system are the individual's central organizing agencies in recognizing the interplay between need satisfaction and specific modes of behavior.

An example of the operation of this model of behavior is provided by the behavior of a hungry infant. The infant's brain receives sensory signals from an empty stomach telling him he is hungry (he has a need). This creates an awareness in his brain of discomfort (giving him a motive). He then begins to cry (behavior) so that his parents will bring him food (his goal). When he eats, his goal is met, and his stomach gives his brain feedback (knowledge of results) that his need has been satisfied. The success of crying gives positive reinforcement to this type of behavior as a means for satisfying the need for food.

Reinforcement and knowledge of results are two important links in this basic model of behavior which management can use to influence the behavior patterns of workers. Knowledge of results encourages goal-oriented behavior and serves as a mechanism for providing reinforcement of such behavior. Knowledge of results makes the worker aware of his performance level and how it compares with organizational standards of work performance (the goal).

A worker can judge his performance level against those of his coworkers. Personal behavior that attains or surpasses these standards is positively reinforced and behavior that is substandard is negatively reinforced. This helps the worker satisfy his internal needs for self-esteem. He can also receive positive reinforcement when his supervisor and fellow workers recognize his higher productivity through the knowledge-of-results technique. Knowledge of results also helps to satisfy the worker's innate need to know what is going on about him, how he performs in relation to others, and if this performance is acceptable.

Reinforcement is related to the "law of effect," which states that persons will tend to repeat behavior that is rewarding, while behavior that has painful consequences will tend to not be repeated.[1] When a worker begins to associate behavior that leads to higher productivity with the satisfaction of his higher-level needs, he is likely to continue that mode of behavior. On the other hand, when a worker begins to associate behavior that leads to low productivity with reduction of need satisfaction, he is likely to discontinue the behavior.

Thus, the mechanism of reinforcement through knowledge of results achieves behavior that is both satisfying to the worker and helps to meet the objectives of the firm through higher productivity. The theory also suggests that the satisfying of higher-level needs will contribute to worker morale.

If a person cannot arrive at the behavior that will satisfy his needs, he is likely to become frustrated. Frustration can be caused by a worker's not knowing how he is doing in comparison to the expectations of management and in relation to his fellow workers.

Studies conducted at Louisiana State University indicate the relationship between knowledge of results and frustration. They state, "without knowledge of progress, members of a group may become aggressive or escape the situation through apathy and boredom."[2]

Morris S. Viteles calls for a positive approach to the avoidance of frustration through the use of positive incentives.[3] Knowledge of results is here regarded as a positive incentive that will reduce frustration and increase employee productivity, satisfaction, and morale. N. R. Maier concurs when he states, "rewards will reduce frustration because they will satisfy higher-level needs and eliminate the causes of frustration."[4]

The behavioral-science technique of "knowledge of results" is analogous to the term "feedback" in cybernetics. It supplies information to the work group on their level which signals corrective action if behavior deviates from standard. It, therefore, is the mechanism through which management can encourage the transition from random behavior to performance. Knowledge of results can be the catalyst for enabling a worker to attain his goals and satisfy his higher-level needs by meeting or surpassing standards for job performance.

Primary studies of the effects of knowledge of results have been undertaken in other areas, mostly in the field of learning.[5] Very little attempt has been made to measure the value of feedback and knowledge and results in the unionized industrial environment.[6] An example of a study made in the field of education was that made by George W. Angell at Michigan State University.[7] The purpose of his experiment was to determine the effect of immediate and delayed knowledge of quiz results on learning in a freshman chemistry class. One group received immediate knowledge of results, the other group received delayed knowledge of results. Each group was composed of 81 students.

Augell found that the group that received immediate knowledge of results scored highest on the final exam. He concluded that knowledge of results was an aid in learning and that performance increased more through immediate knowledge of results.

In a very important study conducted by psychologists from Tufts College, knowledge of results proved to be the important factor in improving the marksmanship or efficiency of 40-mm gunpointers.[8] The purpose of the study was to test the technique to see if it had any value in training the gunpointers for future combat duty in World War II. In the study, 12 gunpointers were divided into 2 groups. Group A was supplied knowledge of results, while Group B received none. Knowledge of results was given to the gunpointers through the use of a buzzer that was set to ring whenever the target was missed. Marksmanship was measured by the percentage of targets missed by each gunpointer.

After three training periods in which Group A received knowledge of results, and Group B received none, it was found that Group A performed better. Group A cut its percentage of missed targets from 60% to 32%. Group B, in comparison, cut its percentage of missed targets from 57% to 55%.

At this stage, the training was reversed for one more training period. Group A received no knowledge of results, while Group B received knowledge of results for the first time. At the end of this period it was found that with the knowledge of results Group B reduced its percentage of missed targets from 55% to 37%. Group A had maintained its rate of 32% missed targets.

The first two phases of the study proved that knowledge of results increased marksmanship efficiency by reducing the proportion of missed targets. In the third phase of the study, the gunpointers were divided into two different types of groups, one group composed of experienced gunpointers, and the other group composed of inexperienced gunpointers. The researchers wanted to determine whether knowledge of results would have different effects on marksmanship improvement for experienced and inexperienced gunpointers. Both groups were given knowledge of results after a control period in which they did not receive any information. The inexperienced gunpointers improved from 61% missed targets to 41%. The experienced group improved from 54% missed targets to 28%. This phase of the study indicates that knowledge of results is an effective technique for increasing performance levels for both experienced and inexperienced gunpointers.

In conclusion, the researchers felt that knowledge of results "is of definite value in improving the gunpointing accuracy of the men. This conclusion appears to hold for trained as well as untrained lateral gunpointers."[9] The researchers observed that when the groups received knowledge of results their level of morale was higher.

In another study closer to the industrial environment, W. V. Bingham, a former professor at the University of Chicago, concluded that knowledge of results stimulated production.[10] He based his conclusion on studies conducted on firemen in an electric-generating plant. He also felt that morale was improved after the introduction of knowledge of results.

The psychologists from Tufts College and W. V. Bingham concluded that morale was increased when knowledge of results was introduced in their studies.[11] Based on their subjective impressions, knowledge of results might positively affect morale.

In an attemptg to evaluate the effectiveness of employing knowledge of results and MBO in a unionized industrial setting, the author conducted two experimental studies to determine the effect on employee productivity in a unionized production department of a mass-production manufacturing plant. The plant was one of Continental Can Co.'s, located in the Midwest. The work layout and methods are highly standardized according to the best available technology. Management realized that the greatest additional gains to be made would have to come through the cooperation and morale of the work force. Within this environment, the technique of knowledge of results was evaluated in two studies.

Knowledge of Results Studies

Study I was made in the press department on the third shift from January 1, 1964, through December 31, 1965. Study II was made in the press and assembly departments on all three shifts from January 1, 1966, through December 31, 1966. Many elements of MBO were involved in the study: goals, goal setting, negotiation, communications feedback, rewards, etc. After a control period in both studies, knowledge of results was introduced. The studies measured and evaluated the performance levels before and after knowledge of results was introduced. Study I used five methods for presenting knowledge of results in comparison to one method used in Study II.

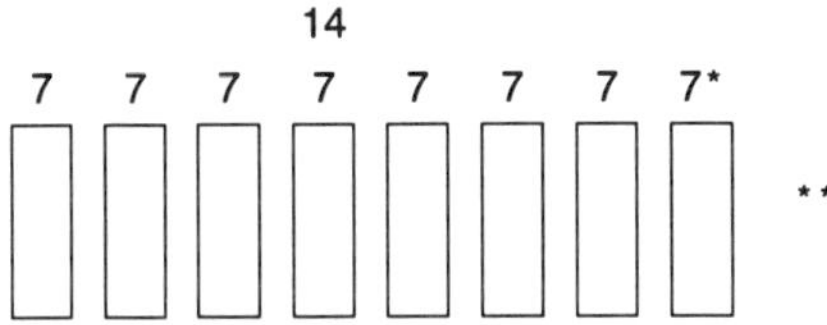

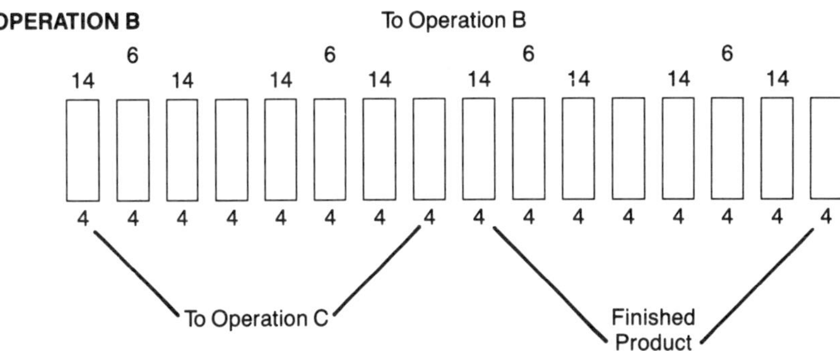

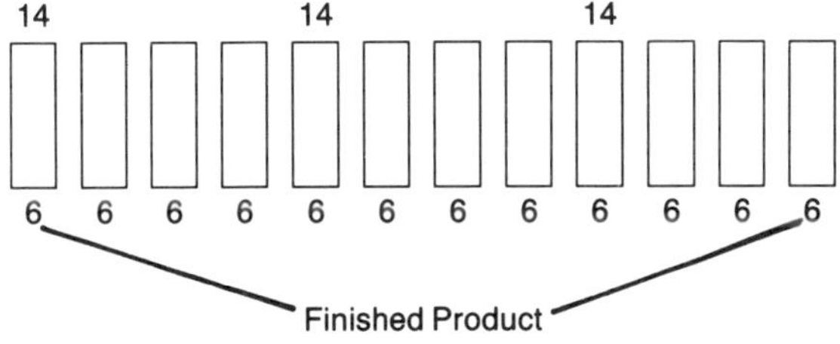

*Worker

**Production line

Figure I: Press department layout

Study I covers a 2-year period from January 1, 1964, through December 31, 1965. It is broken down into three stages: control, preliminary, and full scale implementation. The control stage covers the period when a planned knowledge of results and MBO program were not being used. During this period, existing relative performance levels of the skilled workers were studied. During the preliminary stage, knowledge of results and MBO were introduced into the work environment as the program was being perfected. The full-scale implementation stage covers the period when the more sophisticated and complete methods were used.

Study I was conducted on the third shift of the press department, which is the last shift in a 24-hour operation. The working hours for the shift are from 11:30 p.m. to 6:30 a.m. The press department mass-produces parts that are later assembled in another department or by the customer. The third shift has about 60 of some 200 employees in the department. The employees are organized in groups around the physical layout of the production lines. These work groups are shown in Figure I which represents the number of employees needed for full operation.

Two operations are completed on the raw material before it is brought to the press department. All of the material is altered at Operation A, and is then transferred by trucks to Operation B for fabrication. Approximately 50% of the parts are finished in the press department after Operation B. These parts are taken away by trucks to be assembled later by the customer or in the assembly department. The other 50% of the parts leave Operation B and are transferred by trucks to Operation C where they receive further fabrication. From Operation C, they are taken to the assembly department or shipped to the customer.

The numbers in Figure I represent the employees. The rectangles are the production lines. The magnitude of the number represents the relative wage and skill requirements for the job. The lower numbers indicate lower skilled tasks, and the higher numbers indicate that more skill is needed to perform the job. These numbers are referred to as job grades. Thus job grade 14 is the highest-paying, most-skilled job in the department. Figure I does not include quality control, cleanup, truck drivers, and other personnel. Two supervisors are in charge of this work group on the third shift.

Three national unions represent the work force in the plant. One of these unions represents the workers on the third shift in the press department as well as most of the plant's production workers.

A good communication program is a prerequisite to the effective use of knowledge of results and MBO. Communication channels must be open to supply knowledge of results to the work group. Communication contributes importantly in satisfying higher-level needs. A study by the National Industrial Conference Board indicates that communications can affect attitudes and morale.[12]

In Study I, knowledge of results and MBO were introduced through specially designed communications system, as follows:

- A separate monthly meeting was held with employees in each labor grade. For example, all members of labor grade 14 attended a meeting separate from those held for individuals in labor grade 4. Group performance goals were discussed and set in these meetings.

- A communications center was established, consisting of a group of bulletin boards that were used for posting important information.

- Personal contact by the supervisor with each employee was stressed. Informal conversations, usually on the production floor, discussed progress toward attaining individual and group performance goals. Some meetings were held in the foreman's office.

- Various employee activities were undertaken. A bowling league, golf league, and softball team were organized in an effort to improve morale, communications, working relationships, and to give the satisfaction of participating with fellow employees in social activities.

Through the use of these communications channels, information on goal attainment was presented to individuals and the work group in the following manner:

- The department's efficiency was charted daily on a three-by-four foot line graph that was attached to the bulletin board.

- A form was posted on the bulletin board daily to inform members of the work force about actual production and efficiency as compared to the standard for each production line. The individuals working on each production line were also included on the form.

- Informal contact by the supervisor with persons in the skilled-labor classification (labor grade 14) periodically emphasized individual and group performance statistics and goal sttainment.

- Formal meetings were held with the trainees in skilled-labor grade 14. These men completed a 4,000-hour training program. They had previously completed formal classroom training and were now taking part in on-the-job training. These meetings emphasized their performance levels.

- Performance statistics were always discussed in the monthly meetings with the various labor grades. Shift and department performance levels were compared with goals set for the next period.

Knowledge of results was presented to the individuals and work groups using the five methods mentioned above. This tested the hypothesis that knowledge of results will increase productivity, depending on the following assumptions:

- Changes in the supervisors assigned to the shift had no effect on the shift's performance.

- Factors other than the experimental variable had, at most, random effects on worker productivity. These factors include such variables as union-management relationships, disciplinary actions, and levels and hours of employment.[13]

- The "Hawthorne Effect"[14] had no effect on the outcome of the study. The work group was not aware that a study was being made.

- The general changes in communication techniques and recreation programs for the workers did not have an independent effect on worker productivity.

It must be recognized at this point that the third shift of the press department could not be segregated into a separate entity. Stronger control over the study would have been possible if the work group could have functioned in a closed environment. The study was, however, conducted as part of a normal manufacturing operation. Conversely, this could be a strong point when considering the factors that could affect the study. A more realistic environment does avoid the problems introduced by the artificiality of the laboratory experiment in studies of human behavior.

The ranking of the performance levels of the skilled-labor grade and their crews was made by totaling their performance statistics during the control period and expressing these statistics in the form of an index. The performance statistics were expressed in two factors: an efficiency factor and a quality factor. These factors were arrived at through the use of formulas:

- quality factor = $\dfrac{H + 4S}{P}$

  with
      H = number of parts held for rework
      S = number of parts scrapped
      P = number of parts produced in thousands

- Efficiency Factor = $\dfrac{A - E}{N}$

with

A = daily production-line percent efficiency measuring total parts produced against standard.

A = P/Q x 100, where P = parts produced, Q = standard.

E = daily production-line percent efficiency expected by the immediate supervisor.

N = number of days during the control period.

To arrive at the final index, the quality factor and the efficiency factor were combined using the following formula:

$$\text{final index} = \frac{QF + EF}{2}, \text{ where}$$

QF = quality factor
EF = efficiency factor

After a final index figure was calculated for each member of the skilled-labor grade and his crew, it was ranked with the other indexes. This gave management a clearer picture of the relative performance level and was a basis for taking positive corrective action.

The control stage for the study covered the period from January 1, 1964, through April 30, 1964. Knowledge of results and MBO as a mechanism for encouraging increased productivity was not introduced during this period. During the control stage, a method of ranking the relative performance levels of the skilled labor grade and their crews within the plant was perfected. Criteria for this ranking were based on production-line performance figures during the control period. The performance figures used were (1) production line percent efficiency measuring total parts produced against standard, (2) product quality based on quality control standards, (3) excess spoilage over standard, and (4) the foreman's qualitative judgment of expected line performance.

When completed, the ranking gave management a composite picture of the performance level of the skilled workers and their crews. This information helped to identify individual performance problems and served as a measuring tool to help workers improve.

All statistics for Study I — control, preliminary and full-scale implementation stages — are summarized in Table I and Figure II. Table I presents the performance of the line crews on the third shift for all three stages. It was calculated by taking the average daily output index for the skilled-labor grade-14 workers. The crews were generally made up of the same members with the skilled-labor grade member as the head of the crew. However, vacations, layoffs, absenteeism, sabbatical leaves, sick leaves, and shift changes introduced some variation in crew composition.

Table I. Third-shift press department average daily productivity — index for each skilled employee (and line crew)*

Time Period Skilled Employee (and Line Crew)	Control Stage Average Daily Output Index (Jan.-Apr.) 1964	Preliminary Average Daily Output Index (Oct.-Feb.) 1964-65	Full-Scale Implementation Average Daily Output Index (Aug.-Dec.) 1965
A	105	107	110
B	108	109	109
C	76	92	105
D**	—	80	105
E	71	78	98
F	86	83	96
G	75	76	94
H	80	89	92
I	80	80	91
J**	—	105	87
K**	73	73	86
Summary			
Mean	83.5	88.4	97.0
Median	80.0	83.0	96.0
Range	37.0	36.0	23.0
Standard Deviation	4.07	3.93	2.67

*Index is based on 100 as equal to standard.
**Trainee in skilled labor grade.

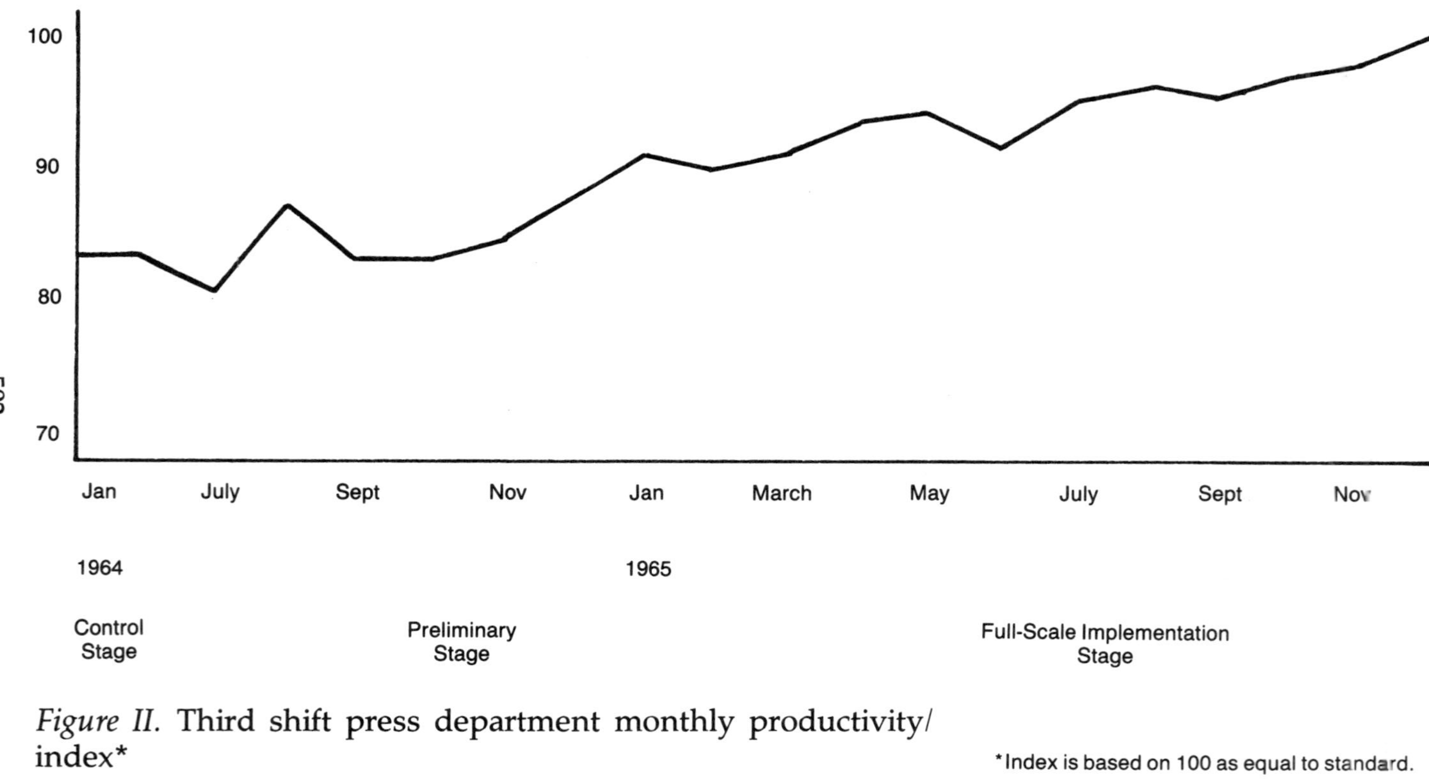

Figure II. Third shift press department monthly productivity/index*

*Index is based on 100 as equal to standard.

Although the entire crew is important, the skilled-labor grade-14 workers do the actual maintenance, minor repair, and play the biggest role in the line's productivity. Each labor crew consisted of from two to five persons, depending on equipment utilization.

Figure II shows the third-shift average monthly efficiency index during the study. It is made up of the average efficiency index for all the production lines during each month.

During the control stage, the third-shift press department efficiency-index mean was 83.5, the median 80.0, with a range of 37.0 and a standard deviation of 4.07.

This stage of the study is called the preliminary stage because it was during this period that the techniques for introducing knowledge of results and some elements of MBO were perfected. This stage covers the period from July 1, 1964, through February 28, 1965. The results of the preliminary stage are measured from October 1, 1964, through February 28, 1965.

The monthly meetings with each labor grade were started during this period. They were geared to the further opening of communications channels. Quality, efficiency, safety, and business trends were the chief topics of discussion. Occasionally, members of the staff and other line departments presented their comments to the groups.

After the meetings became a routine part of the operation, a portion of each meeting was reserved for discussing problems. The meetings proved very beneficial. New ideas were presented, misunderstandings were clarified, better work techniques were introduced, and an atmosphere for the free exchange of ideas was fostered. At each meeting, the group was given feedback on its performance level during the preceding period. Goals and how to achieve them were regularly discussed.

When the communications center was established, it provided another avenue for communicating with the work group. A portion of one bulletin board was used by the department general foreman. All supervisors in the press department used another board to post important information, such as a weekly newsletter, informative newspaper articles, magazine and journal articles, safety posters, and letters written to the employees by upper management. One of the most important uses of the communications center was to serve as a means for presenting daily performance figures.

One portion of the communications center was devoted to graphing the department's daily efficiency. The posting of third-shift performance levels on the bulletin board went through crude stages to arrive at the finished form.
The first stage was merely a board with the heading, "Here's what the third shift did yesterday." The next form showed the performance by production line.

In time, the form became more sophisticated and included more information such as production line, line crew, actual production in units, and efficiency based on standard.[15] Soon, the members of the work force became interested in the form and usually stopped at the bulletin board to check it before reporting to their work stations.[15]

From the results of the performance ranking made during the Control Stage, management had a good idea of which employees had performance problems. These persons were then given a high degree of attention by the supervisor. Their performance trends were continually emphasized. This was always done informally and as part of a conversation on the production floor.

Formal office meetings for this purpose were unsuccessful during the preliminary stage. This kind of meeting seemed to put the person on the defensive, and did not prove to be constructive. After the poor performers started to make progress, this part of the program was expanded to include all members of the skilled classification.

Skilled workers who were taking part in on-the-job training were handled differently. They were rated and counseled periodically in the foreman's office. The progress of their training and the previous month's efficiency were discussed. Each trainee was assigned to work in different areas to further his training. At each meeting a goal was set for the next period's performance level — a joint figure reached by both trainee and supervisor.

The monthly meetings with each separate labor grade enabled the supervisor to reinforce the members of the group as the production goals were being met and the shift efficiency steadily grew higher.

The results of the preliminary stage were determined from performance figures for October 1, 1964, through February 28, 1965. The first few months of this stage were not used in the calculation because the full effects of knowledge of results had not set in. Referring to Table I and Figure II it will be noted that several gains were made during the preliminary stage: (1) The efficiency index mean rose from 83.5 during the control to 88.4 in the preliminary period. (2) The median performance level rose from 80.0 to 83.0. (3) The range improved slightly from 37.0 to 36.0 in the respective periods. (4) The standard deviation reflects the changes by improving from 4.07 during the control period to 3.93 during the preliminary period. (5) It should also be noted that the shift efficiency steadily improved during the preliminary stage.

The last stage of the study is called Full-Scale Implementation because it was during this period that a fairly sophisticated approach had been developed for encouraging production through the mechanisms of knowledge of results and MBO. This stage lasted from March 1, 1965, to December 30, 1965. Performance during this period is measured from August 1, 1965, through December 30, 1965. Again, the later months of the period were more useful for measuring the full effects of knowledge of results during that period.

It appeared that individuals became more aware of the importance of their performance contribution to that of the group. Members of the various line crews continually tried to break existing production records. When exceptional production records were set, the supervisors bought coffee for the workers involved.

During April 1965, the third shift ran over 100% on a regular workday for the first time. The supervisors bought coffee for the entire shift as a reward for meeting the goal. During the next 9 months of the study, the third-shift production efficiency was over 100% 41 more times.

Top production runs were underlined with a marking pen on the daily sheet that was posted with performance information. This practice became the topic of humorous bragging and joshing among the workers. Many members of the skilled-labor classification became so interested in their efficiency averages that they started requesting their totals every week. Some kept their own records.

The greatest gains in efficiency occurred during this period, as noted in Figure II. Referring to the statistics on Table I, the mean efficiency index rose to a peak of 97.0 in comparison with the 83.5 and 88.4 efficiency index means attained during the two previous periods. Gains were also made in other areas: median up to 96.0, range down to 23.0, and the standard deviation reflected these improvements by going down to 2.67 in comparison to the 4.07 and 3.93 during the previous two periods.

Analyzing the individual and group performance levels during the 2-year study supports the hypothesis that knowledge of results is a factor in increasing employee productivity. Significant improvements were made in productivity after the introduction of knowledge of results. All quantitative measures improved:

- Performance-index means rose from 83.5 to 97.0.

- Performance-index median rose from 80.0 to 96.0.

- Performance-index range reduced from 37.0 to 23.0.

- Performance-index standard deviation reduced from 4.07 to 2.67.

- Graphical interpretation shows steady performance increase.

It must also be noted that two of the three trainees and all of the experienced workers in the skilled-labor grade improved their performance. Outside uncontrollable factors contributed to the decline in performance of one of the trainees. This further verifies the conclusions made in the study of the 40mm gunpointers. Both the experienced and inexperienced gunpointers improved their performance after the introduction of knowledge of results.[16] It can therefore be postulated that knowledge of results will improve the performance of both experienced and inexperienced workers in an industrial work situation.

The awareness of their performance gave the employees something to be interested in, it let them know how they were doing, and provided a means for reinforcing constructive, production-oriented behavior. This contributed to better morale through stimulating the satisfaction of higher-level human needs. The outside activities such as bowling, golf, and softball also contributed to better morale. Subjective impressions through observations by the researcher and supervisors all agreed that morale seemed to have increased during the experimental time period.[17] Many statements offered by members of the work group reinforced this observation.

Another supervisor on the first shift in the press department used the knowledge-of-results technique successfully on the work crews at Operation C.[18] He used his own techniques and methods to present the work group feedback on their performance.

The results in Study II were not as dramatic. There was a slight increase in productivity. There was only one method of feedback used in Study II as compared to the extensive goal setting and 5 methods of feedback used in Study I.

An industrial worker must satisfy his higher-level needs within the environment of the industrial workplace. Management can use knowledge of results as a means through which workers receive reinforcement for productive, cooperative behavior. By receiving reinforcement for this behavior and better satisfying their higher-level needs, workers are likely to continue this type of behavior. This is of utmost importance in industry because workers play such a large part in the ultimate success of the firm.

The hypothesis that knowledge of results will increase productivity was based on studies made in other areas, many outside industry. To test the hypothesis, the author conducted two studies covering a period of three years in an industrial environment. Based on the results of these studies it can be postulated that knowledge of results will increase or maintain performance levels in a unionized industrial environment. Support is lent to the hypothesis that knowledge of results will also increase morale and that the more extensive and complete the methods used for presenting knowledge of results the better the payoff in higher productivity.

Notes

[1]Harry S. Broudy and Eugene L. Freet, *Psychology* (New York: Longmans, Green & Co., 1956), p. 274.

[2]Margret W. Pryor and Bernard M. Bass, "Some Effects of Feedback on Behavior in Groups," *Sociometry* (New York: American Sociological Society, March 1959), XXII, p. 57.

[3]Morris S. Viteles, *Motivation and Morale in Industry* (New York: W. W. Norton Co., 1953), p. 91.

[4]N. R. Maier, *Frustration* (New York: McGraw-Hill, 1949), p. 196.

[5]Viteles, p. 144.

[6]Tom Verhave, *"Is the System Approach of Engineering Pyschology Applicable to Social Organizations?" Psychological Record*, II, 1961, pp. 69-86.

[7]George W. Angell, "The Effect of Immediate Knowledge of Quiz Results on Final Examination Scores in Freshman Chemistry," *Journal of Education Research*, 1949, pp. 391-94.

[8]W. C. Biel, G. E. Brown, R. M. Gottsdanker and E. C. Hall, *The Effectiveness of a Check Sight Technique for Training 40mm Gunpointers* (O.S.R.D. Report 4054), Tufts College, 1944.

[9]*Ibid.*, p. 9.

[10]W. V. Bingham, "Making Work Worthwhile," *Psychology Today* (Chicago: University of Chicago Press, 1932), pp. 262-4.

[11]Note 8, p. 10.

[12]"Does Communication Make a Difference?" *Conference Board Management Record* (New York: National Industrial Conference Board, 1952), XIV, pp. 414-16.

[13]Some evidence is available to support this assumption. After the work group had reached a certain stage in the productive and motivational process, outside factors, though important, did not seem to detour their efforts to maintain efficiency. Dramatic changes in outside factors occurred on two

occasions. In January 1965, the entire third shift of the plant became emotionally involved in a situation that concerned the changing of working hours. Shortly after that, in March, the national union declared a strike in which the local union participated.

Manufacturing efficiency during this period remained constant around 90%. It was 6% higher than the previous 3-month period. According to the graph in Figure II, the rate of improvement in performance remained relatively constant during the entire study, including the period between January and March 1965. This further emphasizes the fact that outside factors had little effect, if any, on the outcome of the study.

[14]The "Hawthorne Effect" is referred to when the results of an experiment or study are positive because the group knew they were part of an experiment. The term originated with the Hawthorne Studies.

[15]To test the reaction and get a better idea of how this form was accepted, mistakes were purposely made in production counts, wrong names, etc. Workers were paying very close attention to it. In every case, the error was noticed immediately and pointed out to the supervisors.

[16]Note 8, p. 10.

[17]Throughout this book the knowledge-of-results technique has been emphasized as a means of controlling worker behavior toward higher productivity by reinforcing behavior that satisfies human needs. Knowledge of results will also contribute to increased morale. Dr. Theo Haimann in his book *Professional Management*, declares that it is a manager's function to maintain a high level of morale. Theo Haimann, *Professional Management* (Boston: Houghton Mifflin Co., 1962), p. 456. The results of the studies by Tufts College and Bingham indicated to that knowledge of results increased morale. Note 8, p. 10. Pryor and Bass found that "feedback would increase or at least maintain motivation." Pryor and Bass, see Note 2, p. 56. Rensis Likert found that there was a relationship between high producing supervisors-

knowledge of results-and high morale. Rensis Likert, "Motivation: The core of management," *Personnel Series no. 155* (New York: American Management Association, 1953), p. 9.

[18]Note 8, p. 15.

Appendix B

Blue Collar Management
By Objectives

This Appendix is intended to acquaint the reader with the benefits of management by objectives (MBO) in the lowest levels of the organization. Symptoms of organizational problems will be covered. The organization that recognizes these symptoms will find management by objectives a means for improving its situation.

In these times of unrest in the lower-levels, blue-and-white collar ranks, management is faced with finding an equitable solution to the problem of productivity and job satisfaction. Declining productivity during this century is becoming the concern of all society. As pointed out in Chapter I the productivity annual rate of increase continues to be unacceptably low. Job enrichment and job enlargement have been discussed in the literature as solutions to productivity decline and job dissatisfaction among the lower echelons. This discussion will try to show that management by objectives at the blue-collar level is a far stronger concept in combating productivity and job-satisfaction problems at the lower levels of an organization.

The discussion is based on the experiences of the author, who has successfully implemented MBO at the lower levels of large, complex, unionized, manufacturing operations. And as a consultant to other organizations, the author has completed extensive academic research in the area the over last 6 years.

George Odiorne, in his main address at the Annual International Conference on Management By Objectives at Salt Lake City in August 1974 stated, ". . . Professor Migliore is one of the new pioneers of MBO through his study of applicability at the lower levels of organization."

An organization with the following symptoms has a need for management by objectives at the lowest levels: low productivity; complaints from the work force in almost all areas; and lack of commitment, teamwork, and cooperation.
The work force can be characterized as having an "I don't care" attitude. It seems to take little interest in organization affairs. Lower-level supervision feeds back information to middle management that problems are caused by the people. The major excuse is that the people just won't work.

Management faces many problems when it decides to adopt the management-by-objectives philosophy. Management is not sure what to expect. The literature is full of reports of successes and failures. If MBO is adopted will diminishing returns set in within the management hierarchy? A related question is will diminishing returns set in at all levels below the exempt management levels? This is based on the assumption that the organization had positive results in the first place.

A management-by-objectives philosophy must have a decentralized organization that is built around a profit, revenue, or cost center. It must have management support from the very top of the organization. The management-by-objectives philosophy must be carefully installed into the organization. The assumption is made here that the organization is susceptible to or already has management by objectives.

Diminishing returns will not set in within the management hierarchy. MBO works at management levels for the following reasons:

- Managerial persons benefit from intrinsic nonfinancial awards. The pat on the back by the manager's immediate supervisor is more meaningful under MBO because results are measured against objectives. The manager has an opportunity to satisfy his higher-level needs of recognition, self-esteem, and self-actualization under the MBO system. These intrinsic rewards will increase morale and contribute to the continuity of the MBO system.

- Managerial persons will also benefit from extrinsic rewards. The MBO system, by its very nature, facilitates promotion, pay, bonuses, and job satisfaction. If the MBO system is working properly, career development will be a function of attaining objectives in the contemplated ability to meet objectives at the next-higher level. Much of the uncertainty surrounding promotions will be eliminated. Under properly working MBO, salary advancement will be a function of objectives attainment. Spin-off rewards are an expense account, a bigger office, a company car, and so on. Managerial personnel are career oriented. The MBO philosophy contributes to the establishment of career objectives and a road map to achieve those objectives.

- The MBO philosophy brings out the best of all managerial theories. A study of management and practices during this century reveals that management by objectives has benefited by contributions by many successful managers, consultants, and academicians. Alfred P. Sloan, Jr.; Edward N. Hay & Associates; Peter Drucker; and George Odiorne, to name a few, have all contributed to management by objectives as we know it today. A long list of behavioral scientists beginning with Elton Mayo through Abraham Maslow, Douglas McGregor, and Carl Rogers have contributed theories that support elements of MBO as supporting the human condition.

- Management by objectives takes maximum advantage of all the natural tendencies inherent in man and his organizations. Management must manage in a manner that enables it to take advantage of all the natural tendencies possible so as to devote more time and attention to those fields of the business that are subject to more problems.

Examples of needing more time and attention are in the domains of social responsibility, government and legal lobbying, international trade, and long-range planning. A management tied up with short-term behavioral problems suffers from chronic crisis management.

Turning attention to the nonexempt blue-collar and lower-level white-collar worker, management by objectives will have an immediate, positive result. Part of this can be attributed to the "Hawthorne Effect" — production tends to go up because the workers are aware a study is being conducted. The opportunity to satisfy higher-level needs has now been introduced into their working environment. There is a tendency, too, for the need satisfaction to have a multiplier effect on morale. Before the introduction of management by objectives at their level, they had had little opportunity to satisfy higher-level needs.

Another positive contribution is the fact that the individual has an innate need for discipline. Management by objectives, by its very nature, gives the worker the opportunity to exercise self-discipline, which combats boredom and job dissatisfaction.

Management's inability to use extrinsic rewards causes eventual diminishing returns. The union contract calls for rigid pay scales within job classifications. Management cannot give merit pay increases when individual objectives are attained. Promotions are overly linked to the seniority system due to union contracts. Profit sharing and general programs of this nature are ill timed and not specific enough to meet MBO requirements. A synergistic long-range effect is not attained because important extrinsic rewards do not negate the positive factors due from the intrinsic rewards. It must also be noted that performance and job satisfaction are higher under the management-by-objectives philosophy, and the fact that diminishing returns set in should not keep the organization from adopting the philosophy.

An organization can expect that it will take from six months to two years to get the MBO philosophy working properly at the lower levels. This could be called the developmental stage. During the implementation stage, positive results will continue as a result of benefits of the properly working MBO principles. This has been noted in the second to the fifth years. The diminishing-returns stage will set in during the fourth to the sixth years. This is because the intrinsic rewards will no longer be prime motivators. Management is faced with the inability to use proper extrinsic rewards. Performance will be maintained at a higher level, however. It should also be noted that under normal conditions there will not be negative results from management by objectives.

A spin-off result of using MBO at this level is the effect it has on foremen and leadmen who directly supervise lower-level workers. It forces them to learn to communicate properly. It helps them see the advantages of Theory Y, 9-9 types of management style. It helps make the lower-level manager part of the management team. Another spin-off of using MBO at this level is that workers are responsible for their work and the attainment of objectives. It brings problems out into the open. It provides for job enlargement and job enrichment through greater involvement in their jobs.

Organizations should understand the realistic value of MBO as it will apply to their individual circumstances. Every entity must adapt MBO to its special needs. Each entity has its own format and any attempt to install another form's system to it will ultimately fail. People, tradition, and philosophy of entities, even within the same organization, are different. Special consideration must be given to fitting MBO into these entities. The key is to introduce the philosophy and let the individual managers formulate their own procedures and principles. Total failure is likely to follow if this simple concept is ignored. Every manager must contribute and make it part of his managing philosophy, or management by objectives is surely doomed. MBO is not a cure-all but it will help managers be more effective in their jobs. If we operated in a perfectly balanced, capitalistic system nearing utopia there would be no need for management in the first place.

The strength of management by objectives must be recognized at the lower levels and implemented. Management should plan for and expect accelerating rates of return up to a certain point, say between the fourth and sixth years. By recognizing what is going to take place, management can plan to introduce some type of extrinsic reward in this four to six-year period. This author cannot recommend a solution to the extrinsic-reward problem. Mitchell Fein is one author who is now attacking that problem. We do not necessarily support all of Fein's recommendations but do not have anything better to offer, and, therefore, won't criticize his recommendations. Fein's recommendations can be found in "Rational Approaches to Raising Productivity," publication No. 5 in the Monograph Series, American Institute of Industrial Engineers, Inc.

Management's problem is: If we decide to use MBO at all levels of the organization, how do we get it started? Again, it must be emphasized that no set approach is going to work in every organization. The importance is the fundamentals. Ultimately each foreman and supervisor must work out how he wants to conduct the program within his own entity. He must be given guidelines within which to work, and he must decide how he will function within these guidelines. Suggestions of good practices can be given to help him in formulating his individual approach. What follows is a discussion of a combination that this author has often used successfully.

First, management must inform all the managers, foremen, and leadmen what management by objectives really is. This can be done through seminars, books, program instruction, role-playing, and films. All of these are becoming more and more available. A number of universities hold seminars on MBO: Dr. Richard Johanson, University of Arkansas; Dr. George Odiorne, University of Massachusetts; Bureau of Industrial Relations at the University of Michigan; and the Executive Action Seminar Series at Oral Roberts University. John Humble's book, *Management by Objectives in Action*, is recommended. It is practical, can help the manager understand MBO, and can give him some ideas of how to get it going in his organization. Dr. Glen Varney has an instruction manual on MBO. BNA Inc. has a film series on MBO.

Second, it is of utmost importance that someone in the organization guide the effort. It must have a definite responsibility base. If an outside consultant is enlisted, he should work with someone in the organization who is specifically responsible for starting, monitoring, and staying with the MBO program. The project or "matrix" type of organization can be used. Here, a special group of members of the organization makes a committee or team to work with the consultant. This team cuts across all the organizational lines and reports directly to the top man in the organization. This author has found that if a consultant handles the entire installation, the MBO philosophy will die a quick death after his departure.

The consultant is important, however, as he will educate the organization as to what MBO is, give it insights into problems that other people have had, and answer questions concerning the program. In short, he has an crucial job to do.

Third, communication channels must be open to ensure a free flow of information both up and down the organization. Group meetings should be held to begin the education process for the entire organization. After a general group meeting, separate meetings should be held by job classification. The goal of these meetings is to determine a method for agreeing on the job responsibility in each job classification. This can be done through an open meeting by committee or otherwise. The foremen or managers holding the meetings must stimulate group participation. Plenty of time must be allowed for this. Martha Stuart of Communications, Inc., has a notable education training film called "Shop Stewards," that might well be part of the foremen's training session. At the group meetings and the individual meetings, managers must listen carefully. MBO at the blue-collar level will not work with only one-way communication. Ultimately, a 10 to 30-minute meeting should be held by a supervisor with each individual.

Then comes the fourth step. After the responsibilities in each job classification are agreed on, overall goals for the group must be set in one of the monthly group meetings. It is the supervisor's responsibility to make sure that the goals are set for the group.

After the overall goals are set (for example, the third shift in a manufacturing department might have a goal of 80% efficiency performance for the next month) individual goals must be set in individual meetings with the blue-collar workers. These goals must be realistic, written, measurable, and cover a specific time span. This author has found, both through experience and a longitudinal study in 1972, that these early goals tend to be set too high. The initial goals over the first short periods of time, probably a monthly, should not be exaggerated. A file should be kept on each worker, and should include records of these discussions. Performance, whether in efficiency or whatever measurement the particular job contributes to, should be kept in the file. It is also important to recognize that the goals should be negotiated between the employee and the supervisor.

The authors' experience is that in approximately 90% of the cases these individual meetings are pleasantly anticipated and eagerly accepted by the workers. Some, however, will not respond. The manager must exercise patience in these situations. Sometimes this lack of response is due to the manager. A good part of the session should be reserved for listening by the manager.

The fifth step is the holding of regularly scheduled performance reviews. The first session will not appear to be rewarding. It takes time to build a meaningful interchange. After these individual conferences start, performance reviews and discussions can take place in the workplace. For example, a packing crew might have a 10- to 15-minute lull while waiting for another car to be loaded. The supervisor might discuss performance with a particular member of the crew during this break. These productivity interviews for MBO sessions must be planned and scheduled by the foreman. One of the foreman's goals must be 100% coverage of these interviews monthly. He reports this goal to his immediate supervisor, and he is measured on his attainment of this goal.

However trite it might appear, rewards must be provided to the group. The introduction of rewards makes up the sixth step.

Some rewards include the following:

- A record run board on the bulletin board;

- The foreman can buy coffee for the entire group when a group goal has been met;

- An engraved ballpoint pen for outstanding performance for a crew that changed over a piece of production equipment in record time; and,

- The daily posting of production records.

A longitudinal study published in the Management of Personnel Journal showed that feedback of results spurred performance. Feedback is the seventh step. Every possible means of feeding any significant information must be given to the group, both good and bad. Customer complaints, product shortages, performance review — all of these things must be communicated with the work group. It is only through such open communication that the group will give its attention and get involved in the real problems and commitments that the organization is responsible for.

By using some channel of communication, it is possible for every member of the management hierarchy, to make known to the group that reports to him the results of goal attainment for a particular period. For example, a department manager for a manufacturing operation might be reporting the results of the goal attainment for that department to a division review board. This same presentation, complete with graphical aids, should be made to the work group in a general meeting. Any pertinent information that has been given to the department manager by higher-up management should be routed back to the group, and vice versa.

At the base of the entire MBO philosophy must be a true awareness that each person must be recognized as a human being. A facade won't hold up; people can see through it. A side effect through this recognition and the use of MBO at the lowest level is that a grassroots loyalty will build up in the work force.

This loyalty is the ultimate base of power in any organization. The actual authority to manage is ultimately given to management by this grassroots group. It is little recognized that this is one of the best ways management can cope with union power in the organization. People want to support charismatic leaders. The need to be led is innately human; management must recognize this and supply leadership.

After MBO is in effect, the management team must involve the group in as many decisions as possible. This can be done in many ways. For example, every monthly group meeting should cover as many of the anticipated decisions as possible that must be made by the department manager during this time. The workers will have insights into many of these decisions that management cannot possibly have. Moreover, the workers will be motivated to back up decisions they helped to make.

It is management's responsibility to continue to look for rewards. The situation is continually changing, people change, and the management team is continually changing.

Although MBO is basically a philosophy, it lends itself to methodology. This methodology provides a control mechanism to ensure the long-term success of MBO in the organization.

Every level of management must monitor the progress toward goal attainment. Any method the organization chooses to use is appropriate. This author has found that the organization should devise its own methods to fit its particular needs.

After the first six months, the organization will begin to enjoy the benefits of MBO, which will be expressed through higher productivity and more concern and greater involvement by the work force. For the first times in their careers, first-line supervisors will have time to plan ahead as they will no longer have to rely on "crisis management." The tendency to relax will set in. The basic fundamentals of MBO provide its basic strength. Just as former Green Bay Packer Coach Vince Lombardi emphasized the basic fundamentals of blocking and tackling, managers must emphasize the periodic productivity interview feedback and group meetings. It is as easy to let a momentary crisis cancel a group meeting as it is to skip church on Sunday.

Our spiritual lives pivot on daily prayers and the proper observance of the Lord's Day. The Lombardi brand of football pivoted on blocking and tackling. Likewise, MBO at the blue-collar level must pivot on the individual and group sessions covering mutual goals and problems. Good open communication is the key to making it work.

The biggest danger in the second year is a tendency to relax and not observe these basic fundamentals. There is a natural inclination to slip back to the old way of doing business.

Management by objectives has paid handsome dividends at all levels. An organization can recognize the need for MBO at its lowest level through the following symptoms: low productivity, high waste, and a work force that is characterized as having an "I don't care" attitude. First-line supervisors are overworked, often spending long hours on the job.

MBO capitalizes on and, in a positive way, exploits many of the natural tendencies of men and their organizations. It has survived the test of time since its introduction by Peter Drucker in 1954. The time is ripe to extend the philosophy from the top to the bottom of the organization.

Appendix C

Strategic Production Plan to Support The Firm's Overall Basic Company Plan

Outline

The organization's overall strategic plan is developed according to the following format. The Production Manager, as part of the organization's top management team, has played a vital and integral role in developing this overall plan.

I. Purpose
   A. What is your "reason for being," your "mission," why products are needed, customers served, needs met in marketplace, and scope of the endeavor.
   B. Nationwide and/or local, ethics, profit, or nonprofit.

II. Environmental Analysis
   A. Pulse
   B. Present or past
   C. Industry surveys
   D. Completed studies of future done now.

III. S & W (usually internal)
   A. Human
   B. Facilities/equipment
   C. Patents/natural resources
   D. Financial

IV. Assumptions
   A. Have no control over
   B. Extend environmental analysis
   C. Usually external

V. Objectives and Goals
   A. Specific, time frame, objectives, and goals including

specific time frames measurable in key result areas. Note all rules for objectives.

VI.   Strategy - Two to three strategies for each objective
    A. Thinking stage
    B. Where and how to commit resources
    C. Timing
    D. Pricing policy
    Sales/Marketing
    Manufacturing
    Financial
    Facilities: People/training/morale/public responsibility

VII.   Issues/Problems
    A. Major
    B. Minor

VIII.   Analysis
    A. Industry/competitive/company situation analysis
    B. Functional; marketing, financial accounting, management, production, and people

IX.   Alternative Solutions
    A. List of alternatives
    B. Pros/cons of each

X.   Recommended Course of Action
    A. Alternative Selected
    B. Justification

Now that strategic direction has been set and the production manager has contributed and bought into the plan, then and only then can the production plan be started. Using the same philosophy and basic team principle, the production plan is developed. All staff/line managers that report to the production manager play an active role in the development of the production plan.

The production manager and others then concentrate on a production plan that will support the overall organization.

Production Plan

Purpose of Production Function:

The production function is essentially the implementation of the firm's overall strategy.

The production function mobilizes varied resources to put the firm's strategies in motion.

Environmental Factors Specific to Production:

I. The production function implements the total strategy; production greatly affects the attainment of the other functional plans. Therefore, the production function operates within an environment of subtle internal pressures from other functional areas.

II. The production function operates within an environment of standards and measures
    1) the never-ending hourglass
    2) measuring process parameters on a continuing basis
    3) input vs. output of each production factor

III. Includes latest information of what is going on in production/operation

Production Strengths and Weaknesses:

1) Having in place a complete set of standards and benchmarks for each
    a) operation
    b) process
2) Having in place a seasoned, well-trained work force

Conversely, the lack of either of the above universal strengths would constitute a weakness in the production function.

Production Assumptions:

There are several generic assumptions that we often take for granted; however, we need to list them because the consequences of their not occurring could be severe.

1) All required production factors will be available as needed at current, or near current, prices.

2) All completed production will be distributed to end users and liquidated to cash on a timely basis.

OBJECTIVES

	Last Year Actual	1990	1996
MANUFACTURING/PRODUCTIVITY			
Total Output = labor + materials + energy + capital + miscellaneous input			
Number projects completed			
Number projects scheduled			
Units produced			
Hours worked			
Sales			
Employee			
Labor Productivity			
1. Items produced per employee			
2. Quantities produced per employee-hour			
3. Labor Index = $\dfrac{\text{equivalent employee-hours of output}}{\text{actual total employee-hours}} \times 100$			
4. Labor Prod. Index = $\dfrac{\dfrac{\text{price weighed output (period 2)}}{\text{total labor costs (period 2)}}}{\dfrac{\text{price weighed output (period 1)}}{\text{total labor costs (period 1)}}} \times 100$			
Materials Productivity			
1. Output per constant dollar of total material cost			
Energy Productivity			
1. Output per energy consumer (BTU's)			
2. Energy Productivity Index = $\dfrac{\dfrac{\text{output}}{\text{BTU (constant period)}}}{\dfrac{\text{output}}{\text{BTU (base period)}}} \times 100$			
OR Energy Productivity Index = $\dfrac{\dfrac{\text{output in current period}}{\text{output in base period}}}{\dfrac{\text{BTU in current period}}{\text{BTU in base period}}} = \times 100$			
Capital Productivity			
1. Quantity of output per quantity of capital input			

OBJECTIVES

	Last Year Actual	1990	1996

MANUFACTURING/PRODUCTIVITY CONT.

2. Capital productivity

$$= \frac{\text{quant. of output}}{\text{quant. of capital of input}} = \frac{\text{units produced/day}}{\text{units inventory}} =$$

$$\frac{\text{units produced/day}}{\text{machine (process unit)}}$$

People
1. Manhours worked without lost time from accidents.
2. Various other safety objectives.

Quality
1. Zero defects.
2. Acceptance rates vs. various sampling plans.

About The Authors

R. Henry Migliore, Professor of Strategic Planning and Management, Northeastern State University/University Center at Tulsa. Dr. Migliore teaches at the graduate and undergraduate levels. He is former manager of the press manufacturing operations of Continental Can Company's Stockyard Plant. Prior to that he was responsible for the industrial engineering function at Continental's Indiana plant. He has had various consulting experiences with Fred Rudge & Associates in New York and has served large and small businesses, associations and nonprofit organizations in various capacities. He is also a frequent contributor to the Academy of Management, including a paper at the 50th anniversary national conference.

To date previous articles on management and business subjects have appeared in academic, business and trade journals and magazines. His books, *MBO: Blue Collar to Top Executive, An MBO Approach to Long-Range Planning, A Strategic Plan for Your Life, Strategic Long-Range Planning, Strategic Planning for Church and Ministry Growth, Common Sense Management; A Biblical Perspective, Personal Action Planning; How To Know What You Want And Get It,* and *Tales of Uncle Henry,* describe personal theories and experiences. He contributed to the book, *Readings in Interpersonal and Organizational Communication* and *International Handbook on MBO.* This book, *The Management of Production; A Productivity Approach* is co-authored. *Strategic Management, Strategic Life Planning,* and *Common Sense Management* were published this year by GP/Nichols Publishing. He has also produced "Personal Financial Success," an Oral Roberts Ministry video training kit offered on nationwide television, and video/audio tapes to go with his books and a series of video tapes on strategic planning.

In November 1985, the daily "Managing for Success" cable television program was inaugurated and was on the air until March 1986. It was on Tulsa Cable. He writes occasional columns for the *Tulsa Tribune, Tahlequah Pictorial Press, Collinsville News, Jenks Journal,* and *Muskogee County Times.*

Dr. Migliore holds degrees from Eastern Oklahoma State, Oklahoma State University, St. Louis University, and completed his doctorate at the University of Arkansas. He belongs to the Academy of Management, Planning Executives Institute and is a senior member of the American Institute of Industrial Engineers.

Walt Thrun has a broad background in manufacturing that spans nearly two decades. He has served as Controller, Technical Director, and Manufacturing Manager for such blue chip firms as J.I. Case (a Tenneco Company), Anoconda, and Pepsico, Inc.

Thrun also has a rich background in academics. He taught several years at Oral Roberts University and presently serves on the faculty of Northeastern State University teaching both in the College of Business and Division of Technology.

Thrun's writings on the subject of productivity relative to time are unparalleled in the industry. He began writing for the trade press in 1968 and has been published in a variety of trade magazines ranging from *Industrial Engineering* to *Management Accounting*.

He has participated in numerous symposiums and workshops speaking primarily on productivity issues. He is a member of American Society for Quality Control, American Productivity Center and Production and Operations Management Society.

To contact Migliore or Thrun,
write:

R. Henry Migliore
P.O. Box 957
Jenks, Oklahoma 74037